A Field Guide to Managing Diversity, Equality and Inclusion in Organisations

A Field Guide to Managing Diversity, Equality and Inclusion in Organisations

Edited by

Subas P. Dhakal

Senior Lecturer, UNE Business School, University of New England, Australia

Roslyn Cameron

Professor and Director, Centre for Organisational Change and Agility, Torrens University Australia

John Burgess

Professor of Management, Business and Hospitality, Torrens University Australia

ELGAR FIELD GUIDES

Edward Elgar
PUBLISHING

Cheltenham, UK • Northampton, MA, USA

Published by
Edward Elgar Publishing Limited
The Lypiatts
15 Lansdown Road
Cheltenham
Glos GL50 2JA
UK

Edward Elgar Publishing, Inc.
William Pratt House
9 Dewey Court
Northampton
Massachusetts 01060
USA

Paperback edition 2023

A catalogue record for this book
is available from the British Library

Library of Congress Control Number: 2022942927

This book is available electronically in the **Elgar**online
Business subject collection
http://dx.doi.org/10.4337/9781800379008

ISBN 978 1 80037 899 5 (cased)
ISBN 978 1 80037 900 8 (eBook)
ISBN 978 1 0353 2742 3 (paperback)

Printed and bound by CPI Group (UK) Ltd, Croydon, CR0 4

Contents

Figures

Tables

Contributors

Kenny Abau is International Operations Manager, Air Transport Regulation Division, PNG Department of Transport, Port Moresby, Papua New Guinea. In his current role as manager of all aviation movement operations in the country, he is concerned with the fairness in discharging his duties.

Sujana Adapa is a Professor and Head of UNE Business School at the University of New England. She principally teaches marketing units in the UNE Business School. Her research interests include information and technology adoption, sustainable practices, gender studies covering leadership and entrepreneurship.

Muhammad Ali is Associate Professor at the QUT Business School, Queensland University of Technology, Brisbane, Australia. His research interest areas are workforce demographic diversity and inclusion, work–life programs and corporate governance. He has published his research in journals such as *Human Resource Management, Journal of Management in Engineering, International Journal of Project Management, International Journal of Human Resource Management, Human Resource Management Journal* and *Journal of Business Ethics.*

Lina Alsaree is a PhD candidate at the Queensland University of Technology, Brisbane, Australia, under the supervision of Erica French and Muhammad Ali. Her research is focused on gender equality and diversity initiatives in the workplace and organisational justice theory. She also holds an MPhil in organisational justice at work from Queensland University of Technology.

Mirsad Bahtic is a senior talent specialist based in Vienna, Austria with research interests in the fields of workforce diversity, knowledge management and human resource management, specifically in the areas of organisational behaviour and social sciences. He is passionate about understanding human behaviour in relation to organisational structures, processes and practices. His broad industry exposure in the public and private sectors has enabled him to develop significant practical and theoretical knowledge that he has used to create new business practices which inspire people and create value.

Derek Baker is Professor of Agribusiness and Value Chains in the University of New England and Director of UNE's Centre for Agribusiness, Armidale,

Australia. He has worked extensively in development and research for development programs and in development research management. He has written and published widely on economics, policy, marketing systems and innovation and the value chain.

Marzena Baker is a Researcher and Lecturer with the School of Project Management at the University of Sydney, Australia. She was awarded a PhD and master of business from Queensland University of Technology. She also holds a bachelor of commerce degree from Auckland University. Her passion for workplace equity, diversity and inclusion and promoting women to organisational leadership roles is reflected in her research and publications focused on effective diversity policies, initiatives and practices. Her research produces knowledge capable of helping shape the future of workforce diversity in Australia and beyond.

Sarah Elsie Baker is the Head of Research and a Senior Lecturer at the Media Design School in Auckland, New Zealand. Her research is focused on design methodologies and social justice. She is currently writing a book entitled *Designing Gender: A Feminist Toolkit*.

John Burgess is Professor of Management, Business and Hospitality with Torrens University Australia. He is a visiting professor at Greenwich University, UK. Previous professorial appointments have been held at Curtin University Perth, RMIT University Melbourne and the University of Newcastle. His research publications are in human resource management, industrial relations, labour market analysis and labour regulation. His research interests include transitional labour markets, digital technology and the future of work and working time and well-being.

Philippa Butler is Lecturer of Research Methods in the Institute of Education, Massey University, New Zealand. She has also worked as a research officer and is very experienced at conducting externally funded education research projects. Her teaching interests are in mixed-methods research and research methodology, and her research interests include ethnic group identification and issues of equity in education.

Roslyn Cameron is Director of the Centre for Organisational Change and Agility, at Torrens University Australia. She is Co-Convenor and Founder of the Mixed Methods Research Special Interest Group of the Australian and New Zealand Academy of Management, a board member of the Mixed Methods International Research Association and a member of the Australian Human Resources Institute Advisory Research Panel in Australia. She has been the recipient of several large-scale workforce development research grants and an array of smaller-scale research grants related to skilled migration, work readiness/employability and future skilling/future of work for the Fourth Industrial Revolution, totalling AU$1.9 million, and has over 90 publications.

Kantha Dayaram is Associate Professor in Employment Relations at Curtin University, Perth, Australia. Her research interests are in employment equity and labour force transition in developed and developing economy contexts. Some of her work on gender and employment has been conducted in South Africa, Australia, Bhutan, Myanmar, Mongolia, Indonesia, India and Malaysia. She is a member of the university's gender research network.

Subas P. Dhakal is Senior Lecturer in Management in the UNE Business School at the University of New England, Armidale, Australia. He started his career as a communication officer in an integrated conservation and development project funded by the United Nations Development Programme in South Asia. He has a master's in environment management and a PhD in sustainability and technology policy. His teaching centres on the organisational strategies to solve social, economic and environmental challenges in Asia Pacific/South Asia. His current research interests include the ageing population and society, the future of education and employment and socio-economic resilience in the context of various sustainable development goals. He has received various grants worth nearly AU$450,000. He serves as Editorial Review Board Member of the *Equality, Diversity and Inclusion: An International Journal* as well as a Board Regional Representative for the Australian and New Zealand Academy of Management.

Nikki DiGregorio is Associate Professor in the School of Human Ecology and a member of the Women's, Gender, and Sexuality Studies Executive Board at Georgia Southern University, USA. DiGregorio's scholarship examines the interplay between social policy, language appropriation and the experiences of gender and sexual minorities.

Elizabeth Farrant began as a support worker in 2010 and has since worked across several organisations in the disability sector. She completed her bachelor of commerce (honours) at Curtin University and is currently completing a master's in disability and inclusion at Deakin University while working at policy and systemic advocacy organisation Purple Orange.

Scott Fitzgerald is Associate Professor in the School of Management and Marketing at Curtin University, Perth, Australia. His research interests are located in the areas of industrial/employment relations, sociology and political economy and focus primarily on organisations, professionalism and work in the public sector and in the communication and cultural sectors.

Erica French is Associate Professor at QUT Business School, Queensland University of Technology, Brisbane, Australia. Erica is a researcher in equity, diversity and inclusion and women in project management. Along with her colleagues Lynn Crawford and Beverley Lloyd Walker, she is a winner of the IPMA Research Prize for Outstanding Contribution to Project Management Research for their project "Exploring the Evolution of Project Based Careers". She is Associate Editor with the *Equality Diversity and Inclusion Journal* and a member of their advisory board. Her publications are available at https:// eprints.qut.edu.au/view/person/French,_Erica.html.

Arijana Haramincic is Executive Director with the Government of Nunavut, Department of Family Services, Canada. As a professional social worker for 26 years, she has worked in multicultural and indigenous communities, in both rural and remote and urban environments, and has led numerous transformational and change initiatives. Arijana holds a bachelor's degree in indigenous social work, a master's in social work, a master's in business administration and presently is pursuing a master's in indigenous relations and a PhD with Torrens University Australia focusing on public service leadership and its impact on service outcomes.

Lucy Kalep is a registered nurse and Unit Manager/Coordinator at Kerema General Hospital, Gulf Province, Papua New Guinea. For 34 years she has worked as a midwife, trained midwives and village birth attendants and persevered to achieve equality and fairness in the distribution of services to both urban and rural facilities for effecting safe deliveries of infants and maternal survival.

Ellie Korave is a registered nurse midwife and Associate Lecturer at the School of Health Science, Pacific Adventist University, Papua New Guinea and currently a candidate for a master's in philosophy. She is committed to training competent midwives for the safe delivery and survival of mothers and infants and for the efficient practice of emergency obstetric care.

Jacqueline Larkin is a psychologist with substantial experience in corporate human resources, academia and in her own consultancy business. Her focus is on talent management, career development, mental health and well-being, positive ageing and older workers. She has disseminated her research in the areas of positive ageing and older workers in Australian and international journals, conferences and books, including as an invited speaker/panellist.

Sharlene Leroy-Dyer is a Saltwater woman with family ties to Darug, Garigal, Awabakal and Wiradyuri peoples. Sharlene is Lecturer in Management at the University of Queensland, Australia, where she researches and teaches in the fields of employment relations and the disadvantage that Aboriginal and

Torres Strait Islander peoples face in education and employment. Sharlene would like to acknowledge that her chapter was written on unceded Aboriginal lands. She pays her respect to Elders past and present, and to all those who have walked before her.

Spencer Lilley is an Associate Professor and Director of Learning, Teaching and Equity at the School of Information Management, Victoria University of Wellington, New Zealand. Spencer's research interests focus on indigenous engagement with information and the indigenisation of cultural heritage institutions. Spencer has tribal affiliations to Te Atiawa, Muaūpoko and Ngāpuhi.

Amy Lim is Lecturer in Psychology and the Discipline Lead in Psychology at Murdoch University's Singapore Campus. Her research area focuses on social psychology, where she examines the individual differences amongst women and how these can account for performance differences in women within the fields of science, technology, engineering and mathematics and in the workplace. She also applies modern evolutionary theories to the context of current societal issues. Her recent work revealed the motivations underlying fake news sharing and procrastination during COVID-19.

Jennifer Litau is a social scientist and applied researcher in population and development, health and mixed methods. She was previously Senior Lecturer in the School of Humanities, Education and Theology and is currently Manager for Academic Quality Assurance at the Pacific Adventist University, Port Moresby, Papua New Guinea. In her current role, she researches diversity, equity and inclusion concerns as human rights issues.

McKenzie Maviso is Lecturer in Public Health at the School of Medicine and Health Sciences, University of Papua New Guinea, Port Moresby, Papua New Guinea. His research focuses on nutrition and dietetics, maternal health and perinatal outcomes and behavioural science.

Syed Mohyuddin is Lecturer and Discipline Leader for Human Resources/ Management at the Australian Institute of Business. He holds a PhD in management from Curtin University, Western Australia. He has over 19 years of experience in teaching human resources and management courses in the Middle East and Australia. He worked as a full-time lecturer and a part-time tutor for various management subjects in Curtin Business School. He has also taught at La Trobe University, Mildura Campus, Victoria, Australia. His PhD research was related to the challenges faced by skilled migrants to achieve professional recognition in Australian organisations, one of his core research interests.

Peter Musinguzi is a PhD researcher at the University of New England Business School in its Centre for Agribusiness, Armidale, Australia. He has over eight years of social enterprise professional experience in Uganda and has conducted research in Uganda, Kenya and Malaysia on rural development. His research targets social enterprise performance and how social entrepreneurship facilitates inclusive development.

Lucie Newsome lectures in management and economics and has extensive experience in gender equality research and program development. She has published in the fields of gender and agriculture, gendered experiences of work, gender and entrepreneurship, farm succession, paid parental leave policy and the gendered composition of corporate boards. Formerly, she held senior policy and project roles in the New South Wales and Queensland governments.

Kathryn Pillay is Senior Lecturer in Sociology at the University of KwaZulu-Natal (UKZN), South Africa. Her areas of teaching and research focus on "race", migration, identity and belonging. She was employed as a senior human resources officer at the former University of Natal and thereafter the merged UKZN for five years. Her most recent publication is the co-edited volume *Relating Worlds of Racism: Dehumanisation, Belonging and the Normativity of European Whiteness* (2019). She is also a National Research Foundation rated scholar which in South Africa is an indicator of peer recognition of her research.

Mahan Poorhosseinzadeh is a Senior Lecturer of Human Resources Management at the Australian Institute of Business, Adelaide, Australia. Prior to this, she was an academic in the Department of Employment Relations and Human Resources and a research fellow at the Centre for Work, Organisation and Wellbeing at Griffith Business School. She researches and publishes in the area of women and career progression and women's underrepresentation in senior positions and her research interests include equal opportunity at work, gender and work, women in leadership, flexible work arrangements and inclusive leadership.

Endah Prihatiningtyastuti is a PhD candidate in the School of Management at Curtin Business and Law School, Curtin University, Australia. Endah is a government officer in the Ministry of Women Empowerment and Child Protection in Indonesia.

Anne Pulotu is a registered nurse and health promotion advocate in non-communicable disease prevention. She is a master of philosophy candidate and a researcher in lifestyle and public health promoting healthy lifestyles. She is also a tutor in the School of Health Sciences, Pacific Adventist University in Port Moresby, Papua New Guinea.

Peter Rawlins is an Associate Professor and Director of Academic Programmes for the Institute of Education, Massey University, New Zealand. Peter's research interests are in assessment and mixed-methods research. He teaches in undergraduate and postgraduate assessment as well as a postgraduate mixed-methods research course and a research project course.

Subba Reddy Yarram is Associate Professor in Finance in the UNE Business School at the University of New England, Australia. He primarily teaches finance units. His research covers corporate governance and small business economics/management. He is an active member of the Australian and New Zealand Academy of Management.

Shaun Ruggunan is Associate Professor of Human Resource Management at the University of KwaZulu-Natal, South Africa. Shaun has published on maritime human resources and management education in South Africa. Recently, he has been part of an international project exploring what it means to decolonise management and organisational knowledge.

Peggy Shannon-Baker is an Associate Professor in the Curriculum, Foundations and Reading Department and an affiliate faculty member of the Women's, Gender and Sexuality Studies program at Georgia Southern University, USA. Their scholarship explores the impact of oppressive systems such as racism and heteronormativity on education and research methods.

Alison Sheridan is Emeritus Professor in the UNE Business School, University of New England, Armidale, Australia. She has been researching women's experiences in the paid workforce for nearly 30 years.

Glenda Strachan is a Professor at Griffith University, Brisbane, Australia. Glenda's research focuses on women and work, especially gender equity within organisations. Throughout her career she has developed a body of research on contemporary and historical workplace change, with a special emphasis on gender and equity. Since the 1980s, she has been researching and writing about contemporary developments in equal employment opportunity and diversity policies and practice. Recent research focuses on university employees.

Hilda Tanimia is Specialist Obstetrician and Gynaecologist, Port Moresby General Hospital. She was previously a lecturer at the School of Medicine and Health Sciences, University of Papua New Guinea. Her research interests include sexual and reproductive health, maternal health and family planning issues.

Tasmiha Tarafder is a course coordinator at the School of Communication, RMIT University, Melbourne, Australia. She was awarded a Master's by Research from the University of Canberra, Australia. Tasmiha completed her PhD in Management in 2020 from RMIT University, Melbourne, Australia. Her PhD thesis title is 'inclusive governance for promoting employee well-being: the study of RMGs in Bangladesh.' Her research interests include entrepreneurship, management, occupational health and safety, women in the workplace, health beliefs and attitudes. She has presented research papers at international conferences and has earned highly commended and best paper awards.

Poisy Tava Kae is Deputy Principal Academic of Kerema Coronation Secondary School in Kerema Town, Gulf Province, Papua New Guinea. Poisy's interests lie in treating different students and people equally and fairly.

Renato A. Villano is Professor of Economics in the University of New England Business School, Armidale, Australia, and specialises in the area of applied econometrics, agricultural economics and development economics. His research activities focus on the areas of efficiency and productivity analysis, agricultural marketing, value chain analysis, risk analysis in production systems, poverty measurement and impact assessment.

Peter Waring is Murdoch University's Pro Vice Chancellor for Transnational Education and Singapore Dean. A qualified lawyer, Peter also holds degrees in commerce and management. His research and teaching interests span the business and law fields of employment relations, human resource management, corporate governance, labour law and higher education policy. He has lived in Southeast Asia for the last 20 years.

Preface

We welcome readers to this collection on managing diversity, equality and inclusion (DEI). Many organisations covering the private, public and the not-for-profit sectors have active DEI policies and programs and are subject to meeting legislative standards and reporting requirements around DEI principles. Organisationally, the case for active DEI programs is linked to good business, staff profiles should reflect community and consumer profiles and organisations must conform to community standards around equal opportunity, anti-discrimination and human rights. Supporting these community standards are international conventions that encode human rights including equality and inclusion. DEI extends beyond employment and the workplace and includes access to and participation in basic physical and human infrastructure including health, education, training, transport, housing and communications. Being excluded from these facilities limits the ability to participate in the labour market, and hence being capable of accessing jobs, careers and a basic income. Assessing DEI is thus a holistic process in terms of the criteria assessed and the level of analysis.

The purpose of the book is to illustrate the breadth of DEI research and to inform researchers who are examining DEI topics. There is a wide spread of topics and countries included in the book. There is also diversity among the researchers in terms of age, gender and ethnicity, and in terms of covering early-career and post-graduate researchers through to established researchers. Contributions examine gender, age, disability and ethnicity. They range from organisational case studies to national policy analysis. The research approaches cover standard surveys, interviews and secondary data analyses, and they also include discussions on research processes that consider the personal challenges of DEI research and researching First Nation peoples. Behind DEI programs are the international conventions that are set out later in the prelims.

Acknowledgements

The editors thank the contributors, referees and the publishing staff for their support and patience in helping to bring this collection to fruition.

Abbreviations

AIATSIS	Australian Institute for Aboriginal and Torres Strait Islander Studies
AWARE	Association of Women for Action and Research
B-BBE Act	Broad-Based Black Economic Act
BBA	born before arrival
CCF	Community Capitals Framework
CEDAW	Convention of Elimination of Any Form of Discrimination against Women
COAG	Council of Australian Governments Reform Council
CTG	Closing the Gap
DEA	data envelopment analysis
DEI/DE&I	diversity, equality/equity and inclusion
DM	diversity management
EE Act	Employment Equity Act
EmOC	emergency obstetric care
FIFO	fly in/fly out
GDP	gross domestic product
GEDI	gender equality and diversity initiative
GNH	Gross National Happiness
HIS	health information system
HRM	human resource management
IAS	Indigenous Advancement Strategy
ICT	information and communications technology
ILO	International Labour Organization
IQ	Inuit Qaujimajatuqangit
ISV	Inuit societal values
KPA	key performance area

LGBT/ LGBTQ+	lesbian, gay, bisexual, transgender, queer
LMP	labour market programs
MA	Microboards Australia
MMR	mixed-methods research
NCWC	National Commission for Women and Children
NDIS	National Disability Insurance Scheme
NEP	new economic policy
NGO	non-governmental organisation
NZIST	New Zealand Institute of Skills and Technology
OECD	Organisation for Economic Co-operation and Development
PNG	Papua New Guinea
RMG	ready-made garment
SDGs	Sustainable Development Goals
SE	social enterprise
SMEs	small and medium-sized enterprises
UDHR	Universal Declaration of Human Rights
UK	United Kingdom
UN	United Nations
UNDP	United Nations Development Programme
US/USA	United States of America
WA	Western Australia
WHO	World Health Organization

Principles underlying diversity, equity and inclusion in the workplace and beyond

UNITED NATIONS DECLARATION OF HUMAN RIGHTS (1948)

Article 2

Everyone is entitled to all the rights and freedoms set forth in this Declaration, without distinction of any kind, such as race, colour, sex, language, religion, political or other opinion, national or social origin, property, birth or other status.

Article 23

Everyone has the right to work, to free choice of employment, to just and favourable conditions of work and to protection against unemployment.
Everyone, without any discrimination, has the right to equal pay for equal work.
Everyone who works has the right to just and favourable remuneration. (www.un.org/en/about-us/universal-declaration-of-human-rights)

INTERNATIONAL LABOUR ORGANIZATION FUNDAMENTAL PRINCIPLES AND RIGHTS AT WORK

United Nations Sustainable Development Goals
Goal 3 Ensure healthy lives and promote wellbeing for all of all at all ages.
Goal 5 Achieve gender equality and empower all women and girls.
Goal 8 Promote sustained, inclusive and sustainable economic growth, full and productive employment, and decent work for all. (https://sdgs.un.org/goals)
The International Labour Organization Decent Work Agenda
What is decent work?
It is the aspirations of all people for their working lives: for work that is productive, delivers a fair income with security and social protection, safeguards their basic rights and offers equality of opportunity and treatment, prospects for personal development, the chance for recognition and the chance to have their opinions heard.
The overall goal of the ILO is decent work for all women and men in all countries. This is captured in four strategic objectives: i) fundamental principles and rights at work and international labour standards; ii) employment and income opportunities; iii) social protection and social security; and iv) social dialogue and tripartism. These objectives apply to all workers: women and men in both formal and informal econ-

omies, in waged or working on their own account, in fields, factories and offices, in their homes or in their communities.
ILO Asian Decent Work Decade, Resources Kit, Bangkok: www.ilo.org/wcmsp5/ groups/public/---asia/---ro-bangkok/documents/publication/wcms_098263.pdf

UNITED NATIONS SUSTAINABLE DEVELOPMENT GOALS

Goal 3 Ensure healthy lives and promote wellbeing for all of all at all ages.
Goal 5 Achieve gender equality and empower all women and girls.
Goal 8 Promote sustained, inclusive and sustainable economic growth, full and productive employment, and decent work for all. (https://sdgs.un.org/goals)

THE INTERNATIONAL LABOUR ORGANIZATION DECENT WORK AGENDA

What is decent work?

It is the aspirations of all people for their working lives: for work that is productive, delivers a fair income with security and social protection, safeguards their basic rights and offers equality of opportunity and treatment, prospects for personal development, the chance for recognition and the chance to have their opinions heard.

The overall goal of the ILO is decent work for all women and men in all countries. This is captured in four strategic objectives: i) fundamental principles and rights at work and international labour standards; ii) employment and income opportunities; iii) social protection and social security; and iv) social dialogue and tripartism. These objectives apply to all workers: women and men in both formal and informal economies, in waged or working on their own account, in fields, factories and offices, in their homes or in their communities.

ILO Asian Decent Work Decade, Resources Kit, Bangkok: www.ilo.org/wcmsp5/ groups/public/---asia/---ro-bangkok/documents/publication/wcms_098263.pdf

PART I

1. An introduction to *A Field Guide to Managing Diversity, Equality and Inclusion in Organisations*

John Burgess, Subas P. Dhakal and Roslyn Cameron

INTRODUCTION

What is diversity, equality and inclusion (DE&I)? Since the three elements of the DE&I agenda remain contested in terms of meanings and implications, it is imperative to adopt working definitions for the purpose of this book.

First, Extension Foundation (n.d.) describes diversity as: "the presence of differences that may include race, gender, religion, sexual orientation, ethnicity, nationality, socioeconomic status, language, (dis)ability, age, religious commitment, or political perspective". It is clear from this description that the notion of diversity has multiple layers, and it is not just about being dissimilar from a subjective norm in any given organisation. Second, McGill University (n.d.) compares two similar constructs of equity and equality and suggests that while equality is about equal treatment, equity acknowledges that different types of barriers require different levels of supportive mechanisms to ensure fair access to opportunities and resources. It can be posited that these two different notions are two different approaches to ensure inclusion in an organisation. Third, the University of Pittsburgh (n.d.) portrays inclusion as "the wide variety of shared and different personal and group characteristics among human beings". It means improving the terms of participation for individuals and organisations in different socioeconomic contexts such as disability, race, sexual orientation, etc.

It is also noteworthy to clarify a basic understanding of DE&I management here. The literature uses diversity and DE&I interchangeably to cover the same process. Diversity management (DM) is in general linked to organisational human resource management (HRM) programs to support business objectives. According to Kaputch and Charest (2021):

> Diversity management is usually understood as the official recognition, consideration and support of lifestyles and personal characteristics of all employees by a private firm or an organization. It encompasses the concepts of respect and tolerance and is based on the idea that every individual is unique. In practice, diversity management refers to different awareness measures, providing support for minority groups, communication strategies and general guidelines about the main characteristics of various groups in order to facilitate the acceptance and inclusion of minority group members. The rationale for introducing diversity management is to increase efficiency or profits by underlining what different individuals might contribute to organizations. (p. 3)

The management aspects place the DM agenda in the context of organisational policies and practices, refer to tolerance, inclusion and acceptance and suggest a business case for DM. There is an articulated business case for diversity within organisations. It pays to nurture talent and appeal to diverse clients, to better reflect the wider cultural contexts in which organisations operate and bring diverse perspectives and ideas. It makes business sense to reflect diversity (Thomas, 1996). However, this view of HRM is linked to large organisations in developing economies with HRM divisions. Other employees in small firms or engaged on short-term employment contracts are not part of the DM program. Nor are those who are outside of the workforce, nor are the majority of the population in emerging economies, many of whom are engaged in informal and at-call employment (ILO, 2018).

DE&I management goes beyond the organisations, beyond managerial goals, it extends beyond profit in terms of its benefits and it also extends beyond diversity to incorporate inclusion and equality. Equality requires equal treatment of individuals regardless of their personal characteristics, such as equal pay for equal work. It can be argued that DE&I management is a process that acknowledges population diversity, accommodates difference and attempts to promote equality and inclusion. Many groups suffer from systemic exclusion from the workforce due to limited access to health, education and infrastructure. Inclusion seeks to improve access of groups to the labour market and infrastructure to groups that face barriers in access, such as the disabled. The process extends beyond the formal workplace, it extends beyond developing economies and it is underpinned by social justice principles encoded in international conventions (French et al., 2010; Mor Barak, 2005). Being afforded fundamental human rights, including not being discriminated against at work or in employment conditions, and equal opportunity is embedded within international conventions sponsored by the United Nations (UN) and the International Labour Organization (ILO) (French and Maconachie,

2004). Behind DE&I management there is a framework of international, national and local laws and conventions that support equality and equal opportunity. DE&I embodies more than access to material benefits, it also refers to recognising and encompassing difference, whether it be religion, language, ethnicity or culture (Sakyi et al., 2021).

This book brings together chapters that examine the theories, practices and policies of DE&I management. There is recognition of the segregation and exclusions according to personal characteristics that are present across organisations and workforces across many criteria including recruitment, pay, non-wage benefits, income security, career progression and access to health and safety protection. In one of the world's wealthiest countries, the United States (US), there are deep-seated levels of poverty, and millions of workers in low-pay jobs who are trapped in poverty. Those most at risk of the poverty trap are women, especially black and Hispanic women; even those with human capital attributes such as job experience and post-secondary education find it difficult to move into better-paying jobs (Escotari and Krebs, 2021). Gender has been used as a basis for entry into occupations and professions, for career development and for accessing the rewards from work (Kirton and Green, 2005). Other personal characteristics such as race, age, sexuality, ethnicity, religion and disability have been determinants of access to jobs and rewards (Burgess et al., 2010).

It is clear that DE&I management remains ambiguous, relatively new in the literature and contested in terms of its purpose and operation (Strachan et al., 2010a). There is growing recognition that operationally diversity is extensive in terms of all the characteristics that distinguish individuals and the ways in which diversity is manifested (Sakyi et al., 2021). Behind the DE&I agenda is the concept of identity, how individuals see themselves and how other individuals, organisations and society see them. Identity is grounded in history, culture and institutions. Diversity is multidimensional. It is not single features that are potentially advantageous or disadvantageous in the labour market and workforce, there are multiple factors that operate together to reinforce exclusion or preferential treatment (Sakyi et al., 2021). Combined features such as gender and sexuality, age and disability or religion and ethnicity can compound inequality and disadvantage. It is not simply a matter of identifying how individual factors contribute to diversity, it is also important to consider how they combine and evolve through time. Within diversity research and DM, it is important to recognise how the intersectionality of factors reinforces advantage and disadvantage (Dennissen et al., 2020). With diversity comes inclusion. It is not sufficient to recognise difference, it requires the development and implementation of programs of inclusion from the workplace through to access to social goods and to political participation. Inclusion and tolerance for difference is one factor that has been identified as contributing to dynamic community development (Florida, 2004). Dhakal et al. (2021) observe that unequal female representation remains a prominent challenge in the judiciary amongst developing economies in South Asia and contend that addressing the issue of women's representation in the labour workforce across a variety of sectors and professions, including the judiciary of developing countries like Nepal, is significant from the perspective of the UN Sustainable Development Goals at the national level (p. 236).

Various aspects of DE&I management are constantly in the news such as the recent coverage of bullying, sexual harassment and racism at the multi-national mining company Rio Tinto (Butler, 2022). Claims have been linked to discrimination, harassment and exclusion based on personal characteristics such as gender, ethnicity or race; to programs and policies designed to improve access to the labour force and jobs for identified disadvantaged groups such as First Nations, the disabled, immigrants and the aged; through to campaigns by trade unions and non-governmental organisations (NGOs) highlighting discriminatory practices and poor working conditions in global industries such as shipping and apparel (Clean Clothes Campaign, 2020). According to Kirton and Green (2005), gender and race were the key factors organising access to and rewards in the US and United Kingdom labour market. The advent of social media has given a voice to the disadvantaged and discriminated against, such as the Black Lives Matter and #MeToo movements that highlighted racial discrimination in the US justice system and sexual abuse and exploitation across organisations and the community (Dunn, 2020; Johnson, 2021).

The UN Sustainable Development Goals include several objectives that support DE&I (Sakyi, 2021). Organisations across all sectors, occupations and ownership (public, private, NGOs) are in many countries obliged by statute to develop DE&I programs and to issue regular reports to statutory organisations that are responsible for human rights and equal opportunity. In other instances, the business case for DE&I together with corporate social responsibility and ethical investment funds in the case of private organisations, and organisational charters linked to fundraising for NGOs, support operational DM programs (see Dhakal, 2018; Köllen, 2016). In practice the range, quality, and effectiveness of DE&I policies vary across organisations and in many cases are driven by the reporting requirements imposed by legislation or other stakeholders such as stock exchanges and socially responsible investors (Kollen, 2016; Strachan et al., 2010b). Refer to the annual reports of listed companies and the websites of public-sector agencies and NGOs and you will find a workforce diversity program and report demonstrating the citizenship credentials and the commitment to workforce diversity and inclusion (see Rio Tinto, 2020; World Vision, 2020). For example, Mineral Councils of Australia (n.d.), the leading advocate for Australia's minerals industry, promoting and enhancing sustainability, profitability and competitiveness posits that "Diverse teams are more productive, innovative and creative" and showcases inclusion and diversity across the industry on a dedicated webpage. Professional bodies such as the Australian Human Resources Institute has awards for diversity and bestows these awards on companies and individuals every year (see www.ahri .com.au/awards/select-your-award/workplace-diversity-awards/).

THE DIFFERENT DIMENSIONS, CONTEXTS AND APPROACHES TO DE&I MANAGEMENT

A landmark 2019 Inclusiveness Index Annual Report (Menendian et al., 2019) reflected on the state of exclusion and inequality and asserted that "Religion, ethnicity, skin colour, age, sexual orientation, and race, among other identity groups, are shaping politics everywhere. Societies are polarising around these fundamental axes, as demagogic political leaders promise to keep outsiders away. Xenophobia is on the rise, and anti-immigrant sentiment swells in a period of mass migration" (p. 4). Conceptually, DE&I is complex and linked to synonyms such as equality, inclusion, fairness, equity, balance and empowerment (Sakyi et al., 2021). On the negative side, it is associated with discrimination, exploitation, privilege, segregation and exclusion. Operationally, the multiple dimensions of diversity mean that it is underpinned by different principles (human rights, meeting legislative requirements) and different objectives (non-discriminatory recruitment, equal pay, meeting quotas) (French et al., 2010).

Sakyi et al. (2021) identify globalisation as promoting diversity across multinational workforces and consumers, and effective DE&I programs can support national and organisational competitive advantage. Georgiadou (2019, p. 12) state that the:

> Literature indicates a plethora of benefits associated with the recruitment, retention, and promotion of a diverse workforce, which is representative of today's multicultural society. What seems to still puzzle organizations, though, is how a company can manage diversity, while ensuring inclusion and safeguarding equality. Additionally, organizations must identify practices that are aligned with its culture and vision, so as to implement effectively a business strategy that incorporates and promotes diversity as an asset and an ultimate competitive advantage, not just another tick on a box that legislators and/or policymakers imposed.

There is an extensive management literature that addresses global DE&I within multinational enterprises and examines the management of diverse teams by culture, ethnicity and language; the recruitment and retention of diverse key staff; and talent development and management across diverse groups and in diverse contexts (Özbilgin et al., 2013).

DE&I practice in the main is organisationally based and addresses work and the workplace. However, entry to the workplace is governed by prior access to education, training, health and public infrastructure. The unemployed are outside the workplace and are not part of the organisational DE&I agenda that supports the employed. Across the labour market there is segregation and division, and exclusion from employment, according to personal characteristics such as age, gender, location and ethnicity (Burgess et al., 2010). Hence there are multiple contexts for evaluating diversity that include the workplace, governance and political institutions, communities and the state. Diversity assessment ranges from the micro level of individuals to the macro level of group identification such as women, youth and LGBTQI+. At the macro level it takes in industries and professions, national and international systems. The UN and the ILO, and many NGOs, promote DE&I principles globally. While DE&I management is organisationally based, there are national and community standards to assess regarding the quality of life, and access to services and infrastructure across different groups. Those groups that are disadvantaged in the labour market are also disadvantaged according to other criteria such as access to public services and infrastructure such as education, training, health and communications networks (UNDP, 2020b).

DE&I policies can range from long-term societal programs such as addressing inequality in access to education, health, training and community services; to short-term organisational programs that include non-discriminatory recruitment and promotion programs, and non-discriminatory payment and reward systems. More ambitious approaches include affirmative action and positive discrimination, especially to rectify systemic exclusion such as through quotas for women in senior management roles or in governance positions, or through programs that offer preferential access to post-secondary education and public-sector jobs for First Nations peoples.

By what criteria do you assess the effectiveness of DE&I programs? Is it in terms of representation and inclusivity, or is it in terms of rewards such as pay and employment conditions? Then there is the issue of identifying an appropriate comparator – diversity relative to what? Should it be an average (say wages or labour force participation) or should it be relative to another identified group, for example, white males (Burgess et al, 2010)? A critique of the use of dominant group (male) comparators in the case of labour market disadvantage faced by women is that equality cannot be achieved since biological difference impacts on workplace opportunity (French et al., 2010).

Homogeneity, exclusion and inequality are not static. Through time national demographic profiles change because of the changing age distribution, and through the effects of international migration (Meenat and Vanka, 2017). The challenge of ageing societies in the face of compulsory retirement regimes, rigid working arrangements and social security regimes can restrict the participation of older persons in the workforce (Dhakal et al, 2022). Across organisations and countries, the manifestations of diversity, inclusion and equity differ, and consequently there are differences in the DE&I programs that are present (Georgiadou et al., 2019). These are all important, yet difficult to resolve issues. Through the chapters of the book these issues will recur. Despite the multiple dimensions and challenging analytical issues, the chapters demonstrate diversity in practice within different countries, across different groups, and at different levels.

RESPONSIBILITY, GOVERNANCE, AND THE EFFECTIVENESS OF DE&I PROGRAMS

The influence of DE&I on corporate governance and on corporate social responsibility has been addressed in the literature (El-Bassiouny and El-Bassiouny, 2019). Notwithstanding the limitations of social responsibility as a notion to resolve real-world organisational problems, Dhakal et al. (2020) posit that if understood through the lens of shared values whereby organisations encourage and/or engage with a variety of stakeholders, there is a potential for social responsibility to pursue mutually beneficial or win-win solutions. While we can observe differences across different groups according to educational attainment, wages and working conditions, and participation in decision making and governance roles, what can be done about uneven representation and opportunity? Within organisations the DM agenda is driven by the business case and statutory obligations that include anti-discrimination and equal employment opportunities requirements. Organisations, typically through HRM divisions, are responsible for developing, implementing and reporting on their diversity and inclusion programs, and for compliance with legislative requirements. These processes are replicated in private, public and NGO organisations. The formal reporting processes associated with HRM diversity reporting or reports to stakeholders such as government agencies and shareholders can be assessed and evaluated. However, what happens in the workplace is only one context out of many to assess diversity. The reporting processes are often non-audited and contain gaps, for example, only reporting on full-time ongoing employees and excluding temporary and short-term contract workers, or workers linked to integrated production through international supply chains (French and Simpson, 2010). Such reporting may have more to do with appearance than substance (Strachan et al., 2010a). Other important dimensions impacting on equality and inclusion include human capability (Rola Rubzen and Burgess, 2016) that is captured by access to education, health, infrastructure and community services. Such public goods have a direct impact on the quality of life and on the ability to participate in the labour force. Furthermore, beyond economic participation, there is participation in governance and leadership.

Here the measures of participation may include membership of governing institutions such as boards of directors, and representation in parliaments and executive positions. The Human Development Index developed by the UN Development Programme (UNDP) includes several measures linked to health, education and living standards that can be used to track national human development as well (UNDP, 2020a).

Two problems with the business case for DM are that it is voluntarist, and implicitly if business conditions or results deteriorate, then the case for diversity diminishes. The human rights approach is supported by legislation that prohibits discrimination and promotes inclusion. However, exclusion can be systemic and cumulative across multiple dimensions. It requires more than equal opportunities and anti-discrimination to eliminate the exclusion that is present and faced by First Nations peoples and the disabled (Dyer, 2010; Smith Ruig, 2010). Positive practices and targeted support programs are required to overcome systemic barriers (French et al., 2010). The challenge is how to promote both diversity and equality across the different domains of civil society and achieve gains, as opposed to preventing discriminatory and exclusionary outcomes. Here, affirmative action programs attract criticism that they are discriminatory, however, the advocates of affirmative action argue that positive and immediate action is required to address systemic discrimination and exclusion that is long-standing and as such cannot be remedied by incremental and voluntarist programs. Past behaviours, laws and practices that segregated, excluded and discriminated against particular groups require compensatory actions and programs (Mor Barak, 2005, p. 67). Affirmative action has traction with respect to the exclusion of women from the workforce, First Nations peoples from the workforce, and public goods such as health and education.

Equally challenging is the assignment of responsibility for securing DE&I objectives. Legislative programs such as anti-discrimination and human rights programs require sanctions and enforcement regimes. This is difficult when discrimination is subtle and when victims are reluctant to be identified for fear of reprisal. Within organisations, the research suggests that leadership and commitment to DM programs make a difference (Padavic et al., 2020; Saxena, 2014). Enforcement of DE&I principles can be via NGOs and indirect sanctions such as shareholder and investor activism, consumer activism and social media campaigns. The obstacles to diversity and inclusion programs should also be acknowledged. For example, Mate et al. (2019) identify several key barriers and enablers that affect women's career and leadership development in Australian workplaces such as the competing demands of work and life and male-dominated organisational cultures that discriminate against women in covert ways (p. 857). Prejudices such as racism, sexism and homophobia are present and will generate opposition to diversity programs as privileging certain groups and going against community standards, especially in such areas as sexual preference and religion (Mor Barak, 2005). On another level, spatial exclusion is important. Where you live can determine access to health, education and jobs. Living in isolated communities compounds the exclusion facing First Nations communities. In emerging economies, the capacity to support improvements in jobs, health and education programs is limited and for many countries the support needed to improve opportunity for women, youth, the elderly and those with disabilities is dependent on aid and NGO program support (Rola-Rubzen and Burgess, 2016).

WHY INFORMED DE&I RESEARCH IS REQUIRED

The above discussion highlights the complexity, multiple dimensions, controversy and challenges around DE&I management calls for research to inform policymakers. Informed research serves several purposes. First, it provides benchmarks against which organisations, countries and governments can be assessed. Second, it identifies what programs work and why they work – and if they fail, why they fail. Third, there is the opportunity to inform the research process. How do you go about evaluating diversity programs? What research processes are appropriate? How do you overcome the barriers to research, especially when processes are non-conventional and outside of the paradigms established by funding organisations, journals and universities?

DE&I RESEARCH METHODS

From the chapters in the book a range of research approaches and methods are applied. The level of analysis extends from the individual and personal to the national and aggregate. The information collected and analysed ranges from personal narratives, to interviews, focus groups, surveys, national and international databases. Three elements of DE&I are personal, especially if you face barriers to participation in labour markets and civil society because of personal features and beliefs. Diversity and inclusion are communal where groups of the population are excluded from human capital building infrastructure such as health and education and from the labour force. The analysis of international institutions such as the ILO and UNDP provide international and national analysis of diversity and inclusion, as well as case studies and focused surveys (UNDP, 2020b). The selection of research methods is guided by the research questions, the scope of the research and the focus of the research. In this volume the variety of research methods is both extensive and innovative, especially around the intersectionality and First Nations peoples' research. One overriding challenge in conducting research in this area is that of gaining access to research participants who are reluctant to come forward, especially where there are legal, community and cultural prohibitions on sexuality, gender roles and religious practice. Beyond identification and encouraging participation, there are challenges around confidentiality and protection of the identity of informants. Organisational research that addresses workplace harassment and bullying by race, gender or ethnicity must meet this challenge.

A FIELD GUIDE FOR RESEARCHING DE&I MANAGEMENT

Each chapter informs researchers who wish to conduct research in the identified area covered by the chapter. Through case studies of diversity in country contexts, and micro-organisational contexts, the book provides insights and guidance for the researcher. Case study chapters include research tips, useful websites, further areas of research and guidance to conducting research in the field. The domain of the case studies extends to the theoretical, analytical and policy evaluation process. The research tips have relevance to analysis, practice and policy. Tips for conducting research in the field are also provided as some field research documented in the collection is faced with challenges of remote locations and communication, cultural and language challenges. Other chapters also discuss First Nations research methodologies with traditions that require culturally sensitive approaches to conducting research.

THE STRUCTURE OF THE BOOK

The book is organised into three parts. Part I introduces the book and contains a literature analysis (Chapter 2). Part II contains the research case studies, organised on a country of context basis. Part III includes a detailed policy discussion (Chapter 22) and a conclusion (Chapter 23). The countries included cover both developed economies (such as the US and Australia) and emerging economies like Bhutan and Bangladesh. The workforce groups that are researched include women, the aged, the disabled, First Nations peoples, migrants, LGBT+ and ethnic minorities. The focus ranges from organisational analysis to national analysis. The methods employed include literature analysis, policy documentary analysis, interviews, focus groups, observations, participant mapping and surveys.

Chapter 2 by Dhakal employs a rapid bibliometric analysis of the literature to demonstrate prevalent themes of research, research hotspots and influential stakeholders. These findings have implications for future research directions, organisations and policymakers across countries included in this volume and beyond.

Chapter 3 by Leroy-Dyer examines the exclusion of Aboriginal and Torres Strait Islander peoples in Australia. Since 1967, successive Australian governments have attempted to correct these past policies by enacting policies to redress this disadvantage. One such policy is the "Closing the Gap" strategy announced in 2009. This chapter looks at the purpose of the strategy, what policies have been enacted and what progress has been made.

Chapter 4 by Newsome and Sheridan focuses on women's re-entry into the labour market following periods of unpaid care in regional Australia. The chapter utilises a case study of the Regional Australia Bank to demonstrate how strategic approaches to return to work can support women's career progression and meet labour force shortages in regional areas.

Chapter 5 by Mohyuddin and Cameron explores the DE&I issues experienced by skilled migrants in Australia. The chapter presents two case studies of research conducted with skilled migrants.

Chapter 6 by Larkin examines the ageing workforce in Australia, suggesting that the 50+ segment of the workforce is the most engaged cohort across all generations and, therefore, recruiting, rewarding and retaining workers aged 50+ is critical for organisational sustainability. The chapter offers a case study of Australian universities' response to their ageing workforce.

Chapter 7 by Farrant focuses on "microboards" that have been developed to ensure people with disability engage with community members without disability and express what they need to have to support the life experiences they require. The chapter utilises a community capitals framework to capture key variables that supported five Western Australian microboards.

Chapter 8 by Bahtic, Fitzgerald and Burgess discusses the challenges faced by lesbian, gay and bisexual employees in the mining sector in Western Australia. The chapter addresses the views and experiences of these individuals and provides an additional layer to previous literature by examining an area of research that requires further examination.

Chapter 9 by Tarafder and Burgess is set in Bangladesh and within the context of the ready-made garment sector. Using secondary evidence and interviews with factory managers, this chapter reports on the progress in improving the working conditions of garment workers within the sector since the 2013 Rana Plaza building collapse.

Chapter 10 by Poorhosseinzadeh and Strachan discusses the challenges of conducting equity research in Bhutan. They argue that the knowledge gains in this qualitative study emerged through the ongoing development of the relationship between the research participants and researchers conducted in a cross-cultural setting.

Chapter 11 by Haramincic discusses leadership that supports DE&I and its challenges in the context of Inuit and multicultural workplaces in the newest and largest territory in Canada, Nunavut, more specifically in the field of social services. The challenges of DE&I workplaces are varied and complex, however, embedding cultural values and leading in a culturally congruent and safe manner creates the environment that supports employees of diverse backgrounds.

Chapter 12 by Prihatiningtyastuti, Dayaram and Burgess discusses the challenges involved in women's transition from unpaid informal work to paid formal work in rural Indonesia. The growth opportunities offered by the restructured Indonesian economy have been slow to translate into material gains for women. Regional policymakers fail to include targeted strategies and mechanisms that would sufficiently address inherent employment equity challenges that disadvantage women.

Chapter 13 by Adapa and Yarram explores existing affirmative action policies in a multi-ethnic Malaysian society. The chapter finds that there is a need for revitalisation of the existing affirmative action policies for the betterment of education, employment and business development in Malaysia.

Chapter 14 by Baker examines intersectional gender justice in professional design practice. The chapter explores the barriers to gender justice in professional design practice. It documents systems mapping workshops where gender justice was proposed as a wicked problem.

Chapter 15 by Rawlins, Butler and Lilley asks what organisations can learn from kaupapa Māori research. One area that is particularly challenging is ensuring that the perspectives of minorities and marginalised groups are heard during decision-making processes. Drawing on the concept of kaupapa Māori research (research based on the philosophies of the indigenous people of New Zealand), this chapter argues that in order to fully capture the voices of all those in an organisation, it is critical to be aware of the varied cultural values present in the diverse mix of individuals.

Chapter 16 by Litau, Maviso, Korave, Tava Kae, Kalep, Tanimia, Pulotu and Abau examines the maternal mortality of rural women in Papua New Guinea. A key factor in reducing maternal mortality is the significant role played by effective management by a health system in relation to inputs, mobilisation of health workers, health delivery activities and achievement of health service outcomes. The chapter suggests that DE&I strategies in combination with the Sustainable Development Goals and the organisational systems approach work to address the problem.

Chapter 17 by Lim and Waring examines diversity policies and challenges in Singapore. Drawing upon insights from social psychology, economics and employment relations, the authors argue that in spite of a broad consensus on the merits of greater diversity, there remain substantial cultural, psychological and economic blockages to the achievement of diversity and inclusion.

Chapter 18 by Ruggunan, Pillay and Dayaram examines workplace diversity in South Africa. The chapter suggests that despite a plethora of diversity legislation and some notable quantitative achievements in diversity, a range of tacit and qualitative factors such as organisational culture, professional gate-keeping and overt and covert discrimination contribute to hampering equality, diversity and inclusion in South Africa's labour market.

Chapter 19 by Musinguzi, Villano and Baker reports on a quantitative analysis of social enterprise performance in rural Uganda. The chapter suggests that diversity and inclusion should play a significant role in the design and implementation of social enterprise interventions, particularly in targeting the achievement of the Sustainable Development Goals.

Chapter 20 by Shannon-Baker and DiGregorio examines strategies for supporting LGBTQ+ people in schools in the US. The purpose of this chapter is to discuss how DE&I work in schools can specifically support people who identify as LGBTQ+ and address the issues they face.

Chapter 21 by Sheridan and Adapa investigates the factors contributing to women's underrepresentation in senior roles in accounting firms internationally. Drawing on a qualitative, constructivist approach, the chapter demonstrates how factors operating at the macro, meso and micro levels entrench the gendered processes and structures that privilege men in the accounting profession.

Chapter 22 by French, Ali, Baker and Alsaree argues that globally, gender inequality in the workplace results in extreme poverty and unfair, unjust access to rewards, resources and opportunities for women. While gender equality and diversity initiatives have been identified as a potential answer to addressing inequality, they appear to be failing in their objectives. The challenge remains to better design and implement gender equality and diversity initiatives to achieve substantive outcomes to address injustice. This chapter explores the approach, type and justice perspectives that influence the design and implementation of initiatives.

Chapter 23 by Dhakal, Burgess and Cameron provides a summary of the chapters, highlights some of the interesting insights from the chapters, sets out areas for further research and reflects on the contribution of the collection to conducting research on equity, diversity and inclusion.

REFERENCES

Burgess, J., French, E. and Strachan, G. (2010), Workforce Diversity in Australia. In Strachan, G., French, E. and Burgess, J. (eds), *Managing Diversity in Australia*. McGraw Hill, Sydney, 17–40.

Butler, B. (2022), Bullying, Sexual Harassment and Racism Rife at Rio Tinto, Workplace Review Finds. *Guardian*, February 1. www.theguardian.com/business/2022/feb/01/bullying-sexual-harassment-and-racism-rife-at-rio-tinto-workplace-review-finds

Clean Clothes Campaign (2020), Global Brands, Global Exploitation. https://cleanclothes.org/blog/global-brands-global-exploitation

Dennissen, M., Benschop, Y. and van den Brink, M. (2020), Rethinking Diversity Management: An Intersectional Analysis of Diversity Networks. *Organization Studies*, 41(2), 219–240.

Dhakal, S. P. (2018), Cooperative Enterprises and Sustainable Development in Post-Crisis Nepal: A Social Responsibility Perspective on Women's Employment and Empowerment. *Contemporary Issues in Entrepreneurship Research*, 8, 185–200.

Dhakal, S. P., Mahmood, M. N., Brown, K. and Keast, R. (2020), Airport Social Responsibility and Regional Community Relations: Noisy Elephant in the Sky? *Australasian Journal of Regional Studies*, 26(2), 107–131.

Dhakal, S. P., Shrestha, S. and Dhakal, G. (2021), Gender on the Bench Matters for Sustainable Development: Examining Women in the Judiciary of Nepal through the Lens of Motility. In Crouch, M. (ed.), *Women and the Judiciary in the Asia Pacific*. Cambridge University Press, Cambridge, 235–260.

Dhakal, S. P., Nankervis, A. and Burgess, J. (2022), *Ageing in Asia and the Pacific in Changing Times*. Springer Nature, Singapore.

Dunn, K. R. (2020), Lessons from #MeToo and #BlackLivesMatter: Changing Narratives in the Courtroom. *Boston University Law Review*, 100, 2367.

Dyer, S. (2010), Employing Indigenous Australians: Strategies for Success. In Strachan, G., French, E. and Burgess, J. (eds), *Managing Diversity in Australia: Theory and Practice*. McGraw Hill, Sydney, 137–152.

El-Bassiouny, D. and El-Bassiouny, N. (2019), Diversity, Corporate Governance and CSR Reporting: A Comparative Analysis between Top-Listed Firms in Egypt, Germany and the USA. *Management of Environmental Quality: An International Journal*, 30(1), 116–136.

Escobari, M. and Krebs, E. (2021), *The American Dream in Crisis: Helping Low-Wage Workers Move up to Better Jobs*. Brookings, New York.

Extension Foundation (n.d.), What Is Diversity, Equity, and Inclusion (DEI)? https://dei.extension.org/

Florida (2004), *Cities and the Creative Class*. Routledge, New York.

French, E. and Maconachie, G. (2004), Managing Equity: Structure, Policy, and Justice Influences. *Women in Management Review*, 19(2), 98–108.

French, E. and Simpson, L. (2010), Auditing and Mapping Equity and Diversity: When Counting Is Not Enough. In Strachan, G., French, E. and Burgess, J. (eds), *Managing Diversity in Australia*. McGraw Hill, Sydney, 75–88.

French, E., Strachan, G. and Burgess, J. (2010), Approaches to Equity and Diversity: Conflicting Beliefs and Competing Ideals. In Strachan, G., French, E. and Burgess, J. (eds), *Managing Diversity in Australia*. McGraw Hill, Sydney, 41–56.

Georgiadou, A., Gonzalez-Perez, M. A. and Olivas-Luján, M. R. (2019), Diversity within Diversity Management: Where We Are, Where We Should Go, and How We Are Getting There. In Georgiadou, A., Gonzalez-Perez, M. A. and Olivas-Luján, M. R. (eds), *Diversity within Diversity Management: Country-Based Perspectives*. Emerald Publishing, Bingley, 1–20.

ILO (2018), Five Facts about Informal Economy in Africa. www.ilo.org/addisababa/whats-new/WCMS_377286/lang-en/index.htm

Johnson, B. (2021), How the Black Lives Matter Movement Enhanced Corporate Governance in 2020. *Emory Corporate Governance and Accountability Review*, 8(1), 99.

Kaputch, C. and Charest, E. (2021), Diversity, Equality and Inclusion, Discrimination and Exclusion: Defining the Concepts, Understanding the Debate and Analysing the Political. *Modern Law Review*, 66(1), 16–43.

Kirton, G. and Green, A.M. (2005), *The Dynamics of Managing Diversity: A Critical Approach*. Elsevier, Oxford.

Köllen, T. (2016), Acting out of Compassion, Egoism, and Malice: A Schopenhauerian View on the Moral Worth of CSR and Diversity Management Practices. *Journal of Business Ethics*, 138(2), 215–229.

Mate, S. E., McDonald, M. and Do, T. (2019), The Barriers and Enablers to Career and Leadership Development: An Exploration of Women's Stories in Two Work Cultures. *International Journal of Organizational Analysis*, 27(4), 857–874.

McGill University (n.d.), Equity, Diversity, and Inclusion at McGill. www.mcgill.ca/equity/edi-research/internal-mcgill-resources

Meenat, K. and Vanka, S. (2017), Developing an Empirical Typology of Diversity-Oriented Human Resource Management Practices. *Journal of Management Development*, 36(7), 915–929.

Menendian, S., Elsheikh, E. and Gambhir, S. (2019), *Inclusiveness Index: Measuring Global Inclusion and Marginality*. Berkeley, CA: Othering and Belonging Institute. http://belonging.berkeley.edu/inclusivenessindex

Mineral Councils of Australia (n.d.), Inclusion and Diversity in Australia's Minerals Industry. www.minerals.org.au/diversity-and-inclusion-australia%E2%80%99s-minerals-industry

Mor Barak, M. (2005), *Managing Diversity: Towards a Globally Inclusive Workplace*. Sage, Thousand Oaks.

Özbilgin, M., Jonsen, K., Tatli, A., Vassilopoulou, J. and Surgevil, O. (2013), Global Diversity Management, in Roberson, Q. (ed.), *The Oxford Handbook of Diversity and Work*. Oxford University Press, Oxford, 419–440.

Padavic, I., Ely, R. J. and Reid, E. M. (2020), Explaining the Persistence of Gender Inequality: The Work–Family Narrative as a Social Defense against the 24/7 Work Culture. *Administrative Science Quarterly*, 65(1), 61–111.

Rio Tinto (2020), Annual Report 2020. Rio Tinto, Melbourne. www.riotinto.com/en/invest/reports/annual-report

Rola-Rubzen, M. and Burgess, J. (2016), *Human Development and Capacity Building: Asia Pacific Trends, Challenges and Prospects*. Routledge, Abingdon.

Sakyi, K., Mweshi, G., Musona, D. and Tayali, E. (2021), A Synoptic Review of Theory and Practice of Diversity Management. *International Journal of Human Resource Studies*, 11(1), 204–249.

Saxena, A. (2014), Workforce Diversity: A Key to Improve Productivity. *Procedia Economics and Finance*, 11, 76–85.

Smith-Ruig, T. (2010), The Diversity and Complexity of Disability. In Strachan, G., French, E. and Burgess, J. (eds), *Managing Diversity in Australia: Theory and Practice*. McGraw Hill, Sydney, 205–220.

Strachan, G., French, E. and Burgess, J. (2010a), The Origins and Development of Managing Diversity. In Strachan, G., French, E. and Burgess, J. (eds), *Managing Diversity in Australia*. McGraw Hill, Sydney, 1–16.

Strachan, G., French, E. and Burgess, J. (2010b), Equity and Diversity within Organisations: Putting Policy into Practice. In Strachan, G., French, E. and Burgess, J. (eds), *Managing Diversity in Australia*. McGraw Hill, Sydney, 57–76.

Thomas, R. (1996), *Redefining Diversity*. American Management Association, New York.

United Nations Development Programme (UNDP) (2020a), The Human Development Index. UNDP, New York.

United Nations Development Programme (UNDP) (2020b), Human Development Report 2020. UNDP, New York.

University of Pittsburgh (n.d.), Diversity Statement. www.provost.pitt.edu/university -pittsburgh-embracing-diversity-and-inclusion

World Vision (2020), Annual Report 2020. World Vision, Burswood. www.worldvision .com.au/docs/default-source/annual-reports/wv-annual-reports/annual-report-2020 .pdf?sfvrsn=d4bbb23c_2

2. Bibliometric analysis of diversity, equality and inclusion: a field note

Subas P. Dhakal

INTRODUCTION

Diversity, equality, and inclusion (DE&I) in organisations has been collectively catapulted as a global priority. For example, "leaving no one behind" is the key driving force of the 2030 Agenda for Sustainable Development put together by the United Nations in 2015 (Together2030, n.d. p. 2). Various elements of the DE&I agenda span across the 17 Sustainable Development Goals (SDGs) that aim to ensure the social, economic, and environmental well-being of communities worldwide. In particular, Goal 10 – which promotes the reduction of inequalities within and among countries and aims to "empower and promote the social, economic and political inclusion of all irrespective of age, sex, disability, race, ethnicity, origin, religion or economic or other status" (UNDESA, 2015) – has DE&I implications in an organisational context. On the one hand, DE&I practices in organisations have been found to significantly contribute to their performance (see Chaudhry et al., 2021). For example, organisations of employees with a diverse mix of qualities, experiences, and work styles tend to be informed with a richer set of decision-making tools (see SHRM, n.d.). On the other hand, the DE&I agenda itself spans across multiple fields of inquiry and manifests differently in different contexts. For instance, the potential of information and communications technology (ICT) is considered to be a driver of equity in developed economies like Australia – relative to the metropolitan areas – for the regions (Dhakal et al., 2013, p. 463). At the same time, ICT is often associated with the digital divide and social exclusion in developing economies like Indonesia and Nepal (Dhakal and Tjokro, 2021; Dhakal et al., 2020). In this context, this chapter posits that a meticulous and methodical examination of recent literature on DE&I in organisations through bibliometric analysis can generate useful insights for future studies.

This chapter is structured in four parts, with the next section offering a background to bibliometrics in the context of the DE&I agenda. The subsequent sections describe the methods, results, and discuss implications before making concluding remarks.

THE DE&I AGENDA AND BIBLIOMETRICS

Diversity Equality and Inclusion

In a landmark report, Hunt et al. (2020) state that: "the business case for inclusion and diversity is stronger than ever. For diverse companies, the likelihood of outperforming industry peers on profitability has increased over time, while the penalties are getting steeper for those lacking diversity" (p. 3). However, the misinterpretations of what various elements of DE&I mean and what they truly represent in organisations can stifle DE&I and restrict organisational impact and influence (see Llopis, 2011). Chapter 1 of this volume adopted working definitions of the three elements of the DE&I agenda. These three notions are complementary to each other (Figure 2.1) in the sense that all three contribute to the broader DE&I agenda and highlight the significance of the need to overcome social inequalities caused by unfairness due to various facets of social hierarchy and exclusion. For instance, diverse organisations attract and retain people from multiple perspectives and backgrounds, e.g., gender, ethnicity, age, etc. Various organisations have embedded an inclusive culture to encourage employees to be an integral component of decision-making processes. Making employees feel valued through positive reinforcement and appropriate rewards leads to empowerment and equality. Equity, therefore, represents an outcome when diverse employees, despite their unique circumstances, have equal opportunities and organisational support mechanisms to succeed and grow. Given the DE&I agenda has become a burgeoning priority (UNDESA, 2009), a meticulous and methodical examination of the literature can produce valuable insights for societies and organisations. It is in this context that this chapter employs a literature review approach through a bibliometric analysis of the DE&I literature.

Bibliometric Analysis

Bibliometrics is a quantitative research approach to visualise a big picture based on the review of literature in a specific field. Literature reviews are often carried out to comprehend the extent of existing and/or emerging knowledge in a particular field of research. Although Snyder (2019) highlights the potential of literature reviews to make practical as well as theoretical contributions, there are multiple techniques and approaches to conducting literature reviews with varying purposes (Table 2.1). For example, on the one hand, advances in software applications have facilitated literature review processes and protocols

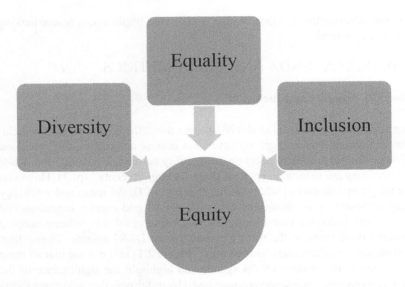

Figure 2.1   Conceptualisation of the DE&I agenda

via automated content analysis through the use of Leximancer and NVIVO software (see Mahmood et al., 2014; Dhakal et al., 2019). On the other hand, Mahmood and Dhakal (2022) suggest that bibliometrics is an analytical technique that allows researchers to assess the magnitude and scope of the literature in a specific field or subfield. Bibliometrics is also different from scientometrics as the latter primarily aims to examine and visualise the impact of literature. Provalis Research (2021) considers bibliometrics and scientometrics as two different analytical techniques to explore the scholarly literature. From the analytical perspective, both bibliometrics and scientometrics differ from other techniques such as content analysis and systematic reviews (Table 2.1) in that the primary emphasis of bibliometrics and scientometrics is the software-based visualisation of literature analysis. In recent years, bibliometrics has become an emerging area of research. A Google Scholar search of "bibliometrics analysis" found 106,000 results in February 2022. When the search was limited for a period between 2011 and the present, there were 17,200 results exemplifying remarkable growth in the previous decade. It is the potential of bibliometrics to unravel factors that foster knowledge advancements of a particular topic or research agenda, such as research clusters, individual researchers, and research institutions (see Mahmood and Dhakal, 2022).

Given that the DE&I agenda has emerged as a priority for organisations worldwide, bibliometric analysis can unravel various elements within the state of current knowledge production, including but not limited to key academic

Table 2.1   *Various approaches to review and analyse literature*

Technique	Description	Purpose	Source
Content analysis	Makes replicable and valid inferences from texts (or other meaningful matter)	To harvest keywords within primary or secondary qualitative data, e.g., grey and scholarly literature; interview transcripts	Hsieh and Shannon (2005); Krippendorff (2018)
Systematic review	Comprises several explicit and reproducible steps and carries out a comprehensive qualitative synthesis of prior studies	To find as much relevant research on the issue of interest using explicit methods to come to a reliable conclusion based on studies examined	Liberati et al. (2009); Griffith University (2022)
Scientometrics	Analyses the quantitative aspects of the production, dissemination, and use of scientific information and collectively visualises the impact of scholarly outputs	To evaluate the magnitude and scope of the impact of a field or subfield of research	Mingers and Leydesdorff (2015); Sharifi et al. (2021)
Bibliometrics	Explores and quantitatively analyses large volumes of written publications	To uncover emerging trends in the field of research, journal performance, and collaboration patterns	Ellegaard and Wallin (2015); Donthu et al. (2021)

institutions, individual researchers, and research clusters. Several bibliometric analyses have been carried out on various aspects within the DE&I agenda. For instance: (1) Najmaei and Sadeghinejad (2019) examined the literature on inclusive leadership; (2) Oswick and Noon (2014) examined trends, patterns, and implications of anti-discrimination solutions (equality, diversity, and inclusion); and (3) Solkhe (2021) reviewed LGBTQ-related workplace policies and procedures. However, these studies do not attempt to address collective policy, practice, and research priorities of the DE&I agenda. This chapter responds to this gap and demonstrates how to conduct a literature review using a rapid bibliometric analysis.

METHOD

The central research question that this chapter asks is: "What research insights can be generated by analysing the DE&I literature using bibliometric analysis?" Drawing on Dhakal et al. (2021) and Mahmood and Dhakal (2022), this chapter relied on a four-stage bibliometric analysis procedure: (1) software selection; (2) database selection; (3) outputs selection; and (4) mapping and visualisation (Figure 2.2). First, two software programs, Microsoft Excel 2018 and VOSviewer 1.6.1.13 (free version), were selected based on factors such as analytical features as well as capabilities of investigators to analyse data and produce graphs of top research outlets, co-occurrence of keyword mapping, and prominent institutions.

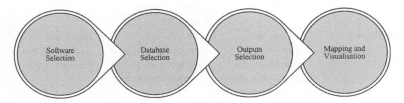

Figure 2.2   *Four-step process adopted for bibliometric analysis*

Second, the Scopus database was selected to capture DE&I-related literature because of its coverage. Third, the literature search was conducted using the four relevant keywords (Figure 2.3) "diversity", "equality", "inclusion" and "organisations" in the title, abstract and keyword sections of published material in the last decade. The search identified a total of 106 research outputs that were selected for the bibliometric analysis. Finally, mapping was carried out to visualise and present findings in terms of the number of publications per year, significant nations, key researchers and research outlets, and emergent topics.

TITLE-ABS-KEY (diversity AND equality AND inclusion AND organisations) AND (LIMIT-TO (SUBJAREA , "SOCI") OR LIMIT-TO (SUBJAREA , "BUSI") OR LIMIT-TO (SUBJAREA , "PSYC") OR LIMIT-TO (SUBJAREA , "ECON") OR LIMIT-TO (SUBJAREA , "ARTS")) AND (LIMIT-TO (LANGUAGE , "English")) AND (EXCLUDE (PUBYEAR , 2010) OR EXCLUDE (PUBYEAR , 2008))

Figure 2.3   *The search code used for a literature search in the Scopus database*

Trend of Research on the DE&I Agenda (2011–2021)

The number of research outputs has steadily increased over the last ten years. As shown in Figure 2.4, two specific years, 2019 (n=18) and 2021 (n=27), had the highest number of DE&I-related articles. One of the potential reasons behind this increase could be the recognition of the DE&I agenda within global priorities such as the 17 SDGs (UNDESA, 2015). In terms of type of output, journal articles (n=78) followed by book chapters (n=17) topped the list. Social sciences (n=65), business, management, and accounting (n=62), and psychology (n=17) were the top three subjects. In terms of number of publications by countries, United States (n=36), Canada (n=31), United Kingdom (n=18), Sweden (n=10), Australia (n=6), France (n=5), Germany (n=4), New Zealand (n=4), Netherlands (n=4), and Spain (n=4) top the list.

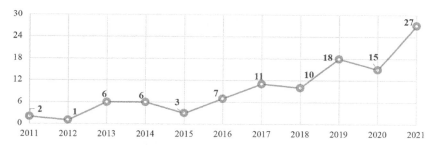

Figure 2.4   *Research outputs between 2011 and 2021*

Top Outlets

The top journals that have published the most articles on the DE&I agenda (n≥2) are depicted in Figure 2.5. The journal *Equality, Diversity, and Inclusion* had the highest number of articles (16), followed by *Personnel Review* with seven articles. Given that (1) *Equality, Diversity, and Inclusion* "offers a platform for critical and rigorous exploration of equal opportunities concerns including gender, ethnicity, class, disability, age, sexual orientation, religion, as well as other nascent forms of inequalities in the context of society" (Anonymous, n.d.a), and (2) *Personnel Review* publishes research that highlights innovation and emerging issues in the field, and the medium- to long-term impact of human resource management policy and practice – including the impact of gender, ethnicity, faith, disability, and other areas of "traditional disadvantage" (Anonymous, n.d.b), this finding is relatively self-explanatory.

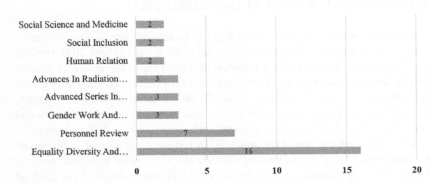

Figure 2.5   *Top contributing journals (n≥2) during a period between 2011 and 2021*

Table 2.2   *Cluster analysis of keywords*

Cluster 1 (24 items)	adult; article; cultural competence; ethics; female; health care; health care personnel; human; human experiment; humans; inclusivity; interview; language; male; middle aged; minority group; organisation; organisation and management; perception; psychology; qualitative research; racism; social inclusion; workplace
Cluster 2 (12 items)	critical; diversity and inclusion; diversity management; equality; gay; gay men; human resource management; lesbian; LGBT; qualitative; sexual orientation; stereotypes
Cluster 3 (10 items)	cultural diversity; discrimination; employment; equity and diversity; ethnic minorities; ethnicity; higher education; organisational changes; race; sport
Cluster 4 (10 items)	feminism; gender; inequality; leadership; managers; men; organisations; politics; post-colonialism; violence
Cluster 5 (7 items)	diversity; exclusion; gender equality; inclusion; innovation; police leadership; quantitative
Cluster 6 (6 items)	national cultures; religion; societies and institution; South Asia; United Kingdom; women
Cluster 7 (5 items)	construction industry; equity; gender diversity; sustainability; sustainable development

Co-occurrence of Keyword Analysis

The co-occurrence of keyword analysis was utilised to evaluate the content and range of research themes represented in DE&I-related research articles. The VOSviewer software was used in order to analyse the literature data. The analysis extracted a total of 74 items across seven different clusters with various research themes. For example, as indicated in Table 2.2, the third cluster included ten research themes: cultural diversity; discrimination; employment;

equity and diversity; ethnic minorities; ethnicity; higher education; organisational change; race; and sport.

A well-connected network of relevant keywords enables a practical comprehension of the connections, trends, and intellectual structure of the areas covered by scientific knowledge creation throughout the years (van Eck and Waltman, 2019). A visual analysis of seven clusters with research themes between 2011 and 2021 is depicted in Figure 2.6. The figure also shows the intensity of publications in the last decade, with a growing number of publications in the later years.

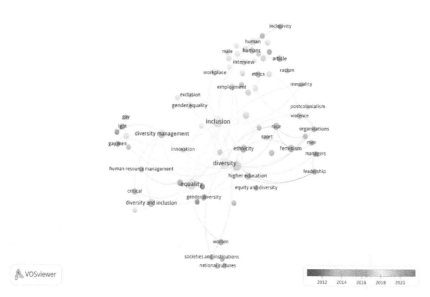

Figure 2.6   *A network map of DE&I-related research themes*

Prominent Researchers and Their Research Outputs

With three research outputs each, Cukier (Ryerson University, Canada) and Gagnon (University of Manitoba, Canada) were two of the prominent researchers. A total of 11 different authors were ranked second with two outputs each, with institutions represented from the United Kingdom, the Netherlands, Malaysia, and New Zealand. Table 2.3 summarises the prominent authors within the DE&I space.

Table 2.4 summarises the most cited outputs (top five), revealing two-fold patterns and commonalities. First, half of the six top-most cited studies were

Table 2.3   Prominent researchers (n≥2)

Ranking	First author	Affiliation	Count
1	Cukier	Ryerson University (Canada)	3
1	Gagnon	University of Manitoba (Canada)	3
2	Adamson	Queen Mary University of London (UK)	2
2	Benschop	Nijmegen School of Management (Netherlands)	2
2	Corenelius	School of Business and Management (UK)	2
2	Fujimoto	Sunway University (Malaysia)	2
2	Hylton	Leeds Beckett University (UK)	2
2	Norman	Leeds Beckett University (UK)	2
2	Pio	Auckland University of Technology (New Zealand)	2
2	Rankin-Wright	Faculty of Social Sciences and Health (UK)	2
2	Syed	Leeds Beckett University (UK)	2
2	Ustabas	Auckland University of Technology (New Zealand)	2
2	van den Brink	Radboud University (Netherlands)	2

related to gender research and specifically address the aspect of equality. Second, three of the six outlets are management-related, highlighting the significance of the DE&I agenda for organisations.

DISCUSSION AND CONCLUSION

This chapter explained how to carry out a literature review using bibliometric analysis of the literature on DE&I in organisations between 2011 and 2021. The analysis presented in this chapter indicates that the past decade has witnessed a sharp growth in the literature on the DE&I agenda. The findings highlight that the utility of bibliometric analysis is a meticulous as well as methodical technique used to examine the DE&I literature. Based on the findings of bibliometric analysis presented in the chapter, the key implications and limitations are discussed.

Evolution and Emergence of DE&I-Related Topics

On the one hand, the analysis indicated that the DE&I agenda began to gain prominence in the literature after 2016. This trend coincides with the 2030 Agenda put forward by the United Nations in 2015. On the other, themes such as cultural competence, health care, health-care personnel, inclusivity, minority group, organisation, organisation and management, perception, racism, social inclusion, workplace, LGBT, sexual orientation, stereotypes, national cultures, religion, societies and institutions, women, equity, gender diversity,

Table 2.4   *Prominent outputs based on citation count*

Rank	Author(s)/date	Title	Journal	Citation
1	Kossek et al. (2017)	"Opting out" or "pushed out"? Integrating perspectives on women's career equality for gender inclusion and interventions	*Journal of Management*	85
2	Mansh et al. (2015)	From patients to providers: Changing the culture in medicine toward sexual and gender minorities	*Academic Medicine*	37
3	Martinez et al. (2016)	Selection bias: Stereotypes and discrimination related to having a history of cancer	*Journal of Applied Psychology*	21
4	Mousa and Puhakka (2019)	Inspiring organizational commitment: Responsible leadership and organizational inclusion in the Egyptian health care sector	*Journal of Management Development*	20
4	Tatli et al. (2017)	Individualization and marketization of responsibility for gender equality: The case of female managers in China	*Human Resource Management*	20
5	Rankin-Wright et al. (2016)	Off-colour landscape: Framing race equality in sport coaching	*Sociology of Sport Journal*	18

sustainability, and sustainable development have dominated the literature. This finding aligns with the six priorities identified under the Vision for an Inclusive Society (UNDESA, 2009). Future DE&I-related research should take these findings into account to shape the agenda in the broader context of SDGs.

The Gap between Developed and Developing Economies

The findings highlight the missing component in the DE&I literature regarding knowledge production and institutions. For example, all ten countries and prominent researchers and institutions included in this analysis are based on OECD economies. In the broader context of the 2030 Agenda, and particularly SDG 17 that seeks to revitalise the global partnership for sustainable development (United Nations, 2020). DE&I researchers and research establishments should take these findings into account and contribute towards shaping the capacity building of researchers and research institutions in developing countries.

Limitations

The analysis presented in this chapter is not free from limitations. First, the Scopus database alone is not representative of the broader literature. The findings based on the available literature, therefore, could have been affected by intrinsic limitations of the Scopus database (see Mahmood and Dhakal, 2022). Second, the literature was searched using four specific keywords. It is possible that the database search might not have been able to retrieve the full extent of the literature (Meyer, 2020). Future DE&I researchers should consider these limitations in designing their research.

The techniques used and results reported in the chapter should be of interest to researchers, research institutions, and policymakers interested in understanding how the various elements of the DE&I agenda have evolved in the context of organisations. By reporting on the results of a rapid bibliometric analysis, this chapter has made a contribution towards distilling the extant DE&I literature in order to identify research needs and future directions.

Implications for Researchers

The DE&I agenda has become a global priority, especially in the context of accomplishing the SDGs. Although it can be contended that the recent DE&I-related literature remains fragmented due to its multidisciplinary nature, the findings indicate that the past decade witnessed a sharp increase in research outputs. The current paucity of DE&I-related studies in organisations presents opportunities for future studies. The study also demonstrates how to conduct a literature review using a rapid bibliometrics analysis.

REFERENCES

Anonymous (n.d.a). *Personnel Review*. www.emeraldgrouppublishing.com/journal/pr ?_ga=2.63715434.433101577.1644878080-1378102026.1640734852

Anonymous (n.d.b). *Equality, Diversity and Inclusion*. www.emeraldgrouppublishing.com/ journal/edi?_ga=2.26285816.433101577.1644878080-1378102026.1640734852

Chaudhry, I. S., Paquibut, R. Y., and Tunio, M. N. (2021). Do workforce diversity, inclusion practices, and organizational characteristics contribute to organizational innovation? Evidence from the UAE. *Cogent Business and Management*, *8*(1), 1947549.

Dhakal, S. P., and Tjokro, S. (2021). Tourism enterprises in Indonesia and the fourth industrial revolution: Are they ready? *Tourism Recreation Research*. www .tandfonline.com/doi/abs/10.1080/02508281.2021.1996687

Dhakal, S. P., Mahmood, M. N., Wiewiora, A., Brown, K., and Keast, R. (2013). The innovation potential of living labs to strengthen small and medium enterprises in regional Australia. *Australasian Journal of Regional Studies*, *19*(3), 101–119.

Dhakal, S., Nankervis, A., Burgess, J., and Prikshat, V. (2019). Challenges and strategies of transition from graduation to work in the post-2020 Asia Pacific and beyond: A comparative analysis of nine countries. In Dhakal, S. (Ed.), *The Transition from Graduation to Work* (pp. 241–253). Springer, Singapore.

Dhakal, S. P., Dahal, D., and Dahal, S. (2020). Nepal. In Nankervis, A., Connell, J., and Burgess, J. (Eds), *The Future of Work in Asia and Beyond: A Technological Revolution or Evolution?* (pp. 167–183). Routledge, London.

Dhakal, S. P., Burgess, J., and Connell, J. (2021). COVID-19 crisis, work and employment: Policy and research trends. *Labour and Industry, 31*(4), 353–365.

Donthu, N., Kumar, S., Mukherjee, D., Pandey, N., and Lim, W. M. (2021). How to conduct a bibliometric analysis: An overview and guidelines. *Journal of Business Research, 133,* 285–296.

Ellegaard, O., and Wallin, J. A. (2015). The bibliometric analysis of scholarly production: How great is the impact? *Scientometrics, 105*(3), 1809–1831.

Griffith University (2022). A guide to conducting a systematic literature review in the education discipline. https://libraryguides.griffith.edu.au/systematic-literature -reviews-for-education/writing-your-systematic-review

Hsieh, H. F., and Shannon, S. E. (2005). Three approaches to qualitative content analysis. *Qualitative Health Research, 15*(9), 1277–1288.

Hunt, V., Prince, S., Dixon-Fyle, S., and Dolan, K. (2020). Diversity wins: How inclusion matters? McKinsey & Company. www.mckinsey.com/featured-insights/ diversity-and-inclusion/diversity-wins-how-inclusion-matters

Kossek, E. E., Su, R., and Wu, L. (2017). "Opting out" or "pushed out"? Integrating perspectives on women's career equality for gender inclusion and interventions. *Journal of Management, 43*(1), 228–254.

Krippendorff, K. (2018). *Content Analysis: An Introduction to Its Methodology.* Sage, Thousand Oaks.

Liberati, A., Altman, D. G., Tetzlaff, J., Mulrow, C., Gøtzsche, P. C., Ioannidis, J. P., … and Moher, D. (2009). The PRISMA statement for reporting systematic reviews and meta-analyses of studies that evaluate health care interventions: Explanation and elaboration. *Journal of Clinical Epidemiology*, 62(10), e1–e34.

LLopis, G. (2011). Diversity management is the key to growth: Make it authentic. www.forbes.com/sites/glennllopis/2011/06/13/diversity-management-is-the-key-to -growth-make-it-authentic/?sh=5bb36bda66f3

Mahmood, M. N., and Dhakal, S. P. (2022). A bibliometric analysis of ageing literature: Global and Asia-Pacific trends. In Dhakal et al. (Eds), *Ageing Asia and the Pacific in Changing Times: Implications for Sustainable Development* (Chapter 3). Springer Nature, Singapore.

Mahmood, M. N., Dhakal, S. P., Wiewiora, A., Brown, K., and Keast, R. (2014). A comparative study on asset management policies and guidelines of different states in Australia. *Journal of Facilities Management, 12*(3), 286–302.

Mansh, M., Garcia, G., and Lunn, M. R. (2015). From patients to providers: Changing the culture in medicine toward sexual and gender minorities. *Academic Medicine, 90*(5), 574–580.

Martinez, L. R., White, C. D., Shapiro, J. R., and Hebl, M. R. (2016). Selection BIAS: Stereotypes and discrimination related to having a history of cancer. *Journal of Applied Psychology, 101*(1), 122.

Meyer, T. (2020). Decarbonizing road freight transportation: A bibliometric and network analysis. *Transportation Research Part D: Transport and Environment, 89,* 102619.

Mingers, J., and Leydesdorff, L. (2015). A review of theory and practice in scientometrics. *European Journal of Operational Research, 246*(1), 1–19.

Mousa, M., and Puhakka, V. (2019). Inspiring organizational commitment: Responsible leadership and organizational inclusion in the Egyptian health care sector. *Journal of Management Development, 38*(3), 208–224.

Najmaei, A., and Sadeghinejad, Z. (2019). Inclusive leadership: A scientometric assessment of an emerging field. In Georgiadou, A., Gonzalez-Perez, M. A., and Olivas-Lujan, M. R. (Eds), *Diversity within Diversity Management* (pp. 221–245). Emerald Publishing, Bingley.

Oswick, C., and Noon, M. (2014). Discourses of diversity, equality and inclusion: Trenchant formulations or transient fashions? *British Journal of Management, 25*(1), 23–39.

Provalis Research (2021). *What Are Scientometrics and Bibliometrics?* https:// provalisresearch.com/solutions-2/applications/scientometrics-bibliometrics-software/

Rankin-Wright, A. J., Hylton, K., and Norman, L. (2016). Off-colour landscape: Framing race equality in sport coaching. *Sociology of Sport Journal, 33*(4), 357–368.

Sharifi, A., Simangan, D., and Kaneko, S. (2021). The literature landscape on peace–sustainability nexus: A scientometric analysis. *Ambio, 50*(3), 661–678.

SHRM (n.d.). *Diversity, Equity and Inclusion*. Society for Human Resource Management, Mumbai. www.shrm.org/resourcesandtools/hr-topics/pages/diversity -equity-and-inclusion.aspx

Snyder, H. (2019). Literature review as a research methodology: An overview and guidelines. *Journal of Business Research*, 104, 333–339.

Solkhe, A. (2021). LGBTQ notion evaluation: A bibliometric analysis and systematic review. *Library Philosophy and Practice*, 1–38.

Tatli, A., Ozturk, M. B., and Woo, H. S. (2017). Individualization and marketization of responsibility for gender equality: The case of female managers in China. *Human Resource Management, 56*(3), 407–430.

Together2030 (n.d.). *Realizing the SDGs for All: Ensuring Inclusiveness and Equality for Every Person, Everywhere*. United Nations, New York. https://sustainabledevelopment .un.org/content/documents/23216Together_2030__Position_Paper__HLPF_2019.pdf

UNDESA (2009). *Vision for an Inclusive Society*. United Nations, New York. www.un .org/esa/socdev/documents/compilation-brochure.pdf

UNDESA (2015). *Transforming Our World: The 2030 Agenda for Sustainable Development*. New York, United Nations. https://sustainabledevelopment.un.org/ content/documents/21252030%20Agenda%20for%20Sustainable%20Development %20web.pdf

United Nations (2020). Goal 17: Revitalize the global partnership for sustainable development. www.un.org/sustainabledevelopment/globalpartnerships/

van Eck, N. J., and Waltman, L. (2019). *VOSviewer Manual: Manual for VOSviewer Version 1.6. 11*. CWTS, Leiden University. www.vosviewer.com/documentation/ Manual_VOSviewer_1.6.11.pdf

USEFUL LINKS

Diversity Council Australia. *Leading Diversity and Inclusion in the Workplace*. www .dca.org.au/

Sweet, L. (2014). *Using NVivo and EndNote for Literature Reviews*. https://staff.flinders
.edu.au/content/dam/staff/documents/using-nvivo-and-endnote-for-literature-reviews
.pdf
United Nations. *Vision for an Inclusive Society*. www.un.org/esa/socdev/documents/
compilation-brochure.pdf
Universities Australia. *Diversity and Equity*. www.universitiesaustralia.edu.au/policy
-submissions/diversity-equity/

PART II

3. Closing the gap on Aboriginal and Torres Strait Islander employment disadvantage in Australia

Sharlene Leroy-Dyer

INTRODUCTION

In March 2009, the Australian Government announced a new initiative to reform and improve Aboriginal and Torres Strait Islander[1] employment outcomes, in which the Australian Government committed to halving the gap between Aboriginal and Torres Strait Islander and non-Indigenous employment outcomes within a decade. Closing the Gap (CTG) is a commitment by all Australian governments to improve the lives of Aboriginal and Torres Strait Islander peoples and provide a better future for Aboriginal and Torres Strait Islander children. An important target, and the one that is the most relevant to this research, was Council of Australian Governments Reform Council (COAG) target 6, which is to halve the gap in employment outcomes between Indigenous and non-Indigenous Australians within a decade (by 2018). This chapter examines labour market policies and programs that have been enacted by governments under CTG to ascertain if these programs and policies have been effective in supplying meaningful employment outcomes and reducing the disadvantage faced by Aboriginal and Torres Strait Islander peoples.

METHODOLOGY

Indigenous methodologies are emerging as a vigorous and active field of knowledge production that involve Indigenous peoples from around the world, who apply their own perspectives and understandings to social research and methodologies (Moreton-Robinson and Walter 2010). Indigenous methodologies are an approach based on Indigenous philosophical positioning and epistemology, the interplay between the method and the paradigm and the extent to which the method is consistent within an Indigenous worldview. It is a more inclusive and culturally acceptable way of doing research that is culturally appropriate and ethically correct for the acquisition and dissemination of knowledge about Indigenous peoples and is based on Indigenous ethics and knowledge that determines how to access knowledge, the tools to gain that knowledge and the theoretical approaches for conducting research (Kovach 2021).

Indigenous research methodologies are based on Indigenous ontologies, epistemologies and axiologies. Indigenous ontologies can be described as Indigenous ways of being, epistemologies are Indigenous ways of knowing and axiologies are Indigenous ways of doing. Ontologies, epistemologies and axiologies underpin Indigenous social research methodologies and make visible what is meaningful and logical in our understanding of ourselves and the world and they are applied to the research process (Moreton-Robinson and Walter 2010).

Aboriginal and Torres Strait Islander research, according to the Australian Institute for Aboriginal and Torres Strait Islander Studies (AIATSIS) (2020), is research that affects or is of significance to Aboriginal and Torres Strait Islander peoples. Included in this are all aspects of research such as planning the research, data collection, analysis and dissemination of the findings of the research, documentary analysis and secondary research and the knowledges that went into the research. In other words, any research "that is about or may affect Aboriginal and Torres Strait Islander peoples, either collectively or individually" (p. 6).

This chapter utilises a qualitative approach, which combines documentary data collection and systematic literature review for the analysis of information relating to closing the gap on Aboriginal and Torres Strait Islander employment disadvantage. Documentary analysis is a form of qualitative research where documents are interpreted by the researcher, therefore giving meaning and voice to the topic (Bowen 2009). It is a systematic procedure for reviewing and evaluating both electronic and printed material. The use of documentary data is important as it provides the capacity to augment and corroborate evidence from a variety of sources whilst developing empirical knowledge. The advantages of documentary data include that data can be repeatedly reviewed and it is unobtrusive, as the data have been collected over a period of time, through many events and settings. A systematic review was used as a research method and process for identifying and critically appraising relevant research, in addition to collecting and analysing data from the research. The overarching aim of the review was to report on the state of evidence about the effectiveness of programs under the CTG umbrella to ascertain what worked and what did not. Reviewing relevant literature helps to understand the breadth and depth of the existing body of work and identify gaps to explore (Snyder 2019).

CONDUCTING CULTURALLY APPROPRIATE AND RESPECTFUL ABORIGINAL AND TORRES STRAIT ISLANDER RESEARCH

It has already been established that Aboriginal and Torres Strait Islander research, is research that affects or is of significance to Aboriginal and Torres Strait Islander peoples, including data collection, analysis and the dissemination of the findings.

The history of research for Aboriginal and Torres Strait Islander peoples is tied to colonisation, where the history of Australia has been told through the eyes of the colonisers. Researchers have argued that Aboriginal and Torres Strait Islander peoples did not have a voice in research and were "dehumanised" as objects of research. Cultural practices and norms were distorted and described in ways that reflected the non-Indigenous researchers' prejudices, beliefs and values (Leroy-Dyer 2016). According to Martin (2003, p. 2), "mistreatment of ourselves and our land, marginalisation from structures and governance and development of misguided policy and programs resulting in feelings of distrust, caution, fear of exploitation and misrepresentation" sums up the effects of past research.

Any research conducted that includes or is about Aboriginal and Torres Strait Islander peoples needs to be conducted in a respectful and consultative way. AIATSIS has developed a research ethics framework structured around four principles: Indigenous self-determination, Indigenous leadership, impact and value and sustainability and accountability (AIATSIS 2020). AIATSIS also identifies for researchers how to apply the ethical framework when conducting research. Implementing an ethical framework requires reflexivity by the researcher with particular attention to recognising and interrogating their role in exercising power and the choices they make to privilege some knowledge and discard others.

In addition to respectful engagement, cultural respect is an important aspect of research into Aboriginal and Torres Strait Islander peoples. Cultural respect is recognising and protecting the inherent rights, cultures and traditions of Aboriginal and Torres Strait Islander peoples. Cultural respect is shared respect and is achieved when research is conducted in a safe environment for Aboriginal and Torres Strait Islander peoples and where cultural differences are respected. The goal of cultural respect is to uphold the rights of Aboriginal and Torres Strait Islander peoples to maintain, protect and develop their culture and achieve equitable outcomes (Leroy-Dyer 2016).

ABORIGINAL AND TORRES STRAIT ISLANDER LABOUR MARKET STATISTICS

Aboriginal and Torres Strait Islanders are not a homogenous group of people. Prior to invasion, there were over 600 nations throughout Australia each with their own territory, language and customs. Most of the problems and disadvantages facing Aboriginal and Torres Strait Islander peoples today stem from generations of oppression and have resulted in a lack of trust of white society. The disadvantage experienced by Aboriginal and Torres Strait Islander peoples in employment, health, housing, and education is a consequence of the widespread destruction of our traditional economic and cultural activities, the dispossession of our lands and waterways, and our subsequent exclusion from mainstream society (Dockery and Milsom 2007).

For Aboriginal and Torres Strait Islander peoples, labour market participation rates, job-related skills, qualifications and income are all well below those of the non-Indigenous population (ABS 2018). The 2016 census found approximately 223,000 Aboriginal and Torres Strait Islander peoples aged 15 years and older were participating in the labour force, a participation rate of 52 per cent as opposed to 64.8 per cent for non-Indigenous Australians. Males (55 per cent) were more likely to participate than females (49 per cent), and the participation rate was higher for people living in urban areas (54 per cent) compared to non-urban (45 per cent) (ABS 2018).

Aboriginal and Torres Strait Islander peoples have relatively low employment rates. The employment to population ratio showed that in 2016, 4 in 10 (42 per cent) of Aboriginal and Torres Strait Islander peoples aged 15 years and older were employed, and those living in urban areas were more likely to be employed (45 per cent) compared to non-urban (35 per cent). Non-Indigenous people were 1.4 times more likely to be employed than Aboriginal and Torres Strait Islander peoples (ABS 2018). Denny-Smith and Loosemore (2020) note that the Aboriginal and Torres Strait Islander employment rate "has improved by less than a percentage point in a decade – to 49%, compared with 75% for non-Indigenous Australians".

Aboriginal and Torres Strait Islander peoples have the highest unemployment rates of any group in the Australian labour market. In 2016, the unemployment rate for Aboriginal and Torres Strait Islander peoples aged 15 years and over was 18 per cent, compared to the unemployment rate for non-Indigenous Australians at 5.7 per cent (ABS 2018). As well as having the highest unemployment rate of any group, Aboriginal and Torres Strait Islander peoples have the lowest levels of education, housing and community services in Australia, which produces adverse social consequences. Aboriginal and Torres Strait Islander peoples (like some other groups of socially disadvantaged people) are 22 per cent more likely to be victims of crime. They often miss out on even basic levels of education and training and are prone to a range of health problems (Burgess and Dyer 2009; Leroy-Dyer 2016).

There is no quick fix or one approach that will reduce labour market disadvantage for Aboriginal and Torres Strait Islander peoples because the disadvantage is not limited to the labour market. There are interconnecting factors that contribute to the disadvantage, such as low levels of education, poor health, inadequate and inappropriate housing, living in remote communities with poor levels of infrastructure, intergenerational trauma, cultural dislocation, cultural genocide and deaths in custody. The disadvantage is multidimensional and intergenerational (Leroy-Dyer 2016).

Since 2008, no progress has been made towards halving the gap in employment outcomes by 2018. Over the decade 2008–2018, the employment rate for Aboriginal and Torres Strait Islander peoples only increased slightly (by 0.9 percentage points), whereas the rate for non-Indigenous Australians fell by 0.4 percentage points, therefore the gap has not changed markedly (Commonwealth of Australia 2020).

LABOUR MARKET POLICIES/PROGRAMS UNDER CLOSING THE GAP

There are several Aboriginal and Torres Strait Islander specific and mainstream initiatives that the Australian Government has implemented to support Aboriginal and Torres Strait Islander peoples into work under the CTG banner. These fall under the umbrella of the Indigenous Advancement Strategy (IAS) and include the Community Development Programme, the Employment Parity Initiative, the Indigenous Procurement Policy, the Vocational Training and Employment Centre as well as Jobactive. The government has put an emphasis on achieving a 26-week employment outcome, as they see this as key to ensuring people remain in the workforce (Australian Government 2021).

Indigenous Advancement Strategy

The IAS is the umbrella strategy the Australian Government uses to fund and deliver a range of programs for Aboriginal and Torres Strait Islander peoples and is administered by the National Indigenous Australians Agency. Funding is allocated yearly for the activities that address the objectives of the IAS in five overarching program streams: jobs, land and economy, children and schooling, safety and wellbeing, culture and capacity and remote Australia strategies. The Australian Government states that the IAS can "achieve real and lasting results to '*Close the Gap*' on disadvantage and ensure all Australians have the same opportunities in life" (Australian Government 2021).

The IAS has come under criticism for a lack of transparency around the funding tender process, funding cuts to the strategy and its inability to produce any real change in the lives of Aboriginal and Torres Strait Islander peoples. In addition, a Senate enquiry found Indigenous organisations were disadvantaged in the tender process. The Australian National Audit Office found the design and implementation of the process was flawed (Thorpe 2018). In response to criticism of the strategy, in May 2021, the Australian Government announced an overhaul of the strategy.

Table 3.1 is a summary of the programs offered under the IAS, what they offer and whether they have been successful in delivering meaningful outcomes to Aboriginal and Torres Strait Islander peoples.

Refreshed Closing the Gap

The CTG initiative has been running for over a decade, with progress against all targets mixed. Some key improvements were made in the areas of education; however, the national Indigenous employment target to halve the gap in employment outcomes between Indigenous and non-Indigenous Australians within a decade (by 2018) was not met and made limited progress.

In 2017, the Australian Government began a process of refreshing the CTG initiative with a new focus on delivering a community-led, strengths-based approach, placing Aboriginal and Torres Strait Islander peoples at the centre of this new strategy. In 2019, COAG and the Coalition of Aboriginal and Torres Strait Islander Peak Organisations signed a formal agreement to work in "genuine partnership". This partnership has jointly developed an agreed framework with new targets in addition to establishing a Joint Council on CTG (Commonwealth of Australia 2020).

The National Agreement of CTG, which was agreed to by all parties on 30 July 2020, has four priority areas and 17 national socio-economic targets to address Aboriginal and Torres Strait Islander disadvantage, with the progress of these targets being monitored by the Productivity Commission. The two new targets that relate to employment are target 7 (by 2031, increase the proportion of Aboriginal and Torres Strait Islander youth (15–24 years) who are in employment, education or training to 67 per cent) and target 8 (by 2031, increase the proportion of Aboriginal and Torres Strait Islander people aged 25–64 who are employed to 62 per cent) (SCRGSP 2020). The Productivity Commission has set up a CTG information repository to support the reporting on CTG outcomes. For targets 7 and 8, there have been no new data available since 2016 (Productivity Commission 2021).

Table 3.1   *The Indigenous Advancement Strategy*

Program	Aim	Criticisms
Community Development Programme – introduced 2015	Mutual obligation program to assist remote job seekers to gain employment and break welfare dependency 83% of participants are Aboriginal and Torres Strait Islanders Engage in 25 hours work for the "dole" per week, 5 days a week (Australian Government 2021)	Limited success – 1% improvement Labelled punitive Modern-day slavery and racist Failed to redress disparity No protections or provisions of other workers Crime, domestic violence increased Mental health issues Huge penalties for non-compliance (70% higher) (Allum 2019, 2021; Allum & Butler 2021)
Employment Parity Initiative (EPI)	Increase Indigenous employment in large companies (3%) Partners need to be champions of change and industry leaders Selected on capacity and track record on Indigenous employment Must purchase from Indigenous suppliers 13 large companies are EPI partners (Australian Government 2021)	Handouts for corporates who can afford to self-fund ($91.7 million) Phased out May 2021 (Allum 2021; Allum & Butler 2021)
Indigenous Procurement Policy	Stimulate business and economic development and foster Indigenous entrepreneurship Access government contracts Create job opportunities Include employment and participation targets Effectiveness measured by increase in the number and volume of Indigenous businesses awarded contracts Gamechanger – driver for Indigenous business (Australian Government 2021)	Inconsistencies in compliance, implementation and monitoring Mandatory targets for participation not met 4% of contracts were reporting Black cladding arose* No stable long-term employment benefits No systematic evidence about what works and what doesn't Needs better evaluation, monitoring and frameworks (Deloitte 2019; Evans & Langton 2021)

Program	Aim	Criticisms
Vocational Training and Employment Centre	Designed to connect jobseekers with 26 weeks employment Works closely with employers, services, individuals and communities to identify training requirements, with a view to long-term employment Five-stage approach: community engagement, work readiness, vocational training, guaranteed job and post-placement support Education and training a prerequisite to CTG High participation (Australian Government 2021)	"Vocational education in Australia is in a state of crisis" (Quiggin 2018, p. 3) Failed experiment in market-led education Government committed to overhaul
Jobactive	Network of organisations funded by government to deliver employment outcomes Not Indigenous specific Funding boosted for up-front intensive employment services for Aboriginal and Torres Strait Islander jobseekers Partnerships to deliver tailored and innovative solutions to employment challenges (Australian Government 2021)	Inappropriate and ineffective Lack of support High case loads Inability to meet individual needs Unable to address barriers "Never receive assistance required to become job ready" (Moore 2018, p. 4) High penalties for breaching (Aboriginal and Torres Strait Islander peoples have 25% higher breaches) Failed those it intended to serve Greater flexibility was needed Cultural competence for providers was needed (Moore 2018; The Senate 2019)

Note: *Black cladding is the practice of a non-Indigenous business entity or individual taking unfair advantage of an Indigenous business entity or individual for the purpose of gaining access to otherwise inaccessible Indigenous procurement policies or contracts.

WHY HAVE LABOUR MARKET PROGRAMS FAILED?

Since recognising the severe disadvantage faced by Aboriginal and Torres Strait Islander peoples, the federal and state governments have offered a range of labour market programs (LMPs) to promote Indigenous employment and training. There are also a range of indirect programs and support offered by Australian Government agencies. The government's stated goals are to determine "how much difference" a program makes, the difference between outcomes for a participant and what outcome would have occurred in the absence of participation (Leroy-Dyer 2016).

In addition, the COAG Reform Council utilises the following indicators to measure the success of the CTG reforms: the employment to population ratio, unemployment rate, labour force participation rate, Community Development Employment Projects participants and off-Community Development Employment Projects job placements, three-month employment outcomes (post-program monitoring), proportion of Indigenous 18–24 year olds engaged in full-time employment, education or training at or above a Certificate III and the number of Indigenous 20–64 year olds with or working towards post-school qualification in Certificate III, IV, Diploma and Advanced Diploma (COAG 2010).

A criticism of the current approach is that it only monitors outcomes. There is a significant body of evidence on what works and what does not work in assisting Aboriginal and Torres Strait Islander unemployed persons to obtain and remain in jobs, and the government is obligated to act on this evidence in the design of LMP policy; however, they have consistently failed to do so.

Successive governments have failed to undertake any systematic evaluation of the effectiveness of any LMP in delivering meaningful employment outcomes for Aboriginal and Torres Strait Islander peoples. Government policy is key to CTG on labour market disadvantage; however, previously implemented LMPs have failed to close the employment gap. Altman and Klein (2018) state that governments have "focused too much on CTG as measured in official statistics" (p. 133), and as a consequence "Indigenous policy is only measured in terms of distinct statistical outcomes, such as whether disparities between Indigenous and non-Indigenous outcomes are declining" (p. 133).

The way in which effectiveness is measured should change to include the holistic factors that contribute to the disadvantage faced by Aboriginal and Torres Strait Islander peoples. In 2002 COAG commissioned the "Overcoming Indigenous Disadvantage Report" to inform Australian governments if their policies, programs and interventions are improving outcomes for Aboriginal and Torres Strait Islander peoples (SCRGSP 2020). The "Overcoming Indigenous Disadvantage: Key Indicators Framework" was developed to focus on outcomes of the lived experiences of Aboriginal and Torres Strait Islander peoples, as opposed to department reports that "tend to focus on service inputs (how budgets are spent) and outputs (the actual services delivered), rather than on the outcomes achieved" (SCRGSP 2020, p. 18). Outcomes, according to SCRGSP (2020), are "crucial to measure whether progress is being made in improving the wellbeing of Aboriginal and Torres Strait Islander peoples and whether the CTG policy objectives are being achieved" (p. 18). Within the developed framework, COAG targets and headline indicators are matched to strategic areas for action, as it is very difficult to measure the progress of broad targets, aspirational outcomes and to hold governments and service providers accountable (SCRGSP 2020). Therefore, utilising this framework has the potential to drive improvements and progress towards the COAG targets.

Limitations of past LMPs included the fact they were short-term fixes by subsequent governments, and policies and programs were often developed using out-of-date census data and thus were destined to fail (Leroy-Dyer 2016). In addition, programs set unrealistic goals that could not possibly be reached, and programs were often outcome driven, hence Aboriginal and Torres Strait Islander peoples were put in the too-hard basket. From the analysis, the two biggest limitations found were that the programs did not cater for remote areas and there was a complete lack of systematic reviewing of the programs. When programs were reviewed, often Aboriginal and Torres Strait Islander peoples were blamed for programs not working (Leroy-Dyer 2016).

WHAT SHOULD LABOUR MARKET PROGRAMS LOOK LIKE FOR ABORIGINAL AND TORRES STRAIT ISLANDER PEOPLES?

What is known from analysing LMPs for Indigenous peoples overseas is that some of the best results came from early intervention programs, such as school programs. According to Karmel et al. (2014), the way to close the gap on Aboriginal and Torres Strait Islander labour market disadvantage is to keep the focus on school participation and retention and on commitment to learning and achievement. Low levels of educational attainment are among the main influences of the employment rate disparity. This is compounded by particularly poor employment outcomes among Aboriginal and Torres Strait Islander peoples with very poor levels of educational attainment (Karmel et al. 2014). A higher proportion of Aboriginal and Torres Strait Islander peoples participate in vocational education and training than non-Indigenous Australians; however, Aboriginal and Torres Strait Islander peoples are also more likely to complete lower-level qualifications than non-Indigenous Australians. Aboriginal and Torres Strait Islander peoples with degrees have employment outcomes largely on par with their non-Indigenous counterparts; however, workplace discrimination and high levels of incarceration play a negative role (Karmel et al. 2014).

Former Australian of the Year Professor Mick Dodson stated that adult literacy is key to closing the gap between Aboriginal and Torres Strait Islander peoples and non-Indigenous Australians (Dodson, cited in Kral 2009). Although Aboriginal and Torres Strait Islander participation and attainment in education and training has increased significantly in recent years, a substantial gap still exists. Education must be the main focus if the gap in employment is to be closed. The under-resourcing of Aboriginal and Torres Strait Islander education has contributed to low levels of English literacy over many decades; low levels of education attainment can create huge obstacles to participation in mainstream employment. Therefore, for some Aboriginal and Torres Strait

Islander peoples, inadequate literacy and numeracy combined with long-term unemployment can put even low-skilled occupations out of reach (Leroy-Dyer 2016).

Savvas et al. (2011) found there was a statistically significant correlation between education and labour market outcomes for Aboriginal and Torres Strait Islander peoples. They found the higher the education levels the more probability of improved labour market outcomes. There are multiple causes for the gap in employment, so looking at the issue holistically is imperative. Year 12 attainment, school attendance, reading, writing and numeracy, as well as secondary education are all important factors that contribute to the gap in employment. Cultural and social factors will also affect the employment gap, whereby "employment and education outcomes can also be influenced by the intergenerational effects of parental income, employment and education levels" (SCRGSP 2020, p. 26).

This would suggest that an LMP that incorporates school and work could reduce labour market disadvantage for Aboriginal and Torres Strait Islander peoples. Other research from overseas found that LMPs featuring targeted training that were small in scale and had an on-the-job component had the best results in reducing labour market disadvantage for Indigenous peoples, such as pre-employment programs run by private-sector employers that have targeted training, are on a small scale and have a work component attached (Leroy-Dyer 2016; Caron et al. 2020).

LMPs in Australia have been developed for the most part as a one-size-fits-all approach and are not tailored to the specific needs of participants. For example, Aboriginal and Torres Strait Islander job seekers needed greater flexibility than is currently allowed and have different needs in LMPs to that of the non-Indigenous population. LMPs that are framed around an Anglo-centric lens do not adequately address Aboriginal and Torres Strait Islander social and economic issues, do not contribute to self-determination and are responsible for the unacceptable gaps between Aboriginal and Torres Strait Islander peoples and non-Indigenous Australians (Leroy-Dyer 2014).

IMPLICATIONS FOR FUTURE RESEARCH

Research is needed that comprehensively evaluates and analyses LMPs in Australia and other colonised countries to gain insight into how we might close the gap and reduce labour market disadvantage for Aboriginal and Torres Strait Islander peoples. Countries such as the United States, Canada and New Zealand also struggle with labour market disadvantage experienced by their First Nations peoples. However, some countries seem more advanced than others in alleviating this disadvantage. A comparative study would provide further insight into what works across countries where First Nations peoples are marginalised, especially in the labour market.

CONCLUSION

The diversity and equity discourse is embedded in the experiences and conditions of employment across a range of personal characteristics including gender, age, sexuality, religion and ethnicity. For Aboriginal and Torres Strait Islander peoples, disadvantage is endemic across the life course, not only employment. A major equity challenge is to support access to and participation in meaningful employment.

This chapter has outlined and critically analysed the major policies that governments have utilised to reduce labour market disadvantage for Aboriginal and Torres Strait Islander peoples. Despite considerable amounts of money being spent in a wide range of employment and economic development programs designed to improve Indigenous employment, the numbers of Aboriginal and Torres Strait Islander peoples involved in mainstream employment have not increased significantly since CTG was initiated.

NOTE

1.   In this chapter I use the term Aboriginal and Torres Strait Islander peoples, as opposed to Indigenous or First Nations. When the term Indigenous is used, it relates to government policy and Indigenous peoples worldwide. In addition, I use the term peoples to signify that Aboriginal and Torres Strait Islander peoples are not one people or nation, but a collective of peoples and nations.

REFERENCES

ABS (Australian Bureau of Statistics) (2018), Census of population and housing: Characteristics of Aboriginal and Torres Strait Islander Australians, viewed 10 July 2021 www.abs.gov.au/statistics/people/aboriginal-and-torres-strait-islander -peoples/census-population-and-housing-characteristics-aboriginal-and-torres-strait -islander-australians/latest-release

AIATSIS (Australian Institute of Aboriginal and Torres Strait Islander Studies) (2020), viewed 25 July 2021, https://aiatsis.gov.au/

Allum, L. (2019), Government releases damning review of its own Aboriginal work-for-the-dole scheme, *The Guardian*, 6 February, viewed 7 July 2021, www .theguardian.com/australia-news/2019/feb/06/a-third-of-remote-aboriginal-work-for-the- dole-participants-say-community-worse-off

Allum, L. (2021), Coalition scraps remote work-for-the-dole program for Indigenous Australians, *The Guardian*, 13 May, viewed 7 July 2021, www.theguardian.com/ australia-news/2021/may/13/coalition-scraps-remote-work-for-the-dole-program-for- indigenous-australians

Allum, L., and Butler, B. (2021), Crown among big companies given more than $90m by government to employ Aboriginal people, *The Guardian*, 5 April, viewed 7 July 2021, www.theguardian.com/australia-news/2021/apr/05/crown-among-big -companies-given-government-funding-to-employ-aboriginal-people

Altman, J. and Klein, E. (2018), Lessons from a basic income programme for Indigenous Australians, *Oxford Development Studies*, 46(1), 132–146.

Australian Government (2021), Indigenous Advancement Strategy, viewed 26 June 2021, www.indigenous.gov.au/indigenous-advancement-strategy

Bowen, G. A. (2009), Document analysis as a qualitative research method. *Qualitative Research Journal*, 9(2), 27–40.

Burgess, J., and Dyer, S. (2009), Workplace mentoring for Indigenous Australians: A case study. *Equal Opportunities International*, 28(6), 465–485.

Caron, J., Asselin, H., and Beaudoin, J.-M. (2020), Indigenous employees' perceptions of the strategies used by mining employers to promote their recruitment, integration and retention. *Resources Policy*, 68, 101793.

COAG (Council of Australian Governments Reform Council) (2010), *National Indigenous reform agreement: Baseline performance report for 2008–09*. Canberra: Author.

Commonwealth of Australia (2020), Department of the Prime Minister and Cabinet, Closing the Gap Report 2020, viewed 16 July 2021, https://ctgreport.niaa.gov.au

Deloitte (2019), *Third Year Evaluation of the Indigenous Procurement Policy*. Canberra: Department of Prime Minister and Cabinet, August.

Denny-Smith, G., and Loosemore, M. (2020), Why we aren't closing the gap: A failure to account for "cultural counterfactuals". *The Conversation*, 13 February.

Dockery, M., and Milsom, N. (2007), *A Review of Indigenous Employment Programs*. Adelaide: National Centre for Vocational Education Research, viewed 8 July 2021, www.ncver.edu.au/research-and-statistics/publications/all-publications/a-review-of -indigenous-employment-programs

Evans, M., and Langton, M. (2021), Research shows procurement policies are a game changer for Indigenous workers, *The Australian*, 20 April, viewed 20 June 2021, www.theaustralian.com.au/business/the-deal-magazine/research-shows -procurement-policies-are-a-game-changer-for-indigenous-workers/news-story/0b bf4ee9602f65c678bffdb1bb53be8d

Karmel, T., Misko, J., Blomberg, D., Bednarz, A., and Atkinson, G. (2014), *Improving Labour Market Outcomes through Education and Training*. Canberra, ACT: Australian Institute of Health and Welfare and Australian Institute for Family Studies.

Kral, I. (2009), The literacy question in remote Indigenous Australia. *CAEPR Topical Issue 06*. Canberra, ACT: Australian National University.

Leroy-Dyer, S. (2014), A review of Indigenous Labour Market programs – why they are unsuccessful in delivering outcomes for Indigenous Australians. Presented to the 2014 Australian Critical Race and Whiteness Studies Association Conference, Brisbane, 4–5 December.

Leroy-Dyer, S. (2016), Private-sector employment programs for Aboriginal and Torres Strait Islander peoples: Comparative case studies. PhD thesis, University of Newcastle.

Kovach, M. (2021), *Indigenous Methodologies: Characteristics, Conversations, and Contexts*, Second Edition. Toronto: University of Toronto Press.

Martin, K. (2003), Ways of knowing, being and doing: A theoretical framework and methods for Indigenous and Indigenist re-search and Indigenist research. *Journal of Australian Studies*, 76, 203–214.

Moore, K. (2018), Submission to Senate Education and Employment References Committee: Inquiry into the Appropriateness and Effectiveness of the Objectives, Design, Implementation and Evaluation of Jobactive, viewed 1 July 2021, https://eprints.qut.edu.au/200177/

Moreton-Robinson, A., and Walter, M. (2010), Indigenous methodologies in social research. In M. Walter (Ed.), *Social Research Method*. Melbourne: Oxford University Press.

Productivity Commission (2021), Closing the Gap Information Repository, viewed 25 July 2021, www.pc.gov.au/closing-the-gap-data/dashboard

Quiggin, J. (2018), The failure of vocational education and training policy in Australia. Submission to the Senate Education and Employment References Committee Enquiry into Vocational Education and Training in South Australia, January, viewed 16 July 2021, https://webcache.googleusercontent.com/search?q=cache: VuIciaongK8J:https://www.aph.gov.au/DocumentStore.ashx%3Fid%3D6eb933e5-e4ce-43b0-963e-0737b48dbe07%26subId%3D562423+&cd=1&hl=en&ct=clnk&gl=au&client=firefox-b-d

Savvas, A., Boulton, C., and Jepsen, E. (2011), *Influences of Indigenous Labour Market Outcomes* (Productivity Commission Staff Working Paper). Melbourne: Australian Government.

SCRGSP (Steering Committee for the Review of Government Service Provision) (2020), *Overcoming Indigenous Disadvantage: Key Indicators 2020*. Canberra: Productivity Commission.

Snyder, H. (2019), Literature review as a research methodology: An overview and guidelines. *Journal of Business Research*, 104, 333–339.

The Senate – Education and Employment References Committee (2019), Jobactive: Failing those it is intended to serve, viewed 19 July 2021, www.aph.gov.au/Parliamentary_Business/Committees/Senate/Education_and_Employment/JobActive2018/Report

Thorpe, N. (2018), Government's Indigenous budget strategy blasted for failures and hundreds of millions to non-Indigenous organisations. *NITV Investigations*, 7 May, viewed 5 July 2021, www.sbs.com.au/nitv/nitv-news/explainer/governments-indigenous-budget-strategy-blasted-failures-and-hundreds-millions-non

KEY WEB REFERENCES

Australian Government, Productivity Commission, Closing the Gap Information Repository: www.pc.gov.au/closing-the-gap-data/dashboard

Closing the Gap: www.closingthegap.gov.au/

Closing the Gap Clearing House: https://aifs.gov.au/projects/closing-gap-clearinghouse

Closing the Gap Report 2020: https://ctgreport.niaa.gov.au

Coalition of Peaks: https://coalitionofpeaks.org.au/

National Indigenous Australians Agency: www.niaa.gov.au/

4. Regional Australia Bank: a case study addressing the triple penalty of regional location, gender and motherhood on women's careers

Lucie Newsome and Alison Sheridan

INTRODUCTION

In Australia, women's participation rates in paid work are influenced by their family responsibilities and their location. While national efforts to enable greater workforce participation of women have been pursued by the Federal Government in recent years, their efficacy has varied across locations. Women's participation in paid work in regional areas lags behind their female counterparts in metropolitan locations (Adapa et al., 2021). Women's re-entry into the labour market following periods of unpaid care work in regional areas is impacted by disadvantages created by the intersection of regional location, gender and motherhood. There can be long-term impacts for women if they remain out of the paid workforce. Their professional skills base deteriorates, making it more difficult to return to the workplace at salary rates commensurate with what they left, and the loss of income has implications for their retirement savings and financial independence. For regional economies, where gender is a principal organising factor and the embedded gendered power relations have real economic and social costs (Farhall et al., 2020), the implications of women's absence from the paid workforce are compounded. Limited availability of suitably skilled labour in regional locations remains an enduring challenge for regional employers (Adapa et al., 2021).

The Australian government has committed to boosting women's workforce participation through a multi-pronged approach, including supporting regional employers to attract and retain women returning to work after a career break (Commonwealth of Australia, 2017). The interdependent contexts of work, households, community and the wider society must be recognised as impacting work–family decisions (Pocock et al., 2009). Certainly, macro-level factors, including government policies, are important environmental conditions impacting women's workforce participation, as are their individual circumstances; but these alone are insufficient to enable women's participation in the paid workforce and financial independence. Attention to what is happening at the organisational and place levels is also necessary if we are to understand career outcomes for regional women.

In this chapter we present a case study of a growing business in the finance industry, Regional Australia Bank, a customer-owned bank which, with its vision to be at the heart of its communities, has actively engaged with the challenges of enabling women's careers in regional locations. Regional Australia Bank was identified as an exemplar regional employer by the Federal Government and, through 2019–2020, worked with KPMG on the government-funded Career Revive initiative, with a specific focus on regional women returning to paid work after a prolonged period. Through this case, we identify the agency exercised by Regional Australia Bank in supporting women's return to work and progress in their careers. Through its strategic positioning at the heart of its communities, its innovative workplace practices, flexibility and commitment to supporting work–life balance and leveraging technology to enable vertical and horizontal shifts not limited by location, Regional Australia Bank is harnessing the value of women's skills and experiences in its communities. This case provides insights into the actions that can be taken by other regional businesses to ensure women careers in regional locations are no longer disadvantaged by their location, gender or family responsibilities.

LITERATURE REVIEW

Understanding the power relationships and structures that impact women's participation in the labour market in regional areas can create better outcomes for organisations in terms of utilising the available workforce (Bryant and Jaworski, 2012). To gain this understanding requires an analysis of organisational processes that 'maintain silence and keep certain issues hidden from view' (Lewis and Simpson, 2007 p. 4). With regard to women's re-entry into the labour market in regional areas, the impact of regional geography, gender and motherhood needs to be made visible.

Accessing secure employment is increasingly difficult in regional Australia (Forbes-Mewett et al., 2020) as it is constrained by low population densities, the isolation of each labour market and distance between regional centres. The geographical proximity of work to residence has been demonstrated to be more important for women than men (Australian Bureau of Statistics, 2016). Women are more likely to relocate to regional areas due to the employment of their partners (Strachan et al., 2002), which may create a mismatch between their skills and those desired by the labour market. It is important that organisations look beyond the perception of skill shortages in regional areas and understand the potential of workers within these communities to meet the organisational needs through further training (Bryant and Jaworski, 2012) or jobs redesigned around existing skill sets. This shift from a mindset of regional economies 'lacking' to one of regional businesses having agency can help to reframe place and employment.

Gendered patterns of employment have traditionally characterised regional areas, with masculine industries such as agriculture and construction constituting the 'norm' (Farhall et al., 2020). Women have been concentrated in particular sectors that are valued less and have less capacity for wage progression (Bamberry, 2016). With the growing importance of the service sector to regional communities (Adapa et al., 2021), women's labour force participation has been increasing and the traditional employment profiles are changing. Further, with advances in technology, there are growing opportunities for employment to be progressively freed from place.

Motherhood increases women's unpaid work, and the negative impact of unpaid work on employment and progression is well established (Australian Human Rights Commission, 2014). Labour force participation following intensive periods of caregiving can be constrained by difficulties in outsourcing care and housework, deskilling, declines in confidence, mismatches between training and education and job opportunities and loss of networks (Cass, 2006). In regional areas, women's opportunity for work is affected by concerns about flexible working hours, access to paid parental leave and affordable childcare (Bamberry, 2016). Reskilling employees who have been out of the labour market due to care responsibilities can facilitate re-entry and help organisations in regional areas meet skills shortages.

Mothers face barriers to career progression once they have re-entered the workforce, with the Australian Human Rights Commission (2014 p. 26) finding that 'discrimination in the workplace against mothers is pervasive'. Mothers in the labour market face stereotyping of male breadwinner/female breadwinner gender roles at home and work and questions regarding commitment to their career and skill level. To balance work and care, women are more likely to seek flexible and part-time work than their partners. In Australia 47.4 per cent of all employed persons are women, and 21.6 per cent of all employed people are women who are working part time (Australian Bureau of Statistics, 2020). Part-time and flexible work is often undervalued, and these workers are likely to be marginalised and excluded from training and career paths, which limits their future earning capacity (Pocock et al., 2009).

Employees with competing responsibilities who seek part-time work are likely to downgrade to lower-skill and lower-paid jobs due to the shortage of part-time jobs in leadership and high-skilled occupations (Preston and Yu, 2015). On an hourly basis part-time workers earn less than full-time workers.

Preston and Yu (2015) found, after controlling for human capital character-istics such as education, the hourly rate of men working full time to be 22.5 per cent more than women working part time. Policies that support the equal treatment of workers regardless of hours worked and job status and the move-ment between part-time and full-time jobs can mitigate the disadvantages of part-time employment. Collective agreements in Australia such as industrial awards incorporate the National Employment Standard right for parents and other workers to request flexibility in their employment, such as moving to part-time work and returning to full-time work. While the recent disruption to work patterns seen through the COVID-19 pandemic accelerated all organi-sations' openness to more flexible work practices (Alon et al., 2020), flexible employment has not been a common feature of regional employment (Adapa et al., 2016).

By understanding the cultural and structural barriers to women's entry and re-entry into regional workforces, organisations can better utilise local labour markets and reduce the disadvantages faced by women in the workforce. Boosting regional employment will require creative organisational responses to skill utilisation, rather than focusing on the individual choices of potential and existing employees (Bryant and Jaworski, 2012). This entails analysing the cultural and social assumptions that underpin organisational practices (Australian Human Rights Commission, 2014).

METHOD

In this chapter we have chosen to use a descriptive case study of an exemplary organisation, Regional Australia Bank, to illustrate processes and practices that appear to have been effective in attracting and retaining women returning to work after a career break in regional communities. The value of an exem-plary case rests with the insights that can be gleaned from it, deepening and extending understanding for other potentially similar cases (Yin, 2012). A case study is appropriate for meeting the purpose of this chapter, which is to under-stand how context shapes organisational workforce decision making. It reveals how local labour markets are shaped by the interplay of social, environmental and economic factors and how this shapes organisational decision making. While not seeking to generalise from the case, the insights gleaned from it may be pertinent to other businesses grappling with the challenge of recruiting and retaining women in regional communities, within Australia and beyond. The penalties of gender, motherhood and regional location are not contained to Australia.

As one of the authors was familiar with the business through her role as a director, we were aware of Regional Australia Bank's activities and had access to its human resources team as well as publicly available documents, to learn more about the processes they had in place. The combination of primary and secondary data helped to flesh out the case. While being an 'insider' helped us to gain access, we were aware of the risks of bias this also entailed. We believe that these risks were minimised by the joint authoring and critical reflections throughout the analysis.

REGIONAL AUSTRALIA BANK AND THE CAREER REVIVE PROGRAM

Recognising the gap between metropolitan and regional women's career outcomes, the Federal Government in partnership with KPMG identified 30 medium to large regional businesses to work on context-specific projects to attract and retain women returning to work after a career break. Regional Australia Bank was selected to be part of the project as it was recognised as an exemplar in having many of the 'foundations' in place for women's career success. It had a senior executive committed to enabling women's careers and, through its Flexible Work Arrangements policy, had long offered a range of flexible working options to all employees – including working from home, compressed hours, flexible start and finish times and extended leave.

As a customer-owned bank, Regional Australia Bank is underpinned by the principle of mutuality and is not driven by shareholder returns alone. Mutuality promotes relational value through collaborative stakeholder relationships, where staff are important stakeholders. Having experienced significant organic growth in the previous decade, as well as pursuing mergers with smaller credit unions in neighbouring regions, at the time it was selected for the project Regional Australia Bank employed 278 staff. Initial benchmarking for the project established that while the wider financial sector has a relatively equal mix of male and female employees (Labour Market Information Portal, 2021), more than two thirds (68 per cent) of Regional Australia Bank's workforce are women. The initial analysis by the project team highlighted that Regional Australia Bank provides opportunities for unqualified school leavers to enter the business, supporting them to acquire a Certificate III in financial services, a requisite qualification for those working in financial services. Many staff entering at the frontline service level have progressed into senior roles. Given the generally lower levels of education in regional communities compared to metropolitan locations (Adapa et al., 2021), this reflects Regional Australia Bank's understanding of place and how it can turn a constraint into an opportunity. Part-time work is used by 28.8 per cent of the workforce, and this is overwhelmingly taken up by women (93 per cent). As permanent employees, part-time staff can renegotiate their hours to full time if it suits them.

In measuring women's and men's salaries within Regional Australia Bank, the significant difference between women's average wages ($62,583 per annum) and men's average wages ($114,086 per annum) was made visible. As 90 per cent of the workforce are covered by the Banking, Finance and Insurance Award 2020, which is underpinned by principles of equal pay for equal work, the gender pay gap is largely from the clustering of women in part-time work and at the lower levels of the organisation. Award wages are common across the industry for lower levels of employees and staff are not discriminated against by gender under the award.

The remuneration of the 10 per cent of staff not covered by the award, made up of the executive team and senior managers, is covered by the remuneration policy. Under this board-approved policy, remuneration is set through an external benchmarking exercise of the identified roles every three years, with Consumer Price Index adjustments in the years between, and is based around the scope of the role and the performance of the incumbent. In addressing the gender pay gap, while not seeking to limit part-time work, the challenge for Regional Australia Bank is to ensure more women are reaching the higher levels of the business.

Regional Australia Bank has physical branches across 37 locations across northern New South Wales, and while its balance sheet has grown significantly over the past decade, the volume of face-to-face activity has declined as customers rely more on electronic access to their savings and the wider range of financial services offered by the bank. At the same time, Regional Australia Bank has recognised the strategic importance of the role it plays as an employer in its communities and the relationships it has with customers. Adapting service delivery to the changing environment has prompted a rethinking of the traditional work practices of full-time workers serving customers in a local branch and significant investment in technology skills across the workforce.

THE CAREER REVIVE PROGRAM

The Career Revive program focused on training women in regional labour markets to assist their re-entry into the workforce. It departed from gender equality programs aimed at quotas or other affirmative action measures to boost women's representation in the workforce. Instead, Career Revive was a creative approach to overcoming the limitations of regional labour markets by utilising, retraining and supporting an untapped labour market – women who had experienced career disruptions due to care responsibilities. This enabled the business to meet workforce gaps and to create an internal labour market to fill higher-level positions as they arose.

In setting up the Career Revive project in Regional Australia Bank, the project team canvassed staff views of maternity leave and the pressures facing women who wished to balance work and careers. To further shape their efforts to enhance women's careers, applying an appreciative enquiry mode the project team had staff complete a short, anonymous survey on what made Regional Australia Bank a great place to work. The appreciative enquiry approach, focusing on the strengths of an organisation, is consistent with the wider culture of appreciation and valuing of staff for which Regional Australia Bank has been recognised through international employer awards (Kincentric, 2020).

As Regional Australia Bank also sought to tap into the wider regional population by creating opportunities for women who had been out of the workforce for an extended period, the challenge was to create an action plan which provided practical support and training to aid women's re-entry into the workforce. Applying a workplace planning lens, Regional Australia Bank identified gaps in its current and future workforce and 'considered the areas of the business that were best suited to support, re-train and retain skilled women from the local community' (Department of Education Skills and Employment, 2021). The project team developed a business case for the Supported Returner Program which was endorsed by the Senior Executive, and resources were directed to supporting women's career advancement, including further developing the online learning and performance programs. Through leveraging technology, location did not limit access to professional development.

DISCUSSION AND PRACTICAL IMPLICATIONS OF THE RESEARCH

Regional economies are commonly framed by a narrative of lacking – of skills and employment opportunities – which limits business opportunities. The focus is often on the paucity of the labour market, including the limited skill sets of individuals in regional communities. Local labour markets are shaped by the interplay of social, environmental and economic factors and this shapes organisational decision making. Navigating the wider environment and enabling employees to flourish as a firm grows is a marker of a successful business.

The actions taken by a business – the strategic priorities set, the workplace policies, including staff development opportunities, remuneration and working arrangements, and how the business leverages technology – are often overlooked when considering enduring issues of limited regional labour markets. For regional businesses in particular, their success rests strongly on their connections within their communities (Adapa et al., 2021). By drawing attention to an exemplar business and the actions taken within the Career Revive project to support women's careers and recognising the importance of the underlying culture in which the project was carried out, we bring into focus the role businesses can play in shifting the narrative of lacking and redressing the career penalties of motherhood and place women face in regional economies.

Strategic Priorities

In committing to enabling women's careers in regional communities through participating in Career Revive, Regional Australia Bank was setting women's employment as a priority, and given its visibility, one it could be held accountable for. With Senior Executive backing and resources directed to achieving its goals – necessary conditions for successful change initiatives – a solid foundation was set. The 2020 Annual Report stated that:

> Regional Australia Bank recognises the important function it plays as a service provider and employer across the geographical footprint it covers, with its vision 'to be at the heart of our communities'. It leverages its strength in relationship banking to fulfil its vision. The success of our business will be determined by how well we extend compassion and share our passion to be the champions for rural prosperity. Being connected with regional Australia and its people is, without doubt, the most compelling and inspiring part of our brand. (Regional Australia Bank Annual Report, 2020, p. 4)

In concentrating on relationship banking, there has been a shift from the historical focus and rewarding of the technical skills underpinning financial services to valuing what have traditionally been framed as 'soft skills' – social and interpersonal skills (good communication), emotional skills (empathy) and behavioural attitudes (a service orientation, involvement and initiative) (Bailly and Léné, 2013). These soft skills are often associated with women's work, and historically have been 'invisible' when it comes to rewards and remuneration (Hatton, 2017) but are growing in demand across a host of professional organisations. With the growth of services in regional economies, the importance of soft skills is increasingly recognised. For Regional Australia Bank, these skills are now embedded in its position descriptions, informing its recruitment and promotion processes. While there is a risk of reinforcing traditional stereotypes in focusing on relational skills as 'women's' skills, Regional Australia Bank has embedded them across all levels of the organisation. Rather than being invisible (and undervalued), these skills are now an integral part of workforce planning, informing recruitment, training and professional development for all roles. For regional women seeking to re-enter the paid workforce, this recognition of many of the skills they have developed through unpaid community roles enables re-entry. Ensuring that the valuing of soft skills remains embedded in organisational practices and policies will be crucial for managing the risks associated with gendered occupational segregation and the often hidden undervaluation of work performed by women.

Innovative Workplace Practices

Regional Australia Bank has a higher share of women employees than finance sector averages and other regional employers. The human resources team recognised the difficulties women in regional areas face in committing to full-time work because of the continuing unequal division of labour in the home, women's disproportionate share of caring responsibilities and more limited child and aged care services, particularly in very small communities, and have offered flexible work practices to staff, including part-time work for the past decade. Part-time working is normalised within the business and, in contrast to much of the wider research on part-time work which shows part timers have less access to training than their full-time counterparts, training and development opportunities are equally accessible to those in part-time and full-time roles.

An openness to entry-level recruitment and the provision of training opportunities to meet industry accreditation requirements and business needs has allowed Regional Australia Bank to 'grow its own' rather than assuming the skills are present across its communities to fill roles at all levels. Recognising this as an existing strength, the Career Revive program included the stories of senior female leaders who had progressed from entry-level roles to senior management. While recruitment from the internal labour market is advantageous in constricted labour markets, it does limit the flow of knowledge, networks and expertise that comes from accessing staff who have worked in diverse markets, sectors and geographies.

Training and professional development are an integral component of Regional Australia Bank's success. Importantly, it has not pursued training designed to 'fix' women – that is training them to be more like the men who have historically held leadership roles and which characterised many of the early efforts by businesses to increase women's representation in more senior roles. Rather, it has reframed its position descriptions to recognise the value of soft skills and designed its recruitment and training activities to select from and develop these. Training has been directed to enabling the skills of middle managers to encourage managers to have conversations about the Regional Australia Bank values and ensuring these values foster diversity and more flexible approaches across all levels of the business.

Employee connection to the firm's strategy and goals, acknowledgement for work well done and a culture of learning and development foster high levels of engagement. In 2020, Regional Australia Bank was awarded Best Employer status by Kincentric, based on its outstanding results with respect to employee engagement. The test for Regional Australia Bank will be addressing the gender pay gap, largely created from women's representation in part-time work. While a benefit of using the Banking, Finance and Insurance

Award 2020 to determine pay and conditions is that equal pay for work of equal value provisions are enshrined in this industrial instrument, employees who are covered by awards are often excluded from collective voice and bargaining arrangements and the larger wage increases that often come from enterprise bargaining arrangements. As the industry and organisation continue to evolve, attention will need to focus on the continuing valuing of soft skills, the movement of part-time workers to full-time work and career progression for workers employed in a part-time capacity for women's career progression to be supported.

Leveraging of Technology

Australia is one of the least densely populated nations of the world and there are vast distances between towns. The sparseness of population away from the coastline and the physical distances between inland regional towns historically has limited career mobility within Regional Australia Bank, as staff were often deeply connected to their communities and reluctant to leave their hometowns. When the business relied so much on face-to-face interaction, the jobs in branches were largely locally based, and the career progression limited by the branch needs. Over the past decade, this has changed significantly as fewer roles are required to deliver the face-to-face services.

By leveraging technology, the physical location of staff members no longer limits their roles to local service delivery as Regional Australia Bank maximises its 'social and environmental returns' (Annual Report, 2020), opening up more career opportunities within the organisation. In realigning the workforce, the branch-based roles are now able to service customers online or through the call centre infrastructure, 'relationship-focused' loans officers are not contained to a single branch and can work remotely and across the geographical locations and the traditional head office roles can be located beyond the four walls of the physical building. In embracing technology to support its service delivery, Regional Australia Bank has opened up career opportunities more widely to all staff. While the leveraging of technology certainly benefits Regional Australia Bank, challenges remain regarding the management of staff's work–life balance, team culture, supervision and workplace health and safety due to flexible work and potentially extensive staff travel. Regional Australia Bank will need to maintain a balance between having a physical presence in rural towns to remain at 'the heart of the community' while creating flexibility for staff and responding to changing modes of banking that do not necessitate physical branches.

Access to training was identified through the Career Revive project as a constraint for those located away from head office and a high priority for supporting women re-entering the workforce after a long absence. Heeding this direct feedback, additional resources were directed to developing online training, mentoring and other transitions to work support. With an organisational culture shaped by its mutual values and valuing of relationships, Regional Australia Bank has been recognised internationally as an exemplary employer. From this strong foundation, Regional Australia Bank committed to enabling women's careers more effectively than it had done – it sought to close the gap between the rhetoric of gender equity and the reality within its own business. While employing more women than the industry averages, there remained a gap between the average wages of men and women. Through the strategic positioning of the business, its openness to innovative workplace practices, leveraging of technology for enabling access to professional development and the breaking down of geographical barriers for roles, Regional Australia Bank demonstrates the importance of connecting the different levels (macro, meso and micro) in redressing the triple penalty of regional location, gender and motherhood. While there is still some way to go, and ongoing risks to manage, the foundations are well grounded. Investing in the development of gender-equal organisational cultures supports the breakdown of gender stereotyping and promotes beliefs that women are committed to their career and able to lead (Australian Human Rights Commission, 2014).

CONCLUSION

Regional women's career opportunities are shaped by the intersection of location, gender and motherhood. The complex interplay of these has drawn public policy attention to the wider societal factors impacting women's careers and there are numerous sites offering career tips for women to develop their careers. Between the macro and the micro, there is the role individual businesses can play in redressing inequality. The actions taken by a business are often overlooked when considering enduring issues of limited regional labour markets. Through the Career Revive project, the Federal Government has drawn attention to those employers who are making inroads into addressing inequality. We believe the lessons learned from our exemplar case, Regional Australia Bank – the strategic priorities set, the workplace policies in place, including staff development opportunities, remuneration and working arrangements, and how the business leverages technology – can spark change for other regional businesses. A key learning from this case study is that it is crucial to take context into consideration when designing workforce development and diversity management programs. Implementing approaches developed for urban contexts would not have had the sustainable outcomes of Career Revive, a program tailored to place. While Regional Australia Bank has laid strong foundations it will face challenges going forward in addressing its gender pay gap while supporting flexible and part-time work. It remains an important example of overcoming the constraints of space and harnessing and building on the available workforce. The insights from this case may resonate with businesses in regional communities beyond Australia where the triple burden of regional location, gender and motherhood can curtail the local labour markets and limit firm growth.

REFERENCES

Adapa, S., Rindfleish, J., and Sheridan, A. (2016). 'Doing gender' in a regional context: Explaining women's absence from senior roles in regional accounting firms in Australia. *Critical Perspectives on Accounting*, 35(March), 100–110.

Adapa, S., Sheridan, A., and Yarram, S. (2021). *Entrepreneurship in Regional Communities: Exploring the Relevance of Embeddedness, Networking, Empowerment and Communitarian Values*. Palgrave MacMillan.

Alon, T., Doepke, M., Olmstead-Rumsey, J., and Tertilt, M. (2020). The impact of COVID-19 on gender equality (0898-2937). www.nber.org/system/files/working _papers/w26947/w26947.pdf

Australian Bureau of Statistics. (2016). Census of population and housing: Commuting to work – more stories from the Census, 2016. www.abs.gov.au/ausstats/abs@.nsf/ Lookup/by%20Subject/2071.0.55.001~2016~Main%20Features~Feature%20Article: %20Journey%20to%20Work%20in%20Australia~40

Australian Bureau of Statistics. (2020). Labour force, Australia, Jan 2020, cat. No. 6202.0. www.abs.gov.au/ausstats/abs@.nsf/mf/6202.0/

Australian Human Rights Commission. (2014). Supporting working parents: Pregnancy and return to work national review – report. https://humanrights.gov.au/our-work/ sex-discrimination/publications/supporting-working-parents-pregnancy-and-return -work

Bailly, F., and Léné, A. (2013). The personification of the service labour process and the rise of soft skills: A French case study. *Employee Relations*, 35(1), 79–97.

Bamberry, L. (2016). Restructuring women's work: Labour market and household gender regimes in the Greater Latrobe Valley, Australia. *Gender, Place and Culture*, 23(8), 1135–1149.

Bryant, L., and Jaworski, K. (2012). Minding the gaps: Examining skill shortages in Australian rural non-agricultural workplaces. *Journal of Management and Organization*, 18(4), 499–515.

Cass, B. (2006). Care giving and employment: Policy recognition of care and pathways to labour force return. *Australian Bulletin of Labour*, 32(3), 240–256.

Commonwealth of Australia, Department of Prime Minister and Cabinet. (2017). Towards 2025: An Australian Government strategy to boost women's workforce participation. https://womensworkforceparticipation.pmc.gov.au/sites/default/files/ towards-2025-strategy.pdf

Department of Education Skills and Employment. (2021). Career Revive case study: Regional Australia Bank. www.dese.gov.au/career-revive/regional-australia-bank -case-study

Farhall, K., Tyler, M., and Fairbrother, P. (2020). Labour and regional transition: Sex-segregation, the absence of gender and the valorisation of masculinised employment in Gippsland, Australia. *Gender, Place and Culture*, 1–19.

Forbes-Mewett, H., Schermuly, A. C., and Hegarty, K. (2020). Aspirational individuals, hopeful communities: Histories and subjectivities of precarity in regional Australia. *Critical Sociology*, 46(4–5), 543–556.

Hatton, E. (2017). Mechanisms of invisibility: Rethinking the concept of invisible work. *Work, Employment and Society*, 31(2), 336–351.

Kincentric. (2020). Best employers program country/market best employers. www.kincentric.com/bestemployers/global-best-employers/market-best-employers

Labour Market Information Portal. (2021). Employment by industry by gender, November 2020. https://lmip.gov.au/default.aspx?LMIP/LFR_SAFOUR/LFR_Industry_Gender

Lewis, P., and Simpson, R. (2007). Gender and emotions: Introduction. In Lewis, P. and Simpson, R., eds, *Gendering Emotions in Organizations: Management, Work and Organisations*. Palgrave Macmillan, pp. 1–15.

Pocock, B., Skinner, N., and Ichii, R. (2009). Work, life and workplace flexibility: The Australian work and life index 2009. Centre for Work+ Life, University of South Australia.

Preston, A., and Yu, S. (2015). Is there a part-time/full-time pay differential in Australia? *Journal of Industrial Relations*, 57(1), 24–47.

Strachan, G., Sullivan, A., and Burgess, J. (2002). Women's work in regional labour markets: Spatial versus industry differences. *Labour and Industry*, 13(2), 91–116.

Yin, R. (2012). *Applications of Case Study Research*, Third Edition. Sage.

USEFUL WEB LINKS

Department of Education, Skills and Investment. (2021). Career Revive case study – Regional Australia Bank. www.dese.gov.au/employing-and-supporting-women-your-organisation/career-revive/case-studies/regional-australia-bank-case-study

Workplace Gender Equality Agency. (2018). Here's how employers can support Australia's working parents. www.wgea.gov.au/newsroom/heres-how-employers-can-support-australias-working-parents

Workplace Gender Equality Agency. (2021). Flexible work. www.wgea.gov.au/flexible-work

5. Researching skilled migrants in Australia

Syed Mohyuddin and Roslyn Cameron

INTRODUCTION

This chapter will explore some of the key issues skilled migrants face in integrating into Australian workplaces and communities and how researching some of these issues in the field can be rewarding, insightful, and challenging. The elements of diversity, equity, and inclusion (DE&I) of researching skilled migration relates to the diversity of skilled migrants and their respective countries of origin and birthplaces and to the levels of similarities/commonalities the skilled migrants share with majority populations within the host country. Issues arise through the difference in languages spoken and the dominant language of the host country, which in turn influences interactions, communications, and understandings. Differences in culture are widely influential in terms of values, customs, traditions, and norms as well as dominant belief systems and roles attributed within families and societies. This richness of diversity also adds a level of complexity across facets of intersectionality and how this manifests in exclusive and inclusive behaviours in societies and workplaces. These intersections cover a myriad of facets, not only ethnic origins but age, gender, marital status, belief systems, sexuality, and disability and a non-English-speaking background to name just a few. Some of the DE&I issues explored relate to subtle and direct discrimination and racism, frustrations in job-seeking activities and career opportunities due to having overseas-acquired qualifications and experiences devalued when compared with those who have Australian qualifications and work experience, and gendered forms of discrimination within migrant groups.

Skilled migration has been a cornerstone to many traditional migration nations' population and skills growth for many decades. For example, Australia has received a significant number of skilled migrants from English-speaking and non-English-speaking countries, with 29.8 per cent of the Australian population overseas born (ABS, 2019b). Traditional migration nations such as Australia, Canada, and New Zealand use a specific point-based system to grant skilled migration visas to fulfil skill shortages in areas where skills demand is not being met by domestic supply.

Today migrants from all over the world and from all continents migrate to developed countries in the hope of securing employment and a new life for themselves and their families. The following regions are some of the most popular destinations for migration: North America, Northern, Southern, and Western European countries, Arab states, Southeast Asia, and the Pacific. Unlike the often traumatic contexts that drive refugee or humanitarian migration, skilled migrants move to host nations by choice, in search of better professional opportunities. Some scholars refer to skilled migrants as self-initiated expatriates which stems from the research traditions of international human resource management (IHRM), a subdiscipline of HRM (Al Ariss and Crowley-Henry, 2013). The motivations to become a skilled migrant are varied and are often referred to as a combination and interplay of push–pull factors. In other words, there are reasons for wanting to leave the country of origin (push factors) and reasons for wanting to migrate to a certain host country (pull factors). However, despite the motivation to migrate skilled migrants will become uprooted from their inherited social and cultural conditions. Hence, they also face the challenge of forms of cultural shock and re-embedding themselves in new social and cultural conditions and workplaces in the host nation. They face the challenge of obtaining recognition of their skills and work experiences acquired overseas. The majority of the skilled migrants hailing from developing countries come to host nations with a belief that they will be benefiting from equal opportunities for all and the policy rhetoric of the host nation's skilled migration programs (Cameron et al., 2019). Further, they also aspire to live in a society which embraces multiculturalism and inclusivity.

This chapter will provide a brief overview of the history of migration in Australia and some key literature and frameworks guiding future skilled migration research before presenting the two skilled migration research case studies which have focused on skilled migration in Australian contexts. The first case study is based on a qualitative PhD study and is therefore a substantive piece of research. The second is based on a study of skilled migration in a regional area in Australia utilising a three-phase sequential mixed-methods research design. Each case provides insights into the research questions driving the studies, the conceptual frameworks developed, the research design and methods applied in the field, key findings, conclusions and limitations. The chapter concludes with key recommendations for researchers and future research directions.

KEY LITERATURE

Brief History of Migration in Australia from 1901

Australia's history of multiculturalism and diversity is relatively recent, as Australia's migration policies up until 1975 were dominated by what was termed "White Australia" policies which were set in place from 1901 and continued until the mid-1970s. These sets of policies were slowly dismantled by successive governments from 1949 to 1975. Australian immigration can be divided into five eras (Mence et al., 2017). Before 1901 the primarily British settlers were brought in due to political and cultural reasons. According to Mence et al. (2017) this was the first era. The second era started when different states and territories of Australia joined to form the federation in 1901. This is also considered the beginning of the white Australia policy. The third era was post-First World War. The fourth era commenced when the Department of Immigration was formally established in 1945 after the Second World War. Australia embraced multiculturalism in 1973 and the white Australia policy was abolished (Mence et al., 2017).

Australia is now home to migrants from all racial backgrounds from different nations of the world. Key Australian Bureau of Statistics figures on migrants reported in 2019 via the Characteristics of Recent Migrants Survey are listed here:

• 1.9 million people in Australia were recent migrants or temporary residents.
• 50 per cent had permanent visas or had become Australian citizens.
• 68 per cent of recent migrants and temporary residents were employed, with a labour force participation rate of 72 per cent. (ABS, 2019a)

Skilled Migration Research: Gaps and Frameworks

Syed (2008) developed a multirelational framework for researching the employment prospects of skilled migrants. He argues for a "relational perspective on employment prospects for migrant workers addressing issues related to diversity and diversity management at macro-national, meso-organizational, and micro-individual levels" (Syed, 2008, p. 28). Table 5.1 summarises this framework and may assist in formulating future research in skilled migration.

An interesting line of inquiry is focused on recruitment. The role of biases and discrimination in the recruitment of migrants has been researched and some of these studies are referred to as "resume studies". Adamovic (2021) undertook a review of resume studies and found that ethnic discrimination depends on the following factors: the applicant; the job; the recruiter; the hiring organisation; the country; and the ethnic group. This review of "resume

Table 5.1   *A relational framework for managing skilled migrants*

Macro level	Meso level	Micro level
Economic and human capital	Organisational	Motivation to migrate
Legal	practices	
– Labour laws and policies	Resources	Lifestyle
– Human rights		Identity and agency
Societal		
– Culture		
– Social support		

Source: Adapted from Syed (2008, p. 40).

studies" resulted in recommendations for future research which included integrating an intervention into a resume study and the use of video applications.

Guo and Al Ariss (2015) from the international HRM field refer to expatriation and expatriation types research as a growing field of inquiry traditionally dominated by international assignees of organisational expatriate research in the international HRM discipline and skilled (im)migration in multiple fields of inquiry (e.g., labour economics, migration studies and human geography). They have identified two research gaps in the studies of migrants: gender-related issues and the role of organisations in managing skilled migrants.

Tharenou (2015, p. 149) identified three main lines of inquiry into what she defines as "investigations into long-term (over one year) skilled (i.e., tertiary educated) international mobility". These three lines of inquiry are: (1) organisational transferees/international assignees/assigned expatriates; (2) self-initiated expatriates and (3) skilled (im)migrants. Tharenou (2015) acknowledges the research in these three lines of inquiry has been integrated over the last ten years, however, they have not been examined comparatively in terms of methodological robustness and rigour. In addition to this, Al Ariss and Crowley-Henry (2013) developed a research map for future studies on self-initiated expatriation-based research becoming developed more in terms of its theorising which is central to this map. The four aspects of the map are: (1) diversity-informed; (2) context-specific; (3) reflexive and (4) methodologically triangulated. Two case studies are now presented.

Table 5.2   *Research aim and questions for "Resolving a crisis of habitus"*

Research aim	Research questions
How does migration to Australia affect the employment experiences of South Asian professionals and managers?	RQ1: To what extent do current theories about the effects of migration on career trajectories provide a useful framework for analysing and understanding the experiences of professionals and managers from South Asia in Australia?
	RQ2: What is the nature of the experience of being a migrant professional/manager from South Asia in Australia?
	RQ3: What are the career challenges faced by South Asian professionals and managers when they migrate to Australia?
	RQ4: How do South Asian managers attempt to overcome the challenges of their new career environment?
	RQ5: In what ways can South Asian managers be assisted in establishing a career following migration?

Source: Mohyuddin (2011).

CASE STUDY 1: RESOLVING A CRISIS OF HABITUS: THE EXPERIENCES OF PROFESSIONALS AND MANAGERS FROM SOUTH ASIA IN AUSTRALIA

To address the key aim of the research and to understand the essence of the lived experience of skilled migrant professionals and managers, the following research questions were explored (Table 5.2).

Conceptual Framework

The key concept of this research was that skilled migrants face a "crisis of habitus" upon migrating from their home countries to Australia. They face this crisis as they are disembedded from their inherited social conditions. Further, they make an effort to resolve this crisis by re-embedding themselves in the new home country, i.e., Australia. Theories of disembedding/re-embedding (Giddens, 1990), habitus (Bourdieu, 1986), acculturation (Redfield et al., 1936) and sense-making (Weick, 1995) were utilised to explain the phenomenon of being a highly skilled South Asian migrant professional and manager in Australia.

Disembedding is the "socially sanctioned" (Bauman, 2000, p. 32) process of individuals removing themselves from their native culture, "from the plot in which they germinated and from which they sprouted" (Gane, 2004, p. 32), as the skilled migrants are uprooted from their home country culture and society.

An individual's habitus is the combination of different forms of capital (Bourdieu, 1986). This includes cultural capital which can exist in three forms:

in an embodied state which includes a person's race or accent; an objectified state which includes a person's way of dressing or art collection; and, finally, in an institutionalised form which is a person's qualifications or degrees earned. Social capital is made up of social obligations which exist as human interconnections and can be convertible in certain conditions into economic capital and, at times, can also be institutionalised in the form of a title of nobility. Finally, economic capital possessed by an individual is a capital that can be immediately and directly converted into money and can be institutionalised in the form of property rights.

Skilled migrants when migrating to new cultural and social settings of the new host country are disembedded from their inherited social conditions. Therefore, their habitus gets alerted and they face a crisis of habitus that they need to resolve. They face non-recognition of their overseas qualifications and experience. They also become an ethnic minority in the host nation. Further, migrants leave their social contacts and networking behind in the home country and joblessness adds to their crisis due to depletion in economic capital.

The resolution of the crisis of habitus was explained by using the theories of acculturation and sense-making. Acculturation is defined as those phenomena which result when groups of individuals who have lived within different cultures come into continuous, first-hand contact with subsequent changes in the original cultural patterns of either or both groups (Redfield et al., 1936, p. 149). According to Sakamoto (2007), acculturation is divided into four categories: integration; assimilation; separation; and marginalisation. While resolving the crisis the skilled migrants can fall into one of these categories.

A process through which individuals rationalise their behaviour on the basis of their interpretation of the environment in which they exist is called sense-making (Salancik and Pfeffer, 1978). From the organisational perspective, people also need to rationalise the events within the organisational environment (Weick, 2001). Therefore, sense-making is a very significant theory to understand the interpretations of skilled migrants when they are exploring the new environments of the country to which they have migrated. Figure 5.1 summarises the conceptual framework of this research.

Research Design and Methods

The research utilised qualitative, interpretive paradigms as the methodology to analyse the data. The qualitative analysis techniques were combined with analysis of narratives. A phenomenological study is the lived experience of several individuals about a concept or phenomenon (Creswell, 1998). In this case, that lived experience was about being a skilled migrant from a non-English-speaking cultural background. A narrative is defined as a spoken or written text which provides an account of an event/action, or

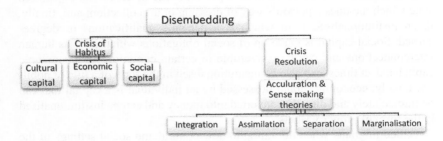

Figure 5.1   *Conceptual framework for "Resolving a crisis of habitus"*

a series of events or actions, chronologically connected (Czarniawska-Joerges, 2004, p. 17). This study utilised the interviews of highly skilled migrant professionals and managers and the interviews were about their experiences. These experiences had a timeline, from arriving in Australia as a migrant to the time when the interview was conducted. Furthermore, it involved their personal and social experiences.

The primary data were collected using purposive sampling (Creswell, 1998). The purpose was to seek the most productive sample to answer the research questions, i.e., individuals who experienced the phenomenon of being disembedded from their inherent conditions as migrants.

Following inclusion criteria, respondents who were selected to be interviewed for this research had the following characteristics:

- Migrated to Australia from Bangladesh, India, Pakistan or Sri Lanka.
- Migration must be part of the skilled-based migration program.
- Must have a minimum of one year of work experience in the home country and at least one year of work experience in Australia.
- Must have professional/managerial qualifications.

The researcher approached 42 individuals for the interviews. The interviews continued until saturation was achieved which was after 21 interviews had been conducted. The interviews were transcribed and coded for analysis. The emerging themes were analysed using the technique of constant comparison.

Key Findings for Diversity, Equality, and Inclusion

The following are the key findings from the common themes that emerged from the participants' interviews:

- Skilled migrants praised Australian society generally as an accommodating society. However, they were also concerned about subtle or overt racism.
- They felt that they were under greater pressure to prove their skills as compared to the locals.
- Females faced deeper crisis as compared to male counterparts due to the home country cultural expectations and norms.
- From an acculturation point of view there was evidence of separation, marginalisation and assimilation, and not much evidence of integration.
- The participants aimed to resolve the crisis of habitus by assimilating into the Australian work environment, even though they found that hard to do.
- Most of the respondents of this study believed that the hardest part of the experience was getting their overseas-acquired skills recognised. Sometimes, when they ended up in jobs that required low skills and they were well compensated, they still yearned for jobs in their relevant profession. Therefore, despite having better economic conditions as part of their agenda, the skilled migrants also wanted jobs that were intellectually rewarding.
- Sense-making was based on migrants' identity, which was further based on their cultural capital.

Limitations and Conclusion

Firstly, there were some methodological limitations in that the participants can construct stories that can support how they interpret the phenomenon under observation. However, this limitation did not undermine the research as the participants hailed from diverse backgrounds and the researcher analysed both where the narratives of the respondents converged and where they differed. Further, the impact of their experience was on the resolution of crisis of habitus. Secondly, the focus of this research was only on those from the South Asian region. Research must be expanded to other regions and more non-English-speaking nations. Limited evidence was found in the extant literature of using a combination of theories of habitus, sense-making, and acculturation to analyse the challenges faced by skilled migrants from non-English-speaking nations in Australia.

Recommendations for Future Research

The researchers who are aspiring to conduct future research on skilled migrants can take the following recommendations into consideration.

The above case study was a triangulation of various qualitative research methods, i.e., phenomenology and analysis of narratives. It is highly recommended to triangulate between both qualitative and quantitative methods. This will not only make the data quite rich but also the researcher can target a bigger sample of participants.

1. As the core focus on the skilled migrant community's perspective was one of the limitations of this case study, it would be a good idea to also develop an understanding of the mindsets of the people who can be the potential employers of the skilled migrants. Focus groups of such executives and managers can be held to gather qualitative data on their perspectives.
2. More in-depth research is required that also takes the factor of gender diversity among the skilled migrants into account.
3. The aspiring researchers need to delve into the unexplored migrant communities in order to take skilled migrant research forward.

CASE STUDY 2: REGIONAL SUSTAINABILITY AND SKILLED MIGRATION

The second case study focused on the contributions of skilled migrants to a regional area. The research aim and research questions are summarised in Table 5.3. Many regions in Australia suffer from a loss of population to larger urban and metropolitan areas such as cities which offer greater opportunities for employment, especially for younger members of the population. This outflow of population, distance from metropolitan areas, and relatively fewer employment opportunities and services can mean that regional areas and regional employers can find it difficult to attract and retain skilled professionals and skilled workforces.

Conceptual Framework

The context of the study is essentially regional sustainability, and the role that skilled migration can play in combatting the issues regions face in ensuring economic and social sustainability through appropriate workforces, skills, and services for the regional population and economy. The Australian Regional Sponsored Skilled Migration visa program has been a key policy and program initiative to assist with these issues and to counter congestion, housing, and infrastructure pressures in our capital cities.

Table 5.3   *Research aim and research questions for "Regional sustainability and skilled migration"*

Research aim	Research questions
The overall aim of this study was to investigate the contributions of skilled migrants and their families to regional businesses and communities and to identify the factors which attract and retain skilled migrants in key workforces in regional areas.	RQ1: What economic, social, and cultural contributions do skilled migrants and their families make to regional businesses and communities?
	RQ2: What are the issues encountered by businesses and communities when employing skilled migrants?
	RQ3: What support do businesses and the community need to provide to ensure they attract and retain skilled migrants and their families in regional areas?
	RQ4: What support do skilled migrants and their families need to better assist them to settle, become active members of communities, and remain in regions?
	RQ5: What are the implications of the study findings for policy and practice?

Source: Cameron et al. (2013).

BOX 5.1

In November 2019, the Australian Government announced changes to our immigration program to strengthen our economy and boost regional areas. Australia's regional migration program consists of:

- Two skilled regional provisional visas that provide a pathway to permanent residence.
- A skilled regional permanent resident visa (from November 2022).
- Additional points under the Skilled Migration Points Test for skilled migrants nominated to live and work in regional Australia.
- More options for international students who graduate from regional universities.

The Australian Government works closely with state, territory, and local governments and local communities to attract migrants to regional areas. Skilled migrants settling in regional Australia have a diverse range of available occupations to match their experience, skills, and qualifications.

https://immi.homeaffairs.gov.au/visas/working-in-australia/regional-migration

The context of the study was framed by the overarching concept of regional sustainability and utilised human capital theory and stakeholder theory to conceptually frame the issues of the role of skilled migrants in regional sustainability through their contributions to regional communities: economic, social, and cultural contributions. Integration and embeddedness into communities (and the HRM practices related to the attraction and retention of human capital to regions and regional workforces) were applied and are depicted in the conceptual framework in Figure 5.2.

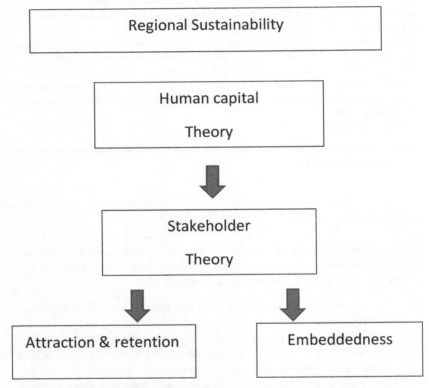

Figure 5.2   Conceptual framework for "Regional sustainability and skilled migration"

Research Design and Methods

The research design employed for this study was a sequential, exploratory mixed-methods design where a combination of qualitative and quantitative data was collected across three phases (Creswell and Plano Clark 2007). The study was undertaken over a nine-month period and sourced data from multiple sources to attempt to paint a picture of the skilled migration population in the region, the workforces and employers of skilled migrants, and the community engagement of skilled migrant populations within the social fabric of the region.

In each phase a combination of qualitative and quantitative data was collected, integrated, and analysed. Figure 5.3 depicts the research design and has applied the new mixed-methods research notation system.

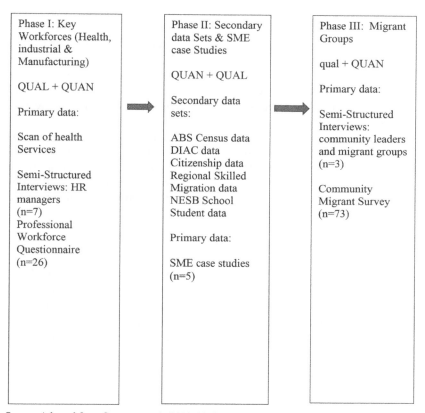

Phase I: Key Workforces (Health, industrial & Manufacturing)

QUAL + QUAN

Primary data:

Scan of health Services

Semi-Structured Interviews: HR managers (n=7) Professional Workforce Questionnaire (n=26)

Phase II: Secondary data Sets & SME case Studies

QUAN + QUAL

Secondary data sets:

ABS Census data DIAC data Citizenship data Regional Skilled Migration data NESB School Student data

Primary data:

SME case studies (n=5)

Phase III: Migrant Groups

qual + QUAN

Primary data:

Semi-Structured Interviews: community leaders and migrant groups (n=3)

Community Migrant Survey (n=73)

Source: Adapted from Cameron et al. (2012, 2013).

Figure 5.3   Sequential exploratory mixed-methods design

The research design was driven largely by the fact there was no single source of data to answer the research questions posed and to try to paint a picture of the contribution of skilled migrants to the region. This likened the research to trying to piece together parts of a larger jigsaw puzzle, with each piece of data collection adding a piece to the puzzle.

Key Findings for Diversity, Equality, and Inclusion

- Skilled migrants contribute economically to regions by providing key professional skill sets, entrepreneurial activities, and population growth.
- Skilled migrants contribute socially through a diversity of cultures (72 cultures represented in the LGA) and positive community self-help structures.
- Skilled migrants contribute culturally through cultural events and activities: welcoming morning teas and the annual multicultural festival.
- Regional businesses are faced with skill shortages and difficulties attracting skilled labour regionally and domestically.
- A strong need for employers and communities to assist with resolving settlement issues associated with housing, schooling, and cultural and linguistic challenges faced by skilled migrants and their families locating to regional Australia is crucial.
- Regional businesses need to tap into existing migrant community organisations and collaborate to improve the settlement and integration of skilled workers and their families. This also includes strategies to combat racism through cross-cultural training, public celebrations of diversity, and building inclusive schools and inclusive workplaces, thereby assisting in skilled migrant regional retention.

Limitations and Conclusions

The study has limitations related to small sample sizes and across multiple sources in relation to the primary data collection. This was also exacerbated by the fact that population frames were small due to the size of regional professional workforces. The secondary data sources contained small samples as well and also incurred limitations across the study. These limitations informed the first recommendation.

Recommendations

1. Need for a national data collection mechanism on skilled migrants and their families which could be used to evaluate current migration policy and inform future migration policy and regional programs.
2. A model should be developed to determine the economic, social, and cultural contributions of skilled migrants and their families to regional Australia.
3. The study recommends a local employer body (e.g., Chamber of Commerce) to provide support to small and medium businesses who are either employing or planning to employ skilled migrant workers.

4. Future research should be undertaken to explore the role of regions in branding and attraction strategies and the utility of developing regional migration plans.
5. A future research agenda should be developed that explores the experiences of skilled migrants and their families in regional communities including regional comparative studies and research focused on the use of skilled migration by small to medium-sized enterprises.

CONCLUSION/KEY RECOMMENDATIONS FOR RESEARCHERS AND FUTURE RESEARCH DIRECTIONS

Researching DE&I issues for skilled migrants is a relatively small field; however, it is a growing field of inquiry which cuts across multiple disciplines such as labour economics and human capital, human geography, migration studies, sociology, political science, international management, HRM (global labour markets and diversity management), and cultural studies, to name just a few. We have provided an overview of some of the issues through two case studies of skilled migration research within an Australian context. Each case study produced a set of recommendations.

The framework developed by Syed (2008) and the identification of research gaps by Al Ariss and Crowley-Henry (2013), Guo and Al Ariss (2015), and Tharenou (2015) echo in a new era of skilled migration research and foci. In addition to this we argue that future research into DE&I issues for skilled migrants needs to acknowledge the intersectionality of these issues for skilled migrants. The categories "skilled migrants" or "self-initiated expatriates" contain within them incredible and complex diversity and intersectionality and to progress this field of research we need to account for and acknowledge this.

The pervading DE&I issues of direct and indirect discrimination, racism, unequal treatment of career capital assets and career opportunities, feelings of marginalisation in workplaces and communities, and experiences of disembeddedness are commonly experienced by skilled migrants and their family members. These issues remain in need of further investigation, especially if intersectionality and diversity among skilled migrant groups are to be acknowledged and taken into account. We have provided some recommendations for resources you may find useful for your field research in respect to skilled migration and skilled migrants.

REFERENCES

ABS (2019a). Characteristics of recent migrants survey. www.abs.gov.au/statistics/people/people-and-communities/characteristics-recent-migrants/nov-2019

ABS (2019b). Migration, Australia. www.abs.gov.au/statistics/people/population/migration-australia/2019-20

Adamovic, M. (2021). When ethnic discrimination in recruitment is likely to occur and how to reduce it: Applying a contingency perspective to review resume studies. *Human Resource Management Review*.

Al Ariss, A. and Crowley-Henry, M. (2013). Self-initiated expatriation and migration in the management literature: Present theorizations and future research directions. *Career Development International*, 18(1), pp. 78–96.

Bauman, Z. (2000). *Liquid Modernity*. Cambridge: Polity Press.

Bourdieu, P. (1986). *The Forms of Capital*. Westport, CT: Greenword Press.

Cameron, R., Dwyer, T., Richardson, S., Ahmed, E. and Sukumaran, A. (2012). *Skilled Migrants and Their Families in Regional Australia: A Gladstone Case Study*. Gladstone: CQUniversity Australia.

Cameron, R., Dwyer, T., Richardson, S., Ahmed, E. and Sukumaran, A. (2013). Lessons from the field: Applying the good reporting of a mixed methods study (GRAMMS) framework. *Electronic Journal of Business Research Methods*, 11(2), pp. 53–66.

Cameron, R., Farivar, F. and Dantas, J. (2019). The unanticipated road to skills wastage for skilled migrants: The non-recognition of overseas qualifications and experience (ROQE). *Labour and Industry: A Journal of the Social and Economic Relations of Work*, 29(1), pp. 80–97.

Creswell, J. W. (1998). *Qualitative Inquiry and Research Design: Choosing among Five Traditions*. Thousand Oaks, CA: Sage.

Creswell, J. W. and Plano Clark, V. L. (2007). *Designing and Conducting Mixed Methods Research*. Thousand Oaks, CA: Sage.

Czarniawska-Joerges, B. (2004). *Narratives in Social Science Research, Introducing Qualitative Methods*. Thousand Oaks, CA: Sage.

Gane, N. (2004). *The Future of Social Theory*. London: Continuum.

Giddens, A. (1990). *The Consequences of Modernity*. 2nd ed. Stanford, CA: Stanford University Press.

Guo, C. and Al Ariss, A. (2015). Human resource management of international migrants: Current theories and future research. *International Journal of Human Resource Management*, 26(10), pp. 1287–1297.

Mence, V., Gangell, S. and Tebb, R. (2017). *A History of the Department of Immigration: Managing Migration to Australia*. Canberra: DIBP.

Mohyuddin S. M. (2011). *Resolving a crisis of habitus: The experiences of professionals and managers from South Asia in Australia*. Unpublished doctoral dissertation, Curtin University, Perth.

Redfield, R., Linton, R. and Herskovits, M. J. (1936). Memorandum for the study of acculturation. *American Anthropologist*, 38(1), 149–152.

Sakamoto, I. (2007). A critical examination of immigrant acculturation: Toward an anti-oppressive social work model with immigrant adults in a pluralistic society. *British Journal of Social Work*, 37(3), pp. 515–535.

Salancik, G. R. and Pfeffer, J. (1978). A social information processing approach to job attitudes and task design. *Administrative Science Quarterly*, 23(2), 224–253.

Syed, J. (2008). Employment prospects for skilled migrants: A relational perspective. *Human Resource Management Review*, 18, pp. 28–45.

Tharenou, P. (2015). Researching expatriate types: The quest for rigorous methodological approaches: Researching expatriate types. *Human Resource Management Journal*, 25.

Weick, K. E. (1995). *Sensemaking in Organizations, Foundations for Organizational Science*. Thousand Oaks, CA: Sage.
Weick, K. E. (2001). *Making Sense of the Organization*. Oxford: Blackwell.

USEFUL RESOURCES

Cameron, R., Mohyuddin, S. and Wijerante, A. (2019). Qualitative research methods for human resources management. In S. Delamont, P. Atkinson, R. Williams, A. Cernat and J. Sakshaug (Eds), *Sage Research Methods Foundations*. London: Sage.
O'Cathain, A., Murphy, E. and Nicholl, J. (2008). The quality of mixed methods studies in health services research. *Journal of Health Services Research and Policy*, 13(2), pp. 92–98.
Zapata-Barrero, R. and Yalaz, E. (2018). *Qualitative Research in European Migration Studies*. New York: Springer.

6.   Valuing older workers? A case study of Australian universities' response to their ageing academic workforce

Jacqueline Larkin

INTRODUCTION

> Age is just an issue of mind over matter. If you don't mind, it doesn't matter.
> (Mark Twain)

An unprecedented ageing workforce is reshaping the future of work and triggering human resource management (HRM) challenges and opportunities. These include the recruitment, reward and retention of older workers, and dealing with the many differences among older workers such as individual characteristics (e.g., how important work is to a person), demographic characteristics (e.g., gender, educational level) and occupational/organisation/job characteristics (Connell et al., 2015). As people live and work longer, they continue to be productive and contribute to society, but to maintain economic growth, employers and governments must recognise and value the benefits that older workers bring to society, communities and workplaces (World Economic Forum, 2019).

Against this backdrop, it is essential to recognise that older workers are not a homogenous group. As such, understanding the diversity, equity and inclusion issues of older workers is highly complex, and needs to be informed by research and evidence to make a stronger business case for diversity, equity and inclusion. Ultimately, greater emphasis should be placed on understanding the knowledge, skills and experience of an older worker, and not their chronological age. This chapter will provide insights from research findings in academia.

There is no one generally accepted definition of an older worker. Authors tend to refer to disparate age categories for older workers, such as 40 plus, 45 plus, 50 plus and 55 plus (McCarthy et al., 2014). For the purposes of this chapter, older workers are those aged 50 years and over, and throughout this chapter, older academics refers to academics in the 50–59 years age bracket.

Although the definition of older academics is based on chronological age, this does not imply a particular life or career stage, as these can be quite separate entities (Larkin, 2016).

People aged in their 50s today are better educated and trained, are healthier and enjoy significantly improved living conditions than in previous generations. In Australia, people are living longer and continue to have one of the longest life expectancies in the world, with an average life expectancy of 80.9 years for men and 85.0 years for women (ABS, 2020). The remarkable improvements in life expectancy primarily due to improved health services, safer working environments and medical and technological advances provide opportunities for older workers to live more purposeful, productive and satisfying lives. Hence, it is reasonable for an individual aged 50 today to have potentially 20 years of working life ahead of them, followed by ten years in retirement.

Yet, despite the increase in longevity and longer working lives, HRM policies and practices on the whole tend to not be well aligned to this changing reality. Furthermore, an ageing workforce is largely ignored or misperceived, and often overlooked as a source of competitive advantage (Milligan et al., 2019). Increasingly, older workers experience diverse economic, social and personal challenges. For example, the Australian Human Resources Institute (2021) revealed that the majority (74 per cent of employers surveyed) were reluctant to employ people over 50. In addition, more than a quarter of Australians aged 50 years and over had experienced age discrimination in the workplace, experience greater difficulty finding subsequent employment when they do become unemployed and, of great concern, a third of those who had experienced age discrimination gave up looking for work (AHRC, 2016). 'It is unthinkable that people who lose their jobs in their 50s may live up to another forty years without paid employment' (AHRC, 2016, p. 6).

The academic workforce is among the oldest and arguably has the most highly qualified professionals within Australia. Over the past three decades, the percentage of academics aged over 50 has been steadily increasing and this age cohort currently represents 40 per cent of Australia's academic workforce (DEEWRS, 2020). While there is no compulsory retirement age in Australia, and national anti-discrimination legislation makes it unlawful for an employee to be dismissed on the grounds of age, the high proportion of academics aged over 50 years suggests that the next two decades for Australian universities presents a time of critical staffing vulnerability, with a key issue associated with knowledge and organisational sustainability.

This overview sets the scene for this chapter, which offers a case study of Australian universities' response to their ageing workforce, specifically academics aged in their 50s. Even though the location of this study is Australia, there is broad international relevance in light of the ubiquitous academic staffing crisis predictions within Organisation for Economic Co-operation and Development countries. The chapter begins by outlining the trend of Australia's ageing academic workforce, the complexities of academic careers and retirement in the Australian context. It then discusses the research method and key findings. The chapter ends with recommendations for HRM policies and practices for an ageing academic workforce, concluding that academics aged in their 50s are a vital and valuable source for Australian universities that should no longer be ignored.

AUSTRALIA'S AGEING ACADEMIC WORKFORCE

Universities have a fundamental role in driving Australia's productivity, research, innovation, global engagement and future economic prosperity (UoA, 2019). In fact, universities contribute significantly to Australia's economic growth. In 2019, international education ranked as Australia's third-largest export industry and generated $37.6 billion (UoA, 2019). Given this, the demographic reality of an ageing academic workforce is one of the critical factors in sustaining universities as well as Australia's economy.

The percentage of academics aged 50 and over of the total Australian academic workforce has been steadily increasing for the past three decades. In 1992, 27 per cent of the total academic workforce was aged 50 years and over, rising to 40 per cent in 2006 and further increasing to 42 per cent in 2015 (DEEWRS, 2015). Despite the pandemic in 2020, academics aged 50 and over represent 40 per cent of Australia's academic workforce (DEEWRS, 2020). Although researchers have long acknowledged the ageing academic demographic profile of universities, the responses by universities have been varied and limited. The absence of an integrated strategy to adequately engage with their older academics is potentially a lost opportunity for universities and for Australia. For this reason, the changing age demographic signals the need for a systematic investigation to provide insights into how universities, their leaders and their HRM policies and practices are responding to this unprecedented human resource challenge and opportunity (Larkin, 2016). The case study discussed in this chapter was designed to make a contribution to this gap in the literature.

COMPLEXITIES OF ACADEMIC CAREERS

An academic career is complex and diverse, ranging from various entry pathways to disciplinary differences. To include factors such as age, gender and career stage only highlights that making generalisations about academic careers can be problematic. Contributing to the complexities of an academic career are the political, economic, structural and technological changes in higher education and their impact on academic work and careers. In Australia, the higher education sector experienced immense structural changes, largely as a result of federal government policy and funding influences. The major structural change since 1990 was the formation of the Unified National System that replaced the binary system of universities and Colleges of Advanced Education. Following the formation of the Unified National System was the changing composition of the academic workforce. Traditionally, the academic demography was largely white, male and Protestant. However, in the last few decades, the academic workforce has become more diverse, due to the steady growth of women pursuing academic careers. For example, the total number of female academics in Australia more than doubled from 1985 to 1991 and as of 2020 females represent almost half of Australia's total academic workforce at 48 per cent (DEEWRS, 2020).

Undeniably, and even more so since the pandemic, the work environment remains competitive and uncertain. Consequently, academic careers have become less secure and this is an increasing trend, as universities strive for greater flexibility in resource allocation in a competitive environment (NTEU, 2018). With the increasing revenues generated by Australian universities, academic work has become more about perceived market value rather than an intellectual pursuit for its own sake. The security of employment that was provided by academic tenured appointments has been substantially replaced by a rapid expansion of continuing, short-term, part-time and casual academic positions. The trend towards academic employment contracts has more than doubled from 11 per cent in 1990 to 23 per cent in 2020 (DEEWRS, 2020), with 63 per cent of the academic workforce employed on a casual basis – in fact, one Australian university has an alarming 76.8 per cent of all employees who are casual or on contract (NTEU, 2018). Consequently, to meet this era of change, universities require HRM policies and practices that are responsive, flexible and agile.

RETIREMENT IN THE AUSTRALIAN CONTEXT

With an unprecedented ageing population, the context within which individuals retire has significantly changed and continues to do so. Thus, the concept of retirement is no longer a permanent exit from full-time work into full-time leisure but can be a gradual, phased or partial process that involves a mixture of paid work and leisure activities (Sullivan and Ariss, 2019). The factors that influence the decision to retire can be categorised in several ways. One approach is referred to as 'push' and 'pull' factors (Shultz and Olson, 2013). 'Push' factors are typically regarded as negative, since poor health and job dissatisfaction from work politics can induce older workers to retire. 'Pull' factors, such as the pursuit of leisure and travel activities that can attract older workers to retire, are typically positive. It is worth noting that the range of factors impacting the retirement decision is further differentiated by gender, as women tend to reach career stages at different ages to men, since their career choices and workforce participation are often moderated by family responsibilities and, consequently, they may delay retirement for financial reasons (Shacklock et al., 2009).

The number of Australians aged 65 and over is expected to more than double by the year 2055, with 1 in 1,000 people to be aged over 100 (Commonwealth of Australia, 2015). With life expectancy continuing to increase, getting closer to the age of 100, and if we continue to retire around the same age as we do currently at 55 years of age, this will mean spending almost half of our lives in retirement. The over-50s population is projected to grow by 3.5 million to 11 million people in the next 20 years, and currently this cohort accounts for nearly 78 per cent of Australia's total net household wealth and 60 per cent of the $1.7 trillion invested in superannuation today (Nance, 2014). Aptly referred to as the 'silver economy', people aged over 50 are one of the richest and fastest growing segments of the population, and will be the major force in wealth, spending and population growth over the next decade (Nance, 2014). Yet, current policies around retirement tend to distort people's choices and attitudes about participating in the labour market and in the main encourage the premature exit of people from the workforce that creates a ripple effect from the individual to the economy. In light of this, there is a critical need for HRM policies and practices to motivate and retain older workers to continue working, and thus, contribute to organisational and economic sustainability.

THE RESEARCH PROCESS/METHODS/ FRAMEWORK

This case study explores the university management perceptions and retirement intentions of older academics. It reports findings from a larger Australian study on career management for older academics (Larkin, 2016). The research is a qualitative two-phase study that purposely incorporated different university types and different academic discipline groups to capture the diversity of Australian universities. Four formal and self-selected university groupings were included: Group of Eight (Go8); Australian Technology Network; Innovative Research Universities (IRU); and Regional Universities Network. Four academic discipline groups were included: Hard-Pure represents the knowledge domain for pure sciences such as physics and biology; Hard-Applied represents the knowledge domain for applied science-based professions such as engineering and agriculture; Soft-Pure represents the knowledge domain for humanities and pure social sciences such as history, philosophy, sociology and psychology; and Soft-Applied represents the knowledge domain for applied social science professions such as management, business, law and education (Becher and Trowler, 2001).

Phase 1 involved the analysis of publicly available institutional HRM policy documents from 16 Australian universities and Australian Universities Quality Agency audit reports for the period 2006–2009 for 21 Australian universities. The findings of Phase 1 informed Phase 2, which involved semi-structured interviews with 52 participants, drawn from three different universities and from the four distinct academic discipline groups. The sample of 52 participants included academics aged in their 50s, academics holding university management positions (senior management such as deputy vice-chancellors and middle-level management such as deans of faculties, heads of schools and heads of departments and administrative staff in senior university human resource positions).

The sample of 52 participants was chosen using purposive sampling and involved the use of publicly available information on selected university websites, and these were combined with the snowball sampling technique on a needs basis (Cooper and Schindler, 2011). Participants were approached via email with an open invitation to participate in the study.

All interviews were conducted at the academic's place of work at a mutually convenient time and date. The interviews followed the same format for each participant, allowing responses to semi-structured questions as well as providing the opportunity to elaborate on their responses and offer further comments. The length of the interviews ranged from 30 minutes to two hours, with an average time for each interview of approximately one hour. All interviews were digitally audio-recorded and then transcribed. All participants and universities were de-identified to preserve anonymity. NVivo software provided a data management tool to facilitate in-depth exploration of the data and was particularly useful in managing the classification of emerging themes. Within the discussion of findings, quotations from interview participants give their academic position, gender, university grouping and number of years in academia. No further identification is provided in the context of preserving individual confidentiality and anonymity.

SELECTED FINDINGS FROM INTERVIEWS WITH UNIVERSITY MANAGEMENT

The document analysis and interviews with university management suggest that older academics are generally 'not on the radar' and 'not a priority at the moment'. Consequently, this age cohort is largely ignored in their workforce planning processes. Below are selected findings from the semi-structured interviews with university management.

The most critical asset for universities, as knowledge-intensive organisations, is the intellectual capital of their academic workforce. However, university management showed little recognition of an ageing academic workforce, nor concern for actively managing the potential loss of institutional knowledge and skills. These senior management perceptions reinforce the document analysis that revealed that universities were inactive in workforce capability planning, with an absence of HRM policies in relation to succession planning, and they generally failed to clearly define the organisation's strategy for its ageing academic workforce. Without a deliberate shift in attitude by senior management to address policy and strategy development to retain the advanced levels of specialised knowledge and experience of older academics, the competitive advantage of older academics is unlikely to be exploited, as evidenced in the following comment: 'I don't think disgruntled, burnt-out academics in their fifties are a priority at all. They're a lost cause' (Dean, male, Go8, 22 years in academia).

One reason to explain the lack of interest and concern for older academics was the opinion that there would be little or no benefit to the university from developing or investing in their careers, as echoed in the following comment: 'It's not the old and grey 50 year olds. It's the 25–35 that need the most help. They need to be given the most assistance and encouragement' (Dean, male, IRU, 24 years in academia).

Overall, the interviews with university management revealed that older academics are not perceived as a valuable resource and, as a result, universities are failing to capitalise on the advanced levels of specialised knowledge and experience of older academics who could potentially create distinctive capabilities that set one university apart from another.

SELECTED FINDINGS FROM INTERVIEWS WITH ACADEMICS

Retirement featured strongly among academic participants when discussing their future career plans. In fact, close to two thirds of academic participants have no intention of retiring. The one third of academic participants who plan to retire or were strongly considering retirement within the next ten years mentioned a range of 'push' and 'pull' factors influencing their retirement decisions. The issues concerning their retirement plans were grouped under five themes, with most academic participants being associated with several of these thematic groups: 'Fifty and Flourishing', 'Fifty and Financially Focussed', 'Fifty and Fit', 'Fifty and Frustrated' and 'Fifty and Flexible'. The following are selected findings for each thematic group.

Thematic Group 1: Fifty and Flourishing

The thematic group labelled 'Fifty and Flourishing' represented the majority of participants, who had no plans to retire because, predominantly, they were highly motivated, strongly committed and passionate about their academic pursuits. Based on the interviews, the intrinsic rewards of an academic career and the core academic tasks of teaching and research were found to be enduring sources of academic career satisfaction and, as a result, they were influential in the decision to delay retirement. A sample comment was: 'The university might have to take me out kicking and screaming. I've always loved writing, academic writing, journalistic writing, whatever. So I would want to continue that for as long as possible' (Senior lecturer, male, IRU, 17 years in academia).

Academic participants' comments about their enthusiasm and passion for academic pursuits, as reasons to delay retirement, suggest there was a distinct sense of engagement, a strong determination and energy amongst older academics who wish to continue with academic pursuits. However, it was interesting that there was a lack of attention by university management to effectively manage older academics, based in part on the perception that older academics are not a valuable resource.

Thematic Group 2: Fifty and Financially Focussed

The thematic group labelled 'Fifty and Financially Focussed' represented those academic participants who have no plans to retire, mainly because they want to build up their superannuation in order to comfortably support themselves in retirement. One key explanation was the lack of accumulated superannuation for this group: entering academia via the sessional pathway. The sessional pathway to academia typically involves being initially employed as a tutor either on a sessional, casual or part-time basis. More female than male participants had entered academia via the sessional pathway and as such were not planning to retire within the next ten years, as echoed in the following comment:

> I wouldn't see myself retiring before the age of 65 and possibly later. I'm nowhere near retiring. I was a casual for 20 years, came into permanent work in academia late. I have a mortgage. In terms of superannuation and in terms of projecting my future, I'm nowhere near as well placed as many of my colleagues who didn't ever leave school and have a very tidy superannuation packet and three houses and are happy to go off and retire at 60. There's just no way I can do that. (Associate professor, female, IRU, 16 years in academia)

Whilst academic pursuits for these individuals may be highly valued, it was their personal financial circumstances that were the key driver to delaying retirement compared with the 'Fifty and Flourishing' group. This finding reinforces that the nature of managing the retirement process is not one-dimensional nor is it a straightforward process.

Thematic Group 3: Fifty and Fit

Health is a common factor influencing an individual's decision to retire and is deemed a 'push' factor in the retirement decision process. The thematic group labelled 'Fifty and Fit' were academic participants who thought that their intention to retire depended upon whether they remained fit and healthy. As the ageing rate is different among people of the same age, universities and their HRM policy-makers will need to abolish their stereotypical and narrow views of age.

Thematic Group 4: Fifty and Frustrated

Academic participants who noted the unsatisfactory state of their working environment as a factor that would induce retirement were categorised into the thematic group labelled 'Fifty and Frustrated'. In this context, the notion of frustration refers to the feeling of being annoyed or irritated as a result of having limited control over changes that impact their work. University management's lack of concern and interest in the career needs of older academics was evident in the interviews. Hence, there is some validity in academic participants' perceptions that the university does little to encourage older academics to continue working as they do not care about them or value their contributions.

Thematic Group 5: Fifty and Flexible

The thematic group labelled 'Fifty and Flexible' reflected those academic participants who expressed a range of 'pull' factors that would positively influence their decision to retire. These 'pull' factors encompassed flexible options such as the financial incentive of having sufficient superannuation, the appeal of more leisure and travel activities and the desire for variable transition to retirement arrangements.

For those whose academic career spanned 25 years or more, their significant accumulated superannuation was a key reason to retire. These academic participants explained that, as they were in the superannuation defined benefit scheme that was financially lucrative, they had the flexibility to choose when they would retire. Under this scheme, a set monthly pension amount is based on a mathematical formula that utilises a combination of employment factors such as employee's average salary leading up to retirement, length of employment and age. Therefore, the higher accrued benefits are a result of the greater number of years of employment. The superannuation defined benefit scheme is considered to be a 'pull' factor in the decision to retire.

Another 'pull' factor in the decision to retire was the university policy of a pre-retirement contract. A pre-retirement contract is typically a fixed-term contract of employment between the university and an employee who has indicated a willingness to commit to a retirement date. The length of the pre-retirement contract will be determined within the context of the individual and university's circumstances and is typically a period between 6 and 24 months. Several academic participants had been offered a pre-retirement contract by their university and, given the extra financial incentive to retire, decided to accept the offer. In addition, the flexible transition-to-retirement arrangements was another 'pull factor' as noted in the following comment: 'I'd like to look at fading out rather than jumping out and gradually cut down those working hours. To stay in the research area and ... gradually just cut down until I stop' (Associate professor, female, Go8, 34 years in academia).

Overall, the interviews with older academics about their retirement plans suggest that the 'one-size-fits-all' approach to retirement decision making is out of date and supports the argument that the decision to retire is multi-faceted and complex. Furthermore, these findings reinforce the view that it is important not to classify an individual into a particular career stage based on age, as careers can unfold in different ways and are not strictly determined by age.

CONCLUSION: KEY RECOMMENDATIONS FOR RESEARCHERS AND FUTURE RESEARCH DIRECTIONS

The essence of universities is to be progressive and knowledge-intensive institutions. Universities would be well positioned to manage the organisational risks, opportunities and sustainability issues associated with an ageing academic workforce. However, the research findings show that universities' HRM approaches to an ageing academic workforce lack an organisational strategic focus. It was evident that the universities' actions to date to cater for the needs of their older academics are deficient. The interviews with university management revealed that they did not perceive older academics to be a valuable resource, and lacked the focus needed to recognise the value and contribution of older academics. Moreover, some negative perceptions about older academics suggesting ageist and discriminatory attitudes and the perceived lack of interest in developing the careers of older academics because there would be little or no return for the university, have tended to undermine the importance and wealth of knowledge and experience of older academics.

The findings also suggested that universities and their HRM policy-makers have little understanding of what motivates older academics as they approach retirement, and that current policies and programs do not adequately support the diversity of retirement plans of older academics. Thus, a better understanding of the full range of factors that either 'push' or 'pull' older academics to retirement is needed, including the diverse retirement plans of older academics, as this would provide some insights for HRM policy-makers to tap into the motivations of this age cohort. This would need universities and their HRM policy-makers to work collaboratively with older academics in order to recognise the diverse career needs and expectations of this age cohort.

The findings with the literature highlight that it is long overdue for universities to move past this reactive approach to their ageing academic workforce to one which pays greater attention to longer-term interests that have mutual benefits for universities and their older academics. Doing so would involve a planned and integrated approach that focuses on the issues associated with an ageing academic workforce that will enhance and continue to foster motivation of their older academics, and this is critical for business and market success. What is also needed is for university management and their HRM policy-makers to establish an active partnership to review and reorient current HRM policies and practices that focus and respond to the different career needs and expectations of older academics and are conducive to retaining the talent of their older academic workforce. For example, HRM policies and practices that accommodate older academics by offering flexible work options that enable work/life balance and provide alternative career options in line with changing life needs and career aspirations.

To conclude, this research has revealed that universities should be more proactive in their HRM approaches to the ageing of their academic workforce, which includes maximising the effectiveness of their older academic workforce by reviewing and reorienting their HRM policies and practices to meet the new demographic realities. The demographic reality of an ageing academic workforce demands a transformation in attitudes to older academics, particularly in terms of recognising their valuable contribution to universities. Universities that respond to the issues associated with their ageing academic workforce will sustain a competitive advantage by capitalising on the accumulated knowledge, experience and wisdom of their older academic workforce (Larkin, 2016). Clearly, this research has highlighted that there is a need for universities to acknowledge and understand that the productivity of an older academic should not be simply viewed as a declining function of age, but to acquire a conviction that older academics do matter. As reflected in the words of one participant in this study: 'Age shouldn't matter, but experience should' (Professor, male, Go8, 19 years in academia).

While this research is restricted to Australian universities, future research could involve the following:

- Universities from different countries, to make comparisons and to determine whether the findings represent the broader international academic community.
- Research in broader contexts in other types of knowledge-intensive occupations that are experiencing an ageing workforce such as specialist medical professions.
- Given the unprecedented ageing global workforce, future research will be fruitful to fully understand the broader challenges and opportunities of an ageing workforce as it is one of the fundamental diversity, equity and inclusive issues influencing organisational policy and practice. Organisations that adopt a proactive approach to fully leverage the knowledge and experience of their older workforce will undoubtedly recognise the competitive advantage of its ageing workforce.

REFERENCES

ABS (Australian Bureau of Statistics) (2020). Life tables. www.abs.gov.au/statistics/people/population/life-tables/latest-release

AHRC (Australian Human Rights Commission) (2016). Willing to work: National inquiry into employment discrimination against older Australians and Australians with disability. https://humanrights.gov.au/sites/default/files/document/publication/WTW_2016_Full_Report_AHRC_ac.pdf

Becher, T., and Trowler, P. R. (2001). Academic tribes and territories: Intellectual enquiry and the cultures of discipline (2nd ed.). Buckingham: Society for Research into Higher Education.

Commonwealth of Australia (2015). 2015 intergenerational report Australia in 2055. www.treasury.gov.au/~/media/Treasury/Publications%20and%20Media/Publications/2015/2015%20Intergenerational%20Report/Downloads/PDF/2015_IGR.ashx

Connell, J., Nankervis, A., and Burgess, J. (2015). The challenges of an ageing workforce: An introduction to the workforce management issues. *Labour and Industry*, 25(4), 257–264.

Cooper, D. R., and Schindler, P. S. (2011). Business research methods (11th ed.). New York: McGraw-Hill/Irwin.

DEEWRS (2015). Department of Education employment and workplace relations: Selected higher education statistics – 2015 staff data. https://education.gov.au/selected-higher-education-statistics-2015-staff-data

DEEWRS (2020). Department of Education employment and workplace relations: Selected higher education statistics – 2020 staff data. www.dese.gov.au/higher-education-statistics/staff-data/selected-higher-education-statistics-2020-staff-data

Larkin, J. (2016). 'Fading @50?' A study of career management for older academics in Australia. Unpublished doctoral dissertation, Macquarie University.

McCarthy, J., Heraty, N., Cross, C., and Cleveland, J. N. (2014). Who is considered an 'older worker'? Extending our conceptualisation of 'older' from an organisational decision maker perspective. *Human Resource Management Journal*, 24(4), 374–393.

Milligan, P., Guzzo, R., Nalbantian, H., Sonsino, Y., and Sung, P. (2019). Are you age-ready? www.mercer.com/our-thinking/next-stage-are-you-age-ready.html

Nance, K. (2014). The silver economy: How the over 50s will reshape financial services. *Journal of Superannuation Management*, 6(1), 30–34.

NTEU (National Tertiary Education Union) (2018). The prevalence of insecure employment at Australia's universities: An examination of Workplace Gender Equality Agency (WGEA) university staffing profiles. www.nteu.org.au/article/The-Prevalence-of -Insecure-Employment-at-Australia%E2%80%99s-Universities%3A-An-Examination- of-Workplace-Gender-Equality-Agency-%28WGEA%29-University-Staffing-Profiles -20526

Shacklock, K., Brunetto, Y., and Nelson, S. (2009). The different variables that affect older males and females' intentions to continue working. *Asia Pacific Journal of Human Resources*, 47(1), 79–101.

Shultz, K. S., and Olson, D. A. (2013). The changing nature of work and retirement. In M. Wang (Ed.), *The Oxford Handbook of Retirement* (pp. 543–558). Oxford: Oxford University Press.

Sullivan, S. E., and Ariss, A. A. (2019). Employment after retirement: A review and framework for future research. *Journal of Management*, 45(1), 262–284.

UoA (Universities of Australia) (2019). Australia has one of the best higher education systems in the world. Data Snapshot. www.universitiesaustralia.edu.au/wp-content/ uploads/2019/06/Data-snapshot-2019-FINAL.pdf

World Economic Forum (2019). Aging workforce isn't a burden – it's an opportunity. www.weforum.org/agenda/2019/01/an-aging-workforce-isnt-a-burden-its-an -opportunity/

USEFUL WEB RESOURCES

Australian Government (2021). Tapping into Australia's ageing workforce: Insights from recent research. June. https://cepar.edu.au/resources-videos/research-briefs/ australia-ageing-workforce-research-insights

Council on the Ageing (2021). State of the (older) nation 2021. June. www.cota.org.au/ wp-content/uploads/2021/06/SOTON21-Full-Report.pdf

Deloitte (2013). The aging workforce: Finding the silver lining in the talent gap. www2 .deloitte.com/ge/en/pages/human-capital/articles/aging-workforce.html

Future of Work Hub (2020). Changing demographics and ageing workforces. January. www.futureofworkhub.info/comment/2020/1/30/changing-demographics-and-ageing -workforces

OECD (n.d.). Ageing and employment policies. www.oecd.org/employment/ageinga ndemploymentpolicies.htm

OECD (n.d.). Work-force ageing in OECD countries. www.oecd.org/els/emp/2080254 .pdf

7. Creating an individualised foundation for genuine community inclusion: evidence from Western Australian microboards

Elizabeth Farrant

INTRODUCTION

The social model of disability moves the concept of being "disabled" from a medical perspective of biological norms and abnormalities to disability as a consequence of the inadequacies of the attitudes, structures and environments that surround people with a disability and exclude them from fulfilling their personhood (Dirth and Branscombe, 2017; Jackson, 2018). To address these inequities, structures such as microboards have been developed to ensure people with disability engage with community members without disability and express what they need to have the life experiences they want. A microboard is created when a small group of people, generally four to six, incorporate a not-for-profit association that supports a single individual in ways that focus on that person's needs and quality of life. Members uphold and support the development of the person's human rights, citizenship and personhood to their full potential, with a focus on communication, social inclusion and community participation. There are more than 1,100 microboards in the province of British Columbia alone (Vela, 2021), however, empirical research is rare and much of the information on what makes a successful microboard is localised to the members involved. Microboards were created in Canada in 1984 as an individualised funding pathway for people who didn't "fit" with existing service offerings (Wetherow and Wetherow, 2004). Australian microboards have only recently begun exploring funding management but have been empowering and supporting focus people and families since 2008 (Microboards Australia, 2016). Microboards were founded on the assumption that the focus person had the capacity, as well as the right, to make decisions and be change-makers in their own life (Malette, 2002; Pedlar et al., 1999; Stainton, 2016). It has been speculated that microboards use a combination of "personal and functional relationships" (Stainton, 2016, p. 8) to maintain sustained and effective engagement. The lack of literature, increasing focus on community participation within the National Disability Insurance Scheme (NDIS) (National Disability Insurance Agency, 2020) and increased use of microboards internationally validates this research and reinforces the need for additional study.

KEY LITERATURE

Much of the microboard literature was not recent, geographically relevant to Australia or peer reviewed, with many available sources lacking depth and containing short mentions of microboards without further discussion. Much of the information on microboards remains unrecorded, existing as intellectual property held in the heads of members or staff in microboard associations. To provide a thorough, consistent and useful analysis of available literature and Western Australian (WA) microboards, the Community Capitals Framework (CCF) was utilised. The CCF was chosen to review the WA microboard community as the identification of seven capitals results in a holistic view of social well-being (Flora and Flora, 2013), in contrast to more typical approaches that use economic factors (Magis, 2010). To this end, literature was reviewed and separated into built, financial, political, human, cultural, natural and social capitals (Flora and Flora, 2013; Himes-Cornell et al., 2018).

Financial capital in the microboard context refers to managing funding. Microboards were initially created as a way to receive individual funding for everyday needs and housing that was not tied to a service provider (Wetherow and Wetherow, 2004). Microboard users were then able to change their support without having to move house, or indeed move house without losing their support (Wetherow and Wetherow, 2004). Microboards and their individualised funding resisted the "commodification of disability" that Pedlar and Hutchison (2000, p. 637) found in other Canadian service providers and increased control and independence for the focus person (Malette, 2002; Pedlar and Hutchison, 2000). Microboards were also less affected by other factors challenging providers, such as competition amongst providers, inadequate resourcing and uncertainty (Pedlar and Hutchison, 2000). Standard assessments such as annual reviews occurred to ensure the appropriate use of funds (Pedlar and Hutchison, 2000), which found microboards to be a positive vehicle for individualised funding in Canada (Pedlar and Hutchison, 2000; Stainton, 2016).

Social capital was very strongly represented in microboard literature. The personal connections between microboard members and the focus person were evident and formed the basis of the strength, quality and sustainability of microboards. Relationships were described as two-way and reciprocal, with benefits for both the focus person and the microboard members (Jay and

Schaper, 2012; Malette, 2002; Pedlar and Hutchison, 2000). Relationships were "voluntary, mutual, and rooted in love, reciprocity, and respect" (Malette, 2002, p. 170). Stainton et al. (2020) described microboards as a "vehicle" (p. 8) on which characteristics such as autonomy, person-centredness, empowerment and interconnectedness can travel to destinations such as social capital and quality of life for people with disability.

Cultural capital was evident in the strong internal culture created by the closeness of relationships and personalised approaches and is defined as the beliefs and values that impact on culture and governance (Flora and Flora, 2013). Member demographics and progressive support approaches were shared elements of cultural capital across the microboard literature. Microboards made up of family as well as friends expanded opportunities for the focus person, because the mix brought different experiences, fresh ideas and new perspectives (Malette, 2002; Pedlar et al., 1999; Women's Research Centre, 1994). Having some members of a similar age to the focus person also helped the microboard to consider age-appropriate goals and activities (Jay and Schaper, 2012; Women's Research Centre, 1994).

Person-centred approaches and supported decision-making were utilised to uphold and enact the person's rights and choices. Person-centred practices focus on the individual whose life is being considered and ensure they are directing their life and not the services and systems around them (Malette, 2002). Supported decision-making occurs when decisions are made by and alongside the individual, rather than for them, maintaining their legal standing while not requiring the individual to make decisions on their own (Browning et al., 2014). Supporters may break down decisions, present information in accessible ways, help to identify options, identify the best times to discuss options, interpret non-verbal communication and infer the person's preferences through observing their reactions (Browning et al., 2021). Stainton (2016) found that both individualised funding and decision-making opportunities increased independence, and each enhanced decision-making capacity. Decision-making for small daily choices along with larger decisions increased quality of life and more faithfully reflected autonomy (Stainton, 2016). Microboards spent time learning the focus person's best communication avenues (speech, signs, pictures, communication devices, etc.) and adopted different decision-making techniques to build decision-making capability (Malette, 2002; Women's Research Centre, 1994). These approaches enabled the focus people to direct their life choices, rather than being told what their life would be.

Access to power, advocacy and ability to create a strong organisational voice form political capital (Flora and Flora, 2013). Canadian microboard association Vela facilitated this access by providing support, teaching advocacy and assisting over 1,100 microboards to discover their own voice (Vela, 2021). Microboard associations helped with initial set-up, education, training, community and capacity building for members and assistance with legal and budget processes. Through its support, Vela helped microboards to imagine life for the focus person outside traditional, and often limiting, support services (Women's Research Centre, 1994).

RESEARCH METHODS

The scarcity of microboard research lent itself to a phenomenological methodology (Liamputtong et al., 2016). At the time of research there were five microboards and focus people in WA with 41 members collectively. Ten microboard members took part in interviews along with five disability-sector professionals who were working or had worked with microboards, for a total of 15 participants. Convenience and snowball sampling were used to identify participants (Liamputtong et al., 2016). Participant information statements were sent to microboard members already known to the author and they shared them with other members and suggested sector professionals to approach. The individualised nature of microboards meant it was essential to gather experiences from members of each of the microboards, with two members from each taking part. Sector professionals were included to provide an external perspective of microboards. The data between the two groups were compared, resulting in a more rigorous set of findings.

The CCF was used to systematically identify and evaluate which capitals were present or absent in WA microboards and how these impacted and interacted with each other (Flora and Flora, 2013; Himes-Cornell et al., 2018). All seven capitals were used to create the interview guide to safeguard against gaps in data collection. Interview guides between the two groups differed slightly, but the core of each question remained. Semi-structured interviews were used to support the exploratory nature of the research and allow expansion or reduction of answers for each participant, while the interview guide maintained consistency and allowed for comparison across interviews.

Participants were supplied with an information statement and ethics approval. All interviewees signed a consent form. Due to the connected and close nature of the WA microboard community, anonymity of data was crucial and complex. Every effort was made to de-identify data, but in some cases, stories were widely known and the subject of the story and/or the teller would be recognisable to other members of this small network. In these cases, those involved were asked for permission to include the story in the final research. Once written, these sections were member checked by those who told the story or were its subject, both for accuracy and to gain final permission for inclusion (Carlson, 2010).

Data were analysed thematically (Liamputtong et al., 2016) in three stages: unrestricted coding of transcribed interviews after each interview;

second-cycle coding to condense common responses and refine/restructure codes; and finally categorising codes under their community capitals. The first cycle aimed to fulfil the first research objective of discovering whether there were commonalities between WA microboards and was done after each interview. Second-cycle coding was completed after all interviews occurred to aid the author in gaining a whole view of the data and make links between interviews. Data were distilled into a responses chart for each interview to aid in identifying the common factors. During distillation, recurring and similar codes were either amalgamated or further delineated. A smaller number of codes across each data set identified key factors.

KEY FINDINGS

> So, a microboard is like a family?
> Well, sort of like that but different. So, like a really good service organiser?
> Sort of like that but different. So, like a group of friends then?
> Well, sort of like that but really different. Like a social club?
> Well, sort of like that but different ...

This quote from a sector professional illustrates some of the complexity in understanding and being part of a microboard. As the findings illustrate, microboards are not a business, or just friends getting together. They are intentional support structures that depend on a number of factors for success. As the first research of its kind into microboards in Australia, the findings begin the exploration into microboards.

Social Capital

Described by a member as the "social glue" that makes things happen, social capital was identified by all participants as a core factor for WA microboards. The relationships between the focus person and the members varied in type and strength. They are influenced by background and demographics of each board's members. Described as a support structure built on love, social capital is a central key to success. Most members identified their relationship with the focus person as the reason they joined and/or sustain the motivation to remain on the microboard through thick and thin. Participants described their relationship with the focus person as reciprocal, feeling they benefitted from being a member just as the focus person benefitted by having them as a member. The benefits varied, their friendships being one common benefit. Witnessing positive change was a strong motivator. A member who joined with little prior relationship with the focus person found their life "expanding enormously as a result" of the relationship with the focus person, other members and even the "cool young people" who were support staff for the focus person.

The microboard represented the first circle of broader community around the focus person. Members then supported the focus person to connect with their own community, and "so the circle widens". These broader connections with the community were highlighted by participants commonly as another benefit. The term "volunteer" was not used or agreed with by participants, described as unsuitable as it carried non-reciprocal tones. Participants explained it as more of a group of people creating a cultural milieu, and then inviting other people to become part of that culture. The reciprocal nature of relationships between the focus person and their members, and between the members themselves, was a strong common thread through each interview. Participants spoke of the importance of actively strengthening the relationships between the focus person and members. "The ones that work really well do a heap of stuff around forming that bond and that community with all of the people involved in it. There's lots of stuff, food and drinks and social stuff and then they get stuff done, which means that there's a sense of progress and success breeds success." One microboard had all the members write down one thing they each wanted to achieve, and together they made it happen for each person. This resulted in all microboard members and the focus person travelling interstate as one member had not previously travelled in an aeroplane. In microboards that work on their relationships, it was described as "like a family. It's hard to describe, but it's a family feeling."

Part of the strength of these relationships was the assumption that changes would happen and flexibility on all sides was a necessity, with the members being "glued together, but we're not stuck". Another participant used astronomy to describe relationships as being in orbit, where the relationships can drift and change but are ultimately orbiting around a central point, the focus person. Some relationships are close and have daily impact, others have a longer orbit but one that nevertheless returns. The flexibility allowed for change, while celebrating the member's contribution whatever it may be, on the premise that it will probably come back around at some point. This flexibility is true for the focus person too. As they grow and change members may or may not be suitable for the microboard; "for [name] there was a time when [they] had less work and less social peers … at the time I was physically more present … it was just a time when our relationship was perhaps stronger as friends". Change is planned for and expected, with members settling into slightly different roles as needed. Commitment is required of members, which may appear contradictory to the amount of flexibility also needed, but the balance doesn't appear overwhelming. A participant commented that it's "a balance, isn't it, between continuity and renewal". An equilibrium must be reached between the responsibilities of being a member and the inevitable fluctuations of life.

Cultural Capital

The traditions and language of a group determines whose "voice" is heard and listened to (Emery and Flora 2006, p. 21). In ensuring the focus person holds the clearest and central "voice", microboards challenge historical norms of the treatment of people with disability. Member demographics play a role in the cultivation of this "voice" along with person-centred approaches to communication and decision-making.

Member Diversity

Diversity among members helped motivate the microboards to think differently, advocate from different perspectives and take advantage of the resulting range of opportunities and ideas. Having friends and family was a good mix. Family provided long-term knowledge of the focus person, what's been tried and what typically does or doesn't suit them. Friends provide fresh eyes, ask basic questions, return to past ideas and suggest completely new ones. An essential part of a microboard was the time spent getting to know the focus person; a depth of knowledge was crucial so family were no longer the primary decision-makers or supporters, communicators or care-givers, widening the circle of people who had a relationship with the focus person and could be a support to them. A participant put it plainly: "if a parent was the driving force behind the microboard after its creation, then it's really not functioning the way I would expect a microboard to be ultimately". Broadening the number of supporters also meant family could move from an emergency state of mind to feeling more comfortable and open to trying new things. This meant "it's not all on their shoulders and [they became] a bit more open to try different things".

A variety of ages of members gave a "unique perspective to the dialogue and the work of the microboard". Intergenerational input was "really, really important", incorporating diverse professional and personal experiences. Having at least one member of a similar age to the focus person provided an inbuilt assessor of the age appropriateness of activities and opportunities and reduced any tendencies to infantilise the focus person. In the same vein, members of the same gender provided useful information to the focus person on what they could expect from life at different stages and provided examples of choices and experiences that different genders might take up.

Approaches to Support

The core belief/assumption every microboard was built on was the focus person having capacity and the right to make decisions and lead their own life.

"Without the belief that with support we can all make decisions, why would you bother?" Examples of WA microboard rules are contained in the Guiding Principles of Microboards Australia (MA), including "all people are assumed to have the capacity for self-determination. The capacity will be acknowledged, respected, and demonstrated in all dealings of the microboard." This tenet was fulfilled through person-centred approaches, a focus on communication and supported decision-making.

Person-Centredness and Communication

Person-centredness in WA microboards meant not making assumptions, asking the focus person even if members thought they knew what the focus person wanted and checking regularly. The reasons for dedication to this approach became clear when the stakes were known. Three microboards felt if the focus person didn't have a support group like a microboard, they could quite easily end up living in an institutional setting, with very limited choices or person-centred practices.

Three of the WA focus people were supported in communication by devices such as iPads; one communicated verbally; and another predominantly used vocal sounds and was exploring other options. All required support to make decisions and were supported by the microboard to make as many decisions as possible. Decisions included choice of staff members, where they lived, worked and their daily activities, among many other decisions. Members often supported the focus person to learn new ways of communicating such as augmented and alternative communication like a Pragmatic Organisation Dynamic Display booklet or an app such as Proloquo2Go (Assistive Ware, 2021). A sector professional framed it in this manner:

> It's just a fundamentally human thing, isn't it, that if you can't make yourself heard, however you do that, then that in itself is an incredibly isolating and disempowering thing. It's significantly more powerful to transition from that to "here are some people who at least attempt to understand me and to speak on my behalf", and it's immeasurably more powerful again to have the group of people gather around you and support you to actually speak on your own behalf.

Members were encouraged to look for communication and see everything the focus person does as a form of communication. After a workshop, a member realised "I've never looked at [their] vocalisations as language. I've never framed it that way. It just shifted everything, that [name] had been working overtime in the best way [they] knew how to try and let us know what [they] needed and what [they] wanted, and [name] had so many different sounds."

Once strong methods of communication were identified, the repercussions could be profound. A professional participant noted that if one of the focus people were treated traditionally by the judicial system, they would be found "unfit to plead, but given the right communication support [name] is well able to communicate what [name] needs, to the point where [name] gives presentations to groups of people at conferences about how [their] life is. So, is that incapable? No, it isn't."

Supported Decision-Making

Substituted decision-making has historically been a common element in support for a person living with disability, meaning the "voice" being heard was not of the person living with disability. The focus on communication and assumption that the focus person had capacity set the foundation for supported decision-making instead. This was especially the case where the focus person would have typically had decisions made for them, often disregarding their own values and goals, and leading to an overall disempowerment of the individual (Pedlar et al., 1999).

One story, shared by eight participants, illustrated how microboards challenged traditional decision-making. To choose the name of their microboard, members worked with support workers and friends over a number of weeks to discuss name options and gather preferences from the focus person and members. The focus person had complex communication needs, meaning typical consent methods, verbal or written, were not appropriate. A video recording of the focus person choosing and pointing to a card with "yes" written on it was submitted, and accepted, as consent for the microboard name.

The United Nations Convention on the Rights of Persons with Disability Article 12 specifies the need to shift from substitute decision-making structures and standards in favour of embedding supported decision-making into legal and everyday processes (Committee on the Rights of Persons with Disability, 2019; Mirfin-Veitch and Richardson, 2017). WA microboards exemplified this shift, with the "voice" being heard, listened to and acted upon being that of the focus person of the microboard, and supported decision-making being further upheld by the internal culture, core approaches and member diversity.

Political Capital

Political capital refers to access to power, powerbrokers and the ability of a community to turn their "norms and values" into standards (Flora and Flora 2013, p. 22). Each WA microboard had a strong connection to the supporting organisation MA, seeking specific support and broader connection as a community. MA provided practical support with start-up steps, including incorporation, as well as ongoing information on regulatory changes and international trends, through a strong connection to Vela Microboards in Canada. Programs offered included an introductory experience into microboards, staff selection and supporting friendships (Microboards Australia, 2016).

MA played a crucial role in the development of all five of the microboards, providing "a massive amount of support to us originally. Honestly, we were handheld for a long time." A professional participant felt that MA created a community of practice for microboards, and was an important safeguard in the establishment, maintenance and development of individual microboards. Participants who joined the microboard after it was established had a less clear idea of the role of MA but knew they could contact them for support whenever needed. MA and the microboard community were "sustenance" for some participants; with MA there was a "sense of what's possible. There's a total acknowledgement of difficulty, but there is also an absolute sense things don't have to remain the way they are and a real willingness to support people to bring about change."

Human Capital

As incorporated entities, WA microboards fell under the requirements of the Associations Incorporation Act 2015. Not all participants were clear about the legal requirements of incorporation, but they were aware that being an incorporated body impacted on the commitment, momentum and sustainability of their microboard. Canadian microboards were initially incorporated in order to self-manage the focus person's funding (Wetherow and Wetherow, 2004). In lieu of this responsibility, WA microboards used the structure and requirements of incorporation to "formalise intent" and create an "intentional community" around the focus person. "The fact that there's a formal structure, a legal structure … clarifies that this is an intentional community of people and that there's clarity around why you're actually doing what you're doing." Incorporation brought a ready-made structure to microboards, requiring members to be registered, rules of association to be created, certain roles to be filled and meeting minutes and financial records to be kept. Without these structures things could get "wishy-washy, dissolved, diluted". One microboard used their annual general meeting as an opportunity for the focus person to consider each member and decide whether they still wanted them as members of their microboard.

Some microboards used the legal structure to agree to a minimum number of meetings per year (usually four to six), establish meeting quorums and enable geographically spread members to organise special trips or attend via a phone/video call. Administrative requirements of the Act could also be a burden and pull attention from the focus person. Members who had little experience of being chair or treasurer could find it difficult to fulfil their role. Some participants "hated" their allocated role and felt unable to make positive input due to their lack of ability and time constraints. One participant joked they were the worst choice for treasurer, as they had been losing money their whole life. Other participants found the new roles helpful in broadening their own experience and approach to the microboard. One participant who took on the treasurer role said, "I haven't had that role before. I've been the secretary. So that's a new role, that kind of makes me think about things differently." While administrative burden was a concern, incorporation generally provided a strong foundation and structure for microboards, to flesh out the hopes, dreams and life of the focus person.

DISCUSSION

Many participants discussed what a microboard could do, rather than how it functioned. These discussions were not included in the final data but illustrated the possible outcomes when key factors worked in unison to successfully support the focus person. These outcomes included creating a share house with housemates chosen by the focus person, a job opportunity with mentoring to learn and retain the role, development of presentations about life and choices resulting in multiple invitations to make public presentations and relocation from less-than-ideal accommodation back to a hometown.

Data from the 15 participants identified social, human, cultural and political capital as the four key factors in microboards, confirming the patterns in existing literature. WA microboards shared these key factors with international evaluations, with one key difference. Financial capital in literature generally referred to individualised funding, which had not been accessed by WA microboards. WA microboards did not have significant financial commitments, and it was not seen as a driving factor. Social capital was the dominant and key factor in both literature and this research. Diversity of members strengthened the dedication to communication, person-centred support and supported decision-making by maintaining focus on the person at the centre and the life they want to lead. Vela and MA performed similar roles, supporting new microboards to navigate legal requirements, instil person-centred approaches and connect to the microboard community.

The Model

Many participants referred to microboards as a "model" or "framework", but no model was yet available in the literature. Figure 7.1 was created based on the data collected from the 15 research participants and microboard literature (Farrant, 2016). The model illustrates the relationships between the key factors evident in WA microboards. The model views the focus person within the context of their microboard, not their wider community, and does not aim to show each part of a person's life. Each microboard is different and is designed that way to provide the best support to the focus person. The model is also dynamic and may change over time to reflect changes in funding, legislative and support norms.

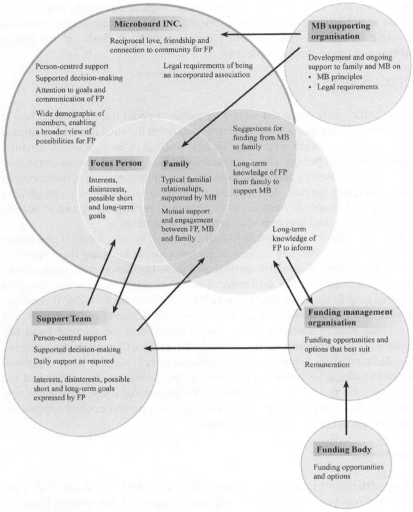

Note: FP = focus person; MB = Microboard.

Figure 7.1   The Microboard model

The model illustrates the major responsibilities and actions of each of the people and groups. The focus person, family and microboard have significant cross-over due to the crucial engagement of family, especially during the set-up of the microboard. Family is distinct from the microboard, however, as not all family members join microboards and microboards should not include only family. The focus person is supported to discover and share their goals, hopes and dreams with their family, microboard and support team. Each group supports the focus person to work towards these goals; the support team may focus on the day-to-day aspects while the microboard considers and supports longer-term goals, with the family supporting both. The national microboard-supporting organisation assists with the development of the microboard, culture, membership, key principles and legal requirements. Ongoing support is provided as further education needs arise and changes occur. The support team are not members while they provide paid support, but play an important role in consistent person-centred support and sharing micro-board principles. The support team learns from the microboard, occasionally attending meetings to give and receive information about the focus person's short-term needs, goals and issues. Funding bodies, typically the National Disability Insurance Scheme in Australia, have been left generic, as the role of funding was not clearly captured in this research.

CONCLUSIONS

The key limitation in this research was access to input from the focus people of WA microboards, due to time limits and the scope of research. Future research should put the voice of the focus person at the centre, to balance the inconsistency of writing about person-centred approaches without including the people at the centre. A measurement of microboard "success" is necessary and could consider microboard impact on community connection, decision-making, employment, housing and plans for the future. The relationship between the NDIS and microboards requires further consideration. Application of the microboard model could be considered in sectors such as aged care and mental health. Comparisons between microboards in different countries may identify key factors that cross international boundaries.

Microboards are a growing and valuable support model that is yet to be fully understood and documented. A legal structure gives the microboard underlying strength, then human relationships, strong culture and community support reinforce and expand on what these groups of people can achieve. Individuals who have historically had very little voice are put at the centre of decision-making and are helped to maintain control of their lives. The individuality of microboards enables optimal support for the focus person, while the key factors provide a replicable framework for others to follow.

The growing use of support structures of this kind and focus on community participation within the NDIS (National Disability Insurance Agency, 2020) may see an increase in community participation, and therefore community diversity, by people who would have previously been given a minimal role in community life. Understanding the factors that support this inclusion is the first step towards diverse and inclusive neighbourhoods, nations and the global community.

Implications for Researchers

The current paucity of microboard research presents multiple opportunities for future study and policy change. Focus on the experiences of the individuals at the centre of the microboard is essential, to capture their insights and preferences. The introduction of the NDIS presents opportunities for Australian microboards to manage funding. The creation of a microboard model provides an opportunity for replication and evaluation of the "success" of a microboard; measuring changes in social inclusion, quality of life and decision-making capacity and frequency. Microboards could provide an alternative to guardianship and a legally recognised process of supported decision-making, deserving examination by policy makers in that space.

REFERENCES

Assistive Ware (2021). Speak up with symbol-based AAC. www.assistiveware.com/products/proloquo2go

Browning, M., Bigby, C., and Douglas, J. (2014). Supported decision making: Understanding how its conceptual link to legal capacity is influencing the development of practice. *Research and Practice in Intellectual and Developmental Disabilities*, 1(1), 34–45.

Browning, M., Bigby, C., and Douglas, J. (2021). A process of decision-making support: Exploring supported decision-making practice in Canada. *Journal of Intellectual and Developmental Disability*, 46(2), 138–149.

Carlson, J. A. (2010). Avoiding traps in member checking. *The Qualitative Report*, 15(5), 1102–1113.

Committee of the Rights of Persons with Disability (2019). Concluding observations on the combined second and third periodic reports of Australia. Geneva: United Nations. https://tbinternet.ohchr.org/_layouts/15/treatybodyexternal/Download.aspx?symbolno=CRPD%2fC%2fAUS%2fCO%2f2-3&Lang=en

Dirth, T. P., and Branscombe, N. R. (2017). Disability models affect disability policy support through awareness of structural discrimination. *Journal of Social Issues*, 73(2), 413–442.

Emery, M. and Flora, C. (2006). Spiraling-up: Mapping community transformation with community capitals framework. *Community Development*, 37(1), 19–35.

Farrant, E. (2016). Exploring Western Australia's microboards: Identifying the central elements of a support model for people with a disability. Unpublished honours dissertation, Curtin University.

Flora, C. B., and Flora, J. L. (2013). *Rural Communities: Legacy and Change* (4th ed.). Westview Press.

Himes-Cornell, A., Ormond, C., Hoelting, K., Ban, N. C., Zachary Koehn, J., Allison, E. H., Larson, E. C., Monson, D. H., Huntington, H. P., and Okey, T. A. (2018). Factors affecting disaster preparedness, response, and recovery using the community capitals framework. *Coastal Management*, 46(5), 335–358.

Jackson, M. A. (2018). Models of disability and human rights: Informing the improvement of built environment accessibility for people with disability at neighborhood scale? *Laws*, 7(1), 10.

Jay, L., and Schaper, M. (2012). Microboards: What are they and how do they work? *Training and Management Development Methods*, 26(4), 401–406.

Liamputtong, P., Anderson, K., and Bondas, T. (2016). *Research Methods in Health*. Oxford University Press.

Magis, K. (2010). Community resilience: An indicator of social sustainability. *Society and Natural Resources*, 23(5), 401–416.

Malette, P. (2002). Lifestyle quality and person-centered support. In S. Holdburn and P. Vietze (Eds), *Person-Centered Planning: Research, Practice, and Future Directions* (pp. 151–179). Paul H. Brookes Publishing.

Microboards Australia (2016). About us. http://microboard.org.au/about-us/

Mirfin-Veitch, B., and Richardson, G. (2017). Exploring Article 12 of the United Nations Convention on the Rights of Persons with Disabilities: An integrative literature review. Donald Beasley Institute. www.odi.govt.nz/assets/Whats-happening -files/exploring-article-12-literature-review-october-2016.pdf

National Disability Insurance Agency (2020). The NDIS in the community. www.ndis .gov.au/community/community-participation

Pedlar, A., and Hutchison, P. (2000). Restructuring human services in Canada: Commodification of disability. *Disability and Society*, 15(4), 637–651.

Pedlar, A., Haworth, L., Hutchison, P., Taylor, A., and Dunn, P. (1999). *A Textured Life: Empowerment and Adults with Developmental Disabilities*. Wilfrid Laurier University Press.

Stainton, T. (2016). Supported decision-making in Canada: Principles, policy, and practice. *Research and Practice in Intellectual and Developmental Disabilities*, 3(1), 1–11.

Stainton, T., Morris, R., and Borja, C. (2020). *Microboards, Social Capital and Quality of Life*. University of British Columbia, Canadian Institute for Inclusion and Citizenship.

Vela (2021). About us. https://velacanada.org/about/about-us/

Wetherow, D., and Wetherow, F. (2004). Microboards and microboard association design, development and implementation. www.communityworks.info/articles/ microboard.htm

Women's Research Centre (1994). Microboards review: A report to Vela Housing Society. www.library.ubc.ca/archives/u_arch/womens.pdf

USEFUL WEB LINKS

Circles of Support and Microboards: https://cosam.org.au/

Microboards Australia: http://microboard.org.au/
Vela: https://velacanada.org/services/microboards/

8. LGB employees and their experiences of fly-in/fly-out employment in Western Australia

Mirsad Bahtic, Scott Fitzgerald and John Burgess

INTRODUCTION TO THE RESEARCH

The challenges associated with working in the mining industry are both physically and psychologically demanding, impacting work and life satisfaction, job performance, relationships and general daily life. While there have been studies dedicated to analysing the growth and impact of fly-in/fly-out (FIFO) employment across various disciplines, from psychology to social sciences (Rainnie et al., 2014) and public inquiries that have addressed FIFO practices on workers, their families and local communities (House of Representatives, 2013; Western Australian Legislative Assembly, 2015), these have solely focused on detailing the experiences of traditional two-parent heterosexual FIFO families (Clifford, 2009). There has been an absence of research on the experiences and well-being of FIFO employees from minority sexuality groups, such as those from lesbian, gay and bisexual (LGB) backgrounds. Employee sexual orientation in the mining industry has generally been an area overlooked in academic literature due in part to the implied assumption that mining is primarily based around heterosexual male employment. This chapter addresses the views and experiences of these individuals and provides an additional layer to previous literature by examining an area of research that is in need of further examination. It highlights the role of sexual orientation in employees' experiences of working in the mining industry under FIFO employment, where employees spend a fixed number of days working in geographically isolated environments followed by a fixed number of days at home (Shrimpton and Storey, 1989). The research reported here is based on a larger study of FIFO work experiences across self-identified LGB and heterosexual workers (Bahtic, 2018).

The typical Australian household is no longer the traditional two-parent family, with census data indicating that a more non-traditional family structure is becoming prevalent across the nation (Australian Bureau of Statistics, 2011). In recognising this diversity, the inclusive definition of family in this chapter (Australian Bureau of Statistics, 2007) includes traditional two-parent households where both parents either share a child/children biologically or the child/children are step or adopted into the family, single-parent families, LGB families, couples without children and single people. Due to such diversity, there is a need for further research on FIFO employment that acknowledges this changing household structure. The following addresses this gap by discussing the contextual factors associated with FIFO employment, impacting employees from these different family types, and in particular focusing on those from sexual minority backgrounds, working in the Western Australia (WA) mining industry. As such, the purpose of this study was to answer the question: how does sexual orientation influence the experiences of FIFO employment?

Sexual orientation relates to heterosexuality, homosexuality and bisexuality. Heterosexual individuals have a sexual orientation towards people of the opposite sex, also known as straight persons. Homosexual individuals are those with a sexual orientation towards people of the same sex, also known as gay men or lesbian women. Bisexual individuals have a sexual orientation towards people from both the same and opposite sex. Although these categories remain the most widely used across research, some academics suggest that sexual orientation is not always as clearly defined within the three categories mentioned, but instead occurs on a continuum. In this chapter, it relates to how a person identifies their sexual orientation, regardless of the sex they were assigned at birth, and as such it encompasses the level of masculinity, femininity or androgyny of a person. By detailing sexual orientation in relation to the mining industry, and specifically to FIFO employment, this study provides an additional layer to previous literature addressing LGB employees in the workplace.

LITERATURE ANALYSIS

Previous literature on LGB employees in the workplace has been extensive, with studies exploring the different challenges faced by LGB employees. In one of the largest Australian studies, Irwin (1999) found that 59 per cent of people sampled felt that they were either victims or witnesses of heterosexism or heterosexist behaviours, 50 per cent were publicly ridiculed by other co-workers and 97 per cent claimed to be the direct or indirect target of verbal or physical harassment. Heterosexism, unlike homophobia, encompasses the broader issues associated with social inequality at the workplace through interpersonal relationships that are typically reflective of cultural values and norms

(Waldo, 1999). As a result of heterosexism, numerous participants identified issues pertaining to stress and depression, and according to Meyer (1995), when stress is combined with an unsupportive and discriminatory work environment, psychological well-being deteriorates, thus increasing the chances of employee mental illness. This form of hostility towards non-heterosexual individuals in the workplace often correlates with hegemonically masculine gender performances (Pascoe, 2012). Emergent research suggests that such negative behaviour towards sexual minorities is true in arenas that are culturally dominated by masculine-type behavioural norms and interaction styles that devalue femininity (Cech and Waidzunas, 2011). These environments harbour heterosexism against sexual minorities in the form of marginalisation, harassment and bullying, discrimination and denial of resources, as the culture promotes what is essentially a male/female sex binary, designating heterosexuality as the only norm (Herek, 2007). In the United States, findings have indicated that between 15 and 66 per cent of LGB employees have experienced sexual orientation discrimination (Katz-Wise and Hyde, 2012). This is a cause for concern, as research has also shown a link between discriminatory behaviour and suicide, with further research by the Department of Health and Human Services of Tasmania (2003) showing that suicide, alcohol and substance abuse were considerably higher among the LGBT population when compared to the heterosexual population, thus indicating a flow-on effect of heterosexism that goes beyond the workplace and impacts the physical and mental well-being of these individuals.

Discrimination based on sexual orientation is a widespread concern in the workplace (Kuyper, 2015). Barrett et al. (2011), in their examination of sexuality disclosure while at work, found that 36 per cent of participants experienced discrimination due to their sexual orientation at one place of work and 34 per cent at two different places of work. The main types of discrimination, similar to research by Willis (2009), included remarks (27 per cent), ridicule (27 per cent) and humour (25 per cent). Additionally, 80 per cent received death threats, 67 per cent were verbally harassed, 33 per cent had their workplace property damaged and 30 per cent were threatened by sexual abuse. Guiffre et al. (2008) also found that discrimination is developed in three main areas that include stereotyping, gender and sexual harassment, with lesbians and bisexual women in particular being affected by these forms of workplace discrimination. LGB employees have invisible stigmas and therefore they can choose whether to disclose or hide their sexual identity from other workers. The anticipated discrimination that is often associated with disclosure may have an even greater impact on individual experiences while at work (Raggins et al., 2007). These findings suggest that because sexual orientation is not readily observable, discrimination requires knowledge of employee orientation, thus potential to discriminate is presumed to be higher when employees disclose their sexuality to others in the workplace.

These studies indicate that heterosexism is still an issue in today's society and has the potential to damage relationships that LGB individuals have with their workplace. Daily experiences of discrimination have been linked to poor psychosocial health (King et al., 2008), physical health (Denton et al., 2014) and overall well-being (Schmitt et al., 2014). However, research has also illustrated the positive benefits, in terms of economic benefits, associated with organisational commitment and support of LGB employees. For example, Day and Schoenrade (2000) found that organisational support and anti-discrimination policies correlated with higher levels of job satisfaction. These studies represent a sample of the vast amount of literature exploring sexual orientation in the workplace. Disclosure or concealment of sexual identity can influence employee job and life satisfaction and mental health, with many participants across the aforementioned studies reporting heterosexism as being the main cause of negative job attitudes and absenteeism (Day and Schoenrade, 2000). However, research studies have been standardised, mainly exploring white- and blue-collar business environments. Further research into more male-dominated workplaces, such as those from the mining industry where research indicates that disclosure or concealment of sexuality can impact on individual well-being (Cain, 1991), could lead to a greater understanding of the impact that high heterosexual work environments can have on employees from LGB backgrounds.

Literature on FIFO employment has been addressed from different backgrounds and perspectives that have examined the impact of extended work schedules on employee and family well-being (Clifford, 2009), health behaviours associated with working in geographically isolated areas for extended periods (Joyce et al., 2013) and the experiences of women working in FIFO employment (Pirotta, 2009). However, all these studies have explored FIFO employment from a traditional two-parent family perspective, with no academic research to highlight the impact such working conditions and environments are having on minority groups and employees from non-traditional FIFO backgrounds. Although previous research is vital in understanding the experiences of working in the mining industry in general, it is evident that a gap exists in the literature that requires further research to address the changing Australian household structure.

There is a growing body of research and public inquiry into understanding FIFO employment and how it impacts on employee lives (Western Australian Legislative Assembly Health and Education Committee, 2015). However, there is limited to no research on sexual minorities involved in the Australian mining industry. Therefore, the present study addresses this gap by detailing the influence of FIFO employment on LGB FIFO employees. These individuals are not only prone to the heterosexual work environment found across mine sites, but they are also more likely to struggle with discrimination and prejudice as a result of their sexual orientation. Although this research is exploratory, it could be vital in the development of better workplace programmes that address the diversity of the mining industry and the needs of LGB workers; it could help detail ways to mitigate issues and stressors, faced by minority groups, resulting from FIFO working; and it may help enhance awareness to more specific employee and family support initiatives that consider all FIFO employees.

RESEARCH PROCESS

The research process was exploratory, attempting to understand the factors contributing to the well-being of FIFO workers and the role played by their sexuality in this experience. The research was interpretive and involved qualitative methods of data collection, largely through semi-structured interviews. The target population of this study consisted of WA FIFO employees residing in the Perth metropolitan area but working in the northern WA mining industry. The commuting distance is around 2,000 kilometres each way. In this research, data triangulation was used to collect information from participants in the same field of FIFO employment, at various life and work stages and from different gender and family types. Due to constrained resources, purposeful sampling was employed to enhance variability of data and participants were selected based on the study objectives. Participants were recruited through email directly by the researcher or indirectly via industry contacts. Support, community and stakeholder groups were also approached to provide access to different participants. To avoid the study interfering with participants' work, the interviews were conducted mainly through email but also via Skype, video chat, telephone and face-to-face discussions. Due to limited resources, purposeful sampling was employed to achieve variability and richness of data, thus leading to a greater understanding of FIFO working and living experience (Charmaz, 2000). Person triangulation was used in this study as data were collected from more than one type of person. Participants included construction and white-collar employees, stay-at-home partners, mothers and fathers all involved in the resources sector, thus leading to greater insight into a variety of FIFO-related contextual factors that covered everything from support services available to employees and their families to workplace practices addressing discrimination and prejudice. Such data were used to support and validate information from the research findings. The sample of participants was separated into two groups that included ten FIFO employees from LGB backgrounds and ten FIFO employees from heterosexual family backgrounds across four different mine sites. The research was subject to an ethics review and clearance before commencing. This chapter reports only on the experiences of LGB employees.

As the study focused on a small sample, a combination of convenience and snowball sampling techniques was implemented to help gather participants. The study adopted convenience sampling during the initial pre-testing of the interview questions with a small group of three FIFO employees. The pilot sample allowed for additional feedback and comments to be made regarding the interview questions and helped modify the final set of questions. Based on this feedback, some questions were edited to express greater clarity and a more refined set of questions was developed for the final interviews. Snowball sampling helped gather a few participants from the target population who recommended others within their work group. The interviews were recorded and transcripts were subsequently generated. After initial and focused coding was conducted, all codes were reviewed to combine codes into themes. Themes were created based on the clustering of similar codes that helped to identify links and interrelationships between the codes. A code structure and hierarchy emerged that detailed the same themes and phenomena. The research was subject to a formal ethics review and participants were assured that their identities would not be revealed in the reporting of the research.

FINDINGS

The study revealed several contextual factors impacting on the experiences of LGB FIFO employees as a result of their sexual orientation. Following the analysis of the interviews, a number of key themes were identified as being important contextual factors that impacted on the employment experience. Each of these factors – workplace culture, support services, bullying and the demands of FIFO employment – are discussed in the following sections. FIFO workers are away from home, communities and support networks for long periods of time; they work and live in proximity with co-workers in an industry that is masculine and heterosexual and they are isolated. Proclaiming LGB sexuality in this context and reporting incidents of harassment only results in further isolation and harassment.

Organisational Culture

Organisational culture was recognised as a driving factor in the way employee attitude and behaviour was shaped. Not only did it impact employee perceptions of organisational support, but it also influenced how individuals interpreted their work environment, with a number of participants detailing a hesitation towards their interaction with co-workers while on site. Across the interviewees it was found that the organisational culture from one mine to the next also differed. Some participants felt that their culture was supportive of employees, while others perceived their culture did not recognise the uniqueness of each individual. "I'm a girl ... in a man's world ... everything here is shaped around a man's life, women don't get much say and that's because their (male) notion of employment has been embedded in the culture for decades," said one lesbian employee. As a result, similar to research by Ozeren (2014), many sexual minorities often chose to conceal their sexual identities around other employees to avoid confrontation and upsetting cultural norms. However, such self-regulating behaviour has been linked to negative outcomes that impact employees' well-being: "we don't really have any policies that recognise our sexual identities ... it can get emotionally draining when your voice cannot be heard" (Lesbian employee). Frank (2001) observed difficulties faced by lesbians in hostile workplace cultures, especially in terms of proclaiming their sexual identity. When men dominate organisational culture, lesbian participants noted that they felt at a greater disadvantage and were more prone to discrimination on account of their gender. As a result, sexual minorities tried to be accepted by other employees by conforming to the norms of the heterosexual environment through concealing their sexual identities.

Culture can instil a level of fear among employees in which they might feel that by expressing their concerns around bullying and harassment with their employer they will be treated differently by other workers, hence their lack of desire to seek formal support. The mining industry, due to the male-dominated work environment, is typically built on a culture of not discussing personal issues as this is not regarded as being manly (Henry et al., 2013).

Support Services

When discussing formal organisational support services, participants claimed that they did not know about the availability of support through their employer, and those that did were hesitant in using such services for reasons indicated above, instead preferring informal support through family and friends. Participants felt that if they were seen taking advantage of support, they would be judged by other workers: "we do have support services ... *I have rarely seen anyone use them*", said one lesbian employee, and another lesbian employee adds: "if I did go to my supervisor for assistance with a work matter or non-work problem, I feel I would be treated differently or looked at differently". McFadden and Crowley-Henry (2017) found that silence was a typical strategy used by LGB employees to avoid getting labelled as troublemakers. Participants in this study described having to keep their feelings to themselves as they feared being isolated and harassed by other employees.

Formal support can potentially improve employee experience of FIFO employment while at work and at home, as the majority of participants claimed that if their employer offered some form of employee or family support, they would be more motivated while on site. Participants claimed that having strong support, such as through a group network, could help lower the demands associated with work and home life, thus reducing individual stress, lowering work–home conflict and improving overall well-being. However, LGB employees were hesitant in seeking support from their employer and often preferred to rely on their family and friends when they felt down or couldn't talk to their employer. They were physically isolated from their loved ones while on site, but also felt mentally isolated from other co-workers, claiming that it was difficult to be open around others in their work group, especially around their sexuality.

Bullying

Despite the changing social and political climate in developed economies, sexual minorities still experience harassment and bullying at work (Guiffre et al., 2008). The participants from this study chose not to report being bullied to their supervisor or manager, as they felt this could exacerbate the potential for further harassment. "Complaining about bullying or any form of harassment is not worth it in the long run ... the formal process in lodging a complaint can be long and people fall victim to this process ... you're named and shamed," said a lesbian employee. Another lesbian employee claimed that people don't want to associate with complainers, thus detailing a reluctance from employees to formally complain. Reluctance to report issues formally can also potentially create further hostility in the workplace, as grievances against colleagues may lead to further problems (Wright, 2013), thus many choose to cope with the bullying in silence.

Workplace attitudes and fear of repercussions embedded in organisational culture might be preventing management from addressing bullying and harassment on site. Employees would rather keep to themselves instead of making a formal complaint, and therefore management is unaware of any bullying experienced by their employees.

The experience of FIFO employment by sexual minorities is hindered via bullying when they openly express their sexuality around others. In a highly heterosexual male-dominated environment, issues of bullying generally tend to get overlooked but can have a drastic effect on employee motivation, morale and productivity. Bullying is a considerably more severe issue in the mining industry, as it is more likely to occur due to distance between the worksite and corporate headquarters where there are formal procedures in place for reporting and addressing bullying behaviour. The problem of distance and isolation is that it is easy for formal policies and processes to be ignored, and for management to remain in ignorance of what transpires at remote workplaces (Paap, 2006).

Physical and Mental Demands of FIFO Employment

The participants claimed that the demands associated with FIFO employment affected them physically and mentally, impacting on their daily routines at work and home. While many of the LGB employees were able to cope with these issues, those new to FIFO employment found that they struggled more than they had initially expected, as one lesbian employee who had been working in FIFO employment for less than a year said: "I cannot be myself … this place [mine site] changes people … I'm already noticing myself acting differently towards others here and at home". She claimed that she has to keep her emotions to herself, as she has seen how others in similar positions get treated. There is an "underbelly" that exists when you first start working in FIFO employment where you are looked at through a different lens because you are new, said another employee.

While most employees struggled to cope with the physical and mental demands associated with FIFO employment, there were a number of individuals that found the demands actually helped strengthen their mental attitude and ability to cope with difficult situations. "My confidence has improved since I started working [in FIFO employment] … my emotions don't zig-zag … my ability to see the bigger picture has become clearer," said a gay FIFO employee. The ability to properly manage all the demands of FIFO employment is not easily achievable but managing such demands can improve individual work satisfaction.

IMPLICATIONS OF THE STUDY

The ability to disclose sexuality at work was influenced by the level of organisational support and inclusive workplace cultures that discourage discriminatory behaviour. Due to the uniqueness of each FIFO employee, it is recommended that organisations strive to develop and adopt transformative policies and practices which recognise a range of minorities based not only on sexuality, but also age, ethnicity and class if they wish to be inclusive and address inequality across the entirety of the organisation (Dickens, 2005).

If organisations in the mining industry were to adopt formal support networks, such as LGB group networks, they could potentially provide a voice for sexual minorities. Networks can act as a collective mechanism in which greater visibility and community for members can be established (Colgan and McKearney, 2012) and promote change in a positive manner. By bringing together sexual minority employees, networks can provide social support in the organisation (Colgan and McKearney, 2012), which has been positively linked to coping strategies and the management of various difficulties faced by these minorities (Willis, 2010). Essentially, a network offers employees an antidote to loneliness in the organisation, and a community where they can be open about their sexuality (Colgan and McKearney, 2012); however, some employees might avoid voicing their concerns as they believe it could lead to further mistreatment or they feel they will be looked at differently by other co-workers (McFadden and Crowley-Henry, 2017). As such, a more nuanced approach to LGB support in such mining organisations is necessary.

RESEARCH FIELD TIPS

When conducting fieldwork that involves sexual minorities that work in workplaces that are heavily gendered and stereotyped it is difficult to access minority workers and to engage with them about their experiences at work. In this case the difficulties are exacerbated by the remote workplaces and FIFO work arrangements that mean it is difficult to physically access the worksites. In a male-dominated workplace such as mining, LGB employees are reluctant to identify themselves and are reluctant to detail their experiences at work. In this research access was gained via support groups, using snowball techniques, and all interviews were conducted away from the workplace.

CONCLUSIONS

Due to their sexuality, and that they work in a highly heterosexual environment, LGB employees struggle to express their true feelings as a fear of being judged and stereotyped means that they choose to conceal their sexual identities from other workers. LGB employees will often choose to remain silent at work because they feel that by being open about their sexuality they will be exposed to social isolation, bullying and prejudicial reactions and discrimination (Ozeren et al., 2016). However, all the participants from this study were able to cope with the challenges associated with FIFO employment and chose to remain in the mining industry because they felt that the difficulties of FIFO working were not severe enough for them to seek employment elsewhere.

Sexual minorities involved in the mining industry differ in terms of their organisational integration and their willingness to be open about their sexuality. Similar to findings from Ozeren et al. (2016), we find that some FIFO employees purposefully choose to avoid disclosing their sexuality to others or voicing their concerns formally, as they believe that it could lead to further discrimination or mistreatment. The ability to disclose sexuality at work was influenced by the level of organisational support and inclusive workplace cultures that discourage discriminatory behaviour. Due to the uniqueness of each FIFO employee, it is recommended that organisations strive to develop and adopt transformative policies and practices which recognise a range of minorities based not only on sexuality but also age and ethnicity if they wish to be inclusive and address inequality across the entirety of the organisation (Dickens, 2005). However, experiences of FIFO employment varied across participant responses, and therefore a potential implementation gap between equality and diversity policies exists across the different mine site locations. Therefore, organisational change in terms of greater equality may not guarantee a working environment that embraces sexual minorities or lowers prejudice or discrimination across the board.

In addressing the issues faced by sexual minorities from this study, managers should aim to voice and encourage the use of formal support services and enforce policies and practices that address equality. They could implement support networks to help sexual minorities voice their concerns and encourage greater visibility as a community that strives to promote change (Colgan and McKearney, 2012). Managers should also reinforce networks, as research has found that top managerial support is essential to the enhancement of employee commitment to the organisation (Day and Schoenrade, 2000). Managerial support should be translated into equality policies that address diversity and implemented across the entire organisation. Colgan and Wright (2011) argue that commitment from the top level might be poorly communicated throughout the organisation, thus lower-level managers might be unwilling to address issues faced by sexual minorities. Our findings suggest that distance between the location of the mine site and the location of the headquarters could also hinder communication and the successful translation of formal policies that are inclusive of sexual minorities in male-dominated workplaces.

Many of the participants noted issues while on site due to daily difficulties they face with discrimination exhibited, either directly or indirectly, by other co-workers that lead to higher levels of stress: "when I have too much stuff on my mind it gets hard to get things done ... there are days when this builds up and trying to complete my duties can get tiresome," said one gay employee. In addition, each participant differed in terms of their personal and social resources, thus influencing their reaction to various difficulties associated with working in the mining industry. For example, some participants were better at coping with harassment or discriminatory behaviour due to them having access to greater levels of support from family and friends. A number of participants felt that having formal social support would offer them a voice in male-dominated work domains, which has positively been linked to promoting change and bringing together sexual minorities (Colgan and McKearney, 2012). Due to the exploratory nature of the study, these results are speculative at best and further research with a more diverse sample is necessary. Moreover, due to the small sample size the findings were difficult to generalise to the wider mining population and therefore the study does not provide an adequate representation of the target population. The study was also limited in that it mainly focused on participants that were open about their sexuality, and further research that addresses employees who actively avoid disclosing such information may provide another perspective on the FIFO environment.

REFERENCES

Australian Bureau of Statistics (2007). 2006 census of population and housing – census tables, Catalogue No. 2068.0. Canberra, ACT: ABS.

Australian Bureau of Statistics (2011). Australian family type. www.aifs.org.au/institute/info/charts/familystructure/index.html#ftype2011

Bahtic, M. (2018). The non-traditional FIFO experience: An exploration of the experiences of non-traditional Western Australian employees and families who work and live FIFO. PhD thesis, School of Management, Curtin University, Perth.

Barrett, N., Lewis, J., and Dwyer, A. (2011). Effects of disclosure of sexual identity at work for gay, lesbian, bisexual, transgender and intersex (GLBTI) employees in Queensland. In Proceedings of the 25th Annual Australian and New Zealand Academy of Management Conference, Australian and New Zealand Academy of Management, Wellington.

Cain, R. (1991). Stigma management and gay identity management. *Social Work*, 36(1): 67–73.

Cech, E. A., and Waidzunas, T. J. (2011). Navigating the heteronormativity of engineering: The experiences of lesbian, gay, and bisexual students. *Engineering Studies*, 3(1): 1–24.

Charmaz, K. (2000). Grounded theory: Objectivist and constructivist methods. In N. Denzin and Y. Lincoln (Eds), *Handbook of Qualitative Research* (2nd ed., pp. 509–535). Thousand Oaks, CA: Sage.

Clifford, S. (2009). *The Effects of Fly-in/Fly-out Commute Arrangements and Extended Working Hours on the Stress, Lifestyle, Relationship and Health Characteristics of Western Australian Mining Employees and their Partners: Report of Research Findings*. Crawley, WA: University of Western Australia, School of Anatomy and Human Biology.

Colgan, F., and McKearney, A. (2012). Visibility and voice in organisations: Lesbians, gay, bisexual and transgendered employee networks. *Equality, Diversity and Inclusion: An International Journal*, 31(4): 359–378.

Colgan, F., and Wright, T. (2011). Lesbian, gay and bisexual equality in a modernizing public sector 1997–2010: Opportunities and threats. *Gender, Work and Organization*, 18(5): 548–570.

Day, N. E., and Schoenrade, P. (2000). The relationship among reported disclosure of sexual orientation, anti-discrimination policies, top management support and work attitudes of gay and lesbian employees. *Personnel Review*, 29(3): 346–363.

Denton F. N., Rostosky S. S., and Danner F. (2014). Stigma-related stressors, coping self-efficacy, and physical health in lesbian, gay, and bisexual individuals. *Journal of Counseling Psychology*, 61(3): 383–391.

Department of Health and Human Services of Tasmania (2003). Gay, lesbian, bisexual and transgender health and wellbeing needs assessment. Tasmania: Blanch Consulting.

Dickens, L. (2005). Walking the talk? Equality and diversity in employment. In S. Bach (Ed.), *Managing Human Resources: Personnel Management in Transition* (pp. 178–208). Oxford: Blackwell Publishing.

Frank, M. (2001). Hard hatted women: Lesbians in the building trades. *New Labor Forum*, 8: 25–36.

Guiffre, P., Dellinger, K., and Williams, C. (2008). "No retribution for being gay": Inequality in gay-friendly workplaces. *Sociological Spectrum*, 28(3): 254–277.

Henry, P., Hamilton, K., Watson, S., and McDonald, M. (2013). FIFO/DIDO mental health: Research report 2013. Perth, WA: Lifeline WA.

Herek, G. M. (2007). Confronting sexual stigma and prejudice: Theory and practice. *Journal of Social Issues*, 63(4): 905–925.

House of Representatives Standing Committee on Regional Australia (2013). *Cancer of the Bush or Salvation for Our Cities*. Canberra.

Irwin, J. (1999). The pink ceiling is too low: Workplace experiences of lesbians, gay men and transgender people. Report of a collaborative research project undertaken by the Australian Centre for Lesbian and Gay Research and the New South Wales Gay and Lesbian Rights Lobby. Sydney: University of Sydney, Australian Centre for Lesbian and Gay Research.

Joyce, S. J., Tomlin, S. M., Somerford, P. J., and Weeramanthri, T. S. (2013). Health behaviours and outcomes associated with fly-in fly-out and shift workers in Western Australia. *Internal Medicine Journal*, 43(4): 440–444.

Katz-Wise, S. L., and Hyde, J. S. (2012). Victimization experiences of lesbian, gay, and bisexual individuals: A meta-analysis. *Journal of Sex Research*, 49(2–3): 142–167.

King M., Semlyen J., Tai S. S., Killaspy H., Osborn D., Popelyuk D., and Nazareth I. (2008). A systematic review of mental disorder, suicide, and deliberate self-harm in lesbian, gay and bisexual people. *BMC Psychiatry*, 8(70): 1–17.

Kuyper, L. (2015). Differences in workplace experiences between lesbian, gay, bisexual, and heterosexual employees in a representative population study. *Psychology of Sexual Orientation and Gender Diversity*, 2(1): 1–11.

McFadden, C., and Crowley-Henry, M. (2017). "My people": The potential of LGB employee networks in reducing stigmatization and providing voice. *International Journal of Human Resource Management*, 1–26.

Meyer, I. H. (1995). Minority stress and mental health in gay men. *Journal of Health Sciences and Social Behavior*, 36(1): 38–56.

Ozeren, E. (2014). Sexual orientation discrimination in the workplace: A systematic review of literature. *Procedia – Social and Behavioural Sciences*, 109: 1203–1215.

Ozeren, E., Ucar, Z., and Duygulu, E. (2016). Silence speaks in the workplace: Uncovering the experiences of LGB employees in Turkey. In T. Köllen (Ed.), *Sexual Orientation and Transgender Issues in Organizations* (pp. 217–232). Cham: Springer.

Paap, K. (2006). *Working Construction: Why White Working-Class Men Put Themselves – and the Labor Movement – in Harm's Way*. London: Cornell University Press.

Pascoe, C. J. (2012). *Dude, You're a Fag: Masculinity and Sexuality in High School*. Berkeley, CA: University of California Press.

Pirotta, J. (2009). An exploration of the experiences of women who FIFO. *Australian Community Psychologist*, 21(2): 37–51.

Raggins, B. R., Singh, R., and Cornwell, J. M. (2007). Making the invisible visible: Fear and disclosure of sexual orientation at work. *Journal of Applied Psychology*, 92(4): 1103–1118.

Rainnie, A., Fitzgerald, S., Ellem, B., and Goods, C. (2014). FIFO and global production networks: Exploring the issues. *Australian Bulletin of Labour*, 40(2): 98–115.

Schmitt M. T., Branscombe N. R., Postmes T., and Garcia A. (2014). The consequences of perceived discrimination for psychological well-being: A meta-analytic review. *Psychological Bulletin*, 140(4): 921–948.

Shrimpton, M., and Storey, K. (1989). Fly-in mining: New challenges for mines managers. *Mineral Resources Engineering*, 2(4): 317–327.

Waldo, C. R. (1999). Working in a majority context: A structural model of heterosexism as minority stress in the workplace. *Journal of Counseling Psychology*, 46(2): 218–232.

Western Australian Legislative Assembly Health and Education Committee (2015). Inquiry into mental illness and suicides of FIFO workers. Perth, WA.

Willis, P. (2009). It really is water off our backs: Young LGBQ people's strategies for resisting and refuting homonegative practices in Australian workplaces. *Gay and Lesbian Issues and Psychology Review*, 5(3): 134–145.

Willis, P. (2010). Connecting, supporting, colliding: The work-based interactions of young LGBQ-identifying workers and older queer colleagues. *Journal of LGB Youth*, 7(3): 224–246.

Wright, T. (2013). Uncovering sexuality and gender: An intersectional examination of women's experience in UK construction. *Construction Management and Economics*, 31(8): 832–844.

USEFUL WEB RESOURCES

Glassdoor (2020), Ten ways to support LGBT employees: www.glassdoor.co.uk/employers/blog/10-ways-support-lgbt-employees/

House of Representatives Standing Committee on Regional Australia (2013). Cancer of the bush or salvation for our cities. Canberra, ACT. www.aphref.aph.gov.au_house_committee_ra_fifodido_report_fullreport.pdf

Western Australian Legislative Assembly Health and Education Committee (2015). Inquiry into mental illness and suicides of FIFO workers. Perth, WA. www.parliament.wa.gov.au/Parliament/commit.nsf/luInquiryPublicSubmissions/D7C40A4EDD680 43E48257D8100196864/$file/23%20FIFO%20Australian%20Community%20of %20Excellence%20COM.pdf

9. Improving workers' well-being through international action: workers in the Bangladesh ready-made garment sector

Tasmiha Tarafder and John Burgess

INTRODUCTION

The purpose of the research discussed in this chapter was to examine the extent to which employment conditions, especially safety, had improved in ready-made garment (RMG) factories due to the international accords and agreements that were reached. The Rana Plaza factory collapsed in 2013, killing 1,132 and injuring more than 2,500 workers. Following the publicity of the disaster, international pressure was placed on the Bangladeshi Government by international agencies, non-governmental organisations (NGOs), and international apparel buyers. There was a concerted campaign to improve working conditions in an industry dominated by low-paid female workers. The research highlights how external stakeholders applied pressure through international agencies and consumer pressure through apparel companies to improve employment conditions characterised by harsh and dangerous working conditions.

In May 2013, a national tripartite plan of action was announced to support fire safety and structural integrity in the RMG sector. There were three categories included in this action plan: legislation and policy, administration, and support activities such as training. The National Tripartite Committee was established in 2013 to ensure and monitor the plan's implementation. The primary purpose of this action included ensuring continuous improvements in labour rights and safety to promote improved labour standards and responsible business.

Further, there is a need for further reform and a regulatory framework within the RMG industries in Bangladesh. In the policy implementation process, the government, buyers, and international stakeholders need to closely monitor the implementation process, especially compliance and enforcement, to ensure outcomes and provide timely adjustments to support sustainability practices in the RMG industrial sectors and local businesses. Future research could examine the effectiveness of protocols for protecting workers, especially supporting safety, in countries with a large RMG sector, such as China and Vietnam. At the policy level, the problem of the effective enforcement of employment conditions and safety standards remains, and there is scope for benchmarking against international protocols that apply elsewhere. There is scope to assess the effectiveness of the ongoing international apparel protocols in forcing a change in the application and effectiveness of regulations that support employee well-being and safety in the sector.

The RMG industry in Bangladesh developed and grew on access to cheap inputs and cheap labour. Foreign investment, free trade, and trade preferences with the large apparel markets in North America and Europe have supported the expansion of the industry, making Bangladesh one of the world's largest exporters of apparel products after China. Employment in around 5,000 RMG factories is approximately 4 million, dominated by female process workers, many originating from rural areas (Ahmed et al. 2014; Asian Development Bank 2013; Bajaj 2010; Rahman et al. 2013). The RMG sector is the largest export sector for Bangladesh. The sector's employment increased by over 1 million in the last decade, and over the same time, export value nearly tripled to around US$30 billion in 2020. There is extensive sub-contracting and tailored design and manufacture within the sector to meet the needs of buyers and retail chains across the globe.

Poorly educated, migrant, and poor women from rural areas have become the primary workforce in the RMG industry (Akhter et al. 2017b). The social setting of Bangladesh is patriarchal, like other South Asian countries, thus gender inequality continues to dominate every aspect of social and economic life, business owners in the RMG sector have strong political ties to the government, and corruption and limited enforcement of factory regulations are widespread (Khan et al. 2002). These gender differences are manifested through bullying, harassment, and authoritarian working practices that result in unpaid hours, long working hours, and poor and dangerous working conditions (Mondal 2020). Prior to the Rana Plaza building collapse, the minimum RMG employee wage was less than $40 a month for working 15 hours a day, six days a week (Al Bhadily 2015). Bangladesh's RMG wage level is one of the lowest globally, lower even than South Asian wage levels. The Bangladeshi worker minimum wage per hour is US$0.15, compared to Cambodia's $0.33, Pakistan's $0.41, India's $0.51, China's $0.55, Vietnam's $0.85, and Thailand's $1.75 (Al Bhadily 2015). Human Rights Watch (2015) reported that in Rana Plaza, 3,639 mainly female workers worked for about 13 to 14.5 hours a day, with just two days off each month before the building collapse. They earned about $0.24 a day. There were also underage employees as "helpers" and "junior workers", aged between 12 and 14 years. They were paid 0.12 cents and 0.22 cents an hour, respectively. In the textile industry, many companies use the piece-rate wage system. Although the nominal wages of these companies are higher than the minimum wage, workers need to work overtime to complete high work quotas to reach the minimum wage (Wang 2018).

Behind the apparent success of the RMG industry were the reality of poor employment conditions, low pay, child labour, and dangerous working conditions supported by poor governance and safety regulations (Mujeri and Mujeri, 2021). Reported hazards include fires, building collapse, deafness from machine noise, fatigue and tiredness from long working hours, and factory injuries from machines (Mahmud et al. 2018). Accidents, deaths, and hazards at work have been common in RMG establishments. The two most notable were the fire at Tazreen Fashions in November 2012, which killed 124 workers and left more than 200 seriously injured. The second was the collapse of the Rana Plaza building in April 2013, which took the lives of 1,129 workers and left more than 2,500 seriously injured (Khan and Wichterich 2015). The sub-contracting system meant that contractors were always under pressure to meet tight deadlines, reduce costs, and avoid factory safety regulations (Baumann-Pauly et al. 2015; Khan 2018). The process of sub-contracting and resub-contracting undermines monitoring and inspection and places pressure on small enterprises and their employees.

The primary reason for the Rana Plaza disaster in 2013 was a low investment in health and safety at work, inadequate supervision and regulatory enforcement, and a poorly maintained workplace (Boudreau et al. 2018). The Interior Ministry of Bangladesh found that Rana Plaza was built with inferior quality building materials. The weight and operation of the garment manufacturing equipment contributed to the collapse of the building (The Guardian 2013). Many other accidents and worker deaths had previously afflicted the RMG industry (Ansary and Barua 2015; Haque and Azmat 2015). The absence of a systematic process in the industry to support employee well-being and weak enforcement of workplace regulations, especially around occupational health and safety, contributed to these disasters (Tanha et al. 2021).

Enforceable building and fire safety regulations were absent before the 2013 Rana Plaza building collapse and other industrial accidents such as the 2012 Tazreen fire in Bangladesh. In response to these tragedies, several global apparel brands started in 2012 to formulate private mechanisms linked to contracts with suppliers to strengthen weak fire safety regulation or improve enforcement by the government (Baumann-Pauly et al. 2015). Several leading international apparel brands initiated a new approach to fire safety issues in the garment sector, including Calvin Klein and Tommy Hilfiger (Sharon 2015). The deadly Tazreen fire in November 2012 began to catalyse a more collective response on the part of brands. However, it was not until Rana Plaza in April 2013 that there was a broader international response by agencies and apparel brands to address the shoddy work and safety conditions in the industry. Within a month of the Rana Plaza collapse, 43 brands (mainly from Europe) had joined to form Accord on Fire and Building Safety in Bangladesh (Baumann-Pauly et al. 2015). Meanwhile, 17 American and Canadian brands and retailers worked to form the Alliance for Bangladesh Worker Safety, which was launched in July 2013 (Baumann-Pauly et al. 2015). The objective of both agreements was to address the safety issues in Bangladesh's RMG industry through factory inspections and reporting and understanding the contacts to regular audits of workplace and employment conditions (Islam et al. 2016).

In the wake of the Rana Plaza incident in 2013, the RMG industry in Bangladesh faced significant pressure from home and abroad to improve garment workers' occupational health, safety, and building structure (Rahman and Rahman 2020). Employee well-being also became a serious issue for discussion, with extended hours, low pay, stress, and fatigue found across the sector (Akhter et al. 2017a; Lerche 2012). The International Labour Organization, the Government of Bangladesh, and the Bangladesh Garment Manufacturers and Exporters Association employers signed a tripartite agreement to improve employee well-being that includes improving inadequate infrastructure, reducing inefficient and corrupt processes within the industry, and improving employment conditions and labour standards (Nuruzzaman 2013).

LITERATURE REVIEW

The focus of the research is on examining how external stakeholders can improve employee well-being. In the RMG sector, around 90 per cent of workers are low paid, poorly educated, and female workers are from rural areas of Bangladesh (Mohiuddin 1998). After the Rana Plaza disaster, the global safety governance bodies led the industry to ensure workplace safety; thus the involvement of external stakeholders such as ACCORD, ALLIANCE, buyers, international labour federation, NGOs, and trade unions (Akbar 2018). The research suggests that stakeholder pressure can improve well-being if supported by effective governance mechanisms with conditions that recognise and support employee voice (Kaufman 2015).

Employee well-being relates to employment, workplace, and employment conditions (Tov and Chan 2012). Poor well-being at work contributes to low commitment, depression, absence, and turnover (Kowalski and Loretto 2017). The employee well-being literature focuses on an individual's job satisfaction beyond pay and conditions but includes physical and mental health at work (Kowalski et al. 2015). Well-being is a total package of satisfaction, having a sense of control over life and having a purpose in life so that one can create the space for an individual to respond to various challenges that he or she needs to face and creates the path for achieving resources and capabilities (Fredrickson 2001).

Having mechanisms that support employee voice support well-being since employees can transmit grievances and identify conditions that impinge on safety and well-being (Myers et al. 2018; Yunus and Yamagata 2012). Without a voice, grievances and potential dangers in the workplace are unknown or can be ignored. Voice also supports participation which enhances self-esteem among workers in the organisation. Workplace communication processes and participation promote social networking for voice or reaching out to those who need to voice their concerns and interests (Lloyd 2007). In the RMG sector, voice has been absent, formally through trade unions and informally through workplace communications and feedback mechanisms. The vulnerability and harsh working conditions compound what these women workers face in the RMG sector (Akhter et al. 2017a; Yuan et al. 2015).

Moreover, as many workers have limited education, their ability to understand and comprehend workplace safety notices and formal communications from management is limited. Having limited numeracy and literacy skills can be a barrier for employees in the RMG sector to comprehend the importance of following and maintaining safety procedures (Brooks 2016; DIFE 2016). Having less formal school education can also impede applying employee rights in the workplaces, which means even if employee rights are violated, they do not have the ability or access to mechanisms to report violations or voice opposition to poor and dangerous working conditions (Brooks 2016).

The second component for protecting and enhancing employment conditions is governance mechanisms that ensure compliance with workplace safety regulations and minimum employment standards. The three dimensions of governance (transparency, accountability, and the rule of law) have been linked to the sustainability and viability of the RMG sector (Amin 2015). The previous disasters within the sector, including fires and building collapses, demonstrated that building and safety regulations had been ignored through a combination of corruption, limited enforcement, and ignorance (Huq et al. 2016). Without adequate governance mechanisms that support labour and safety regulations, employee safety and well-being and the international reputation of the RMG sector are compromised. The Organisation for Economic Co-operation and Development (OECD 2015, 2016) has argued that effective and enforceable governance of workplace safety and labour standards improves well-being and life satisfaction (Helliwell 2014). Key to effective governance is the role of public institutions and officials through developing transparent and participatory public policy practice, ensuring accountability for those who are responsible for safety and labour standards, removing corruption, and increasing engagement with key stakeholders (OECD 2015).

Engagement with and pressure from key stakeholders is the critical process that has driven improved workplace safety and labour conditions in the RMG sector. Stakeholder theory (Freeman 1984) suggests that effective and engaging relationships between the stakeholders are crucial for the long-term sustainability of organisations. Stakeholder theory moves beyond the narrow view of organisations as defined by the interest of owners and their representatives, as captured by shareholder value (Winkler 2014). Stakeholder theory recognises that organisations represent a coalition of interest or internal stakeholders (such as shareholders, employees, suppliers, and consumers) and external to the organisation such as government, community organisations, and regulatory agencies (Pinto 2017). Additionally, many organisations such as public-sector agencies and NGOs have multiple and diverse stakeholder structures. What is relevant for the RMG sector was that following the publicised disasters that afflicted the industry, it was a range of stakeholders, within and outside of RMG businesses, and within and external to Bangladesh, that applied direct pressure to the Government of Bangladesh and to the RMG sector to improve workplace safety and employee conditions (Huq et al. 2016).

The lens of the stakeholder theory is relevant to this chapter to help explain how powerful external stakeholder groups may influence employee well-being strategies of the RMGs. This research considers how influential stakeholders of the RMGs in Bangladesh (ALLIANCE, ACCORD, buyers, union members, including government, NGOs, and consumer and activist groups) may pressure the apparel industry sector to ensure well-being responsibilities through effective governance initiatives and demonstrate its transparency, the rule of law, and participation in society. Thus, pressure from stakeholders who can exercise power and authority over RMG suppliers can be a source of improved employee well-being.

THE RESEARCH PROCESS

The qualitative phase of the study included one-to-one, in-depth telephone interviews with 14 RMG managers, using semi-structured questions. The reason for selecting managers is that they are responsible for developing and implementing formal policies, procedures, and strategies. They are responsible for employee supervision, complying with workplace legislation and other agreements and mechanisms that govern the workplace. Fourteen managers of the three RMG factories in Dhaka were interviewed, as they are responsible for workplace conditions and enforcement of regulations. The interviews were conducted by phone and were semi-structured. For reasons of access and confidentiality, the interviews could not be conducted at the workplace.

The RMG managers included floor managers, human resource managers, compliance managers, and general managers responsible for the planning, development, implementation, and monitoring of programs and policies that impact the operations of the factories, including workplace, employee, and safety management. Thus, the interviews with the managers provided detailed insights into the practice and implementation of governance mechanisms and well-being practices post-Rana Plaza.

The interview instrument was developed to address the research questions and draw on the managers' experience in responding to the post-Rana Plaza regulations imposed on factories and workplaces. The interview protocol was pre-tested to check the suitability of the interview questions. The pre-test of the qualitative phase ensured the alignment of the study's research questions, the wording of the questions, and, above all, the time management of the interview protocol (Castillo-Montoya 2016). The research process was subject to an ethical review and clearance from the human ethics committee of RMIT University.

The interviews were recorded and transcribed into English. The transcriptions were analysed to identify emerging themes that were relevant to answering the research questions. Interview transcriptions were examined line by line during coding and categorised to identify contradictions and consistency (Strauss and Corbin 1998). Transcribed data initially were filed and indexed, ready for using NVivo qualitative analysis. Principal codes related to each of the research questions were identified and allocated by the researchers just as in manual analysis. However, the software allows for automated indexing, searching, and creating sub-codes in the form of "trees". This means that a large and complex dataset can be more readily organised and analysed. NVivo generated new themes through its categorising system, bringing order to the primary data (Welsh 2002). Clustering codes generated emerging themes into more general categories. Emergent categories were then reconstructed through analysis to generate more or develop those already listed (Johnson et al. 2007). The NVivo process thus helped develop a broader understanding of the empirical context and helped determine emergent themes. When main themes and sub-themes were identified, the research turned to thematic coding.

FINDINGS

The broad findings of the research indicated that employment conditions had improved post-2013, especially in terms of legislated wage increases and improvements in factory safety. Since 2013, the minimum wage for factory workers had increased from US$39/month to US$66.49 (5,300 Tk) with an increase of 76.67 per cent in the wake of the Rana Plaza tragedy (Elahi et al. 2019; Farhana et al. 2015). A manager commented:

> Although the salary has increased a little bit after 2013, it is not enough. Dhaka is an expensive city. The salary of the workers is low. However, there is another problem. If the workers' salary increases, then the product will be expensive, and then the buyers will go to other cheap countries. There is enormous competition. India wants to beat us. It is a challenge to be happy with this low salary. A low salary is also the primary reason workers become unhappy and call for strikes.

Concerning governance, the managers indicated that regulations had tightened and that factory conditions were regularly audited. However, due to compliance costs and the ability to evade regulations, many regulations were either only partially met or ignored. One factory manager commented:

> The issue to comply did not exist even three years ago. At that moment, I faced challenges from three or four sides while changing the compensation structure and designing some issues related to benefits ... It was a challenge that my employee would either accept or reject the payment structure when the new structure would be implemented. My building had no electrical compliance. In this case, obtaining a license from the government, going according to government procedures, to get a result was also a challenge for me.

The transition of RMG industries from non-compliance to compliance with regulations was a challenge for owners and managers (Haque and Azmat 2015; Rahim 2012). The physical transformation after 2013 of the RMG industries after years of neglect by owners of buildings and garment enterprises previously not held accountable for ensuring safe workplaces was a difficult one to make. However, the natural barrier was to shift from non-compliance to compliance. Non-compliance is also a significant issue targeted by the corporate social responsibility programs of international buyers (Haque and Azmat 2015; Huq et al. 2014).

Compliance with external regulations often involves coaching workers to provide auditors with information suggesting conformity with regulations: "workers are trained up in such a way so when the buyers or auditors come and inquire about salary or benefit the workers can give positive feedback as people like us rehearse them". This quote indicates that following and strictly practising legal provision is the top priority of the external stakeholder of the RMGs, which ensures the overall well-being of the employees. However, employees and managers are trained to falsify or provide incomplete information to inspectors. Due to buyer pressure, however, workplace safety has improved:

> Regarding safety, our company is far ahead. Our fire safety doors at the workplace are costly and even in 1400 degree Celsius; it does not melt in 48–72 hours so that fire does not transfer one floor or one room to the other. Almost 80 per cent of work is done putting on safety doors, which is very expensive. The audit teams come and do the risk assessment and suggestions, and accordingly, we work. The buyers' group ensure that there are more than two exit doors on every floor or workplace. So, if 100/200 workers are working, then our factory can evacuate all the workers within 5 minutes. Our stairways are very wide so that 4–5 people can walk down shoulder to shoulder.

In terms of consultation, all managers suggested that employee grievance procedures had improved, mainly through suggestion boxes and immediate managers, but without trade union involvement. Workplace Consultative Committees was one of the developments across the industry post-Rana Plaza. These were intended to identify plant and workforce problems, especially around occupational health and safety. However, the committees' effectiveness was questioned by one manager who saw it as endorsing prior decisions made by management. A manager commented: "I know at the junior (management) level, there is no discussion, and it does not matter whether he is a corporate guy or a worker. Decisions are imposed. This is a fact. Decisions are always top-down."

CONCLUSIONS

Following the 2013 Rana Plaza disaster, the RMG sector in Bangladesh was under pressure from international external stakeholders to improve workplace safety and working conditions in the sector. A series of reforms and audit processes were implemented to improve safety and working conditions. This chapter reported on the views of frontline managers in three plants located in Dhaka regarding the changes in working conditions and the ongoing challenges and obstacles to improvements. Overall, there have been improvements to safety and working conditions, such as wages, however, there is still evidence of corruption and evasion of new codes governing safety. Moreover, long hours of work, evening work, intensification of work, and fatigue remain a challenge to workplace safety.

RESEARCH FIELD TIPS

Since the research was focused on the management response to the changes in legislation governing RMG factories, accessing participants was difficult.

Social media was used to identify managerial groups in the RMG sector, and from initial contacts, a snowball technique was used to identify further participants. The researcher was familiar with the national context and fluent in Bengali. Interviews were conducted off site to ensure confidentiality and to protect the identity of informants. Through personal contacts through social networking sites, such as Facebook (Zikmund et al. 2013), the researcher was introduced to various RMG groups, manager groups, legal groups, and NGOs associated with RMGs. Snowball sampling requires researchers to initially select a few research participants and ask them if they know others who might meet the criteria of the research sample and might be interested in participating (Liamputtong 2006).

By becoming a member of various RMG managers' Facebook groups, the researcher found an opportunity to interact with employers or managers from various levels of the RMG sector who had different types of work experiences (Zikmund et al. 2013). Furthermore, when the researcher got the opportunity to interact with employers or managers through social network sites, they functioned like an online focus group or interview (Zikmund et al. 2013). Moreover, these managers whom the researcher got to know from Facebook interaction provided extensive contextual information on labour law, its amendments, and practicality in actual work experiences in the RMG sector that became an essential resource for the study.

REFERENCES

Ahmed, F.Z., Greenleaf, A. and Sacks, A. (2014), The paradox of export growth in areas of weak governance: The case of the readymade garment sector in Bangladesh, *World Development*, 56, pp. 258–271.

Akbar, S. (2018), Responsibility and accountability for workplace safety in the Bangladesh garments industry. Unpublished PhD thesis, RMIT University, Melbourne.

Akhter, S., Rutherford, S. and Chu, C. (2017a), What makes pregnant workers sick: Why, when, where and how? An exploratory study in the ready-made garment industry in Bangladesh. *Reproductive Health*, 14(1), pp. 1–9.

Akhter, S., Rutherford, S., Kumkum, F.A., Bromwich, D., Anwar, I., Rahman, A. and Chu, C. (2017b), Work, gender roles, and health: Neglected mental health issues among female workers in the ready-made garment industry in Bangladesh. *International Journal of Women's Health*, 9, p. 571.

Al Bhadily, M. (2015), Does the Bangladesh Accord on Building and Fire Safety provide a sustainable protection to ready-made garment workers? *Review of Integrative Business and Economics Research*, 4(4), pp. 158–177.

Amin, K.M. (2015), The ready-made garments (RMG) sector of Bangladesh: Exploring sustainability dimensions. Doctoral dissertation, BRAC University.

Ansary, M.A. and Barua, U. (2015), Workplace safety compliance of RMG industry in Bangladesh: Structural assessment of RMG factory buildings. *International Journal of Disaster Risk Reduction*, 14, pp. 424–437.

Asian Development Bank Report (2013), Bangladesh quarterly economic update. Dhaka.

Bajaj, V. (2010), Bangladesh, with low pay, moves in on China. *New York Times*, 16.

Baumann-Pauly, D., Labowitz, S. and Banerjee, N. (2015), Closing governance gaps in Bangladesh's garment industry: The power and limitations of private governance schemes, SSRN 2577535.

Boudreau, L., Heath, R. and McCormick, T. (2018), Migrants, information, and working conditions in Bangladeshi garment factories. IG Centre. www.theigc.org/wp-content/uploads/2018/06/Boudreau-et-al-2018-Working-paper.pdf

Brooks, M.L. (2016), Triangulating a sustainable safety culture in the readymade garment industry of Bangladesh. Walden Dissertations and Doctoral Studies Collection.

Castillo-Montoya, M. (2016), Preparing for interview research: The interview protocol refinement framework. *The Qualitative Report*, 21(5), pp. 811–831.

DIFE (Department for Inspection for Factories and Establishments) (2016), Status of building assessment. Dhaka. http://database.dife.gov.bd

Elahi, S., Hosen, M.D. and Nizam, M.E.H. (2019), Comparative analysis in RMG industries before and after Rana Plaza incident in Bangladesh. *Journal of Textile Engineering Fashion Technology*, 5(4), pp. 202–211.

Farhana, K., Syduzzaman, M., and Munir, M.S. (2015), Present status of workers in ready-made garments industries in Bangladesh. *European Scientific Journal*, 11(7).

Fredrickson, B.L. (2001), The role of positive emotions in positive psychology: The broaden-and-build theory of positive emotions. *American Psychologist*, 56(3), pp. 218–226.

Freeman, R.E. (1984), *Strategic Management: A Stakeholder Perspective*. Boston, MA: Pitman.

Haque, M.Z. and Azmat, F. (2015), Corporate social responsibility, economic globalisation and developing countries: A case study of the ready-made garments industry in Bangladesh. *Sustainability Accounting, Management and Policy Journal*, 6(2), pp. 166–189.

Helliwell, J.F. (2014), How can subjective well-being be improved? In F. Huppert (Ed.), *Well-Being: A Complete Reference Guide* (pp. 1–21). Chichester: Wiley.

Human Rights Watch (2015), Whoever raises their head suffers the most: Workers' rights in Bangladesh's garment factories. www.hrw.org/report/2015/04/22/whoever-raises-their-head-suffers-most/workers-rights-bangladeshs-garment

Huq, A.F., Stevenson, M. and Zorzini, M. (2014), Social sustainability in developing country suppliers: An exploratory study in the ready made garments industry of Bangladesh. *International Journal of Operations and Production Management*, 34(5), pp. 610–638.

Huq, A.F., Chowdhury, I.N. and Klassen, R.D. (2016), Social management capabilities of multinational buying firms and their emerging market suppliers: An exploratory study of the clothing industry. *Journal of Operations Management*, 46, pp. 19–37.

Islam, M.S., Rakib, M.A. and Adnan, A. (2016), Ready-made garments sector of Bangladesh: Its contribution and challenges towards development. *Journal of Asian Development Studies*, 5(2).

Johnson, R.B., Onwuegbuzie, A.J. and Turner, L.A. (2007), Toward a definition of mixed methods research. *Journal of Mixed Methods Research*, 1(2), pp. 112–133.

Kaufman, B.E. (2015), Theorising determinants of employee voice: An integrative model across disciplines and levels of analysis. *Human Resource Management Journal*, 25(1), pp. 19–40.

Khan, M.E., Townsend, J.W. and D'Costa, S. (2002), Behind closed doors: A qualitative study of sexual behaviour of married women in Bangladesh. *Culture, Health and Sexuality*, 4(2), pp. 237–256.

Khan, M.R.I. and Wichterich, C. (2015), Safety and labour conditions: The accord and the national tripartite plan of action for the garment industry of Bangladesh. Global Labour University Working Paper, 38.

Khan, Z. (2018), Transnational labour governance: A critical review of proposals for linkage through the lens of the Rana Plaza collapse in Bangladesh. *Canadian Journal of Law and Society/La Revue Canadienne Droit et Société*, 33(2), pp. 177–197.

Kowalski, T. and Loretto, W. (2017), Well-being and HRM in the changing workplace. *International Journal of Human Resource Management*, 28(16), 2229–2255.

Kowalski, T., Loretto, W. and Redman, T. (2015), Special Issue of *International Journal of Human Resource Management*: Well-Being and HRM in the Changing Workplace.

Lerche, L. (2012), *Quantitative Methods*. Amsterdam: Elsevier.

Liamputtong, P. (2006), *Researching the Vulnerable: A Guide to Sensitive Research Methods*. London: Sage.

Lloyd, C.B. (2007), *World Development Report 2007: Development and the Next Generation*. Washington, DC: World Bank.

Mahmud, S., Mahmud, R. and Jahan, M.N. (2018), Health issues of female garment workers: evidence From Bangladesh. *Journal of Population and Social Studies*, 26(3), pp. 181–194.

Mohiuddin, G.M. (1998), Requirement of technical competence in RMG industry in the open market of 2005. Keynote paper at BATEXPO, 98, BGMEA, Dhaka, 16–18 October.

Mondal, L.K. (2020), From dispossession to surplus production: A theory of capitalist accumulation in neoliberal Bangladesh. Doctoral dissertation, Virginia Tech.

Mujeri, M.K. and Mujeri, N. (2021), *Structural Transformation of Bangladesh Economy: A South Asian Perspective*. New York: Springer Nature.

Myers, F., Dickie, E. and Taulbut, M. (2018), A rapid evidence review: Employee voice and mental well-being, Edinburgh: NHS Health Scotland.

Nuruzzaman, M. (2013), Improving competitiveness of ready-made garment (RMG) industry of Bangladesh-Analysis of supply chains. Thesis, Curtin University.

OECD (2015), *Universal Basic Skills: What Countries Stand to Gain*. Paris: OECD Publishing.

OECD (2016), *The Governance of Inclusive Growth*. Paris: OECD Publishing.

Pinto, J. (2017), A multifocal framework for developing intentionally sustainable organisations. *Current Opinion in Environmental Sustainability*, 28, pp. 17–23.

Rahim, M.M. (2012), Legal regulation of corporate social responsibility: Evidence from Bangladesh. *Common Law World Review*, 41(2), pp. 97–133.

Rahman, P.M.M., Matsui, N. and Ikemoto, Y. (2013), *Dynamics of Poverty in Rural Bangladesh*. New York: Springer.

Rahman, S. and Rahman, K.M. (2020), Multi-actor initiatives after Rana Plaza: Factory managers' views. *Development and Change*, 51(5), pp. 1331–1359.

Sharon, A.A. (2015), Workers' Safety in Bangladeshi Readymade Garments Industry. Laurea University of Applied Sciences: Laurea Otaniemi.

Strauss, A. and Corbin, J. (1998), *Basics of Qualitative Research Techniques*. Thousand Oaks, CA: Sage.

Tanha, M., Michelson, G., Chowdhury, M. and Castka, P. (2021), Organisational responses and varieties of employee safety in the shipbreaking industry in Bangladesh. *Journal of Safety Research*, 80, pp. 14–26.

The Guardian (2013), Bangladesh factory collapse blamed on swampy ground and heavy machinery. www.theguardian.com/world/2013/may/23/bangladesh-factory -collapse-rana-plaza

Tov, W. and Chan, D. (2012), The importance of employee well-being. *Business Times*, Singapore Management University, September 25, 14–21.

Wang, C. (2018), The problems and reforms of labour relations since the implementation of labour contract law. Working paper.

Welsh, E. (2002), Dealing with data: Using NVivo in the qualitative data analysis process. *Forum Qualitative Sozialforschung/Forum: Qualitative Social Research*, 3(2).

Winkler, A.L. (2014), An exploration of broad employee ownership and responsible stakeholder management in B corporations. Doctoral dissertation, Rutgers University-Graduate School-New Brunswick.

Yuan, T., Zhang, T. and Han, Z. (2015), Placental vascularisation alterations in hypertensive disorders complicating pregnancy (HDCP) and small for gestational age with HDCP using three-dimensional power Doppler in a prospective case-control study. *BMC Pregnancy and Childbirth*, 15(1), p. 240.

Yunus, M. and Yamagata, T. (2012), The garment industry in Bangladesh: Dynamics of the garment industry in low-income countries: Experience of Asia and Africa. Interim report. www.iiav.nl/epublications/2002/Womens_employment_in_the _textile_manufacturing_sectors_of_Bangladesh_and_Morocco.pdf

Zikmund, W.G., Babin, B.J., Carr, J.C. and Griffin, M. (2013), Business Research Methods. Cengage Learning Australia.

USEFUL WEB RESOURCES

Clean clothes Campaign: Rana Plana, https://cleanclothes.org/campaigns/past/rana -plaza

International Labour Organization (2015), Bangladesh Rana Plaza compensation scheme: Technical report on the scheme design and operationalisation, and lessons learnt, www.ilo.org/wcmsp5/groups/public/---ed_protect/--- soc_sec/documents/publication/wcms_431795.pdf

International Labour Organization (2019), Bangladesh move towards employment injury insurance: The legacy of Rana Plaza, Report, www.ilo.org/wcmsp5/groups/public/---ed_emp/documents/publication/wcms_632364.pdf

Odhikar, Broken dreams: A report on the Rana Plana collapse, http://odhikar.org/broken-dreams-a-report-on-the-rana-plaza-collapse-2

Transparency International (2018), Bangladesh, Report, www.ti-bangladesh.org/beta3/index.php/en/

10. Challenges of conducting equity research in the field: the example of Bhutan

Mahan Poorhosseinzadeh and Glenda Strachan

INTRODUCTION

The representation of women in Bhutan's professional workforce continues to increase but still they remain underrepresented as managers and professionals and technical workers. As a similar situation exists in Australia, we were eager to examine the obstacles to women's career advancement in Bhutan and whether there were similarities with the Australian context. The opportunity to research gender equality in Bhutan arose when in 2018 a group of Bhutanese managers (men and women) attended Griffith University to undertake a three-week Australia Awards South and West Asia Short Course Award on Evaluating Workforce Learning and Development Initiatives. The program was funded by the Australian Government Department of Foreign Affairs and Trade and gender, diversity and social inclusion were its primary focus. We designed and delivered the diversity program which included a final component which was delivered in Bhutan. One of the main requirements of the program was the inclusion of a Gender and Social Inclusion Specialist which was as a result of the Bhutanese government looking to strengthen the technical and advisory capacity of the Gender Experts Group through the completion of courses and training (National Gender Equality Policy, 2019). Therefore, we attended most of the workshops to ensure that the gender perspective and relevant gender theories were embedded in the content. We delivered sessions specifically targeting gender mainstreaming including a workshop on women's career progression in Australia which asked the participants to compare this to the transition of women to management positions in Bhutan. One of the authors was a constant contact of the group in Australia while the other travelled to Bhutan to participate in the course there. We established a rapport with the participants while they were in Australia and their enthusiastic response to our discussions resulted in extending our research on gender equity to examine the careers of managers and professional women in Bhutan. In particular, we explored the obstacles to women's career advancement. We conducted interviews with the participants while they were in Australia and followed through in Bhutan where the participants provided us with further contacts with managers in Bhutan's capital Thimpu. Our participants were very supportive and enthusiastic about our research. When visiting Bhutan, one of the authors met with several nationally recognised women who had been prominent in the development of women's rights. They were extremely supportive of our project because of the limited amount of research into gender equity which had been conducted in Bhutan.

In conducting our research in Bhutan, we used similar questions to those developed for our Australian study, but we were immediately confronted with a challenge. The research questions we had developed, focused on gender equity and gender discrimination, did not elicit answers from our participants in Bhutan as readily as we expected and compared with our experience in Australia. Our interviewees – both women and men – responded that they did not believe gender discrimination existed in Bhutan or their organisation. We would have gained limited insights into gender equity and gender discrimination in Bhutan if we had not probed further. Only after additional questions and examples from the Australian context were some interviewees able to expand on the situation in Bhutan.

This raises interesting questions for cross-cultural research. Do all research framing/questions/issues translate into a different cultural context? Is it not just that Bhutanese culture is different but that concepts such as gender equity are less widespread, and the development of research questions requires more consideration? Possibly it is not only related to the question of gender research but also a cultural issue. The questions we reflected on included: Can we as researchers make a meaningful contribution to examining gender equity in Bhutan? Can we be "cultural interpreters"? In this discussion, we want to emphasise the "analytical lens and subjective role of researchers rather than factual/spatial levels of analysis" (Cooke, 2018, p. 5) because "a researcher's cognitive understanding of what they see" underpins the conceptualisation and interpretation of the data (Cooke, 2018, p. 5). We conclude in this chapter that it is not just that Bhutanese culture is different but that concepts such as gender equity are less widespread and so the development of research questions needs to understand and take this into consideration. Therefore, it is not only a gender issue and a cultural issue but also an issue of awareness. Our experience undertaking cross-cultural research in Bhutan was extremely rewarding but also prompted us to reflect on our position as researchers, issues we discuss in this chapter. Particularly, it explores challenges associated with conducting cultur-

Table 10.1   2021 Gender Gap Index

Rank out of 156	Bhutan	India	Bangladesh	Nepal	Pakistan	Sri Lanka
Overall rank	130	140	65	106	153	116
Economic participation	130	151	147	107	152	132
Education	117	114	121	134	144	88
Health	131	155	134	113	153	30
Political empowerment	137	51	7	61	98	90

Source: World Economic Forum (2021).

ally grounded equity research. We highlight that the overriding challenges are present across all dimensions of equity research.

LITERATURE REVIEW: GENDER IN THE CONTEXT OF SOUTH ASIA

The pattern of gender inequalities varies across time and space with differences and similarities both between and within nations which are continually changing. South Asian countries' unique traditions, beliefs, work settings and organisational practices present diverse and distinctive gender issues. The 2021 Gender Gap Index examines a range of pertinent national statistics and places Bhutan at 130 out of 156 countries (World Economic Forum, 2021). In comparison, Australia ranks 50, the United Kingdom 23, New Zealand 4 and Iceland 1. Table 10.1 shows a breakdown of the scores for South Asian countries. While Bhutan shares similar rankings with many of these countries, it is out of step when it comes to the category of political empowerment which measures the participation of women in parliament. Bhutan held its first democratic parliamentary elections in 2007 and in 2021 eight out of 47 members of the National Assembly were women (National Assembly of Bhutan, 2021).

Women in South Asia are recorded as having low labour force participation, with many women contributing economically in the rural and unorganised sectors of work and as unpaid family members contributing to family enterprises. Like most countries, the formal labour markets are characterised by vertical and horizontal segregation and lower earnings for women. Women's representation in trade unions and policy-making levels of government is low and this raises concerns about the importance given to these issues at the national level. The basic legislative framework of equal employment opportunity laws exists across South Asia and, indeed, India was the first country in 1950 to introduce reserved places in employment for the most disadvantaged castes and tribes and name this affirmative action. As occurs in most of the literature on gender equity, commentators focus on the gap between policy and practice and there remains a great variety between the outcomes for women in different regions, industries and organisations (Strachan et al., 2015).

Women and Work in Bhutan

Bhutan is a Himalayan country geographically positioned between India and China. Historically a remote kingdom, it has never been ruled by a colonial power and has been able to preserve its own identity with a unique culture distinct from its neighbour India (Strachan et al., 2015). The country is predominantly Buddhist, the religion of approximately three-quarters of the population, with its roots as a matriarchal society, while Hinduism predominates in some geographical regions. The country has been a constitutional monarchy since 2008. In 2020, Bhutan's population was 771,608 (Bhutan Population, 2020) with almost two-thirds living in rural areas, predominantly in the broad river valleys (Rinzin et al., 2007).

The majority of the rural population are subsistence farmers (Choiden, 2016) and the majority of women work in the primary sector of the economy, largely on family farms and in cottage industries. Since 2002, the manufacturing, mining, hydropower generation and construction industries have grown but the economy remains dependent on agriculture and forestry (Choiden, 2016). Women's labour force participation is increasing as they transition into the non-rural workforce, with many employed as doctors, engineers, pilots and in other professions (Wangdi, 2019), but women still form the largest group of workers in agriculture. Despite their increasing representation in the professional workforce, women remain underrepresented as managers, professionals and technical workers (Choiden, 2016).

Buddhism's influence in Bhutan is significant, impacting both its culture and economic philosophy. The current national policy is based on the Gross National Happiness (GNH) Index which emphasises social welfare (Wangdi, 2019) and is designed to measure the collective happiness and well-being of the Bhutanese people (National Commission for Women and Children, 2021). Following the establishment of the GNH Index, Bhutan achieved a reduction in poverty and improvement in education, justice, basic health, gender equality and access to clean water and sanitation.

The Constitution of the Kingdom of Bhutan 2008 provides an overarching framework and foundation within which gender equality is enshrined (National Gender Equality Policy, 2019). An integral part of this governance model is policies that promote women's rights, including the provision of child day-care facilities in urban areas, maternity and paternity leave, the provision of flexible work practices to suit breast-feeding mothers and measures that encourage the retention of women in higher levels of education (National Gender Equality Policy, 2019). According to the National Commission for

Women and Children (NCWC), however, "women continue to shoulder the burden of home, care-work and employment" and "the persistence of gender stereotypes" remains (National Gender Equality Policy, 2019). As a result, the NCWC engaged with business associations to design a Gender Equality Policy to facilitate women's representation in non-traditional positions and senior management (Choiden, 2016). In 2018, the Royal Civil Service Commission developed a Five-Year Plan to promote women in leadership positions. As part of this plan, they developed two key performance indicators: "number of interventions to promote women in leadership positions in the civil service" and "number of gender interventions in the civil service" (National Gender Equality Policy, 2019, p. 3). Following Bhutan Civil Service Rules and Regulations (2018), the NCWC adapted different strategies to enhance women's participation in leadership roles (National Gender Equality Policy, 2019). As can be seen, policy discussions around gender equity are relatively recent in Bhutan. In addition, in this study the Department of Foreign Affairs and Trade (the program sponsor) has been instrumental in engendering change (in individual consciousness and actions, in economic standards, in politico-social structures and in cultural practices).

METHODOLOGY

Research Process

Both researchers are experienced in conducting research on gender and diversity in numerous Australian organisations. In our research in Bhutan, we opted for semi-structured interviews and participant observations with the researcher taking comprehensive field notes. Our position is that "Doing qualitative field studies is not simply empirical but a profoundly theoretical activity" (Ahrens and Chapman, 2006, p. 299), as humans invent the concepts, models and patterns to make sense of experiences, and we persistently change these constructions through the light of new knowledge (Schwandt, 2000). A critical social constructivist approach tries to understand the social constructed nature of reality (Denzin and Lincoln, 2000). This approach argues that knowledge is not something that researchers can easily describe or explain, rather it is viewed as socially constructed through interactions and language (Schwandt, 2000; Tracy, 2013).

Using the tools of institutional ethnography we aimed to observe managers in Bhutan as members of a society to uncover the culture shared within the broader social context (Creswell, 2014). In this way, Geertz (1983) describes researchers as "cultural interpreters" who provide vivid descriptions that reveal beliefs, values and action in the society and organisation. Consequently, through the observation we aim to develop a better understanding of the "reality" of Bhutan's workplaces/organisations as socially constructed through the interaction of social and national beliefs, values and actions in the broader society.

We recognise that an interview is a social event (Atkinson and Hammersley, 1998), displays cultural particulars (Silverman, 2013) and is determined by discursive relations and situatedness. The researcher influences the data collection and analysis (Ting-Toomey and Dorjee, 2018) with the interviewee/s also participating in the knowledge-building activity. Interviewees are informed by a knowledge of social sub-systems operative in that culture, but constant adaptations of the interview process are needed to suit each individual situation in relation to the participants' subjectivities. Objectivity, implying neutrality and detachment, is not possible on the part of the interviewer or the interviewee (Lincoln and Guba, 1985). Face-to-face responses are not simply given to the questions, but reflect the interplay between how participants perceive the researcher posing those questions and themselves in that particular social context. Understandably, the implications of the participants' (interviewee/interviewer) subjectivities in intercultural interviewing gain more complexity because of this additional factor of "communicating across cultures" (Ting-Toomey and Dorjee, 2018).

Appreciation of the cultural context was developed through our immersion in the literature on Bhutan, as well as discussions with the course participants during the delivery of the course. Our contact with the participants continued after they had left Australia through social media and a WhatsApp group. This preparation and experience contributed to building a close connection and rapport. The importance of building a relationship with interview participants is critical for data collection and analysis (Owen-Smith and Coast, 2017) as is creating "a good setting that will encourage a trusting, comfortable and secure climate" (Basch, 1987, p. 433). As interviewing is a multi-phase activity and involves interacting in many ways, an understanding of the interviewees' culture by the interviewer is important. As researchers, we could observe the participants taking notes at different stages during the program. This assisted with the interpretation of the data as we were better positioned because of our knowledge of the relevant patterns of social interaction required for gaining access and making meaning. It would be ideal to include a Bhutanese scholar as part of the research team, however, in this case, the participants told us to go ahead and undertake the research by ourselves. A couple of participants are willing to review our research draft and so we gain their involvement in this way. This is one of many examples where researchers in the field have to be flexible.

Research Methods in the Bhutan Project

In Australia we built relationships with the Bhutanese participants and through them, when visiting Bhutan for the post-program component, we were able to approach numerous senior managers in the private and public sectors and conduct semi-structured interviews. Some of these interviewees were women who were instrumental in getting gender issues on the government agenda and were well versed in the issues. In total, 27 semi-structured interviews were conducted with Bhutanese male and female participants from both public and private sectors.

This chapter is mainly focused on the process of the research (see Figure 10.1) and researchers' reflections and experience in this process. The interviews were conducted in English and took approximately one hour. They were recorded and transcribed, and the information gathered from the interviews was de-identified with each participant assigned a pseudonym. The Bhutan field notes were a significant part of the data analysis as they captured the researchers' feelings and thoughts before and after conducting interviews. Initially, primary cycle coding was undertaken, followed by secondary cycle coding or "focused coding" where the research team examined the primary codes and started organising and categorising the data into interpretive concepts. This was followed by "thematic coding" which includes interpreting the codes based on the theories used (Tracy, 2013). By being conscious of the need to be reflexive, "researchers focused on representing the views of the participants as authentically as possible, while at the same time responding to their own issues, feelings, and experiences" (Holgate et al., 2006, p. 322).

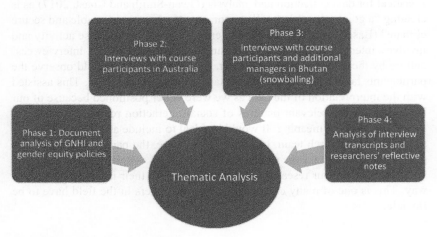

Figure 10.1   Research process

Reflections on the Research Methods

Researchers' field notes were a significant part of their data analysis. The field notes captured their feelings and thoughts before and after conducting each interview which had been informed by spending three weeks with these groups during the short course in Australia and then two weeks visiting in Bhutan. By being conscious of the need to be reflexive, researchers focused on representing the views of the participants as authentically as possible, while at the same time responding to their own issues, feelings and experiences (Holgate et al., 2006, p. 322). Ramazanoglu and Holland (2002) identify and differentiate reflexivity as an act of critical consciousness located in the subjectivity of the researcher, since it involves "reflecting critically on the consequences of your presence in the research process" (Ramazanoglu and Holland, 2002, p. 158). As a result, the researcher's acknowledgement of their standpoint in the project was a crucial aspect of this research (Holgate et al., 2006; Merriam et al., 2001). This is an important methodological and theoretical standpoint (Yuval-Davis, 2012) and it doesn't mean that researchers do not trace their unconscious research output (Wickramasinghe, 2009).

The researchers also needed to be flexible in their approach. As is common for research in the field, opportunities arise and at other times some ways of proceeding with the research are not possible. In this research on Bhutan, the researchers had to make some adjustments to the questions by adding further probing questions. Participants suggested that other managers would be interested in becoming interviewees, so these individuals were approached, thus widening the pool of participants via a snowballing approach. A variation to the Ethics Clearance was gained to enable this.

The research team from Australia asked several of the participants who were knowledgeable about women and work issues in Bhutan if they would like to be part of the research team. They all declined, saying they were pleased the Australian researchers were undertaking this work. A couple of them said that they would be happy to peruse drafts of the work, and these offers would be followed up. This is another example of the flexibility needed in field research. The ideal might be to have a cross-country team of researchers, but this is not always achievable.

FINDINGS

Key Learning about Bhutanese Participants

After interacting with the managers from Bhutan in Australia for three weeks, one member of the research team conducted interviews in Bhutan. Our experience interviewing the Bhutanese participants in Bhutan was different to conducting interviews with the Bhutanese participants in Australia. Almost all the Bhutanese participants were supportive of the research and were open to discussing gender equality issues during the interviews. Through the qualitative interviews in Bhutan, we became conscious of the different elements of Bhutan's culture that had been unknown to us. The researcher who went to Bhutan was overcome by the difference in culture. Coming from Australia where economic goals trump other social goals in employment, Bhutan felt different. Economic goals did not seem to subsume all else as an emphasis on social well-being and the preservation of culture were important. We hypothesised that the approaches to supporting women's employment and family life come in part from this emphasis on social well-being.

Prior to completing the Australian course, male and female participants responded in ways similar to the senior male manager interviewed in Bhutan. Gender issues rarely came up in the discussion and even after prompting many claimed that there were no gender issues in Bhutan and they had a very egalitarian/matriarchal society.

The following give some insight into how, without prompting, gender issues were not raised. This participant was a male senior manager in the private sector, interviewed in Bhutan, who had not participated in the Australian course but was aware that gender was a focus for us. Despite their brief knowledge of the research focus, most of the interviewees did not refer to any gender issues unless prompted by a question.

> *Interviewer*: As you have seen in the information sheet, our focus in this study is about women's career progression, so I wondered about your thoughts on women's career progression and women getting to management, whether there is any difference in their careers to those of men?
> *Participant*: Bhutan is one nation where gender bias or gender equality and inequality is not there. We consider, as long as he or she is capable, the place, or the position is open for all. Of course, again in saying that doesn't mean that we would employ a woman for a job that requires a little bit of more of … heavy manual work otherwise there is no bar, no restriction at all.

In contrast, and as expected, another participant (a female manager working for NCWC in Bhutan), focused on gender issues from the beginning of the interview without any prompting. This participant was very knowledgeable about gender issues in Bhutan and in other countries.

> *Interviewer*: Can you tell me about the societal and cultural expectations of women in Bhutan?
> *Participant*: Culturally what Bhutanese expect of women is … they expect women to take care of the children, expect the food to be ready when the husband and the kids come back from school and office, wash their clothes, be socially involved in all the family activities and gatherings. Just be a good wife, that is what is culturally

expected. Also culturally it is also expected that, say in the family, if you live in a family with your husband, your mother and your father and everybody, you are expected to serve your husband and do the cooking and everything. If you find a husband cooking and things like that, people don't say anything of course but ... people say, it does not look good when your husband is cooking, especially if it is in front of his mother or the older people say, grandparents, they say, it doesn't look good, things like that. It still happens in my family that when me and my husband go to our grandparents' house which is in another district of Bhutan. So, they always tell my husband to sit above or to eat or they ask me to serve for my husband. It is still there in small ways, culturally. Socially I think it's, I think people are now viewing women at par with the men, they view what men can do they can do as well, socially. But culturally, that cultural stigma is still there that women are supposed to be seen as home makers.

Some interviewees reflected on the differences in culture and attitudes towards women where religion was a factor, especially comparing the regions where Hinduism predominates compared to those regions of Bhutan and in its national policies influenced by Buddhism. For example, one of the participants (male manager, public sector, from Southern Bhutan), agreed with the attitudes towards women in families in some regions of Bhutan:

> The case of southern and some parts of the middle central region of the country, the role women play in society is very minimal, just normal house chores and then agricultural work which does not involve hard labour. ... Most of the districts and the administrative blocs of the country are isolated and far flung and then they do not have any *modern* concepts and ideas inherited. So, I still feel that there is the dominance of the societal belief that women are inferior.
>
> For women still in those villages ... like where I belong ... they perform the basic roles of the household and family care. Yes, there is a policy in which the primary level of education is compulsory for both genders and ... most of the ... males and females complete class 12. Then after that, by the time they have to go to college ... the people in the villages cannot afford to pay for the children and then in the Hindu tradition ... it is seen as women will marry and they will be with ... the husband. So, the husband's parents will take care of her. ... Most of the parents do not put their resources and capital into educating their daughters.

The influence of GNH policies on gender equity policies was less clear for participants. Growing up under the influence of these policies made it difficult for participants to judge their impact. Most participants did not really have an answer, leading us to speculate that they did not understand a world where economic interests predominate. There are, however, workplace policies and practices in both the public and private sectors which promote an equitable workplace for women and women with children.

KEY LEARNING FOR THE EQUITY RESEARCHERS IN A CROSS-CULTURAL CONTEXT

This project, as with other qualitative studies, was underpinned by our background as researchers. Acknowledging our standpoint in the project was crucial (Holgate et al., 2006). In researching gender equity in Bhutan, we tried to remain conscious that we are a research team comprised of researchers from Middle Eastern and Australian cultures, but all working in Australian universities. As such our knowledge is embedded in a western understanding of, and influenced by, western notions of gender equity. Therefore, the acknowledgement of one's own position in relation to the research assists the reader in two ways. First, the reader gains an insight into a methodological approach that recognises the processes of intersectionality (gender, race, ethnicity, nationality, origin, culture and age), and second, it provides further information that enables the reader to question the effect this may have on the research (Holgate et al., 2006).

The researchers lived in Australia and were familiar with the Australian setting, however, despite our immersion in the literature about Bhutan and interactions with Bhutanese managers over the course of a three-week program, and despite having knowledge of global theorisation on feminist research, our backgrounds did not necessarily translate to Bhutan's historical and cultural context. From our reading of literature on Bhutan we concluded that many of the employment issues women faced were the same as in Australia and other western countries, that is that women are underrepresented in male-dominated occupations and management. We also understood the theory of the policy of GNH. What we could not fully comprehend, before arriving in Bhutan, was the impact of the philosophy behind Bhutan's national development policies and how that played out culturally. First impressions on arriving in Bhutan were that it was a very different society compared to Australia, particularly as social issues were prioritised over economic issues. Our knowledge of the critical role of feminist internationalisms and gender mainstreaming (Wickramasinghe, 2009) led us to conclude "the distinctive role of theory in qualitative research as relating to expression of a subjective reality more than clarification of an objective one" (Ahrens and Chapman, 2006, p. 299).

As researchers in the gender, equity and diversity space we are conscious of differences in cultures between countries and within them. For instance, from our earlier research interviewing female and male senior managers in Australia, we understood that each group experienced different situations and cultures. Although one of the research team has worked in an Asian country, during the course of the research on Bhutan we came to understand and were confronted by a distinct, different and unknown culture. Despite our extensive preparation, including understanding Bhutan's inclusion of happiness and well-being in national planning through the GNH Index, we were unaware of how this would be reflected in people's attitudes.

DISCUSSION AND KEY RECOMMENDATIONS

Given our immersion into the literature on Bhutan, and discussions with Bhutanese participants in Australia, we believed we had prepared ourselves adequately for conducting interviews in Bhutan. The experience of interviewing managers in Bhutan – both male and female – however, was similar to our experience of conducting interviews with male senior managers in Australia. Our interviews in Bhutan, with both women and men, would have been very short if we had not asked further probing questions about discrimination or provided Australian examples and asked the participants to reflect on these. In some ways, it was similar to interviewing male senior managers in Australia, as the men in Bhutan and many of the women denied the existence of employment discrimination. Unless we probed further our understanding of gender equity and discrimination would have been limited. After the interviews and on reflecting on the Bhutan experience, we hypothesised that perhaps it was because we were women and from a different cultural background, and so as outsiders we were distanced from the experience of the participants. Our experience in Bhutan contrasted starkly with that of interviewing women managers in Australia. In these interviews, we only had to mention the words "discrimination" and "gender equity" for our participants to talk at length about their own experiences and those of their organisation.

After returning from Bhutan, thinking on our experiences interviewing managers, we reflected that perhaps we had not considered enough that the framing of the questions we were posing may not transfer as readily to a different cultural context. We had not adequately factored in or considered the cultural differences or cultural applicability of our research terms when conducting our research. Reflecting on the Australian experience, after our Bhutan interview experience, we hypothesised that in the Australian context discussions about "discrimination" and "gender equity" have existed in the social landscape for decades and therefore was a question easily understood. Through social attitudes and awareness of the issue, our Australian female participants had lived experience of, and were alert to, observing these issues in their organisation. As researchers, we critically contemplated and demonstrated our subjectivity. This has been confirmed by Wickramasinghe (2009, p. 55) who stated, "new developments in epistemology/theory and research methodology, influenced by sociological and cultural studies, have exploded the myth of objectivity and theorised on the significance of the researcher's role in the research process".

On a very practical level, unexpected things happen when you are in the field and you are required to be flexible and make some new decisions about the conduct of the research project. Opportunities for further research might open up, or avenues that you wanted to pursue might close. A very important issue with all changes is to consider the consequences for the Ethics Clearance details for the project, and to seek a variation to this clearance if necessary.

In this study, we have discussed the challenges in conducting international, cross-cultural research on gender equity and our focus has been on the research process and our experiences with different sociocultural backgrounds from those of participants. A number of learnings were drawn from this experience which highlight the importance of such a study. In particular, we highlighted the challenges of conducting equity research in a different context. Our study also emphasised the necessity of facilitating a cross-cultural research process that is appropriate in the given sociocultural context.

Bhutan is the vehicle for illustrating the challenges of conducting research framed in a different context. Therefore, our key recommendations are mainly based on conducting equity research in other countries:

- The need for researchers to critically contemplate and demonstrate their subjectivity – by writing reflexively. It is also important to critically reflect on how researchers position themselves in writing up the research as well as the extent to which their identities construct and position their work.
- The benefits of undertaking in-country fieldwork. The particularities of the Bhutan historical and cultural context meant that global theorisations on methodology were not always appropriate to the local context. Researchers need to be aware, as Mohanty (2003, p. 461) argues, that there cannot be a unified global perspective of women because "a place on the map is also a place in history". In this instance, perhaps it is useful to consider Narayan's (2004) argument on how positivism has its uses in India, despite being condemned in western feminist debates for not being able to portray the experience-based politics that are central to feminisms.
- The need for flexibility in the research process. This allows the researchers to remain open and adapt their research approach if required. Opportunities might open up for the researchers when conducting a study in a different context and researchers might have to look for alternatives when conducting research in the field.

REFERENCES

Ahrens, T., and Chapman, C. S. (2006). Doing qualitative field research in management accounting: Positioning data to contribute to theory. *Handbooks of Management Accounting Research*, *1*, 299–318.

Atkinson, P., and Hammersley, M. (1998). Ethnography and participant observation. In Denzin, N.K., and Lincoln, Y.S. (Eds), *Strategies of Qualitative Inquiry*. Thousand Oaks, CA: Sage, 248–261.

Basch, C. E. (1987). Focus group interview: An underutilized research technique for improving theory and practice in health education. *Health Education Quarterly*, *14*(4), 411–448.

Choiden, S. (2016). *The Economics of Happiness: Insights into Gross National Happiness in Bhutan*. Brisbane: Queensland University of Technology.

Cooke, F. L. (2018). Concepts, contexts, and mindsets: Putting human resource management research in perspectives. *Human Resource Management Journal*, *28*(1), 1–13.

Creswell, J. W. (2014). *Research Design: Qualitative, Quantitative and Mixed Methods Approach* (Fourth ed.). Thousand Oaks, CA: Sage.

Denzin, N., and Lincoln, Y. (2000). *Handbook of Qualitative Research*. Thousand Oaks, CA: Sage.

Geertz, C. (1983). *Local Knowledge: Further Essays in Interpretive Anthropology*. New York: Basic Books.

Holgate, J., Hebson, G., and McBride, A. (2006). Why gender and "difference" matters: A critical appraisal of industrial relations research. *Industrial Relations Journal*, *37*(4), 310–328.

Lincoln, Y. S., and Guba, E. G. (1985). *Naturalistic Inquiry*. Thousand Oaks, CA: Sage.

Merriam, S. B., Johnson-Bailey, J., Lee, M. Y., Kee, Y., Ntseane, G., and Muhamad, M. (2001). Power and positionality: Negotiating insider/outsider status within and across cultures. *International Journal of Lifelong Education*, *20*(5), 405–416.

Mohanty, C. T. (2003). "Under western eyes" revisited: Feminist solidarity through anticapitalist struggles. *Signs: Journal of Women in Culture and Society*, *28*(2), 499–535.

Narayan, U. (2004). The project of feminist epistemology: Perspectives from a non-western feminist. *The Feminist Standpoint Theory Reader: Intellectual and Political Controversies* (pp. 213–224). Hove: Psychology Press.

National Committee for Women and Children, Royal Government of Bhutan (2021). Annual report 2021. www.ncwc.gov.bt/publications/NCWC%20Annual%20Report1644810656.pdf

Owen-Smith, A., and Coast, J. (2017). Understanding data collection: Interviews, focus groups and observation. *Qualitative Methods for Health Economics* (pp. 59–91). Oxford: Oxford University Press.

Ramazanoglu, C., and Holland, J. (2002). *Feminist Methodology: Challenges and Choices*. Thousand Oaks, CA: Sage.

Rinzin, C., Vermeulen, W. J., and Glasbergen, P. (2007). Public perceptions of Bhutan's approach to sustainable development in practice. *Sustainable Development*, *15*(1), 52–68.

Schwandt, T. A. (2000). *Three Epistemological Stances for Qualitative Inquiry* (Second ed.). Thousand Oaks, CA: Sage.

Silverman, D. (2013). *Doing Qualitative Research: A Practical Handbook*. Thousand Oaks, CA: Sage.

Strachan, G., Adikaram, A., and Kailasapathy, P. (2015). Gender (in)equality in South Asia: problems, prospects and pathways. South Asian Journal of Human Resources Management, *2*(1), 1–11.

Ting-Toomey, S., and Dorjee, T. (2018). *Communicating across Cultures*. New York: Guilford Publications.

Tracy, S. (2013). *Qualitative Research Methods: Collecting Evidence, Crafting Analysis, Communicating Impact*. Oxford: Blackwell Publishing.
Wangdi, K. (2019). *Perceived Sources of Happiness: Things Bhutanese Think Would Make Them Live a Truly Happy Life*. Thimphu: Centre for Bhutan and GNH Studies.
Wickramasinghe, M. (2009). *Feminist Research Methodology: Making Meanings of Meaning-Making* (Vol. 2). New York: Routledge.
World Economic Forum (2021). Global gender gap report 2021. www.weforum.org/reports/ab6795a1-960c-42b2-b3d5-587eccda6023
Yuval-Davis, N. (2012). Dialogical epistemology: An intersectional resistance to the "Oppression Olympics". *Gender and Society*, *26*(1), 46–54.

WEB RESOURCES

Bhutan Population (2021). Worldometer: www.worldometers.info/world-population/bhutan-population/
Nam, C. W. (2020). World economic outlook for 2020 and 2021. In *CESifo Forum* (Vol. 21, No. 2, pp. 58–59). Munich: ifo Institut-Leibniz-Institut für Wirtschaftsforschung an der Universität München: www.econstor.eu/bitstream/10419/226405/1/CESifo -Forum-2020-02-p58-59.pdf
National Assembly of Bhutan (2021). Royal Government of Bhutan: www.nab.gov.bt/en/
National Gender Equality Policy (2019). Royal Government of Bhutan: www.gnhc.gov .bt/en/wp-content/uploads/2020/02/National-Gender-Equality-Policy.pdf

11. Diversity, equity and inclusive lessons from a workplace in the Canadian Arctic

Arijana Haramincic

FIELD RESEARCH CONTEXT

Located in the Arctic Circle, Nunavut is the largest territory in Canada, with 2 million square kilometres, that comprises one fifth of Canada. The population of Nunavut is approximately 38,000 of which 85 per cent are Inuit (Indigenous people of this land). There are 25 communities accessible only by plane during the year and by boat during the summer months. Living and working in this environment has unique challenges and offers learning opportunities about Inuit culture, leadership and its impact on the diversity, equity and inclusion (DEI) in the workplace.

Managing social services in Nunavut entails challenges because of environmental, social and historical issues, including colonialism, geographic isolation and Inuit culture within a multicultural Canadian society.

In Nunavut, child welfare services are delivered by the Department of Family Services, a diverse group of professionals. The department employs 57 per cent Inuit, and another 43 per cent are professionals from diverse social, cultural and linguistic backgrounds. This creates an interesting and complex dynamic within the workplace. This chapter reflects on DEI in the field of social services and will focus on observations and reflections regarding leadership and management practices in a highly diverse workplace within an Indigenous environment in the public sector, delivering child welfare services. This is an opportunity to highlight lessons learned based on a culturally and environmentally specific context and the importance of culturally safe and congruent leadership practices.

The study concludes with the specific strategies that support Inuit knowledge and Inuit societal values, thus promoting a culturally safe public service to Nunavummiut, aspiring to be free of racism and discrimination.

INTRODUCTION

Diversity and multiculturalism in the workplace are realities in today's world, regardless of the geographical location, and are not a unique phenomenon to Canadian society. Modern societies embrace such dynamic opportunities and maximize the benefits within and for workplaces. Colonialism, racism and discrimination in workplaces have been ongoing realities for Indigenous peoples and people of colour in Canada (RCTC, 2015), which has a profound impact on the workforce.

These concepts are discussed from the perspective of Nunavut's geographical, political and socio-economic position, approaches to leadership and management and its impact on the workforce. The observation of leadership and its influence on creating a culture that maximizes Inuit and multicultural aspects found in these workplaces is explored.

Understanding diversity, equity and multiculturalism and its impact on the workforce is critical to understand the dynamics that motivate and enhance employees' performance and productivity and thereby improve overall organisational success while promoting DEI. Workplace diversity, how it is perceived and is understood, depends on and influences society in general, social interaction and therefore work relations (Prasad and Mills, 1997). Political, economic, historical and social contexts impact our understanding of diversity and equity, on the individual and communal levels. Historically, power influences and workplace relationships were based on hierarchical models. These models exaggerate the imbalances and power and control and therefore special attention needs to be given to strategies that bring balance and empower historically marginalized groups (Prasad and Mills, 1997).

Leadership and management approaches in diverse and multicultural settings is a conversation to be considered by employers to ensure DEI is supported and the barriers for marginalized groups are removed. The focus of this chapter is to discuss leadership approaches that support DEI in the workplace. The concept of culturally based/communal leaderships through collaborative and engaging action learning/action research is explored as a strategy to allow for continuous, flexible adjustments to leadership in the public sector. It is proposed that this will allow for the ever changing diverse ethno-cultural employee group to thrive while developing respectful and productive workplace interactions within Indigenous and northern environments.

Location and People

Indigenous peoples are the descendants of the original inhabitants of North America and account for approximately 3 per cent of Canada's population, with a population growth twice that of non-Indigenous people (Canadian Government, 2021). The Canadian Constitution recognizes three groups of Indigenous people: First Nations, Inuit and Metis (Chappell, 2001). Within Canada, Inuit primarily live within four regions with the majority residing in Nunavut. Inuit (meaning "the people") have lived in Canada for over 10,000 years, travelling from Siberia across the Bering Strait, then moving to what is today northern Canada, becoming the first Inuit People of Canada (Chappell, 2001; RCAP, 1996).

On 1 April 1999, Nunavut was created by separation from the Northwest Territories following 30 years of negotiations with the Canadian Federal Government. Inuit, prior to contact with the Europeans, were self-sufficient, living in small, nomadic, autonomous groups. They provided for their basic needs by fishing, hunting and gathering food. Their society was based on customary law that supported communal wellbeing and flexibility, utilising social pressures to affect appropriate behaviours when necessary. In the twentieth century, as contact with non-Inuit cultures increased, the Inuit culture adapted to the modern world. In the early 1960s, through the Canadian Government's policies, many Inuit were forcibly moved to permanent settlements in southern communities that offered access to education, health care and modern amenities.

Socio-economic Position

There are 38,780 Nunavummiut (residents of Nunavut) living in the territory, with an average population growth of 0.5 per cent and 40 per cent of the population receiving government income assistance. The unemployment rate is 13.1 per cent. The territory has the highest number of youth suicides in North America and there are presently 3.74 per cent of children receiving child welfare services and 2.39 per cent of children in care (CWRP, 2021; DFS, 2020). There are 41.24 per cent of Nunavummiut younger than 19 years of age; the average age is 27.7 and the median age is 25.1 (Canadian Government, 2021). Overcrowding, lack of housing, poverty, food security and family violence are present in all communities. Lack of critical resources to address the generational trauma caused by colonisation, forced settlement, residential school systems and the capacity to resolve these challenges have been a long-standing concern in the territory. This socio-economic picture can be positively influenced by the right leadership style and approaches. Leadership based on an autocratic style depends on power dynamics and continued colonisation, discrimination and exclusion of Inuit from the workforce, governance and politics. The leadership that focuses on supporting DEI, such as integrative, collaborative and community-based leadership styles and approaches, empowers and enhances self-reliance and self-determination.

The chapter now reviews the literature on leadership in an Indigenous and multicultural context followed by a description of the methodology employed to explore the challenges outlined. Findings are discussed and the chapter concludes with limitations and recommendations for future research.

LITERATURE REVIEW

Leadership

Leadership as a phenomenon has been extensively researched. However, leadership as it relates to DEI within a blended Indigenous and multicultural context has received little attention.

The success of organisational, economic and political systems depends on leadership effectiveness and its impact on overall organisational outcomes. Effective leadership is critical for success, organisational effectiveness and overall performance. Leadership has been defined as an ability to influence employees (followers) in an organisation to be motivated to work towards a common goal (Plsek, 2001). Organisations have always searched for ways to improve performance and achieve better outcomes, better service delivery and improved societal outcomes, and one of the answers to this challenge is developing and improving leadership capacity. There is a consensus among researchers that organisational performance can be improved through leadership practices, as well as overall organisational outcomes (Van Wart, 2003, 2013). Leadership has been extensively studied from the perspective of social, business and behavioural sciences (Parris and Peachey, 2013). However, the question about model, type and/or style of leadership, specific to Indigenous and multicultural environments, that produces effective and efficient outcomes, has not been clearly answered.

Those who are interested in leadership in diverse, multicultural and Indigenous environments face a distinctive, but equally compelling, challenge. There is a dearth of studies focused on mainly Indigenous and multicultural leadership, especially in the context where both are equally prominent; therefore, understanding the unique contributions and possible strategies to impact the workforce in a meaningful and productive way is important.

Traditional Inuit Leadership

Traditional Inuit culture is about fostering healthy communities by promoting the personal leadership skills, interests and or/abilities of individual community members (Preston et al., 2015). It is guided and rooted in the eight Inuit Societal Values (ISV) that the Government of Nunavut since 1999 continues to advocate in advancing the workplace environment and move forward towards achievement of its objectives as set in Turaaqtavut (Nunavut Government, 2017, 2021):

1. Inuuqatigiitsiarniq: Respecting others, relationships and caring for people.
2. Tunnganarniq: Fostering good spirits by being open, welcoming and inclusive.
3. Pijitsirniq: Serving and providing for family and/or community.
4. Aajiiqatigiinniq: Decision making through discussion and consensus.
5. Pilimmaksarniq/Pijariuqsarniq: Development of skills through observation, mentoring, practice and effort.
6. Piliriqatigiinniq/Ikajuqtigiinniq: Working together for a common cause.
7. Qanuqtuurniq: Being innovative and resourceful.
8. Avatittinnik Kamatsiarniq: Respect and care for the land, animals and the environment.

The connection to the land is evident in all aspects of the Inuit lifestyle which is connected through activities to all four seasons. Inuit engage in a different way with each other and the nature depending on the time of year. In general, spring and fall are times to hunt and travel, and winter is time to spend with family, tell stories, play games and learn about Inuit oral history and Inuit legends (Preston et al., 2015). In addition, associated with the land and environment, gender roles or gender balance are important (Kuniliusie, 2015; Preston et al., 2015). In general, Inuit women cook, sew and care for children, while the men hunt caribou, seal, birds and sea animals. Elders play an important role in Inuit society, they are decision makers and knowledge keepers demonstrating their leadership through wisdom and transfer of knowledge. However, the role and leadership of elders is complex and diverse depending on their own history and specific experiences that formed them as individuals. Therefore, Inuit have an inherent understanding that there is no one way of being and/ or doing; there are many diverse ways of ensuring the balance and harmony. Their survival has been successful because of their adaptability to change, historically with the changes of the season and more recently with social and political advancements.

In regard to Inuit worldview, Inuit Qaujimajatuqangit (IQ), meaning traditional life, articulates the beliefs, values, skills and knowledge that are components of a traditional and modern Inuit way of life. The workplaces in Nunavut focus on incorporating IQ in everyday practices. These values form the features of Inuit leadership. Relationship building and kinship responsibilities are critical ways of practising leadership. Furthermore, community service, connection to the land, promotion of language, culture and family are core values. Therefore, there is a blend of what is in non-Inuit culture known as a transformational style of leadership, rooted in collective value and co-determined outcomes aimed at social equality and change, and servant leadership, attending to community needs. Inuit leadership is a more fluid type of leadership, meaning that the person who has a skill in a certain area steps forward. It is understood that everyone in the community has an obligation to be a leader and a successfully led community is a collection of all these different leaders, their skillsets and raising them at the right time (Pauktuutit, 2006; Preston et al., 2015; Purich, 1992). Through the experiences of colonialism, Indigenous people learned to protect themselves by holding onto the traditional ways of being and leading which are critical components in ensuring that effective leadership within the Indigenous context honours traditional ways.

MULTICULTURAL LEADERSHIP

Multiculturalism can be described as a social and behavioural view of society that honours, appreciates, tolerates and promotes multiple cultures and identities situated within the context of a particular community/region/country. It is a view that through an attitude of tolerance, acceptability, respect and hospitality offers a positive strategy towards resolving the challenges of racial difference, cultural diversity and social inequality (Olanrewaju et al., 2017). More specifically, managing and valuing diversity enhances the overall individual and organisational performance (Mazibuko and Govender, 2017). Workplace diversity is associated with higher organisational benefits (Joubert, 2017). For instance, cultural diversity is associated with organisational advantages, such as strengthening the organisation's culture, improving the company's global reputation, increasing creativity and innovation and building loyalty among customers of different origins (Franken, 2015; Shen et al., 2015). It is also associated with increases in productivity, goal attainment, creativity, client-focused services and an interesting work environment (Joubert, 2017), as well as work team cohesion (Trivedi, 2008). In addition, when diversity is managed effectively, employees learn more about each other so that communication is improved, with less stereotyping and discrimination among the employees (Joubert, 2017). Organisations promoting initiatives based on a multicultural ideology can be expected to be particularly attractive to minorities, because diversity is acknowledged and retained (Verkuyten, 2005).

Leading in a culturally congruent manner, the ability to adhere and use the ISV is critical in ensuring the workforce is developing and moving in a cohesive way forward and aligned with the vision for Nunavut as set in Turaaqtavut, a guiding document for Nunavut's 5th Legislative Assembly (Nunavut Government, 2017). Ensuring the presence of either multicultural leadership alone and/or Inuit-specific ways of leading is not sufficient in the present Nunavut context. Leadership within workplaces over the past 20 years has moved on the continuum from non-Inuit (mostly European) to Inuit, ignoring both the multicultural and Indigenous aspects of the workforce. Integrating Inuit leadership with multicultural leadership theories will honour all aspects of the present workforce.

Integrated Leadership

Integrated leadership has been emerging as an approach to leading that honours diversity, supports equity and ensures inclusion. To gain a better understanding of public leadership and its influence on followers, Van Wart (2003) suggested that comprehensive models be developed that combine various leadership theories and approaches. Fernandez et al. (2010) designed and tested an integrated five-factor leadership model that included task-, relations-, change-, diversity- and integrity-oriented leadership and found a significant relationship between integrated leadership and public service program performance.

The integrated leadership model is based on private-sector research. Tummers and Knies (2016) highlighted four public leadership roles that are particularly relevant in public organisations. The first three roles (accountability, rule following and political loyalty) are bureaucracy-specific approaches that relate to the leaders' obligations under this system. The fourth (network governance) was added to acknowledge the importance of managing networks and the prominence that networks are gaining in the public sector. Tummers and Knies (2016) argued that a leader can move from one role to another depending on the situation and that these four approaches are subdimensions of a larger "public leadership" construct. Considering the basis of Inuit-specific leadership and the lessons regarding leadership in multicultural settings, the integrated leadership style, both internal to the leader and with other leaders, may be the most successful approach for diverse workplaces contributing to greater equity, inclusion and therefore effectiveness and efficiency.

METHODOLOGY

The chosen methodology for this research is a multimethod, combined quantitative and qualitative approach across two phases. The first phase was a review of the literature available regarding Inuit and/or multicultural leadership in support of DEI. The second phase was a review of observations of leadership in the present context through reflective journaling, enhanced by integrative thinking in synthesising and arriving at recommendations.

Reflection, both in private and professional life, is an important activity. It is a crucial cognitive practice in the research field and is aligned with Indigenous research methodologies.

This chapter and the lessons learned have been based on the reflective practice approach, field observations and reflective journaling regarding

Indigenous and non-Indigenous leadership practices of self and others for the period of 24 months in Nunavut and over the past 10 years in the province of Ontario, Canada. The reflections look at leaders in relation to followers. Through journaling the opinions were formed based on observation on how leaders through supporting DEI in Indigenous and multicultural settings create positive outcomes. A critical focus was given to ensure engagement in thoughtful relationships with individuals observed and the context of inquiry in Nunavut's public social services field. This chapter not only provides a report of the findings of the observations but also questions and explains how those findings are constructed. This approach has allowed information arriving from a variety of individuals (frontline social workers, supervisors, managers, directors, elders, community leaders, multidisciplinary professionals) to be incorporated and synthesized in the key findings and observations.

The data from reflective journaling were reviewed and analysed from the lens of the integrative thinking theory (Riel and Roger, 2017; Roger, 2007), thus allowing for the perceived opposing or different views on leadership – Indigenous versus multicultural – to be integrated in a unique concept. Further, the dialogue, storytelling and talking circle approaches were utilized to validate the information and reflections. Participation in ceremonial Indigenous activities, such as smudging, qulliq lightning, meal sharing, berry picking and ice fishing, and in multicultural festivals such as Black History Month, contributed to the observations of spontaneous leadership styles inherent in different cultures.

Table 11.1 shows specific reasons for choosing this method of data collection, with the most compelling being that of mirroring support for DEI principles.

The above purposes are strongly aligned with the ISV and as such reflective journaling, as a research method, lands itself as a non-intrusive and non-oppressive approach to be utilized. Reflective journaling allows for the transparency of experiences, opinions, thoughts and feelings while supporting the research design, data generation, analysis and interpretation process (D'Cruz et al., 2007) from a variety of research perspectives from constructivist, feminist, race-based, interpretivist, poststructuralist perspectives and decolonising (Pillow, 2003; Tuhiwai-Smith, 2012). While reflective journaling remains focused on achieving the required methodological rigour and paradigmatic consistency, it is also aligned with the Indigenous research methodologies that empower historically marginalized populations and provide for a critical transparent self-reflection of the researcher, their effect on the research process (what and how they influenced changes on the research design, methods used and approaches taken), while holding the accountability for the outcome of research to be for and with the Indigenous communities (Tuhiwai-Smith, 2012).

Table 11.1   Methodology alignment with Inuit Societal Values

Reflective journaling	Inuit Societal Values alignment
Better understand learning processes of self and others within the Indigenous/Inuit and multicultural context	Inuuqatigiitsiarniq: Respecting others, relationships and caring for people
Promote active involvement in the learning for self and other, thus role modelling equity, diversity and inclusion	Pilimmaksarniq/Pijariuqsarniq: Development of skills through observation, mentoring, practice and effort
Contribute to personal and communal ownership of learning	Pijitsirniq: Serving and providing for family and/or community
Enhancement of professional practice or the professional self in practice while participating in the process	Piliriqatigiinniq/Ikajuqtigiinniq: Working together for a common cause
Promote valuing of the self towards self-empowerment and empowering others through awareness and participation	Pilimmaksarniq/Pijariuqsarniq: Development of skills through observation, mentoring, practice and effort
Increase creativity and intuition through group involvement and empowerment	Qanuqtuurniq: Being innovative and resourceful
Understand that writing represents learning	
Be an alternative "voice" for others, synthesizing and reflecting on the experiences of self and others	Piliriqatigiinniq/Ikajuqtigiinniq: Working together for a common cause
Foster reflective and creative group interaction, supporting Indigenous modalities such as talking circle, gatherings, elder support, story telling	Qanuqtuurniq: Being innovative and resourceful

The reason this methodology was chosen is due to its alignment with both the multicultural and Indigenous aspect of the context in which the leadership is being observed, to minimize subjective bias and to have an opportunity to critically examine those, while respecting empowering and acknowledging all the voices in the process. The core elements of DEI, such as respect for diverse opinions, encouraging marginalized voices, focusing on inclusion and removing barriers to equity, have been implemented and considered during the reflective journaling.

KEY FINDINGS

Child welfare and child protection services are delivered directly through the Department of Family Services. The department hires community social services workers with a background in social services and/or social work. Hiring and retaining qualified staff has been an ongoing challenge for the department. The need for services is beyond the local capacity of the available workforce, and therefore many are brought in from other parts of Canada, often immigrants and from varied ethnocultural backgrounds. These individuals bring diverse educational and experiential backgrounds, creating a unique blend of Inuit and non-Inuit approaches to the practice of child welfare and workforce management in general. In order to ensure the alignment and effectiveness of all workers, strong leadership and management is required that understand the subject matter and dynamics of leading in both Inuit and multicultural environments, supportive of DEI, thus willing to explore the most effective approaches leading to the best outcomes for children, youth, families and communities.

Working in the Arctic in isolated, fly-in only communities, challenges individuals on both personal and professional levels. Further, historical traumas and the inability to have regular supervision, team meetings, face-to-face connection with other members of the team exaggerate the feelings of lack of support and lack of reaffirmation to build confidence and ongoing staff professional development. All these factors result in high turnover, high stress and high burnout. In addition, many supervisors, managers, directors and executives were promoted into their positions early in their careers, often with minimal training in management and/or supervision, training addressing DEI in the workplace and minimal support through coaching and mentoring.

Seven key themes emerged from the research: need and openness for further education related to leadership and DEI in an Inuit and multicultural context; cultural immersion; practising shared leadership with a mentoring and coaching component; community engagement; cross-cultural communication; embedding ISV in leadership approaches; and integrating Inuit and multicultural leadership styles.

Through the observation of present leaders, it has been noted that many expressed a desire for and are open to receiving further education related to their duties. The motivation and eagerness of employees and management to take Inuit cultural competencies training have been high among staff, and the individuals that have taken the training are more open to embracing and understanding the Indigenous context, showing higher levels of compassion towards clients and colleagues. Non-Inuit supervisors who have taken training/ courses in Inuit history and/or Inuktitut/Inuinnaqtun expressed greater appreciation and respect towards the Inuit culture and people, assisting them to lead in a more culturally safe and congruent way. In turn, the elders and Inuit staff responded in a positive way towards their colleagues who are learning the language, attempting to communicate simple everyday expressions and making an effort to continue learning. Both Inuit and non-Inuit employees expressed appreciation for cultural days, finding different ways to learn the way of the Inuit and embrace the Arctic lifestyle, such as fishing, hunting and dog sledding. Both Inuit and non-Inuit employees express that their supervisors, managers and senior managers in their view set the culture of the team, and have the ability to encourage DEI within the team. The following examples have been identified as demonstrating DEI in the workplace: encouraging sharing of diverse opinions through regular supervision, team meetings, clinical discussions, problem solving, dialogue and openness to learn from mistakes. Sharing leadership responsibilities for different projects and programs, as well as delegating meaningful tasks, has been identified as a welcome strategy to empower and, also, many identified that leaders who spend time mentoring and coaching through mutual learning strategies are identified as supportive and interested in individual growth and the development of employees. Furthermore, a willingness to be involved in community life, volunteering and contributing to the land and its people outside of the work environment, has been identified as one of the characteristics that assists in building trust and relationships that are based on mutual respect.

The high turnover rate in leadership resulted in a certain level of mistrust; demonstrating interest in the community, through community participation, supports a genuine desire to become its member. Leaders who are involved in community life have shown better ability to engage with and develop both personal and professional relationships. Furthermore, the ability to advocate for DEI and challenge the status quo has clearly been identified throughout the review by both employees and management. The ability of leadership to continuously and actively challenge historical ways that continue colonisation, oppression, discrimination and racism, such as unequal pay for women, the exclusion of Indigenous and people of colour from leadership opportunities or the lack of accessibility for individuals with disabilities, is a trait that many identified as necessary. Supervisors and managers, while agreeing with the same points, identified a lack of knowledge, skill and confidence to support DEI in the most effective way. They expressed that attention and role modelling of DEI as it relates to leadership, such as strategies that encourage the engagement of diverse individuals, remove barriers to equity and support inclusion. The specific tool that was identified as helpful was an equity lens, which is a simple questionnaire when decisions are being made: Who is this benefiting? Who is it excluding? Whose voice needs to be heard to ensure DEI? Leaders asking these questions, prior to finalising a decision, pausing before the next stage in the process or using them as an evaluation tool in quality improvement processes have been perceived in a positive way, demonstrating cultural sensitivity and advocating for change towards equity and inclusion.

There is a difference in how different ethno-cultural groups communicate not only the language but also the manner and expressions. The Inuit way of communication is through storytelling, sharing and is primarily verbal. Some non-Inuit employees will communicate in a more direct way thus missing the impact of the different communication style. Also, the way language is used varies from culture to culture, and the same or similar expressions can be misinterpreted. Developing leaders' ability to understand cross-cultural communication and understand the impact of his/her own communication style, developing sensitivity and openness to listen for understanding and engagement, is important in order to ensure messages are received and interpreted in the way they were meant. There are four official languages in Nunavut: English, French, Inuktitut and Inuinnaqtun. For the majority of the public-sector employees, English is a second language and the primary language of communication day to day in a workplace. This at times creates challenges to communicate essence and meaning. Further attention to cross-cultural communication with specific strategies to prevent miscommunication would be supportive and encouraging of diverse voices to be heard and involved in decision making, program design and/or problem resolution.

Therefore, the most successful leaders emerging through this review are not identified by their cultural background but by their ability to respect each employee's strengths, being willing to approach leading as a learning process, being willing to spend time coaching and mentoring, are facilitators of change, are able to consider a variety of viewpoints, are community minded and support innovative solutions where all involved feel empowered and respected.

The approach to leadership that has demonstrated the most effective outcomes based on the observations is embedded in ISV, thus being wholistic, collaborative and dependent on local/community-specific resources and the visions which support DEI approaches to managing workplaces: respect, empowerment, focus on learning and improvement rather than deficits and criticism. This has been evident through the positive outcomes of strategies such as IQ (cultural) days, minimising isolation through the use of virtual platforms, regular check-ins, addressing personal and professional growth, a robust training system, attention to challenges of cross-cultural communication, attention to welcoming, inclusive spaces through visual signage and transparent, motivating and encouraging team discussions. Further, the blending of honouring both multicultural and Inuit strategies to leading, such as allowing time for sharing and awareness of each other, has increased trust and improved teamwork.

The realities of the north, such as isolation, low population density, a need for a specialized workforce and access to education, brought Inuit and individuals of diverse ethnocultural backgrounds to work together in and for the territory. This unintended blending of the workforce creates a unique opportunity to draw on strengths and benefits that arrive from a diversity of views and educational and experiential backgrounds. Firmly grounded in ISV, guided by IQ and drawing on the linkages with the multiple and differing approaches to community development, child welfare and social services can provide for the new approaches that are constructed for Nunavummiut through applying a mixture of theoretical approaches such as social constructivism (Carpenter and Brownlee, 2017) and general systems (Ridel-Bowers and Bowers, 2017). Thus, there is a need to have the ability to develop a leadership approach that is responsive to the needs of employees in the Arctic, being flexible to move from crisis to maintenance and back again, in a fluid and uninterrupted way. The interest in, and higher level of understanding of similarities and differences in both Inuit and cross-cultural communication, leadership and management approaches has demonstrated a positive impact on the workforce. The ability for managers and leaders to envision, create and implement the organisational culture that is based on mutual respect and openness has also been identified as a positive trait to bring cohesiveness, effectiveness and efficiency among employees.

DISCUSSION/RECOMMENDATIONS

The Canadian Arctic is a unique environment from historical, geographical, cultural and socio-economic perspectives. Embracing this can be both rewarding and challenging as this territory has continued to mature since its formation 22 years ago. Approaches to leadership that are respectful and acknowledge all its aspects are necessary. Leadership from all levels that provides solutions to support DEI in Arctic workplaces needs to be specifically designed, developed and delivered holding all options with equal light through integrative thinking and reconfiguring them to create new value/new leadership approaches. Colonisation and continued systemic legacy barriers continue to impact Indigenous people in Canada. Many Inuit continue to live with traumatic experiences, such as the residential school system, overcrowding and family violence which impede, if they are not attended to, their fulsome participation in the workplace. Decolonisation and Indigenisation of workplaces will support stability, equity and inclusion of all employees. Empowerment, self-determination, cross-cultural communication, collaboration and adaptation to the changing realities in the workplace are critical. A multicultural workforce alignment with the employer's vision and ISV is required in order for the integration of their own contributions to Nunavut.

Therefore, leadership's first task is to gain an awareness and understanding of the complex issues that face Nunavut workplaces and implement strategies towards decolonising and indigenising workplaces, removing legacy barriers that prevent Inuit employment and building openness and adaptability to embrace the benefits of shared/integrated aspects of the workforce. Further utilising an integrative approach in leadership, advocating for Inuit values and the values of a multicultural workforce with respect and creating new choices/ opportunities/values/solutions are necessary for sustainable effective workplaces. An approach to leadership in Nunavut that embodies the characteristics of ISV, equity and holism while supporting Inuit self-determination, mutual respect and diversity has the potential to produce better outcomes for all, while supporting, motivating and empowering all members of the present workforce.

Future research could consider expanding and complementing lessons learned by conducting participative research through action learning and action research, in order to bring Inuit and diverse voices to share their experiences, benefits and shortfalls. This approach would further inform specific educational strategies that can be implemented into training present and future managers and leaders in Nunavut.

REFERENCES

Canadian Government (2021). Statistics Canada. Aboriginal Peoples in Canada: First Nations People, Metis and Inuit, 31 March. www12.statcan.gc.ca/nhs-enm/2011/as -sa/99-011-x/99-011-x2011001-eng.cfm

Carpenter, D. E., and Brownlee, K. (2017). Constructivism: A Conceptual Framework for Social Work Treatment. In F. Turner (Ed.), *Social Work Treatment: Interlocking Theoretical Approaches* (pp. 96–116). New York: Oxford University Press.

Chappell, R. (2001). *Social Welfare in Canadian Society*. Scarborough, ON: Nelson Thomson Learning.

CWRP, C. W. (2021). Child Welfare Reserach Portal. Nunavut Statistics, 19 April. www.cwrp.ca

D'Cruz, H., Gillingham, P., and Melendez, S. (2007). Reflexivity, Its Meanings and Relevance for Social Work: A Critical Review of the Literature. *British Journal of Social Work*, 37, 73–90.

DFS (2020). Director of Child Welfare Annual Report 2019/2020. Iqaluit: DFS.

Fernandez, S., Cho, Y. and Perry, J. (2010). Exploring the link between integrated leadership and public sector performance. *Leadership Quarterly*, 308–323.

Franken, S. (2015). *Personal Diversity Management*. Wiesbaden: Springer Gabler.

Joubert, Y. (2017). Workplace Diversity in South Africa: Its Qualities and Management. *Journal of Psychology in Africa*, 27(4), 367–371.

Kuniliusie, M. (2015). Arctic Coton and Stratified Identity of Inuk Educational Leaders. In F. Walton and D. O'Leary (Eds), *Sivimut: Towards the Future Together: Inuit Women Educational Leaders in Nunavut and Nunavik* (pp. 57–70). Toronto: Women's Press.

Mazibuko, V. J. and Govender, K. (2017). Exploring Workplace Diversity and Organizational Effectivness: A South African Exploratory Case Study. *SA Journal of Human Resources Managment*, 2–10.

Nunavut Government (2017). *Turaaqtavut*. Iqaluit: Nunavut Government.

Nunavut Government (2021). Inuit Societal Values. 28 March. www.gov.nu.ca/ information/inuit-societal-values

Olanrewaju, I., Loromeke, R. and Adekoye, R. (2017). Multiculturalism, Value Differences, and Cross-Cultural Conflict in Nigeria. *Journal of African Union Studies*, 6(1), 39–62.

Parris, D. L. and Peachey, J. W. (2013). A Systematic Literature Review of Servant Leadership Theory in Organizational Contexts. *Journal of Business Ethics*, 377–393.

Pauktuutit (2006). *The Inuit Way*. Ottawa: Pauktuutit Inuit Women of Canada.

Pillow, W. (2003). Race-Based Methodologies: Multicultural Methods or Epistemological Shifts? *Counterpoints*, 195, 181–202.

Plsek, P. E. (2001). Complexity, Leadership, and Management in Healthcare Organisations. *BMJ*, 746–749.

Prasad, P., and Mills, A. J. (1997). Understanding the Dilemmas of Managing Workplace Diversity. In P. Prasad (Ed.), *Managing the Organizational Melting Pot: Dilemmas of Workplace Diverisity* (pp. 3–30). London: Sage.

Preston, J. P., Rowluck, W., Claypool, T., and Green, B. (2015). Exploring the Concepts of Traditional Inuit Leadership and Effective School Leadership in Nunavut (Canada). *Comparative and International Education*, 44(2).

Purich, D. (1992). *The Inuit and Their Land: The Story of Nunavut*. Toronto: James Lorimer and Company.

RCAP, T. R. (1996). *Looking Forward, Looking Back* (Vol. 1). Ottawa: Canada Communications Group.

RCTC, T. R. (2015). *Final Report of the Truth and Reconciliation Commission of Canada, Volume 1: Summary: Honouring the Truth, Reconciling for the Future*. Toronto: Lorimer.

Ridel-Bowers, N., and Bowers, A. (2017). General Systems Theory. In F. Turner (Ed.), *Social Work Treatment: Interlocking Theoretical Approaches* (pp. 240–247). New York: Oxford University Press.

Riel, J., and Roger, M. (2017). *Creating Great Choices: A Leader's Guide to Integrative Thinking*. Boston, MA: Harvard Business Press.

Roger, M. (2007). *The Opposable Mind*. Boston, MA: Harvard Business Press.

Shen, J., Chanda, A., D'Netto, B. and Monga, M. (2015). Managing Diversity through Human Resource Management: An International Perspective and Conceptual Framework. *International Journal of Human Resource Management*, 235–251.

Trivedi, P. (2008). Respecting Diversity through Acknowledging, Valuing and Using Diversity and Challenging Inequalities. Chichester: Wiley.

Tuhiwai-Smith, L. (2012). *Decolonizing Methodologies*. Dunedin: Otago University Press.

Tummers, L. and Knies, E. (2016). Measuring Public Leadership: Developing Scales for Four Key Public Leadership Roles. *Public Administration*, 94(2), 2–34.

Van Wart, M. (2003). Public-Sector Leadership Theory: An Assessment. *Public Administration Review*, 63, 214–228.

Van Wart, M. (2013). Lessons from Leadership Theory and the Contemporary Challenges of Leaders. *Public Administration Review*, 73, 553–565.

Verkuyten, M. (2005). Ethnic Group Identification and Group Evaluation among Minority and Majority Groups: Testing the Multiculturalism Hypothesis. *Journal of Personality and Social Psychology*, 88(1), 121–138.

USEFUL WEB LINKS

Canadian Government, Many Voices One Mind: A Pathway to Reconciliation: https://www.canada.ca/en/government/publicservice/wellness-inclusion-diversity-public-service/diversity-inclusion-public-service/knowledge-circle/many-voices.html

Hofstede Insights' cross-cultural comparisons: https://hi.hofstede-insights.com/national-culture

Regroupement québécois des organismes pour le développement de l'employabilité, Understanding Inuit and Work: An Examination of Cultural Factors to Develop

Tailored Employment Services: https://axtra.ca/wp-content/uploads/2016/05/Understanding-Inuit-and-Work-An-Examination-of-Cultural-Factors.pdf

12. Examining gender mainstreaming in Indonesia: a feminist policy analysis

Endah Prihatiningtyastuti, Kantha Dayaram and John Burgess

INTRODUCTION TO THE RESEARCH

One of the measures of assessing regional policy initiatives that target women's work transitions from the informal to the formal economy is to use gender equity and inclusion indicators. This chapter looks at a set of seven questions from a feminist policy perspective that has been used to measure and evaluate regional policymaking in terms of its effectiveness in improving the standing of women in the economy and the community. The seven questions include problem identification, formulation, translation, implementation, and evaluation of development programs initiated by the state or regional governments. These questions concern value orientation, multiple identities, equality, special treatment, gender neutrality, role change, and gender relations. As indicators they are important (see Figure 12.1) because they examine the policymaking strategies and implementation developed by regional governments in Indonesia, such as by those in the Gunungkidul and Sleman districts of Java, the regions reported in this chapter.

The first question looks at value. Value orientation investigates how the policy pays attention to social justice, as well as values the inherent dignity of women as part of their citizenship (McPhail, 2003). State market control questions how the policy considers women's unpaid labour and care work as a profession (McPhail, 2003).

The second question relates to multiple identities. The existing studies on feminist policymaking still apply the assumed standards for all women (such as middle class, productive age, Muslim, married). Meanwhile, the multiple-identity perspective explores how regional policy addresses the various identities of women, such as class, age, religion, and other identity classifications (Mansfield et al., 2014). This discussion also examines whether regional policy prevents or promotes the multiple-identity perspective in determining the position of women's work transitions in their context.

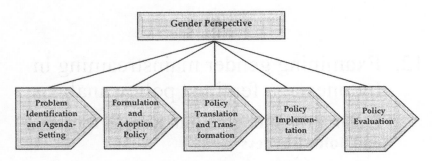

Source: Adapted from Anderson (2014), Dye and Dye (1992), and McPhail (2003).

Figure 12.1   Integration of a gender perspective into the public policymaking process

The third question of equality investigates how the policy affects gender equality and equal treatment of women and men (Lombardo et al., 2009; McPhail, 2003). Here, it discusses the extent to which regional policy has achieved gender equality. Moreover, as an indicator it explores whether regional policy has treated people similarly or differently, and whether the local policy has paid attention to gender differences to achieve equality.

The fourth question addresses equal treatment or protection. Under some conditions, special treatment or protection is needed to achieve equal treatment. The government has developed alternative policy approaches that seek equal treatment, by proposing special treatment for women based on their physical and social differences from men. Protection or special treatment here refers to the way in which the policy gives special treatment or protection to women as manifested in their regulations and programs (Kanenberg, 2013; McPhail, 2003). The ensuing discussion examines whether any special treatment or protection to increase women's participation is visible in their development.

The fifth question is about gender neutrality. Gender neutrality explores how the current policy brings out or hides women or gendered issues, as well as the solutions that it created (Silvey, 2004). The neutral policy is a double-edged sword. On the one hand, it could support women's access to a precious service. On the other hand, it can go against women's interests when men have greater access to benefit from this policy as women may be less able or willing to attain this access. The gender-neutral policy can work for women though it may disproportionately affect them.

The sixth question is linked to role change. Whether the alternative policy provides the opportunity for role change is one indicator to assess whether this policy utilises the feminist framework. The analysis investigates whether this alternative policy has a goal towards role change or not. Also, this analysis examines the kind of shifting role proposed to increase the opportunity for success (McPhail, 2003).

The seventh question regards power analysis. Power relation changes are commonly used to identify whether an alternative policy works within the feminist framework. Power analysis investigates how women participate in the designing, shaping, and implementing of the regulation, policy, and program in the development process at the grassroots level. Power analysis also tries to understand whether the applied policy empowers women. Furthermore, power assessment questions whether the policy operates to empower women and affect the gender power relation (McPhail, 2003).

RESEARCH APPROACHES

To address the public policy process outlined in Figure 12.1 a qualitative and exploratory comparative case study approach was applied that examined the lived experiences of women in the two provinces as outlined in Table 12.1. Qualitative research involves multiple data collection methods. These methods can include interviews with relevant stakeholders and the analysis of key planning documents. They can also include regional development planning documents, manpower development, and regional reports on sustainable development goals. The interviews were conducted with a range of stakeholders, from relevant districts such as regional development planning agencies, district manpower, women's empowerment, family planning boards, and non-government individuals or non-government organisations. Table 12.1 illustrates various qualitative approaches that can be adopted and provides an outline of why these perspectives would be considered suitable for researching regional gender policies and practices.

THE IMPORTANCE OF WOMEN'S FORMAL WORK IN REGIONAL INDONESIA

Formal work is closely interlinked with power in decision making and the capacity to accumulate assets and resources such as land. Where there are limited opportunities for formal employment, women continue to be marginalised in the economic and political spheres. According to the Indonesian National Labour Force Survey (Survei Angkatan Kerja Nasional/Sakernas) (Indonesia, 2015), the number of women in the informal sector (61.37 per cent) was higher than their counterparts in the formal sector, which is only 54.34 per cent (Indonesia, 2015). Only a few studies have paid attention to women's transition from informal to formal work (Rothenberg et al., 2016). This study focuses on the transition from informal work to formal work within regional

Table 12.1   Research approach applied to the regional case studies

	Perspective	Justification
Methodology	Qualitative	The collection and analysis of research data look into words, rather than quantification, to explore and understand the social reality and to produce the theory.
Strategic methodology research	Exploratory case study	The research applies in-depth exploration of individual, group, or contemporary phenomena.
Technique and procedure	In-depth interview Participant observation Focus group discussion	The observation, semi-structured interviews, and focus group discussions have proved to be reliable methods for collecting rich empirical data and information.
Perspective	Feminism	The research emphasises women's views and aims to investigate imbalanced power relations that marginalise and oppress women's position.
Position	Insider-outsider	The study adapts to insider and outsider positions to gain a basic understanding of the cultural and social background, language certainty, and accessibility.

Indonesia. The study is relevant and important since, firstly, involving women in economic activities has a positive impact on their empowerment status (Khan et al., 2016). Secondly, transitioning women's work from informal to formal work helps support local and national economic growth at a macro level, as well as acting as an important apparatus to reduce poverty (Sari, 2016).

Women's empowerment is defined as a "female's capacity to exercise choices and agency in key areas of their lives" (Kabeer, 2012). According to Kabeer (1999), the process of empowerment consists of three steps: resources, agency, and achievement. Resources, such as money, education, and human, are noted as preconditions for empowerment (Kabeer, 1999). Agency is "the capacity to negotiate with power in whatever form – as complicity, compromise, deviance or resistance – and with power in whatever motivation – whether it be intentional or unintentional, voluntary or involuntary, self-expression, self-interest, or group interest" (Parker and Dales, 2014, p. 165). Agency is the capacity to determine one's goals and to act to achieve these goals, for example, in critical thinking abilities and making independent resolutions (Kabeer, 1999). Moreover, achievement refers to outcomes such as educational achievements, enhanced labour force participation, and good health status (Kabeer, 1999). Samman and Santos (2009) argue that agency is a direct indicator of empowerment, whereas resources and achievement are indirect indicators of empowerment. While education access, employment, and property ownership provide potential for women's capacity to make choices, agency is arguably the most important step within the empowerment process because it reflects women's actual capacity to make choices (Kabeer, 1999).

Located within the literature that investigates women's agency in a developing Muslim country context and taking into consideration that Muslims are a majority in Indonesia, this study attempts to examine the working opportunities for and obstacles to rural Muslim women exerting agency in a regional or grassroots context, especially in accessing formal work in care sectors.

THE RESEARCH CONTEXT

This study applied exploratory case studies to two regional areas in Indonesia, namely, Gunungkidul and Sleman of the Yogyakarta Special Region. The two sub-case studies provide an understanding of diverse and detailed features at the grassroots level to examine policies (Mohajan, 2018; Yin, 2011). In this study, case studies in the specific areas as stated above provide relevant context to investigate complex sociocultural constructions that enable or challenge women's status and roles, and how policies at the grassroots level inhibit or encourage women's labour force participation in their communities. In addition, this study seeks to provide a detailed exploration of why the transition from working in the agricultural and industrial sectors to the service sector has not resulted in a significant positive impact on women's employment in the national and regional contexts. The regions are illustrative of the transformation taking place in Indonesia from agriculture towards other industries and from the informal to the formal economy. They offer opportunities for women to transition to the formal sector, however, as with many other regions of Indonesia, there are a range of structural barriers that impede this transition.

The selected case studies, Gunungkidul and Sleman, were identified based on their similarities and differences in location characteristics. Gunungkidul and Sleman are of Javanese ethnic background. The similar ethnic backgrounds of these regions will help to understand how norms and ethnic culture influence women's labour force participation and work transition. Their similarities also extend to the various levels of economic development. These two regions have experienced economic structural changes from being primarily in the agricultural sector to moving to secondary- or tertiary-sector employment. Sleman is located in the southeast part of the province of the Special Region of Yogyakarta. The district comprises 574,82 square kilometres or 18 per cent of the area of the Special Region of Yogyakarta. The Merapi eruption in 2010 had a severe impact on Sleman in the spheres of environmental damage, social economy, and agriculture (Kusumasari, 2015). Agricultural land usage has decreased due to the shift from agricultural to other industries (Sleman District, 2016).

Gunungkidul is a district of Java, Indonesia. Gunungkidul is one of the five districts in the province of the Special Region of Yogyakarta. It is located in the southeast part of the province. Drought and water scarcity are persistent problems in Gunungkidul (Martias, 2015). Vulnerability to these natural conditions contributes to the high poverty rate (Antriyandarti et al., 2018). Gunungkidul has also experienced socioeconomic transformation. The contribution of the agricultural sector to regional gross domestic product declined from 34.17 per cent in 2012 to 25.77 per cent in 2014 (Gunungkidul District, 2016). In contrast, the tourism industry's contribution to Gunungkidul's regional gross domestic product has slightly increased from 5.16 per cent in 2012 to 5.71 per cent in 2014 (Gunungkidul District, 2016).

RESEARCH INTO REGIONAL WOMEN'S EMPLOYMENT TRANSITIONS

The literature and findings in this section provide an insight into a doctoral study that explored women's transition into and participation in formal paid employment (Prihatiningtyastuti, 2021). The selected sub-case studies, Gunungkidul and Sleman, were identified based on their similarities and differences in location characteristics. Gunungkidul and Sleman are of Javanese ethnic background. The similar ethnic backgrounds of these regions will help to understand how norms and ethnic culture influence women's labour force participation and work transition. Their similarities also extend to the various levels of economic development. The two regions have experienced economic structural changes from being primarily in the agricultural sector to moving to other secondary or tertiary sectors as an alternative to improving people's welfare. Differences between the cases include the distance from the central provincial government, environmental characteristics, and the level of well-being. Sleman is closer to the central provincial government compared to Gunungkidul. Sleman has more extensive water resources and more fertile lands. In contrast, Gunungkidul is more remote with a poor water supply. In addition, Sleman citizens are comparatively wealthier and highly educated, whereas Gunungkidul is suffering from scarce infrastructure, lower education, and less income.

These two case studies applied a gender perspective framework to assess women's formal work participation. This study argued that regional policymaking for development failed to consider women's position as active subjects or main actors as they are perceived as not being able to articulate their voice and make effective choices to contribute to sustainable (economic) growth. In particular, regional governments place women as underutilised human capital resources in the local development context, which contributes to a potential loss in individual, family, and community income and welfare.

Table 12.2 presents a compilation of the concepts used by the policymakers in the research by Prihatiningtyastuti (2021) that sets out the detailed analysis and findings from the interviews. The compilation is based on interviews that were undertaken with a range of relevant stakeholders. It provides a description of how the terms and concepts of the feminist policymaking framework have been adopted, translated, integrated, and implemented into policy. It also outlines the progress of such policies.

Gender mainstreaming guided policies towards women in both provinces. Gender mainstreaming is:

> the process of assessing the implication for women and men of any planned action, including legislation, policies and programmes, in all areas and at all levels. It is a strategy for making women's as well as men's concerns and experiences an integral design, implementation, monitoring and evaluation of policies and programmes in all political economic and societal spheres so that women and men benefit equally, and inequality is not perpetuated. The ultimate goal is gender equality. (UN Economic and Social Council, 1997, p. 2)

Regional development planning documents between 2016 and 2021 in Gunungkidul and Sleman districts noted the achievement of gender equality and women and girls' empowerment as key objectives of regional development. This goal was further reiterated by some government stakeholders in the Gunungkidul district, that women should be provided with resources to empower them in decision-making processes. This includes providing access to actively participate in regional development policy processes and decision making. Women's active participation and contribution to regional decision making was seen as important, especially given the challenges that women experience. In the Sleman district, several development issues were identified, such as (1) respect, protection and fulfilment of women's basic rights in social, economic, cultural, and political life were lacking; (2) limited gender mainstreaming in the formulation of laws and regulations, institutions and budget policies existed; (3) the trafficking of women and children; and (4) the occurrence of violence against women and children. In the Sleman district a gendered perspective was adopted in four of its programs (Sleman District, 2016). These programs are: (1) synchronisation of policies to improve the quality of life of children and women's program; (2) strengthening of gender and child mainstreaming institutional program; (3) improving the quality of

Table 12.2   Regional development framework in supporting women's transition from informal to formal work

Main themes	Sub-themes	Aggregate dimension
Women empowerment concept	Considering	Applying gender perspective in formulation and adoption policies in a development planning document.
Women's access	Integrating	Translating and transforming gender perspective into programs and activities designed in the development process.
Women's participation		
Women's control		
Women's advantage		
The utilisation of gender-based data		
The utilisation of gender-empowerment measure index		
Participation in planning regional development	Serving women as an active agent of development	Implementation of progress and activities.
Bottom-up planning and financing		
Non-attendance in training	Serving women as passive objects/beneficiaries of development	
Top-down planning and financing		
Ignoring women's contribution	Ignoring women's existence and rights	
Ignoring care work and workers		
Ignoring women's needs		
Limited finance	Poverty feminisation or economic marginalisation	Monitoring and evaluation.
Limited capacity to make choices	Gender inequity	
Subjectivity		
Discrimination		
Exploitation		
Violence		

Source: Fieldwork, Prihatiningtyastuti (2021).

life and women's protection program; and (4) enhancing participation and gender equality in the development program. In addition, within each of these four programs the Sleman government district set performance indicators that needed to be achieved for reducing violence against women and children (Sleman District, 2016).

In the Gunungkidul district, policy documents highlighted gender issues and continued violence against children and girls. Importantly, these documents noted that gender mainstreaming (Gunungkidul District, 2016) had not been optimally implemented and cited examples where there were a limited number of women employed as service workers, sales workers, and agricultural labourers. As part of its policy formulation, the government of Gunungkidul had applied strategies that enhanced and strengthened gender mainstreaming. These included setting performance targets/indicators that needed to be achieved (Gunungkidul District, 2016).

Prihatiningtyastuti (2021) applied a feminist policymaking framework to examine how regional policymakers applied the gender (equality and inclusion) initiatives. The study found that the policymakers in the Gunungkidul and Sleman districts used an integrationist approach rather than an agenda-setting approach that mainstreams gender. The integrationist approach applies a gender perspective to existing policy paradigms, which has been associated with technocratic applications of mainstreaming (Verloo, 2005) and the inclusion of gender experts in policy machineries (Barnett Donaghy, 2004; Rees, 2005). It has been argued that integrationists tend to adopt Beijing's agendas for women's empowerment without fundamentally changing the way their organisations work (Sweetman, 2015), while agenda-setting approaches attempt to transform existing policy paradigms. The latter is said to be achieved by making changes in the decision-making structures and processes, prioritising gender objectives among competing issues, reorientation of the mainstream political agenda, and rearticulating the ends and means of a policy from a gender perspective (Lombardo et al., 2017).

Regional offices in the Gunungkidul and Sleman districts, such as the Office of Manpower and Social Services, the Regional Development Planning Agency, the Regional Office of Education, the Regional Health Office, and the Regional Office of Women Empowerment and Child Protection, have specific programs with budget allocations that target poverty eradication. However, prior studies found that there was a lack of coordination among the regional offices (Nugrahani and Rejeki, 2018). They used different interpretations on how the budget should be allocated and areas that needed to be prioritised. While some regional offices allocated smaller portions of the budget to address poverty eradication initiatives, other regional offices prioritised their budget allocation towards gender-neutral programs (Hasan et al., 2019; Nugrahani and Rejeki, 2018). The regional officers in the Gunungkidul and Sleman districts paid greater attention to physically visible violence against women in the domestic and public spheres over other forms of violence. There appeared to be a lack of awareness that violence against women was broader and included forms such as early-age marriage, multiple burdens, exploitation, and family and workplace discrimination. As a result, it has been noted that there is a gap between the impact of grassroots gender-mainstreaming efforts and achieving women's equity rights (Sweetman, 2015).

GENDER EQUITY AND INCLUSION APPROACHES

In researching initiatives that address women's equity and inclusion, a mix of approaches can be adopted. Various scholars note that gender equity and inclusion approaches are not mutually exclusive (Squires, 1999; Verloo, 2005). Integrationist and agenda-setting approaches are associated in practice and, thus, policymakers are encouraged to adopt both approaches. The inclusion strategy is essentially an integrationist approach, whereas the agenda-setting approach might be transformative. When regional policymakers employ an agenda-setting approach, they need to understand and consider the needs and issues of women's rights at early stages of the public policymaking process; that is, from the problem identification and agenda-setting phases (Jahan and Mumtaz, 1996). It is argued that only then can policymakers obtain a solid understanding of the source of unequal power relations and act accordingly. Jahan and Mumtaz (1996) described that combining an integrationist and agenda-setting approach would involve necessary changes in decision-making processes and structure, in prioritisation of strategies, in articulating objectives, in the positioning of gender issues amidst competing concerns that may emerge, and in the need to improve communication to build a solid support base for men and women. The agenda-setting approach does not only encourage women to play a proactive role but also focuses on targets that achieve gender equity and inclusion. Simultaneously, it encourages policymakers to grant primacy to groups and organisations that strengthen women's agency and, in the bigger picture, encourages building institutional capacities that enable aid recipients to recognise, set, and implement their own agendas.

IMPLICATIONS OF THE RESEARCH FOR ANALYSIS, PRACTICE, AND POLICY

Regional Indonesia presents an ideal case for researchers to examine women's transition from unpaid informal work to paid formal work. These contexts also highlight how gender mainstreaming occurs or should occur. Male and female employment has shifted from agriculture to manufacturing and service sectors, leading to improved social status, employment conditions, and wages (Booth, 2016; Matsumoto, 2016). The data used by Matsumoto (2016) suggest that female labour force patterns are responsive to the opportunities provided in the labour market, with young, educated women in urban areas having improved their participation in formal employment (Matsumoto, 2016; Schaner and Das, 2016).

In contrast to urban labour market transformation, in Indonesian regional locations such as Gunungkidul and Sleman districts, while the transition is occurring, it is at a much slower pace, with regional women being subjected to a range of barriers to paid employment together with a lack of inclusive decision-making processes (Prihatiningtyastuti et al., 2020; Suprobo, 2019). The growth opportunities offered by the restructured Indonesian economy have been slow to translate into material gains for women. Indonesia's Human Development Index for women is lower than their male counterparts, at 66 per cent compared to 71.5 per cent (UNDP, 2018). The Human Development Index summarises the indicators of long-term progress in three core dimensions of human development: access to education, a long and healthy life, and a decent living standard (UNDP, 2018). Indonesia's Gender Inequality Index is 0.45, ranking 104 out of 160 countries (UNDP, 2018). The Gender Inequality Index reflects gender-based inequalities in three dimensions: reproductive health, economic activity, and empowerment (UNDP, 2018). These international metrics indicate a marked gap in gender equality in Indonesia's economic and civic domains. Additionally, the 2017 Indonesian National Labour Force Survey (Survei Angkatan Kerja Nasional/Sakernas) (BPS, 2018) shows the number of women employed in the informal sector (61.37 per cent) was higher than their male counterparts in the formal sector (54.34 per cent). There is also a high rate of women's employment in low-paid and insecure jobs (Tusianti and Abdurrahman, 2018). These data therefore present opportunities to under-take further research into women's transition into formal paid work, particu-larly since the composition of the female labour force in Indonesia has changed since the late 2000s (Matsumoto, 2016). The existing regional development planning documents in Gunungkidul and Sleman districts note social justice and women's dignity as part of the nation's citizenry (Prihatiningtyastuti et al., 2020). However, in the translation and implementation stages of the devel-opment programs, regional policymakers fail to include targeted strategies and mechanisms that would sufficiently address inherent employment equity challenges. The implications for researching regional women's transition to paid, formal work in Indonesia is therefore threefold: (1) policy intentions; (2) policy implementation, monitoring, and review; and (3) women's agency and capacity to be included in decision-making processes.

CONCLUSION

The case studies used by Prihatiningtyastuti (2021) illustrate that Indonesian regional development planning agencies developed well-intentioned policies to address gender equity and inclusion, in both the Gunungkidul and Sleman districts. These districts employed the gender analysis pathway as an instru-ment in regional development planning. This instrument analyses the gender gap using four key dimensions – access, participation, control, and benefit of development – between men and women and marginal groups (Fithriyah,

2017). However, the research findings show that policy formulation on its own (however well intentioned) is insufficient in addressing initiatives such as women's employment transitions from unpaid informal work into paid formal work. The study provides researchers with suggested approaches that can be adopted for future research. Importantly, for researchers looking to undertake studies on gender equity and inclusion topics within an Indonesian or similar context, the focus needs to shift beyond policy formulation and include effective governance, adequate policy monitoring and review. Women's agency and capacity to be included in decision-making processes are fundamental to national equity and inclusion agenda setting.

RESEARCH FIELD TIPS

In researching regional gender policies, a critical gender policy perspective is a way to analyse gender mainstreaming initiatives that are undertaken by regional development planning agencies in Indonesia. This approach requires accessing policy documents, being fluent in local languages, conducting a textual analysis of the documents, and analysing the processes that support the implementation of policy programs. To do this, the researcher must be familiar with the cultural and policy context of the research, be able to access the relevant policy documents, apply a framework of evaluation, and examine the policy process from development to implementation to review. This requires familiarity with the regions, the language, and the culture; the policy process; the sources of documentary information relevant to the research; and access to and engagement with the stakeholders associated with the policy process.

REFERENCES

Anderson, J. E. (2014). *Public Policymaking*. Nelson Education.
Antriyandarti, E., Agustono, Barokah, U., Darsono, Fajarningsih, R., Marwanti, S., Rahayu, Wt., Supardi, S., Sutrisno, J., Ferichani, M. and Khairiyakh, R. (2018). Poverty alleviation system of dryland farm community in karst mountains Gunungkidul, Indonesia. IOP Conference Series: Earth and Environmental Science, 200, No. 1, p. 012062. IOP Publishing.
Barnett Donaghy, T. B. (2004). Applications of mainstreaming in Australia and Northern Ireland. *International Political Science Review*, *25*(4), 393–410.
Booth, A. (2016). Women, work and the family: Is Southeast Asia different? *Economic History of Developing Regions*, *31*(1), 167–197.
BPS (Badan Pusat Statistik, Central Bureau of Statistics) (2018). The Indonesian National Labour Force Survey 2017. Jakarta.
Dye, T. R., and Dye, T. R. (1992). *Understanding Public Policy*. Prentice Hall.
Fithriyah, F. (2017). Indonesia's experience: Implementing gender responsive planning and budgeting. *Indonesian Journal of Development Planning*, *1*(1), 59–75.

Gunungkidul District, Regional Body for Planning and Development (2016). *Peraturan Daerah No. 7 th 2016 tentang RPJMD Kabupaten Gunungkidul tahun 2016–2021* [*The middle term of region development planning 2016–2021*].

Hasan, A. M., Anugrah, B., and Pratiwi, A. M. (2019). Analisis Anggaran Responsif Gender pada Program Perlindungan Sosial di Indonesia: Studi Kasus di Dua Kabupaten dan Kota. [Gender-responsive budget analysis on social protection program in Indonesia: A case study in two districts and a city]. *Jurnal Perempuan* [*Women Journal*], *24*, 26. https://pdfs.semanticscholar.org/a4d2/3d7be3d01e81f79d a0c495c329239d52a704.pdf

Indonesia (2015). *The National Medium Term Development Plan 2015–2019*. Jakarta.

Jahan, R., and Mumtaz, S. (1996). The elusive agenda: Mainstreaming women in development [with comments]. *Pakistan Development Review*, *35*(4), 825–834.

Kabeer, N. (1999). Resources, agency, achievements: Reflections on the measurement of women's empowerment. *Development and Change*, *30*(3), 435–464.

Kanenberg, H. (2013). Feminist policy analysis: Expanding traditional social work methods. *Journal of Teaching in Social Work*, *33*(2), 129–142.

Khan, A., Dayaram, K. and Rola-Rubzen, M. F. (2016). Labour participation and women's empowerment: Implications for capacity building of women in potato production in Pakistan. In M. F. Rola-Rubzen and J. Burgess (eds), *Human Development and Capacity Building Asia Pacific: Trends, Challenges and Prospects for the Future*. Abingdon: Routledge.

Kusumasari, B. (2015). Women's adaptive capacity in post disaster recovery in Indonesia. *Asian Social Science*, *11*(12), 281.

Lombardo, E., Meier, P., and Verloo, M. (2009). *The Discursive Politics of Gender Equality: Stretching, Bending and Policy-making*. Routledge.

Lombardo, E., Meier, P., and Verloo, M. (2017). Policymaking from a gender+ equality perspective. *Journal of Women, Politics and Policy*, *38*(1), 1–19.

Mansfield, K. C., Welton, A. D., and Grogan, M. (2014). "Truth or consequences": A feminist critical policy analysis of the STEM crisis. *International Journal of Qualitative Studies in Education*, *27*(9), 1155–1182.

Martias, I. (2015). Reframing water scarcity issues in Gunungkidul: From local environmental problems to global-national water policy discourses. 3rd IIFAS Conference: Borderless Communities and Nations with Borders, 1198.

Matsumoto, M. (2016). Women's employment in Indonesia: Gaining more from structural transformation. In S. Dasgupta and S. S. Verick (eds), *Transformation of Women at Work in Asia: An Unfinished Development Agenda*. New Delhi: Sage.

McPhail, B. (2003). A feminist policy analysis framework. *Social Policy Journal*, *2*, 39–61.

Mohajan, H. K. (2018). Qualitative research methodology in social sciences and related subjects. *Journal of Economic Development, Environment and People*, *7*(1), 23–48.

Nugrahani, T. S., and Rejeki, S. (2018). Three pillars approach as gender perspective and poverty alleviation model. *Jurnal Penelitian Kesejahteraan Sosial*, *14*(2), 123–136.

Parker, L. and Dales, L. (2014). Introduction: The everyday agency of women in Asia. *Asian Studies Review*, *38*(2), 164–167.

Prihatiningtyastuti, E. (2021). Exploring women's participation and transition into formal employment: Case studies in regional Indonesia. Unpublished PhD thesis.

Prihatiningtyastuti, E., Dayaram, K., and Burgess, J. (2020). Skills development and challenges for regional women, in K. Dayaram, L. Lambey, J. Burgess, and T. W.

Afrianty (eds), *Developing the Workforce in an Emerging Economy: The Case of Indonesia*. Routledge.

Rees, T. (2005). Reflections on the uneven development of gender mainstreaming in Europe. *International Feminist Journal of Politics*, 7(4), 555–574.

Rothenberg, A. D., Gaduh, A., Burger, N. E., Chazali, C., Tjandraningsih, I., Radikun, R., Sutera, C. and Weilant, S. (2016). Rethinking Indonesia's informal sector. *World Development*, 80, 96–113.

Samman, E. and Santos, M. E. (2009). Agency and empowerment: A review of concepts, indicators and empirical evidence. Prepared for 2009 Human Development Report in Latin America and the Caribbean.

Sari, N. P. (2016). Transformasi pekerja informal ke arah formal: Analisis deskriptif dan regresi logistik [Transformation of informal to formal workers: Descriptive analysis and logistic regression]. *Jurnal Ekonomi Kuantitatif Terapan*.

Schaner, S. and Das, S. (2016). Female labor force participation in Asia: Indonesia country study. Asian Development Bank Economics Working Paper Series 474.

Silvey, R. (2004). Transnational domestication: State power and Indonesian migrant women in Saudi Arabia. *Political Geography*, 23(3), 245–264.

Sleman District, Regional Body for Planning and Development (2016). *Peraturan Daerah No. 9 th 2016 tentang RPJMD Kabupaten Sleman tahun 2016–2021* [*The Middle Term of Region Development Planning 2016–2021*].

Squires, J. (1999). *Gender in Political Theory*. Polity Press.

Suprobo, H. Y. (2019). Sleman evaluate gender mainstreaming implementation in five villages. https://jogjapolitan.harianjogja.com/read/2019/11/14/512/1024662/sleman -evaluasi-pengarusutamaan-gender-di-lima-desa

Sweetman, C. (2015). Gender mainstreaming: Changing the course of development? In A. Coles, L. Gray, and J. Momsen (eds), *The Routledge Handbook of Gender and Development* (pp. 48–58). Routledge.

Tusianti, E. and Abdurrahman. (2018). Ketimpangan gender dalam penyerapan tenaga kerja formal di Indonesia [The gender gap in formal employment in Indonesia]. Conference: Kongres ISEI ke XX Bandung.

United Nations Economic and Social Council (1997). Coordination of the policies and activities of the specialized agencies and other bodies of the United Nations System. www.un.org/womenwatch/osagi/pdf/ ECOSOCAC1997.2.PDF

UNDP (United Nations Development Programme) (2018). Human Development Report 2018.

Verloo, M. (2005). Displacement and empowerment: Reflections on the concept and practice of the Council of Europe approach to gender mainstreaming and gender equality. *Social Politics: International Studies in Gender, State and Society*, 12(3), 344–365.

Yin, R. K. (2011). *Applications of Case Study Research*. Los Angeles, CA: Sage.

USEFUL WEB RESOURCES

Ford, M. (2018). Investing in women. https://investinginwomen.asia/wp-content/ uploads/2018/01/Investing-in-Women-Indonesia-Country-Context-Paper-1-1.pdf

ILO (2018). Care work and care jobs for the future of decent work. www.ilo.org/global/ topics/care-economy/care-for-fow/lang--en/index.htm

Indonesia Central Bureau of Statistics (2018). Labour force survey (SAKERNAS) 2017, February. ///C:/Users/14385694/Downloads/ddi-documentation-bahasa-802%20(2).pdf

13. Affirmative action and equality, diversity, and inclusion in Malaysia

Sujana Adapa and Subba Reddy Yarram

INTRODUCTION

Malaysia was a British colony before independence in 1957, known as the Federation of Malaya with 11 states from what is now known as the Peninsular Malaysia. The formation of Malaysia took place in 1963 with Sabah, Sarawak and Singapore joining the federation. In 1965 Singapore separated from the federation and became an independent country. The population of the country is ethnically diverse with the dominant Malays (also loosely referred to as Bumiputeras) accounting for 60 per cent, Chinese accounting for 25 per cent and Indians and others accounting for the remaining 15 per cent (Ratuva, 2013). Reference to distinct ethnic group divisions is common in Malaysia – Malays, Bumiputeras, Malaysian Indians and Malaysian Chinese. Other popular categorisations relate to "Bumiputeras" versus "non-Bumiputeras" and "Indigenous" versus "immigrant" communities (Lee, 2017), leading to non-inclusivity.

Malaysia experienced severe social riots in 1969 that caused over 200 deaths. This led to the adoption of affirmative action policies through a new economic policy (NEP) in 1971. The reason for the riots and affirmative action policies was attributed to a disproportionate distribution of corporate assets between various ethnic groups. Non-Bumiputeras owned 30 per cent of corporate assets as opposed to only 2.5 per cent owned by Bumiputeras, with the remainder owned by foreigners. The target and focus of affirmative action policies were achieving a significant improvement in the economic interests of Bumiputeras (Lee, 2017). NEP modified into the National Development Policy from 1991 to 2000, the National Vision Policy from 2001 to 2010 and the New Economic Model in 2009. The New Economic Model is the current model and aligns with Malaysia's Vision 2020 objectives. The aim of Vision 2020 is to transform Malaysia's country status from the existing developing nation to a developed country (Lee, 2017). Vision 2020 also aligns with other objectives such as economic competitiveness, national unity, a skilled

Table 13.1   National policies and purposes – Malaysia

Year	Policy	Purpose
1971–1990	New Economic Policy	State-oriented program to eradicate poverty and to reduce economic gaps/disparities.
1991–2000	National Development Policy	Development in Malaysia and enhance the export market.
2001–2010	National Vision Policy – Vision 2020	Focus on economic, social and government transformation in Malaysia.
2008	One-Malaysia	Promote national unity among different ethnic groups in Malaysia.
2009	New Economic Model	Attain the status of a high-income country.

Source: PMO (2019).

workforce, a knowledge economy and overall growth. Table 13.1 presents the national policies and the purposes of these policies.

The affirmative action and associated policies are devised to support the disadvantaged and to manage the existing socioeconomic inequalities (Stewart et al., 2008). These policies are evident in the areas of education, employment, business creation and/or business development for the uplift of disadvantaged groups and for the better handling of prevailing discrimination. The assessment of the effectiveness of the affirmative action policies in Malaysia seems to be complex and difficult due to the existing ethnic divide and prevailing socioeconomic inequalities. The purpose of affirmative action policies has been less successful than anticipated in Malaysia due to continued inequality, lack of diversity and non-inclusiveness of different ethnic groups in Malaysia. The overall objective of the national unity considered as prestigious in the Malaysian context from Vision 2020 as the previously formulated affirmative action policies is questionable and debatable (Le, 2016).

There are concerns around the formulation and implementation of the affirmative action policies and lack of objectivity to attain the goals of these policies (Lee, 2017). This chapter presents an overview of the existing status of these policies to answer the following research question: "What is the impact of the existing affirmative action policies on the critical areas of education, employment and business creation in Malaysia?"

The next section provides literature syntheses, then a brief discussion of the methodological approach is presented, followed by results and discussion. The last section of the chapter presents the conclusion.

LITERATURE SYNTHESES

The affirmative action policies as outlined in the NEP in Malaysia supposedly need to improve the economic status of individuals, reduce poverty and increase economic growth leading to reduced ethnic disparities. The increase in the economic status of individuals largely attributed to the general increase in the individual salary levels and national unity to date remains debatable. The ethnic differences are closely aligned with religion that resulted in the formulation of economic, educational and cultural policies that are perceived to be discriminatory by the majority of the Malaysian population (Ratuva, 2013).

Article 11 of the Constitution indicates freedom for all religions and Article 3(1) refers to Islam as the official religion in Malaysia (Haque, 2003). The religious statements included in the Constitution informally suggest that conversion of individuals from other religions to Islam is encouraged. However, conversion from Islam to other religions is not encouraged and attracts punishment and penalties. State-based initiatives such as the following of Islamic laws, the establishment of the International Islamic University and Islamic banking became common practice in Malaysia. Certain initiatives attracted political and religious significance such as the Muslim Youth Movement, the Islamic Representative Council and the Islamic Party. Language and religion became intertwined amongst the ethnic groups. Table 13.2 presents information on the religions in Malaysia (DOSM, 2010). These policies resulted in the widening of inequality and non-meaningful diversity and inclusivity initiatives. Under the NEP formulated in 1971, excessive government intervention was evident. During the pre-colonial period, the Malays had the right to land. Under the British colonial system, changes to land rights allowed the British and the Chinese to own land. Later, the British introduced the Malay Reservation Act when the Malays were given designated areas for lease and mortgage (Haque, 2003). In 1957, under the ethnic preferential policies arrangement, the king was authorised to delegate to relevant authorities; this resulted in the reservation of quotas, incentives and licenses for the Malays. The First Outline Perspective Plan (1971–1990) emphasised a 30 per cent ownership for Malays engaging in industrial activities. Malay-operated businesses received assistance and support through government institutions and the State Economic Development Corporation. Malays also had access to state trust funds to actively participate in the corporate sector.

The affirmative actions proposed by the governments often are referred to as preferential policies across many countries in the region. These policies are aligned towards the encouragement of ethnic minorities to integrate with the ethnic majority to enhance the economic status of the identified minorities. However, in Malaysia, the preferential policies referred to as special rights in

Table 13.2   Religion in Malaysia

Religion	Percentage
Islam	61.3
Buddhism	19.8
Christianity	9.2
Hinduism	6.3
Confucianism	1.3
No religion	0.7
Other religion	0.4
Unknown	1.0

Source: DOSM (2010).

the Constitution are oriented towards the ethnic majority – the Malays – with objectives such as economic growth, business representation, creation of wealth and political domination (Haque, 2003). These special rights focused on the Malays attracted significant agitation from the Malaysian Chinese and the Malaysian Indians in the 1970s. The tradeoff to offer citizenship to non-Malays by the Malaysian government enabled the ethnic minorities residing in the country to tolerate the privileges allocated to the Malays (Le, 2016).

The macro environmental framework is important for the economic growth and development of the country (Sridhar et al., 2016). For example, the political factors in a country enable or hinder the country's institutional capacity and operations due to the impact exerted on the country's tax systems, tax administration and corruption levels, to name a few. Economic factors determine the purchasing power parity of individuals and businesses residing in the country and also influence foreign direct investment to a greater proportion. Sociocultural factors exert greater influence on the cultural norms and societal expectations of individuals as well as business performance. Technological factors are key to enhancing the self-efficacy levels of individuals and promoting the growth of new and innovative businesses. Legal and regulatory factors determine the law, rules, regulations, policies and procedures in the country (Sridhar et al., 2016). In Malaysia, national symbols of pride such as Petronas, Proton, Malaysian Airlines, Telekom and Tenaga are a few companies that emerged as a result of several macro-environmental factors with limited economic success.

Inequalities in the extant literature are explained using horizontal and vertical inequality frameworks. Horizontal inequalities refer to differences and inequalities between identified groups with common identities. Vertical inequalities refer to the individual differences. Horizontal inequalities are more evident in Malaysia due to prevailing interethnic differences and the categorisation is most commonly based upon history, religion and language. Extant literature highlights that direct, indirect and integrationist approaches are commonly followed by leaders and policymakers in handling horizontal inequalities effectively (Stewart et al., 2008). Direct approach refers to the formulation of direct policies with specifications relating to quotas in education and employment and provision of specialised business benefits for targeted groups. Indirect approach includes policies developed for designated groups such as anti-discrimination, regional development, sectoral support, etc. (Le, 2016). Integrationist approach focuses upon offering incentives for promoting better integration practices such as multicultural communities or schools, cross-cultural activities, etc.

The Malaysian context and existing structural components that enhance and/or hinder the identified ethnic groups affirms the importance of context specificity. It is envisaged that the institutional theory provides a valid explanation when exploring the underlying reasons leading to inequality and exclusionary practices. Institutional theory guides social behaviour by emphasising the existing structures, norms, rules, processes and procedures in a specific context. Institutions provide certain prescriptions for social acceptability and encourage compliance (Webb et al., 2015). These prescriptions foster firms in the country to exhibit behaviour as per the institutional norms to produce desirable outcomes such as economic growth, employment creation, wealth maximisation and increased profits. Institutional theory supports the legal structures and policy formulation (Webb et al., 2015). The Constitution, various amendments to the Constitution, articles and the state present legal, government and political structures that provide special rights in the form of preferential treatment for Malays and Bumiputeras.

METHODOLOGY

Qualitative analysis is deemed appropriate to source information from the available secondary data given the sensitivity of the topic, including affirmative action, national policies and ethnic groups. Sourcing information related to the context and the phenomena under exploration (de Vaus, 2001) is invaluable. Secondary data are sourced from various documents as presented in Table 13.3.

Researchers recognise policy analysis as a research method to deeply understand the context and draw inferences from policy relevance (Browne et al., 2019). The three approaches of policy analysis are: traditional (objective analysis of the existing policies and identifying the best solutions); mainstream (interaction of various actors in policymaking); and interpretive (social construction of problems to policy framing and representation). An integrated approach was undertaken in this chapter using a combination of all the three

Table 13.3   *Secondary data sources supporting the research*

Source	Number	Information retrieved
Journal articles	28	Malaysian context
		Direct, indirect and integrationist approaches
		Institutional framework
		Structural, political, economic and social factors
		Macro-environmental factors
		Affirmative action
		Preferential policies
		Special rights
Books	10	Malaysian context
		Information from pre-colonial, colonial and post-colonial periods
		Ethnic divisions
White papers (publicly available)	14	British rule
		Ethnic riots and preceding/succeeding changes
		Aristocracy influence
		Institutions (formal and informal)
Government reports (publicly available)	20	Rural versus urban divide
		Education, employment and business policies
		Preferential treatment
Websites (mainly government websites)	15	Malaysian population density
		Access to education, employment and businesses
		Ethnic divisions and ethnic conclaves
Newspapers (only English newspapers)	12	Ethnic tensions
		Business ownership
		Government changes
Others (magazines, blogs, vlogs, etc.)	10	Racial composition
		Religion statistics
		Social class division
		Occupational segregation
		Workforce participation

policy analysis approaches. The analysis related to criteria such as authenticity, credibility, representativeness and meaning to the problem under investigation (de Vaus, 2001). The secondary data obtained are organised into macro and micro themes of importance identified from the systematic syntheses of extant literature on affirmative policies and associated equality, diversity and inclusion criteria in Malaysia (Table 13.4; Miles and Huberman, 1994).

Table 13.4   Macro and micro research themes

Macro themes	Micro themes
Structural factors	Rules
	Regulations
	Values
	Beliefs
	Hierarchy
	Aristocracy
Political factors	Constitution
	Articles
	Amendments
	Government
	State
	Governance
	Policies
Economic factors	Capital
	Wealth distribution
	Ownership
	Land
	Labour
	Growth
Social factors	Religion
	Social class
	Work
	Safety
	Accessibility
	Demographics

RESULTS AND DISCUSSION

Structural, political, economic and social factors contributed to the existing ethnic, race, gender, caste, class and religion-based diversity that is commonly visible in contemporary Malaysia (Lee, 2017; see Figure 13.1). The impact exerted by these factors as a result of the existing affirmative action policies on education, employment and enterprise/business development (Le, 2016) by different ethnic groups in Malaysia is presented below.

Structural Factors

The NEP in 1971 had the original objective of achieving national unity, harmony and integrity. This objective was to be achieved through action on poverty and accelerating structural change in society that corrects economic

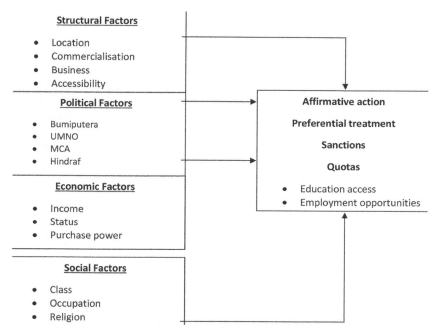

Figure 13.1   Factors contributing to preferential treatment in Malaysia

imbalances and eventually leads to the elimination of the identification of race with economic status. The affirmative actions aimed at improving equality, diversity and inclusion in Malaysia continued with subsequent economic policies. These policies not only failed to be effective due to a short-term focus, but the resultant enforcement of legislation related to education, employment, ownership and enterprise development also caused ethnic and economic disparities alongside gender, class, caste and religion issues. Varghese and Gomez (2018) identify the shortcomings of the 10th Malaysia Plan, 2011–2015, as the proposed initiatives for inclusion are limited.

The structural issues relate to stereotypical perceptions towards ethnicity. Malays pursued the traditional agrarian type of activities and concentrated in the rural locations. Malays occupied hierarchical aristocratic positions and served as administrative corporals. During the colonial era, the British allowed Chinese immigrants to be involved in commercial sectors and tin mining. Malaysian Chinese are identified to be dominant in enterprise/business creation and development (Gul et al., 2016). Under the British administration, Indians traditionally were brought into the country as labourers to work on rubber plantations and estates. Indians then lived in estate areas and partially moved towards urban or town areas. Indians are identified with low-level administrative services in the government sector.

Until Malaysia attained independence from British rule, around 60 per cent of the Chinese lived in urban areas, whereas 80 per cent of Malays lived in rural and regional areas in Malaysia (DOSM, 2010). The location of the ethnic groups determined access to education and subsequent occupations held by different ethnic groups in the country. The intersections of the ethnic groups with other dimensions such as language, location and class influenced the nature and type of education that individuals in Malaysia were exposed to. Thus, the education received by individuals in Malaysia further determined the employment and business development opportunities available to different ethnic groups in Malaysia presenting a case of ethnic disparity.

Political Factors

The political structure in Malaysia has been complex since independence. After Malaysia gained independence in 1957 from colonial rule, the Alliance Coalition comprised of the elite and the colonial government consisted of the United Malays National Organisation (UMNO), the Malaysian Chinese Association and the Malaysian Indian Congress, representing the three ethnic groups. The power of the Alliance Coalition was held and led by UMNO (Le, 2016). The political ethnic representation continues to produce further inequality in the political space between Malays and non-Malays. The Federal Constitution of Malaysia attributes a "special position" to Malays by way of explicitly following the direct approach of the horizontal inequalities frame- work. Malays and the natives of Sabah and Sarawak states benefit from the reservation of quotas in various sectors.

The socioeconomic disparities widened between Malays and Chinese just after independence, resulting in the 1969 ethnic riots. After the riots, the growth policies formulated in Malaysia shifted from the objective of economic growth to the redistribution of wealth to reduce income inequalities between the ethnic groups. As a result, the Alliance Coalition was renamed Barisan Nassional in 1974 with the merging of major opposition parties and the emer- gence of civil liberties groups Hindraf (Hindu Rights Action Force) and Bersih (Coalition for Clean and Fair Election). The Malay Administrative Service offers ethnic quotas in a ratio of 4:1 (Malays to non-Malays). Malays are rep- resented more in external affairs, the judicial system, civil services and in the cabinet. Government assistance for Malays allowed Malay representation to be predominant in business ownership (Saari et al., 2015).

The political structure in Malaysia is not equitable. The policies and proce- dures outlined in the Malaysian political arena are largely in favour of Malays and Bumiputeras (Lee, 2017). The existing affirmative policies and programs involving political decisions mainly focus upon the socioeconomic uplift of Malays and Bumiputeras and exclude the other two ethnic groups with a lack of sufficient inclusive measures. The extent of bureaucracy, level of regulation and deregulation and government stability and/or instability profoundly impact the areas of education, employment and business development in Malaysia.

Economic Factors

The formulation of NEP was mainly oriented towards poverty reduction. Jomo (2004) states that while this objective of poverty reduction was met in Malaysia, the reasons are attributed to the general increase in the quality of life and salary levels throughout the world. The existing policies in Malaysia are often criticised due to the preferential agreements embedded within economic development that favour one ethnic group over the other. The other criticism in Malaysia relates to missed opportunities to revise the NEP policies, specifically the policies associated with racial preference, when revised in 1991 and 2000 (Le, 2016). Scholars identify that certain groups such as estate workers, rural peasants, contract labourers and public workers were largely ignored by the government in devising the NEP and associated policies.

A lack of appropriate measures to achieve Bumiputera quota in terms of the share capital and eradication of interethnic economic inequalities in the original policies was criticised (Jomo, 2004). The official documents fail to present information related to ethnic preference subsidies offered to Bumiputeras. Affirmative action policies oriented towards the uplift of the economic situation of ethnic groups in Malaysia have only been partially achieved and resulted in persisting economic inequalities. Within the Malaysian Constitution, Article 153 specifically mentions the preferential treatment sanctioned towards Malays and indigenous groups (Guan, 2005). Under colonial rule, the British engaged in the promotion of preferential treatment as Malays were selected and trained to be part of an elite workforce. Later, in 1948, the Federation of Malaya agreement allowed permits and licenses granted for Malays alone to promote business development, enterprise initiation and increase ownership (Le, 2016).

The quotas and/or lack of quotas included within the affirmative action policies explicitly included or excluded certain ethnic groups, mainly Chinese and Indians, whereby business formation and continuation rested with Malays, not due to business expertise but due to preferential agreements in place. All public universities in Malaysia reserve 55 per cent of their places for Malay students. Tertiary graduate enrollments of the Malay students increased exponentially over the past three decades resulting in the growth of a Malay professional class. The steady increase in the number of Malays pursuing university education in the 1990s and after indicates that more Malays today are in professional occupation categories. Further, state privatisation programs allowed for Malay ownership in companies to grow exponentially up to 20.6 per cent resulting in the emergence of a corporate Malay community (Guan, 2005).

Social Factors

Various social factors also play an important role in determining the effectiveness of the existing affirmative action policies in Malaysia. The workforce employed in Malay-owned companies predominantly includes Malays only. Malay ownership dominates large companies, and the Chinese dominated the small and medium-sized enterprises sector in Malaysia. The principles of equal opportunity are largely ignored, and favouritism exhibited towards specific ethnic groups has resulted in the recruitment of a workforce from the same ethnic background, resulting in the emergence of ethnic conclaves (Guan, 2005). The disposable income of the individuals and/or households shows the social class status and rank as these dimensions directly link to the attainment of quality education and employment opportunities.

The state in Malaysia has offered generous scholarships, relaxed admission criteria and promoted training facilities for Malays. The university system is based on the allocation of quotas for Malays. The Education Act (1961) facilitated many Chinese secondary schools to convert the medium of instruction from Chinese to Malay and English. Malay is identified as the national language as per the National Language Act (1967) and as the medium of instruction in the public education system in the country (Hsu et al., 2018), replacing the four major education systems (on the basis of language – Malay, Mandarin, Tamil and English) prevalent in the country during the 1970s and 1980s (Menon, 2009). The government made several attempts towards progressing a unified education system with limited success. The Malaysian government initiated similar interventions during 1995 and 2000 as part of the Vision School Program, also with minimal success.

Religious beliefs held by the different ethnic groups in Malaysia are ingrained through organisational practices as most businesses favour recruiting individuals with a similar ethnic background in order to avoid conflict (Lee, 2017). The recruitment of individuals from other ethnic backgrounds in businesses dominated by a specific ethnicity will potentially impose restrictions not only on the nature and type of work carried out on a day-to-day basis but also a limit on the career progression of individuals. On one side, by way of recruiting individuals from different ethnic backgrounds, businesses may be aligning with the principles of diversity. However, the prevailing social conditions imposing restrictions on individuals' careers and type of work instil inequality and non-inclusivity. These asymmetries in human capital lead to discrepancies in social capital that restricts the achievement of the objectives of the existing affirmative action policies in Malaysia. Social factors that potentially confound the effectiveness of affirmative action policies need to be carefully considered by the Malaysian government to reduce interethnic differences and contribute to the overall wellbeing of all ethnic groups. The wealth and social class accumulated further determine the ownership of businesses in Malaysia that trigger ethnic differences. The Malaysian government has implemented measures and policies to promote business ownership among ethnic groups as the existing policies favour preferential treatment. McCrudden (2015) notes that affirmative action policies focused on positive discrimination, inclusionary measures, targeting underrepresented groups and preferential treatment explain the partial embeddedness of equality, diversity and inclusion in management practices in Malaysia.

CONCLUSION

Ethnic disparities have seemed to persist in Malaysia since the colonial period. The measures taken by the Malaysian government through the formulation and implementation of affirmative action policies in the country seem to have deepened the existing ethnic disparities. Whilst the affirmative action policies met some original objectives of enhancing the socioeconomic conditions of Malays and Bumiputeras to some extent, much needs to be attained. Available information indicates that in order to attain the goals of Vision 2020, attention needs to be directed towards the effective incorporation of equality, diversity and inclusivity measures in affirmative action policies. The affirmative action policies need to be revitalised by way of linking the objective of the policy to the targeted soft and hard metrics. Measures to reduce positive discrimination and excessive preferential treatment are necessary. The revitalised affirmative action policies need to close the urban and rural divide and also need to reduce the gap between different ethnic groups. The impact exerted by other intersecting variables such as language, religion, location and occupation need to be considered carefully alongside interethnic differences.

Effective measures to potentially reduce the existing interethnic differences through a horizontal inequalities framework need to be considered by the Malaysian government. For example, until now the focus of the Malaysian government on the incorporation of a direct approach to a larger extent and the embracement of an indirect approach to a lesser extent to reduce ethnic differences seems to have had limited effect. Therefore, the ministries and the government need to pilot the effectiveness of an integrated framework by way of embracing direct, indirect and integrationist approaches in order to enhance the effectiveness of revitalised affirmative action policies. Affirmative action policies need to link to the broader areas of education, employment and business creation and/or development for minimising the impact exerted by the identified macro-environmental factors. Education, employment and business development are identified to be the core areas that relate directly to economic growth, market competitiveness and international trade. The incorporation of equality, diversity and inclusion measures in the revitalised affirmative action policies potentially allows Malaysia to achieve the objectives of Vision 2020 in terms of national unity.

Although this chapter systematically analysed various public documents, government reports, scholarly academic articles, websites and white papers, one of the limitations of the study is the presentation of the results on the basis of the available secondary data. Future research studies need to gather first-hand information from primary data sources through feasible qualitative or quantitative approaches or even obtain data through mixed-methods research in order to enhance the robustness and rigour of the study. Also, the results presented in this chapter are specific to the Malaysian context and therefore cannot be generalised to other country contexts with interethnic disparities. Affirmative action policies can be evaluated in other country contexts such as Sri Lanka in the Southeast Asian region where ethnic disparities are prominent. The identification of the structural, political, economic and social factors leading to ethnic disparities provides important implications for the negotiation of existing preferential treatment and the allocation of sanctions and/or quotas. The revitalisation of the existing affirmative action policies and the incorporation of equality, diversity and inclusivity measures may need openness from different ethnic groups. Further embeddedness of these policies is essential for overcoming positive discrimination and preferential treatment.

REFERENCES

Browne, J., Coffey, B., Cook, K., Meiklejohn, S. and Palermo, J. (2019). A guide to policy analysis as a research method. *Health Promotion International*, 34(5), 1032–1044.

de Vaus, D. A. (2001). *Research Design in Social Research*. London: Sage.

DOSM (Department of Statistics) (2010). *Population Distribution and Basic Demographic Characteristic Report 2010*. Putrajaya.

Guan, L. H. (2005). Affirmative action in Malaysia. *Southeast Asian Affairs*, 1, 211–228.

Gul, F., Munir, S. and Zhang, L. (2016). Ethnicity, politics and firm performance: Evidence from Malaysia. *Pacific-Basin Finance Journal*, 40, 115–129.

Haque, M. S. (2003). The role of the state in managing ethnic tensions in Malaysia: A critical disclosure. *American Behavioural Scientist*, 47(3), 240–266.

Hsu, P. L., Maccari, E. A., Mazieri, M. R. and Storopoli, J. E. (2018). A bibliometric review of institutional theory on higher education institutions. *Future Studies Research Journal: Trends and Studies*, 10(3), 383–401.

Jomo, K. S. (2004). The new economic policy and interethnic relations in Malaysia, Geneva: United Nations Research Institute for Social Development, Paper No. 7.

Le, N. H. (2016). *An Assessment of the Implementation of Affirmative Action in Education in Malaysia.* Masters Programme in Economic Growth, Innovation and Spatial Dynamics, Lund University.

Lee, H. (2017). *Majority Affirmative Action in Malaysia: Imperatives, Compromises and Challenges.* Ottawa: Global Centre for Pluralism, Institute for Southeast Asian Studies, 1–24.

McCrudden, C. (2015). Affirmative action: Comparative policies and controversies. *International Encyclopedia of the Social and Behavioural Sciences,* J. Wright (Ed.). New York: Elsevier, 248–255.

Menon, J. (2009). Macroeconomic management amid ethnic diversity: Fifty years of Malaysian experience. *Journal of Asian Economics,* 20(1), 25–33.

Miles, M. B. and Huberman, A. M. (1994). *An Expanded Sourcebook: Qualitative Data Analysis* (2nd Ed.). London: Sage.

PMO (Prime Minister's Office) (2019). National anti-corruption plan 2019–2023. www.pmo.gov.my/wp-content/uploads/2019

Ratuva, S. (2013). *The Politics of Preferential Development: Affirmative Action and Trans-Global Study.* Canberra: ANU Press.

Saari, M. Y., Dietzenbacher, E. and Los, B. (2015). Sources of income growth and inequality across ethnic groups in Malaysia 1970–2000. *World Development,* 76(December), 311–328.

Sridhar, R., Sachithanandam, V., Mageswaran, T., Purvaja, R., Ramesh, R., Senthil Vel, A. and Thirunavukkarasan, E. (2016). A political, economic, social, technological, legal and environmental (PESTLE) approach for assessment of coastal zone management practices in India. *International Review of Public Administration,* 21(3), 216–232.

Stewart, F., Brown, G. K. and Langer, A. (2008). Policies towards horizontal inequalities, in Steward, F. (Ed.), *Horizontal Inequalities and Conflict: Understanding Group Violence in Multiethnic Societies* (pp. 301–325), Basingstoke: Palgrave Macmillan.

Varghese, M. and Gomez, E. T. (2018). Representations of inclusiveness in social assistance programmes of the 10th Malaysia Plan, 2011–2015. *National Identities,* 1–17.

Webb, J. W., Pryor, C. G. and Kellermanns, F. W. (2015). Household enterprise in base-of-the-pyramid markets: The influence of institution and family embeddedness. *Africa Journal of Management,* 1, 115–136.

14. Beyond demographic diversity: towards intersectional gender justice in professional design practice in New Zealand

Sarah Elsie Baker

INTRODUCTION

Over the last few years, popular discourse such as the #metoo movement has brought the prevalence of gender inequality to the fore. Design has been included in this critique of the patriarchy, with questions being raised over the lack of female designers receiving industry accolades, corporations being criticised for designing objects that perpetuate gender stereotypes and authors drawing attention to gender blindness in tech culture. For example, in her book *Invisible Women: Exposing Data Bias in a World Designed for Men*, Caroline Criado-Perez documents how the design of artefacts including digital assistants, seat belts and breast pumps all reflect and perpetuate the dominance of male experiences over female ones. The bias of design, she argues, is due to a gender data gap in which men are the default. For Criado-Perez, the solution is to diversify the workforce. She writes basic errors would surely be 'caught by a team with enough women on it' (2019, p. 176).

Indeed, Criado-Perez is correct that women are underrepresented in design and creative technology. For example, in Aotearoa, New Zealand, where this study is based, 65 per cent of design students in tertiary education are female, while only 45 per cent find work in the industry (Arnett-Philips, 2020). Lack of parity intensifies in senior positions with 11 per cent of creative directors identifying as female (Arnett-Philips, 2020).

In this chapter I argue that while the involvement of women in professional practice is an essential starting point in addressing the gender bias of design, unfortunately the path to gender justice is not that simple. The chapter begins by documenting academic accounts of gender and design. It finds that the majority of texts assume that increased employment, recognition and visibility of women will address inequality. Using the lens of intersectional gender justice, I argue that design principles and practices often reinforce heteropatriarchal power structures and hierarchies. Thus, diversifying the workforce is not enough to challenge workplace inequalities or to alter the biases of products, services and systems. With this in mind, the research frames gender justice in professional design practice as a wicked problem made up of complex and interconnected issues which make it difficult to solve. Drawing on participatory systems mapping workshops, the research sets out to map barriers to gender justice in professional design practice in Aotearoa in order to identify leverage points for intervention beyond demographic diversity.

WOMEN, DESIGN AND GENDER

It was not until the mid-1980s that gender emerged as a topic for discussion in design research. In the seminal text, 'Made in Patriarchy: Towards a Feminist Analysis of Women in Design', the design historian Cheryl Buckley (1986) observed how women's interventions had been consistently ignored or framed as craft. She writes that the 'selection, classification and prioritization of types of design, categories of designers, distinct styles and movements, and different modes of production, are inherently biased against women' (1986, p. 3). Buckley explores how, within the context of patriarchy, design disciplines are gendered and hierarchised with women associated with 'decorative' practices, while 'technical' design disciplines such as industrial design were coded as male and afforded higher status. Buckley's arguments are a critique of dominant design histories, and she incites researchers to address the paucity of information about women. For Buckley, gender equality can be achieved by making female designers and their conditions visible.

It was also in the 1980s that the first primary studies of gender in the design industries emerged. In their 1989 paper 'Divided by Design: Gender and the Labour Process in the Design Industry', Jenny Lewis and Margaret Bruce reflect on gender hierarchies in graphic and industrial design. Like Buckley, they observe that women's contributions as designers have been overlooked. They propose that the absence of women is reflected in the gendered inadequacies of products and aim to find solutions to address this. Lewis and Bruce identify three 'hurdles' that women face in professional design practice. The first barrier to entry is 'getting qualifications', the second hurdle is 'getting a first job in design' and the third is 'becoming a success' which involves 'getting management experience', 'getting prestigious work contacts' and 'gaining awards' (1989, p. 16). They offer practical solutions for reducing the gendered division of labour which includes targeted recruitment of female design students and training on gender issues.

Since the 1980s there have been surprisingly few academic texts exploring gender and design (notable exceptions include Attfield, 2000 and Kirkham,

1996). However, in the last few years, the gender bias of design has received more attention. Like the arguments made in the 1980s, many recent discussions propose that the solution to gender inequality is to increase the employment and recognition of women. For example, in her recent revisiting of 'Made in Patriarchy', Buckley (2020) maintains that there is still a need to focus on women (rather than gender justice more generally). Quoting Sara Ahmed, Buckley suggests that 'in a world in which human is still defined as *man*, we have to fight for women and as women' (2020, p. 23). She writes that there is a need to fight for 'all who travel under the sign women' as a tactical priority and, by doing so, challenge some of the design industry's embedded assumptions (2020, p. 23). Buckley's call for increased visibility of women is echoed by the recent work of Caroline Criado-Perez in which she suggests that 'we must acknowledge – and mitigate against – this fundamental bias that frames women as atypical … it's time for us to finally start counting women as the entirely average humans that they are' (2020, para. 13).

NON-BINARY IDENTITIES AND INTERSECTIONAL GENDER JUSTICE

Focusing on the visibility of women as a strategy to challenge gender inequality raises a number of problematic issues that I now consider. In the first instance, the category 'women' does not account for people who fall outside the binaries of man/woman, and thus is unlikely to address the needs of people of all genders.

Even when it is used inclusively, as in 'all who travel under the sign women' (Buckley), unity under the binaries of man/woman cannot be assumed. Gender is a complex 'biopsychosocial construct' that is comprised of identity (a sense of who one is), role (how one interacts according to gender norms), expression (how gender manifests through clothes, hair, etc.) and experience (how one navigates the world according to their gender) (Barker and Iantaffi, 2019). Each of these elements do not necessarily align. For example, while my own gender expression may be read as feminine and I use the category female if required, on the whole I do not experience myself as gendered. This may, in part, be a product of privilege. I did not feel the full weight of my gender until I entered the workforce and became a parent. Nevertheless, I do not feel an affinity with the category 'woman' and any fight for recognition of women may not feel inclusive of my experience. Thus, as these reflections highlight, gender cannot be defined outside of other categories including sexuality, age, ethnicity, class, disability and nationality. My position as an English, bisexual, white, middle-class, non-disabled, 41 year old living in Aotearoa influences my gendered experience affording me certain privileges and/or oppressions depending on the context.

These reflections about the complexity of identity can be understood through the lens of intersectionality. The theory of intersectionality is a tool for exploring the interlocking systems of power that impact upon us. First defined by Kimberlé Crenshaw (1991), intersectionality demonstrates how the experience of being a member of more than one social group should not just be understood as being a member of each, but as a compound. For example, the experience of being an indigenous woman is not just about being a woman and being indigenous, it is a compound of the two. Indigenous women experience a different form of sexism from white women and as a result are often overlooked in feminist political projects. As Crenshaw (1991) notes: 'the failure of feminism to interrogate race means that the resistance strategies of feminism will often replicate and reinforce the subordination of people of colour, and the failure of antiracism to interrogate patriarchy means that antiracism will frequently reproduce the subordination of women' (p. 1252). By implication, when Criado-Perez speaks of 'women as entirely average humans', which women is she referring to and how would we go about designing for them? Surely this approach to design would simply reassert norms and stereotypes, albeit those attached to the category 'woman' rather than the category 'man'?

The assumption that the increased employment of women in design would inevitably lead to equality should also be challenged. Emphasis on diversifying the workforce negates many of the systemic inequalities inscribed in the everyday experience and culture of design. For example, in primary research completed from 2005 to 2008, Suzanne Reimer (2015) found that design professionals felt gender divisions were 'getting better' because of the increased employment of women. Reimer argues that this disavowal of structural power relations was actually part of hegemonic masculinities that continued to be central to the work culture of United Kingdom (UK) design agencies.

Design masculinities were rehearsed through 'the normalisation of long and unpredictable hours; and via relationships developed in the work setting and with clients' (2015, para. 60). She writes that it is assumed that creative work is all encompassing and that ideal employees must be obsessive or perfectionist and thus willing and able to work at all times. Creative skill in design, she finds, is coded as masculine, and male managers 'repeatedly denied that women possessed legitimate expertise in creative or technological production' (2015, para. 46). Similarly, rapport building which is crucial to pitch for new business and satisfy clients was conceptualised as a male activity. Reimer finds that for many of her participants it was 'unquestioningly assumed that men … [would] best be able to relate to other men' (2015, para. 22). Indeed, when many women take on a 'double shift' at work and at home, rapport building through attendance at social events such as afterwork drinks becomes more difficult. Reimer argues that while creativity, knowledge, innovation and craft may seem gender neutral, they rest on assumptions about a masculine subject.

In addition, just because someone inhabits a particular body or identifies with a particular category such as 'woman', it does not necessarily mean that they will act in a certain way. For example, not all women are nurturing, a quality traditionally (and problematically) coded as female. Thus, rather than viewing experience as a foundation for knowledge (i.e. based on a fixed notion of what it is to be a woman), experience should be thought of as informing positions that are continually evolving. This means that it is possible for a 'straight white man' to offer a diverse perspective if he has had a diversity of experience. Of course, design studios and boardrooms full of 'straight white men' are not adequate. Based on experience it is more likely that a female Māori designer would better understand the complex intersections of racial and sexual discrimination, for example. However, demographic diversity alone is not enough to foster gender justice, changes to values, environments and processes are also vital.

Therefore, rather than focusing specifically on equality for women, I strive for, and adopt, the concept of intersectional gender justice. This approach maintains that the systemic redistribution of power, opportunities, and access for people of all genders will only be achieved by the dismantling of harmful structures such as heteropatriarchy, white supremacy, and settler colonialism. Thus, while the analysis of Buckley and Criado-Perez is convincing, I do not believe gender hierarchies in design will be dissolved by 'fighting for women'. Instead, we need to deconstruct the binaries of sex and gender that manifest themselves in design cultures.

As a field and as an industry, design has been (and arguably still is) heavily reliant on modernist discourse that reproduces binaries including male/female, mind/body, self/other, subject/object and nature/culture and their associated hierarchies (Escobar, 2018, p. 25). These are binaries that are also foundational to patriarchal culture (Escobar, 2018, p. 121). Thus, I would argue that design needs to dismantle hierarchies by working towards the proliferation of gender identities, expressions and experiences in all their possible manifestations. This long-term vision is focused on 'justice' rather than 'equality' and 'equity' because it not only aims to address imbalanced social systems but also pursues sustainable and equitable access for future generations.

Before it is possible to dismantle harmful structures, however, it is necessary to understand the current state of gender-based experiences in design. Thus, the chapter uses Reimer's arguments regarding the hegemonic masculinities at work in UK design agencies as a point of comparison and considers what power relations might be at play in professional design practice in Aotearoa. Exploring how values, environments and processes act as barriers to gender justice is complex, however. One way of tackling this complexity is by framing gender justice as a 'wicked problem'.

METHODOLOGY: GENDER JUSTICE IN PROFESSIONAL DESIGN PRACTICE AS A WICKED PROBLEM

The wicked problem approach was conceived by Horst Rittel in the 1960s (Buchanan, 1992, p. 15). Rittel was critical of the linear model of problem solving that was being explored by designers at the time. In its most basic formulation, this rational approach sees problem definitions logically determining problem solutions. As Daniela K. Rosner (2018) notes, design methodologies continue to be shaped by this logic. Indeed, it is this type of approach that conceptualises gender inequality in design as simply solved by employing more women.

Instead, as critics of the linear model point out, design thinking and decision making involves multiple issues, stakeholders, contexts and changing conditions. Thus, Rittel argues that the majority of design problems are wicked problems. Wicked problems are 'a class of social system problems which are ill-formulated, where the information is confusing, where there are many clients and decision makers with conflicting values, and where the ramifications in the whole system are thoroughly confusing' (Rittel, quoted in Buchanan, 1992, p. 15).

The most recent incarnation of the wicked problem approach as a design methodology is in transition design. The central premise of transition design is that there is a need for societal transitions to be more sustainable and equitable futures and design practices are essential to this transformation (Irwin et al., 2015, p. 1). The wicked problem approach is used in transition design together with systems thinking in order to explore issues such as climate change, biodiversity and crime. It is argued that wicked problems are essentially systems problems, and thus systems mapping is used to understand issues within their larger systems contexts with the view to formulating interventions. As the instructors of the Transition Design Seminar 2021 write, 'if wicked problems are like a tangled ball of yarn', then mapping systems is like showing 'us which threads to pull on to begin untangling it' (Transition Design Seminar, 2021b, para. 3). Lines of connection, they write, can become dense and can reveal 'leverage points for change where solutions have the potential to solve many issues simultaneously' (Transition Design Seminar, 2021b, para. 3). Therefore, analysing wicked problems using systems mapping is an action-oriented methodology that aims to identify the most effective sites to intervene with design projects. In this approach, wicked problems are understood as governed by positive and negative feedback loops. This means that understanding the dynamics within the complex system is paramount otherwise design interventions can amplify negative effects.

Table 14.1   Self-identified categories by participant

Designer	Gender	Sexuality	Age	Ethnicity
1	Female	Gay	42	New Zealand European
2	Female	'Straight', monosexual	29	Cook Island/New Zealand European
3	Cis-woman	Lesbian	22	New Zealand European/Māori
4	Cis-woman	Non-binary	33	New Zealand European/Chinese
5	Female	Heterosexual	58	New Zealand European/Māori

METHOD: SYSTEMS MAPPING WORKSHOPS

The primary research completed for this chapter mapped barriers to gender justice in professional design practice in systems mapping workshops with five designers. By collectively mapping systems, multiple participants can learn together in 'reflection-in-action' (Simonsen and Robertson, 2013, p. 2). The method provides the means for stakeholders to achieve a shared understanding of the complexity of the problem. It also allows for all human and non-human elements (barriers in this case) to be explored at the same time. This strength means that participatory systems mapping is currently predominantly used in the fields of environmental science and sustainability studies. Even examples from transition design tend to focus on climate change and its effects. Therefore, the research documented in this project is currently unique in using a wicked problem approach and participatory systems mapping to explore gender justice.

It is recognised that five participants is a small number, however, participatory systems maps are a product of their specific contributors and their contexts, rather than meant as a representative sample. As Sarah Elsie Baker and Rosalind Edwards (2012) find, the valid number of participants for a study is dependent on its purpose. In this case, once possible sites for intervention have been identified in the systems map, they can then be explored with a wider group if required.

The designers were found via personal networks. All were interested in gender justice in design and self-identify as women. As such, it is acknowledged that the map is a reflection of the thoughts and experiences of a specific group of female designers. They were all based in Auckland and work within what can largely be framed as media design (graphic design, branding, interactive design and social innovation). More detail regarding the categories with which the women identified can be found in Table 14.1.

The online workshop took place via Zoom and used the relationship mapping software Kumu. Kumu offers templates that allows teams to map stakeholders, systems, social networks, community assets or concepts. The systems mapping template enables participants to contribute to an online system map posting issues via sticky notes, linking topics and creating causal loops with arrows. Originally intended to take two hours, the workshops were decreased to one hour due to the commitments of the participants. The fact that participants were so time poor is discussed in more detail below. The workshop was run using a similar process to that documented by Pete Barbrook-Johnson and Alexandra Penn (2021) in their discussion of participatory systems mapping as method. The focal factor of gender justice in professional design practice was introduced using recent industry statistics. Using the categories of infrastructure/technology issues; policy/governance/legal issues; social/psychological issues; business/economic issues; and environmental issues from the transition design framework (Transition Design Seminar, 2021a), participants brainstormed barriers to equality as they saw them. Participants spoke about what they thought were general inequalities in industry as well as those issues that had affected them personally.

MAPPING GENDER JUSTICE IN PROFESSIONAL DESIGN PRACTICE: REPETITIVE DYNAMICS

The map in Figure 14.1 shows all the barriers to gender justice in professional design practice in Aotearoa that were raised in the participatory workshops. Five areas have been identified and represented as loops: repetitive dynamics that play out 'over and over again and end up acting as either significant drivers of change or maintainers of the status quo' (Alford, 2017). The five areas of time pressures, division of labour, self-worth and judgements of value, a lack of champions and ingrained binaries were discussed for the longest amount of time during the workshops. Findings in each area point to a 'how might we' question (Ideo, 2021). These questions are posed as starting points for future design interventions.

Time Pressures

One of the first issues that participants mentioned was the extra familial duties that many women take on. This included looking after children and elderly family members, and greater responsibilities in terms of household chores. Participants in same-sex relationships felt that while their responsibilities were less than their 'straight' counterparts, they still seemed to take on more than many of their male colleagues. Participants thought that obligations outside work clashed with the demands of being a designer. While there have been

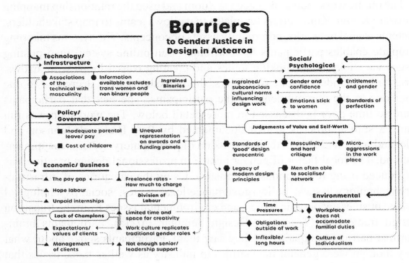

Source: Designed by Kolcha.

Figure 14.1   Barriers to gender justice in design in Aotearoa

changes to more flexible working practices in design agencies particularly in light of Covid-19, professional design practice tends to involve long hours especially when working towards tight deadlines. For freelancers there is even greater flexibility, but hours tend to be made up by night shifts, early starts or weekends in order to complete projects. Familial responsibilities also mean that women are less able to network and socialise in order to make a name for oneself. For example, one participant spoke about missing out on Friday drinks at the studio and how that meant she felt 'out of the loop'.

Discussions of the long and unpredictable hours involved in design resonate with Reimer's findings in the UK and reinforce her argument that hegemonic masculinities continue to structure the work culture of design. The expectation to work long hours affects people of all genders and is particularly challenging for parents. Work cultures that are incompatible with parental responsibilities maintain gender inequality because women (as the majority of primary carers) are likely to have to make compromises regarding their careers. These compromises also mean that men are less able and/or willing to take on a more active role. While a problem in all industries and evidence of the importance of adequate parental leave, the inequities of familial responsibility are more acutely felt in work cultures with long and unpredictable hours. Thus, how might we challenge the long hours culture in design? What would a 'slow' design movement look like in the present moment, and how could this co-exist with the demands of capitalism?

Divisions of Labour

According to the participants, the demands of family life also influenced the types of creative work that freelancers would take on. For example, one participant spoke of a friend who since becoming a solo parent only takes on relatively small uncomplicated jobs because she does not have the capacity (physical and mental) for more creative projects. This was reiterated by another freelance designer who mentioned it was difficult to carve out the long periods of time necessary to concentrate on branding work.

For those working in agencies, divisions of labour were rehearsed in slightly different ways. For example, participants thought that female junior designers were often more likely to be expected to make coffee and set up for client meetings. A recent female design graduate also spoke about the surprise that some clients had when they found out about her skills in interactive design and coding. Therefore, while the gendered hierarchies of design disciplines might not be quite so distinct as when Buckley and Lewis and Bruce were writing in the 1980s, technical skills such as coding continue to be read as masculine. The associations of the technoscientific with masculinity mean that women are less likely to be offered work on innovative projects using cutting-edge technology, and may be less likely to take these projects on because they lack the conditions for creativity. This results in reduced involvement in high-status projects, fewer submissions to design awards and fewer opportunities for promotion. Most importantly, it means that women have less chance to challenge inequality through their design work and change gendered experience for the better. Thus, how might we create spaces for all designers to have the opportunity to work on high-status creative projects?

Judgements of Value and Self-Worth

When mapping gender justice in professional design practice as a wicked problem, participants also referred to the indeterminacy of the value of design work. Some spoke about how a narrow notion of 'good' design continued to make projects with more 'feminine' aesthetics less likely to get awards or secure funding. Participants with Māori and Pacific heritage spoke of the time taken to get the confidence to embrace their own cultural identity in their design work. It was noted how awards panels and funding bodies had tried to broaden their understanding of what constituted 'good' design in recent years. Despite these efforts, it was felt that the legacy of European modernist aesthetics continued to influence what was deemed as valuable. Thus, how can we interrogate and break down standards of 'good' design? What new judgement criteria should we create?

The indeterminacy of the value of design also meant that freelancers found it difficult to know what to charge for their work. One participant told the group that she knew she undercharged for her brand strategy projects but had not put up her fees. Others spoke of how white men in the industry had a greater sense of entitlement and confidence. For example, a recent graduate described how her fellow female classmates felt they had to perfect their portfolios while her male counterparts only worked on them until they were 'good enough'. As Reimer found, the ideal designer is conceptualised as an obsessive perfectionist and discussion in the workshops would suggest that this burden is unequally experienced by women. The internalisation of patriarchal design ideologies made the participants feel that they had to be extra confident and 'sell' their ideas more strongly than their male counterparts. Yet this was a fine line to tread because, as one more experienced designer suggested, 'emotions stick to women' and one could easily be cast as too aggressive. Thus, female designers find themselves in a 'double bind': not confident enough in their own abilities or overly assertive and aggressive. Participants thought that concerns about self-worth were intensified by working alone and when in competition with other designers. Thus, how might we encourage self-worth in those who are marginalised without viewing a lack of confidence as an individual character flaw? What training or organisational structures could be put in place to educate people about gender and judgements of value in design?

Lack of Champions

All participants, apart from one who works in social innovation, work for commercial clients. As such, the expectations of clients influence their design decisions. For example, a designer might deviate from gender norms in something as simple as colour choice or the order of gendered symbols, but if a client disagrees, they may ask for it to be changed. If designers feel the client is conservative, they may avoid taking risks in the first place. In agencies, creative work may be signed off by senior managers or creative directors before it gets to the client. This can limit the potential designers have to challenge gender norms. For example, one participant spoke of design work they produced which included depictions of different family forms including a lesbian couple. They were asked by the creative director to take out this image before it was shown to the client because it was assumed to be too radical. The participants felt that the representation of a diverse family could have been 'sold' to the client and they spoke of the need for management support and leadership. Therefore, while the design justice movement argues for the need to put communities of users at the centre of design work and this is an honourable goal (see Costanza-Chock, 2020), in commercial contexts it is often clients and preconceived notions of their tastes that influence outcomes. This frequently means that gender norms are reproduced despite designers' wishes. Thus, how might we increase the number of champions of gender justice in the design industry? How can designers move away from reproducing gender norms while also satisfying their clients?

Ingrained Binaries

All participants involved in the mapping workshop indicated their interest in gender justice. As such, they were aware of gender-related issues including the challenges faced by gender-diverse people. For example, it was recognised that statistics about gender in design in Aotearoa do not acknowledge trans and non-binary people. This barrier to gender justice was included on the map. Participants were also aware of the problematic cultural norms reproduced in design work. Yet, at the same time, as evidenced above, much of the discussion associated typical behaviours with either men or women. One participant remarked how 'if men were in this workshop, we'd have to change our language to #not all men!' Participants sometimes rephrased their language and said 'people who identify as women'. However, the conversation would often revert back to men/women binaries and associated behaviours. This finding may have been different if there were transgender people and/or non-binary people present, and it is one of the limitations of the study. What the finding does highlight, however, is the extent to which binary language and gender norms are ingrained into everyday experience. It also sheds light on why normative gender associations made in design work may go unchecked. Thus, how might we enable designers to reflect on their own gender identities and to check their assumptions about others?

CONCLUSION: TOWARDS INTERSECTIONAL GENDER JUSTICE

The map and repetitive dynamics explored here reiterate many of the arguments made by design researchers. This includes the legacy of modernist discourse with its patriarchal norms, the challenges posed by the long hours culture and the division of labour in professional design practice along gendered lines. What is notable is how the complexities of gendered experience that have been identified by academic research since the 1980s have had seemingly little impact on commercial professional practice until now. With the recent increase in interest in diversity and inclusion in industry, it is the best possible time to bridge the gap and intervene.

With this in mind, the systems mapping workshops completed for this chapter set about identifying projects with the most potential to create change. Articulated as 'how might we' questions, possible projects include exploring the idea of a slow design movement, creating tools for reflection and checking assumptions about users, breaking down standards of 'good' design and creating new criteria for evaluation, and establishing spaces for people of all genders to work on high-status creative projects. The inclination might be to jump straight into outlining solutions, but this would replicate the linear design methodology that I have been critical of in this chapter. The next stage in this action-oriented research project will be to explore the viability of projects in each theme with users who self-identify with a range of identity categories. This participatory approach aims to design artifacts that are appropriate to context and that resist singular or essentialising points of view. Indeed, projects may be relatively local and small scale. In Aotearoa, for example, projects will explore how mātauranga Māori (Māori knowledge) and kaupapa Māori research approach (Māori research methodology) can inform the design process. By activating projects together with other initiatives globally, however, impacts could be greater than the sum of their parts.

Indeed, one of the strengths of participatory systems mapping is that participants reflect on their own experiences within a wider context and are directly involved in determining appropriate interventions. This moves away from the notion of the designer and/or academic researcher as expert and is an advantage in action research that aims to collaborate with industries or communities. In organisations, for example, participatory systems mapping could be fruitful for anyone wanting to make a positive culture shift by exploring the complexities of diversity and inclusion with employees. Once produced, ownership of the maps themselves can be taken over by stakeholders as they become living documents that change over time.

Like all methods, participatory systems mapping has its limitations. The systems maps produced in workshops are only representative of the stakeholders involved and thus could miss crucial elements others may consider central to the problems at hand. Therefore, I would also recommend recording the session to allow for analysis of what was (or was not) mentioned. In this study, the recording was particularly useful to analyse the discussion and use of gendered categories such as man/woman.

To summarise, the analysis of gender inequality in design in Aotearoa explored in this chapter may look similar to the findings of authors such as Buckley and Criado-Perez. However, the potential design interventions look very different from the calls simply to employ more women in design and creative technology, or to create products specifically for women. This is not to suggest that these appeals are irrelevant. Diversity of experience is more likely to be found by engaging demographically diverse employees and users.

However, the visibility of women, transgender and non-binary people, and recognition of the injustices they experience, is just the first step towards intersectional gender justice. If we want a future where people of all genders have equal power, opportunities and access, then we need to design environments and embrace processes and value systems that go beyond gender binaries. The challenge for researchers, then, is to explore how binaries manifest in their own field or organisation, and to work with stakeholders to produce tools appropriate to their contexts.

REFERENCES

Alford, C. (2017) How systems mapping can help you build a better theory of change in 'Too Deep'. https://blog.kumu.io/how-systems-mapping-can-help-you-build-a-better-theory-of-change-

Arnett-Philips, N. (2020) Field guide 2020: Towards openness. *Design Assembly.* https://designassembly.org.nz/2020/09/11/field-guide-2020-towards-openness/

Attfield, J. (2000) *Wild Things: The Material Culture of Everyday Life.* Berg.

Baker, S. and Edwards, R. (2012) How many qualitative interviews is enough. http://eprints.ncrm.ac.uk/2273/4/how_many_interviews.pdf

Barbrook-Johnson, P. and Penn, A. (2021) Participatory systems mapping for complex energy policy evaluation. *Evaluation*, 27(1), https://journals.sagepub.com/doi/full/10.1177/1356389020976153

Barker, M. J. and Iantaffi, A. (2019) *Life Isn't Binary: On Being Both, Beyond and Inbetween.* Jessica Kingsley Publishers.

Buchanan, R. (1992) Wicked problems in design thinking. *Design Issues*, 8(2): 5–21.

Buckley, C. (1986) Made in patriarchy: Toward a feminist analysis of women and design. *Design Issues*, 3(2): 3–4.

Buckley, C. (2020) Made in patriarchy II: Researching (or re-searching) women and design. *Design Issues*, 36(1): 19–29.

Contanza- Chock, S. (2020) *Design Justice: Community-Led Practices to Build the Worlds We Need.* MIT Press.

Criado-Perez, C. (2019) *Invisible Women: Exposing Data Bias in a World Designed for Men.* Random House.

Criado-Perez, C. (2020) We need to close the gender data gap by including women in our algorithms. *Time Magazine.* https://time.com/collection/davos-2020/5764698/gender-data-gap/

Crenshaw, K. (1991) Mapping the margins: Intersectionality, identity politics, and violence against women of color. *Stanford Law Review*, 43(6): 1241–1299.

Escobar, A. (2018) *Designs for the Pluriverse: Radical Interdependence, Autonomy and the Making of Worlds.* Duke University Press.

Ideo (2021) 'How might we'. Design Kit. www.designkit.org/methods/3

Irwin, T., Kossoff, G., Tonkinwise, C. and Scupelli, P. (2015) 'Transition design 2015'. https: design.cmu.edu/sites/default/files/Transition_Design_Monograph_final.pdf

Kirkham, P. (eds) (1999) *The Gendered Object.* Manchester University Press.

Lewis, J. and Bruce, M. (1989) Divided by design: Gender and the labour process in the design industry. *7th Annual UMIST Conference.* https://digital.hagley.org/08065464_divided_by_design

Reimer, S. (2015) 'It's just a very male industry': Gender and work in UK design agencies. *Gender, Place and Culture: A Journal of Feminist Geography*, 23(7): 1033–1046.

Rosner, D. K. (2018) *Critical Fabulations: Reworking the Methods and Margins of Design*. MIT Press.

Simonsen, J. and Robertson, T. (eds) (2013) *Routledge International Handbook of Participatory Design*. Routledge.

Transition Design Seminar (2021a) Wicked problems: Anatomy and dynamics. https://transitiondesignseminarcmu.net/classes-2/mapping-wicked-problems/#1482254259729-27721fa6-4857

Transition Design Seminar (2021b) #1 Mapping. Wicked problems. https://transitiondesignseminarcmu.net/assignments/#1483987943689-016372b2-8b49

USEFUL WEB RESOURCES

Gender

Rewriting the Rules: www.rewriting-the-rules.com/blog/
The Genderbread Person: www.genderbread.org/

Wicked Problems and Systems Mapping

Disruptive Design: https://medium.com/disruptive-design/systems/home
Donella Meadows Project: https://donellameadows.org/archives/leverage-points-places-to-intervene-in-a-system/

15. What can organisations learn from kaupapa Māori research?

Peter Rawlins, Philippa Butler and Spencer Lilley

INTRODUCTION

Managing diversity, equality and inclusion in organisational settings is a complex and multi-faceted problem. One of the areas that is particularly challenging is decision making and ensuring that the voices of minority, and often marginalised, groups are heard during the decision-making process. Commonly, decisions are made by managerial teams that are not representative of all members of the organisation. This can easily lead to decisions that are inclusive of the majority but exclude the minority, reinforcing a lack of equality too often found in diverse organisations. The question is, then, how do we gather a full range of views that can inform a robust policy and decision-making process? Drawing on the example of kaupapa Māori research, this chapter argues that it is important to be cognisant of the differing cultural values inherent in the diverse mix of people in an organisation. Research designs that privilege these values are more likely to capture the full range of voices in that organisation.

To advance this discussion, we will draw on two examples of research conducted within one Aotearoa New Zealand university. The research projects themselves are tangential to our main argument, which is that research projects should be designed to draw on the principles and values of effective research with Māori. Put simply, applying these values to research designs means that, within a given community, the initiation of research, the selection of the researcher team, the research questions, the way the research is conducted, the way the data are analysed and interpreted, and the ownership and distribution of new knowledge all come from within the community. Integral to this is the need for the community to see tangible and ongoing benefits from the research, through a continued research relationship.

To more fully understand the arguments we are making in this chapter, it is important to provide a brief history of the complexity of the relationship between Māori (New Zealand's indigenous population) and non-Māori. An understanding of this complex relationship, and the inherent distrust it has created, is important to the central thread of our argument and helps explain why Māori have traditionally not taken part in Western research methodologies. We will then unpack a number of key Māori concepts related to research involving Māori and examine how an understanding of these might inform key aspects of research design. We will then briefly explain the design of two examples of research projects conducted within one Aotearoa New Zealand university and how these illustrate and support our arguments for research to be informed by kaupapa Māori principles and values.

A BRIEF HISTORY

Aotearoa New Zealand is a young country, both geographically and in human terms. Historians believe that Māori first started arriving in New Zealand from Eastern Polynesia about 1,000 years ago. The first European to have contact with New Zealand was the Dutchman Abel Tasman in 1642, but it wasn't until the Englishman James Cook travelled to New Zealand in 1769 that Europeans first started to come in larger numbers. By the 1830s, the Bay of Islands district had become the centre for trade and was popular for its ability to provide whalers with access to fresh water and food. Unfortunately, it also became notorious for debauchery, prostitution, violence, and other lawless activities (King, 2003). With an increasing level of settlement, demand for land and other resources started to escalate and led to increasing tension between Māori and non-Māori. This resulted in 13 chiefs writing to King William IV of the United Kingdom in 1831 to seek an alliance and protection from other foreign powers. This letter resulted in the appointment of James Busby as the British resident in the Bay of Islands with a mandate to control the behaviour of the Europeans. Busby worked with rangatira (chiefs) in helping them to assert their independence from foreign interventions. This was strongly motivated by Busby's concerns over increasing interest by the French in New Zealand land (Walker, 2004). The resulting 1835 Declaration of Independence, He Whakaputanga, was signed by 52 chiefs and recognised the sovereignty of the Confederation of United Tribes (Te Whakaminenga) by the British Crown (Orange, 2015). It was seen by Māori as a way to address the challenges posed by European contact, to strengthen an alliance with Great Britain, and to assert their authority to the wider world. Significantly, it affirmed that sovereign power and authority over the land resided with Te Whakaminenga, and that no foreigners could make laws. Although some have argued that He Whakaputanga did not represent the majority of Māori, it has been seen as a foundation for the assertion of indigenous rights.

Despite He Whakaputanga, rampant demand for land and other resources continued, as settlement of New Zealand became an increasingly attractive option for those from Great Britain wishing to have an opportunity to own land. By 1839, it had become apparent that the Crown had to take action to ensure that the lawlessness of Europeans could be controlled and that the rights of Māori could be protected. This led to the Treaty of Waitangi (Te Tiriti o Waitangi) being drafted and signed in 1840. Of note is the fact that the actual document was prepared in English and then translated very quickly into te reo Māori (Māori language). During this translation, terms were used that have proven to be problematic and are at the heart of tensions that exist over modern interpretations of the treaty's intention. For example, the terms 'kawanatanga' (governance) and 'sovereignty' were used as equivalents. In the Māori version of Te Tiriti there is the phrase: 'tuku rawa atu ki te Kuini o Ingarangi ake tonu atu te kawanatanga katoa o o ratou wenua'. This literally translates to: 'give absolutely to the Queen of England forever the complete governance over their land'. In the English version the text reads: 'cede to Her Majesty the Queen of England absolutely and without reservation all the rights and powers of sovereignty'. While the distinction between these two phrases may seem negligible to someone looking with Western eyes, the difference is stark when viewed from a Māori world view, Te Ao Māori. Walker (2004) suggests that it would have been unacceptable to rangatira to relinquish their mana (authority) to another power, especially to someone who they did not know. Walker (2004) believes that the translators decided to use words that would be acceptable to Māori and therefore they were more likely to sign. These choices resulted in the English and Māori versions of Te Tiriti having quite different meanings. When doubts were raised at the time, about whether the chiefs understood what they were signing, Governor Hobson claimed it was 'no fault of mine ... I have done all that I could' (Orange, 2020, p. 43). Although more than 500 chiefs signed Te Tiriti, only 39 signatures were made on an English version.

Another significant tension lies in the understanding of the concept of whenua. For Māori, whenua means land and also placenta. After birth, the placenta and the pito (umbilical cord) are buried on whānau (family) land, which Mead (2016) states establishes a spiritual link between the land and the child. In Te Ao Māori, whakapapa (ancestral links) is at the heart of the relationship between whenua and all other living things. Tangata (people) and whenua (land) therefore belong together, and their relationship is alive and connected – hence they are tangata whenua (people of the land). In Te Ao Māori, Māori act as guardians of the land for future generations and, although they might give others access to and use of the land and its resources, occupation and use would revert back to them when no longer required. For the British, land was something that was measured and marked out in portions that anyone could buy and sell over and over again. The notion of ownership was quite different between the two groups. This was summed up by Nōpera Pana-kareao in 1840: 'Ko te atarau o te whenua i riro a te Kuini, ko te tinana o te whenua i waiho ki ngā Māori. Only the shadow of the land goes to the Queen; the substance remains with us' (Orange, 2020, p. 49).

Te Tiriti o Waitangi was designed to formalise the relationship between the Crown and Māori. However, disputes over the different intent and interpretation of the two versions is at the heart of continuing tensions between Māori and non-Māori and distrust by Māori of the intentions of the Crown and those who represent it. These tensions are deep-seated, and extend to all relationships between Māori and non-Māori, including research relationships.

RESEARCH WITH MĀORI

Europeans have been researching Māori since James Cook's first voyage in 1769. This has led some Māori to claim that they are the most researched people in the world (Smith, 2021). Much of this research has been done *by* Europeans *to* Māori, with the findings reflecting data that had been analysed using a Western perspective. Consequently, a tradition of research about Māori has developed that addresses the interests of the majority group of predominantly non-Māori researchers (Bishop, 1999; Smith, 2021). Such research has 'left a foundation of ideologically laden data about Māori society, which has distorted notions of what it is to be Māori' (Smith, 2021, p. 222).

An example of this is the fascination that was held over the inferiority/superiority of Māori and Europeans. Craniometry – skull measurement – was used to conclude that the smaller skull size of Māori demonstrated that they were less intelligent. As one early traveller wrote:

> It was ascertained by weighing the quantity of millet seed skulls contained … that New Zealanders' heads are smaller than the heads of Englishmen, consequently the New Zealanders are inferior to the English in mental capacity … The memory they possess is the memory of boyhood; and their minds may be compared to mirrors … incapable of retaining any sense of the past … The faculty of imagination is not strongly developed among them, although they permitted it to run wild in believing absurd superstitions … This analysis shows that the Zealanders have the minds of children. (Thomson, 1859, pp. 81–84, cited in Hokowhitu, 2004, pp. 266–267)

Additionally, judgements of the 'validity' of such research is made in terms of the non-Māori researchers' own cultural world view (Bishop, 1999). Such research often comes across as Europeans trying to solve the 'indigenous problem'. Linda Tuhiwai Smith (2021) states that problematising the indigenous is a Western obsession, and so for many indigenous communities they have become the focus of research that is 'deficit' based. Accordingly, many Māori have raised concerns over how research is conducted and to whom

Table 15.1   *Three approaches to research with Māori*

	Kaupapa Māori research	Māori-centred research	Research involving Māori
Focus	Māori interests	Cross-cultural	Non-Māori interests
Researchers	Māori are key members	High involvement of Māori	Predominantly non-Māori
Participants	Māori	Significant number of Māori	Some Māori involvement
Analysis	Te ao Māori lens	Māori and non-Māori perspectives and concepts	Non-Māori lens
Benefits	Māori communities	Māori and non-Māori communities	Non-Māori communities

Source: Adapted from Rawlins et al. (forthcoming).

researchers are answerable (Bishop, 1999; Pihama, 2010; G. H. Smith, 2015; Smith, 2021). Who has control over the initiation of research? Who decides on the research procedures, evaluations, construction and distribution of the newly defined knowledge resulting from research? Who 'owns' this new knowledge and how will such knowledge be of benefit to those who have taken part in the research?

To try and redress this imbalance, a number of influential Māori researchers have developed Māori research methodologies. These research methodologies shift the focus to Māori ways of understanding and interpreting the world and can be defined in three distinct categories: 'research involving Māori', Māori-centred research, and kaupapa Māori methods (Bishop, 1999; Cunningham, 2000; G. H. Smith, 2015). The three approaches to research with Māori are summarised in Table 15.1.

Research involving Māori recognises that although Māori might be involved either as participants or researchers, they are not the focal point of the research, and the analysis of research results is unlikely to have been conducted using a Māori cultural perspective. The outcomes of the research are more likely to benefit non-Māori communities rather than Māori communities.

Māori-centred research typically has a higher involvement from Māori, where they are leaders or senior members of the research team, where significant numbers of Māori are research participants, and where some analysis of results uses Māori perspectives, but not exclusively. Māori-centred research provides a project team with the ability to draw on a diverse set of methodologies and analytical lenses to collect and interpret data. Although not all team members might be Māori, those leading the project are likely to be highly skilled researchers who are able to operate effectively in both Western and Māori research environments. In the design and analysis, they can decide which approach is more appropriate and will provide the best outcomes for their Māori participants (remembering that not all participants will necessarily be Māori), and not remain wedded to one approach over another. This relates to the Māori concept of tino rangatiratanga (self-determination), whereby the team exercises its autonomy to choose what is right for the research, while at the same time providing their Māori participants with an opportunity to express their own notion of self-determination in how they implement the findings.

Kaupapa Māori (Māori-focused) methods are described as research conducted *with* Māori by Māori researchers. In its purest sense, research is initiated by Māori, the research team is predominantly Māori, and research results are analysed using a Māori lens to create Māori knowledge. Kaupapa Māori methodologies are also entrenched firmly within values espoused by tikanga Māori (Māori customs). Within Te Ao Māori, the concept of kaupapa Māori embraces the validity and legitimation of Māori language, knowledge, and culture (G. H. Smith, 2015). Applying this concept to research informs an approach where Māori are the focal point and where the research results and outcomes primarily benefit Māori.

Regardless of the approach taken to Māori research, a critical aspect is the relationship between the research team and the participant community. The concept of kanohi kitea (the face seen) is extremely important here to ensure that the research team members are active participants in the community when appropriate. This connection should not last for the duration of the project only; there should be an intention to develop an ongoing relationship formed around the sharing of Māori values, particularly those of manaakitanga (respect), whanaungatanga (connecting), whakamana (give prestige to), and tauutuutu (reciprocity).

APPLYING THE PRINCIPLES OF KAUPAPA MĀORI RESEARCH

A key feature of kaupapa Māori research is that it is conducted by Māori, for Māori communities, about issues that are important to Māori. It aims to make a positive difference for Māori. Linda Tuhiwai Smith (2021) cautions that, in a New Zealand research landscape, it is not a research approach that can be adopted by non-Māori researchers, or at least not on their own without partnership and leadership from Māori researchers. However, the values and principles that underpin kaupapa Māori research (L. T. Smith, 2015, 2021; www.rangahau.co.nz/rangahau/) can be applied more broadly. Different researchers highlight different principles, but there are some key concepts that are considered core to an understanding of kaupapa Māori research. We focus on mana, rangatiratanga, whakapapa, whanaungatanga, te reo, and tikanga Māori below, and outline how they can be applied to research within an organisation.

Mana refers to the prestige, dignity, or status of an individual. In terms of research, mana recognises the rights of participants to be informed and to make decisions about the research process. Mana also refers to the continued development of an individual as they acquire new skills and knowledge and are empowered to determine their future pathways.

The principle of rangatiratanga can be interpreted as autonomy or self-determination. It refers to the idea that the organisation or group being researched is not the 'object' of the research, but instead is a true partner that shapes the way that the research takes place. The principle of whakapapa relates to notions of identity that are broader than the common definition of 'genealogy' would imply. In research terms, this is about research that reflects the organisation or community in which it is taking place, where relationships between participants and researchers and between group members and leaders are paramount. The principle of whanaungatanga is about relationships, kinship, and a sense of family connection – a relationship through shared experiences and working together which provides people with a sense of belonging. In establishing whanaungatanga, Māori prefer to initially deal with people 'kanohi ki te kanohi' (face to face). This implies that establishing and maintaining relationships is key to effective research.

The principle of te reo, or 'language', can be thought of in utilitarian terms: that research be conducted in the language of the community or organisation, with research tools, information sheets, and consent forms that have been translated into the appropriate language. More broadly, it relates to the importance of communication, and the notion that there needs to be shared understandings about the purpose and outcomes of the research. It also refers to the idea that language and knowledge are intertwined. Some ideas can only be expressed and fully understood in their original language.

Finally, the principle of tikanga Māori refers to cultural practices, behaviours, obligations, and protocols. This relates to research that is conducted in ways that are appropriate for the community or organisation that privileges group values and ways of understanding the world. Collectively, these values shape research that is responsive to a group's diverse needs and expectations. Research that draws on these principles is by the community, with the community, and for the community. In Aotearoa New Zealand, some of these principles have been encoded in *Te Ara Tika: Guidelines for Māori Research Ethics* from the New Zealand Health Research Council (Pūtaiora Writing Group, 2010). These guidelines focus on whakapapa and mana, as well as tika (the purposefulness or validity of research: will the research achieve its aims and be of benefit for Māori?), and manaakitanga (cultural and social responsibility: will the research uphold the dignity and mana of all parties?). Other countries and cultural contexts have their own version of such ethical guidelines. For example, in Australia the National Health and Medical Research Council has produced guidelines for *Ethical Conduct in Research with Aboriginal and Torres Straight Islander Peoples and Communities* (2018). The six principles contained within these guidelines are spirit and integrity, cultural continuity, equity, reciprocity, respect, and responsibility. Together, these six principles respect indigenous Australians' ways of viewing the world, the importance of relationships, and the importance of research that respects and empowers communities for the benefit of those communities.

TWO ILLUSTRATIVE EXAMPLES

The following examples present two research projects that have been recently conducted within Massey University. In discussing these, we do not wish to suggest that this research is either Māori-centred or kaupapa Māori research. What we are arguing is that certain design aspects of these research projects can help us better understand how we might gather the voices of all within an organisation, including those who have traditionally been marginalised. In particular, if the initiation of the research, selection of researchers, research questions, data gathering and analysis, ownership and distribution of new knowledge, benefits of the research, and ongoing research relationships are controlled by the community being researched, then the research is more likely to capture the full voice of that community.

Massey University is the primary distance university within New Zealand and also operates campuses across three main locations. The focus and results of these studies are tangential to our arguments, but sufficient detail is provided to allow the reader to more fully appreciate the arguments we are trying to make.

Case 1

The first of these illustrative cases concerns the trialling of an external, commercial, online, on-demand learning support platform. The university already provided a range of learner support services (e.g. library service, consultation with learning and/or writing advisor, assignment pre-reading service, writing and referencing support). Having both distance and on-campus students means that providing sufficient learning support services, at times that suit learners, can be challenging. To address this challenge, Massey University adopted a mixed model of provision where in-house support was complemented by the introduction of an external online and on-demand platform to address learners' needs. Prior to the introduction of the external platform, if students needed to access an in-house learning support person, they were required to do this during general office hours. With the introduction of the external platform, students had the means to access one-to-one support outside of office hours (e.g. evenings and weekends). The trial of the external platform was conducted

Table 15.2   *Ethnic groups of respondents compared with Massey figures*

Stated ethnicity[a]	Percentage in sample (n=500)	Massey University student population (2018) (n=30,145)[b]
Māori	8%	9%
Pacific peoples	4%	4%
Asian	11%	12%
Pakehā/New Zealand European	63%	64%
Other	14%	11%

Note: [a] A chi-square test showed no significant differences between the observed and expected counts for ethnic groups; [b] see www.educationcounts.govt.nz/statistics/tertiary-participation.

within nine first-year courses across a range of disciplines and a range of course offerings (campus based and distance).

Coincident with this trial, a study was initiated by the university to investigate learners' perceptions of both the existing in-house learning support services and the recently introduced external platform. Essentially, the university was trying to evaluate whether the introduction of the external platform was worth the relatively large annual license fee. Rather than approach an outside organisation to evaluate the trial, three researchers from within the university were approached to conduct the study. The study adopted a mixed-methods design comprised of two phases: an online survey towards the end of the semester and a series of follow-up interviews.

Traditionally, Māori and Pacific peoples have not responded well to surveys as they often have no prior relationship with the researchers (Poppelwell et al., 2018). In this case, the researchers, although they worked for the university, were not known to the students in the trial courses. Cognisant of the importance of whanaungatanga, the researchers used the course lecturers, who did have a relationship with the students, to introduce the research team and encourage the students to take part in the survey. The purpose of the research was clearly explained to the students, specifically that the research was for internal purposes only and was conducted to make decisions around the provision of existing learner support services as well as the added value of the new external platform.

When examining the demographics of the survey participants, an observation was made that the proportion of Māori and Pacific participants in the sample was closely representative of the proportion of these students across the university (see Table 15.2). This was unusual and caused us to question why this might be the case.

While the findings of the study are not important here – in short, the university decided not to implement the external platform across all courses at the university – the research design was important in gathering the full range of voices across the student body. Specifically, in relation to the research principles discussed earlier, this research was initiated by the university solely to examine whether the existing provision of learning support was fit for purpose. The initial introduction of the research was by the students' own course lecturer. The established relationships of the lecturers acted as a bridge to allow the researchers to introduce themselves and the study to the students. The findings were used for internal decision-making purposes and resulted in changes to the way learner support was provisioned. As a result, we argue that the benefits of the research supported an ongoing and positive relationship between the students and the university.

Case 2

The second illustrative case relates to research carried out in 2020, again at Massey University. In March 2020, due to the Covid-19 global pandemic, the New Zealand Government introduced an alert-level system and put the country into an initial six-week lockdown. The high degree of uncertainty around how long the country might be in lockdown and what might happen afterwards meant that schools and universities had to pivot to online teaching, learning, and assessment. As part of these changes, Massey University decided to replace all paper-based, face-to-face examinations with a variety of technology-enhanced assessments. The university had been working on a range of online assessments to replace paper-based exams for some years. With the global pandemic, there was an opportunity to undertake research to inform this broader project. As such, we were commissioned to investigate students' and lecturers' views on the changes to assessment brought about by the pandemic.

A mixed-methods approach was undertaken, involving three phases. The first phase was a survey of students who were impacted by the changes. The second phase was a survey of lecturing staff who had made a range of changes to their assessments. The third phase was to interview college-level decision makers throughout the university. Once again, the primary purpose of this research was to inform internal decision making. Consistent with the principles of kaupapa Māori research, it was important to establish a relationship with the participants (whanaungatanga) and to clarify the purpose of the research, who owned the findings, and what those findings would be used for. Accordingly, the two senior leaders within the university who had initiated the research (the provost and the deputy vice chancellor, students and alumni) actively endorsed the project to the various participant groups. Students and staff members received a personalised email inviting them to take part in the research. A summary of the findings was made available to participants, and the results were used to inform the university's assessment policy and practices.

Table 15.3   *Ethnic groups of respondents in Covid-19 research compared with Massey figures*

Stated ethnicity	Percentage in sample	Massey University student population (2020) (n=30,500)[a]
Māori	11%	12%
Pacific peoples	4%	5%
Asian[b]	20%	10%
Pakehā/New Zealand European	55%	63%
Other	10%	10%

Note: [a] See www.educationcounts.govt.nz/statistics/tertiary-participation; [b] a chi-square test revealed that there were significantly more students who identified with an Asian ethnic group than expected in the survey sample ($\chi2 = 324.987$, df = 4, p<.001).

For the purposes of this discussion, we will look at the ethnic group breakdown of the student survey respondents. In total we had 4,134 valid student responses to the survey, of which 4,022 provided their ethnic group (see Table 15.3).

As can be seen, the proportion of students who identified as Māori in the survey very closely approximated the proportion of those who identified as Māori in the wider university. The same is true for those identifying themselves as Pacific peoples. As discussed previously, Māori and Pacific peoples are usually not well represented in surveys, but we can see in this research that they are. We argue this is because of the pre-existing relationship they had with the university and their lecturers, and the fact that they were likely to see tangible benefits from engaging in this survey and making their opinions known. The knowledge that their opinions were asked for and taken seriously by the university is likely to enhance students' mana and support ongoing relationships between students and the university.

DISCUSSION

The central argument of this chapter is that research which is informed by principles that are respectful of the wider community in which an organisation sits will more effectively capture the diverse voices within that organisation, particularly those of minority groups. The illustrative examples we have given here are consistent with the principles of kaupapa Māori research. We argue that the underlying values can be applied to research in many different contexts, within Aotearoa New Zealand and internationally.

Specifically, for effective research about an organisation, the locus of power and control over the research, issues of initiation, benefits, representation, legitimation, and accountability should be internal to that organisation. The initiation and design of the research should come from within the organisation (rangatiratanga). There should be a pre-existing relationship between the researchers and potential participants of the research (whanaungatanga), rather than outsourcing the research team. The findings should be owned by the organisation, who determines how those findings are used (rangatiratanga). There should be clear benefits to the participants of the research that supports an ongoing relationship with the organisation (mana, tauutuutu). The research should foster a sense of identity and belonging within the organisation (whakapapa).

While we argue that these principles are central to effective research in organisations, they are not always applied. To illustrate this point, in 2019 the New Zealand Government announced that the 16 polytechnics in New Zealand would be merged into one, the New Zealand Institute of Skills and Technology (NZIST), also known as Te Pūkenga. In July 2020, the Minister for Education, Chris Hipkins, said that the organisation 'needs to ... leverage off the extensive expertise that already exists within NZIST'.[1] On the surface this stance would seem to be consistent with the arguments we have put forward in this chapter. The statement appears to recognise that within the NZIST, there are the skills and expertise to develop its operating model. Despite this, NZIST has spent approximately 2 million dollars contracting a professional services company and, in particular, its indigenous Māori section, to co-design the operating model. This is inconsistent with the aforementioned stance taken by the minister and seems a missed opportunity for building mutually beneficial relationships within the organisation.

It is important to stress that conducting research that is consistent with the principles of kaupapa Māori research is complex. In our illustrative examples, given that Massey University has made a commitment to being Te Tiriti led, the minority group of primary interest is Māori. As such, for both Māori and the university to benefit further from the research, there should be strong involvement of Māori from the very beginning of the research process to ensure that their perspectives are incorporated into the research design. Our research would have profited from focus groups or hui (gatherings/meetings) with Māori. These could have been conducted using tikanga Māori principles, including the use of a facilitator able to switch between English and Te Reo Māori, so all views were captured and nothing was lost in translation. Analysing the data collected from these hui using an indigenous lens would then ensure that culturally important thematic data were available for further consideration and reporting in the results of the project. The perspective coming from these results would then be distinctive and would ensure that Māori were incorporated into the decision-making processes. The benefits accrued from these perspectives would be able to be universally applied to all participant communities where appropriate.

In an environment where population profiles are becoming increasingly ethnically more diverse, it is no longer appropriate to conduct research just from a Western perspective. To do so will continue to perpetuate policies and decisions that benefit those who fit in with the majority view and will fail to include the voices of other groups, including indigenous peoples.

RECOMMENDATIONS FOR FUTURE APPROACHES TO RESEARCH

Conducting responsible research in diverse environments requires a research team to adopt a strong mindset right from the beginning of the design process. Of key importance is to ensure that the research team has the cultural capacity to conduct research with the different participant communities. This mindset should be guided by questions such as:

- Who has initiated the research?
- Who are the likely participant communities that need to be consulted?
- What cultural factors need to be considered when distributing research instruments?
- From what perspective will the research responses be analysed?
- How can culturally appropriate analysis be included?
- How will the results or outcomes of the research benefit the different communities represented in the responses?
- What mechanisms will be used to ensure that response communities receive information about the study?

Giving due consideration to these questions will greatly assist in ensuring that all perspectives are captured when conducting research in diverse environments.

NOTE

1.   See www.stuff.co.nz/national/education/124113179/mega-polytech-to-spend-2 -million-on-consultants-and-hosts-staff-workshop-at-a-wellington-golf-course.

REFERENCES

Bishop, R. (1999). Kaupapa Māori research: An indigenous approach to creating knowledge. In N. Robertson (Ed.), *Māori and Psychology: Research and Practice. The Proceedings of a Symposium Sponsored by the Māori and Psychology Research Unit*. University of Waikato, Māori and Psychology Research Unit.
Cunningham, C. (2000). A framework for addressing Māori knowledge in research, science and technology. *Pacific Health Dialog*, 7(1), 62–69.

Hokowhitu, B. (2004). Tackling Māori masculinity: A colonial genealogy of savagery and sport. *The Contemporary Pacific*, *16*(2), 259–284.

King, M. (2003). *The Penguin History of New Zealand*. Penguin.

Mead, H. M. (2016). *Tikanga Māori: Living by Māori Values*. Huia Publishers.

National Health and Medical Research Council. (2018). *Ethical conduct in research with Aboriginal and Torres Strait Islander peoples and communities: Guidelines for researchers and stakeholders*. Commonwealth of Australia. www.nhmrc.gov.au/about -us/resources/ethical-conduct-research-aboriginal-and-torres-strait-islander-peoples- and-communities

Orange, C. (2015). *The Treaty of Waitangi*. Bridget Williams Books.

Orange, C. (2020). *The Treaty of Waitangi: Te Tiriti o Waitangi. An Illustrated History*. Bridget Williams Books.

Pihama, L. (2010). Kaupapa Māori theory: Transforming theory in Aotearoa. *He Pukenga Kōrero*, *9*(2), 5–14.

Poppelwell, E., Esplin, J., Doust, E., and Swansson, J. (2018). *Evaluation of the primary care patient experience survey tool: Final report prepared for the Ministry of Health*. Sapere Research Group.

Pūtaiora Writing Group (2010). *Te ara tika: Guidelines for Māori research ethics: A framework for researchers and ethics committee members*. Health Research Council. www.hrc.govt.nz/resources/te-ara-tika-guidelines-maori-research-ethics-0

Rawlins, P., Butler, P., Lilley, S., and Hartnett, M. (forthcoming). What can mixed methods partnerships learn from kaupapa Māori research principles? In C. Poth (Ed.), *The Sage Handbook of Mixed Methods Research Designs*. Sage.

Smith, G. H. (2015). The dialectic relation of theory and practice in the development of kaupapa Māori praxis. In L. Pihama, S.-J. Tiakiwai, and K. Southey (Eds.), *Kaupapa rangahau: A Reader. A Collection of Readings from the kaupapa rangahau Workshop Series* (2nd ed., pp. 17–27). Te Kotahi Research Institute.

Smith, L. T. (2015). Kaupapa Māori research: Some kaupapa Māori principles. In L. Pihama, S.-J. Tiakiwai, and K. Southey (Eds.), *Kaupapa rangahau: A Reader. A Collection of Readings from the kaupapa rangahau Workshop Series* (2nd ed., pp. 46–52). Te Kotahi Research Institute.

Smith, L. T. (2021). *Decolonizing Methodologies: Research and Indigenous Peoples* (3rd ed.). Zed Books.

Walker, R. J. (2004). *Ka whawhai tonu matou: Struggle Without End*. Penguin.

KEY RESOURCES

For further reading on kaupapa Māori research, please see the following resources.

Pihama, L., Tiakiwai, S.-J., and Southey, K. (Eds). (2015). *Kaupapa rangahau: A Reader. A Collection of Readings from the kaupapa rangahau Workshop Weries* (2nd ed.). Te Kotahi Research Institute.

Pūtaiora Writing Group. (2010). *Te ara tika: Guidelines for Māori research ethics: A framework for researchers and ethics committee members*. Health Research Council. www.hrc.govt.nz/resources/te-ara-tika-guidelines-maori-research-ethics-0

Rangahau: www.rangahau.co.nz/rangahau/

Smith, G. H., Hoskins, T. K., and Jones, A. (2012). Interview: Kaupapa Māori: The dangers of domestication. *New Zealand Journal of Educational Studies*, *47*(2), 10–20.

GLOSSARY OF MAORI TERMS

He Whakaputanga	The 1835 Declaration of Independence
Hui	Gathering/meeting
Kanohi ki te kanohi	Face to face
Kanohi kitea	The face seen
Kaupapa Māori	Māori-focused
Mana	Prestige, dignity or status of an individual
Manaakitanga	Respect
Pito	Umbilical cord
Rangatira	Chiefs
Rangatiratanga	Exercising chieftainship/self-determination
Tangata	People
Tangata whenua	People of the land
Tauutuutu	Reciprocity
Te Ao Māori	The Māori world
Te Pūkenga	New Zealand Institute of Skills and Technology
Te reo Māori	Māori language
Te Tiriti o Waitangi	The Treaty of Waitangi
Te Whakaminenga	The Confederation of United Tribes
Tikanga Māori	Māori custom
Tino rangatiratanga	Self-determination
Whakamana	Give prestige to
Whakapapa	Ancestral links/genealogy
Whānau	Family
Whanaungatanga	Connecting
Whenua	Land

16. Organisational implications for DEI strategies against maternal mortality in Papua New Guinea's Gulf province

Jennifer Litau, McKenzie Maviso, Ellie Korave, Poisy Tava Kae, Lucy Kalep, Hilda Tanimia, Anne Pulotu and Kenny Abau

RESEARCH FOCUS, CONTEXT AND DEI

Maternal mortality, the death of a woman while pregnant or within 42 days after delivery (Haupt et al., 2011), is an inevitable outcome of Papua New Guinea's (PNG) national health system's culture of inadequate input hence poor activities and output, outcomes and impacts achieving United Nations (UN) Sustainable Development Goal (SDG) 3.1 and key performance area (KPA) 5 of the country's 2011–2020 National Health Plan. This chapter focuses on the intentional integration of diversity, equality, equity and inclusion (DEI) processes in the health system, to mediate a shift in thinking and practices for the achievement of KPA 5 and/or for enacting practical bridging in leadership performance gaps in the health system and the achievement of SDG 3.1. This chapter specifically focuses on how the determinants of maternal mortality have significant impact not only on the health of individuals but how the health or medical system responds to women versus men, poor versus rich, rural versus urban, young versus old, etc. Three research questions will be answered in this chapter:

RQ1. What are the health determinants of maternal mortality?
RQ2. What are the non-health determinants of maternal mortality?
RQ3. How does the interplay of health and non-health determinants contribute to maternal mortality?

Community narratives of the Gulf province demonstrate how the failure of the health system's leaders in providing equitable access and adequate coverage of medical care for pregnant women leads to death. The maternal mortality ratio, the conventional measure for maternal mortality, denotes the number of women who die, including abortions from pregnancy or childbearing-related complications, in a given year per 100,000 live births in that year. In the absence of vital registration systems, accurate maternal mortality data of PNG is lacking hence mathematical modelling and national health information system (HIS) and facility-based data have been utilised to produce estimates of maternal mortality ratios (Haupt et al., 2011; Mola and Kirby, 2013; Zureick-Brown et al., 2013). Mola and Kirby (2013) report estimates offered from 1990 to 2012 and argue that since the World Health Organization's (WHO) 1996 estimate of PNG's 930/100,000 live births in 1990, all subsequent international estimates have been underestimates. Based on contextual considerations, they advocate for the reliability of national estimates of 438/100,000 live births in 2009 from HIS and 394/100,000 live births in 2009 from facility-based surveys, and 460/100,000 live births in 2010 from HIS.

How can the health system incorporate components of DEI to address/ reduce maternal mortality rates? Berer (2012, p. 5) laments the existence of maternal mortality as a violation of the most basic women's right to life. Maternal health-care access or availability is unequal between and within countries. Equality means "sameness", equal treatment opportunity (Kossek and Pichler, 2006) or taking affirmative action through opportunity provision (Kelly and Dobbin, 1998). It implies that diverse groups including mothers of poor, rural, illiterate or minority background are marginalised and treated differently. Equality awards preferential or selective treatment based on people's surface-level demographic attributes of age, sex, disability differences, etc. Diversity embraces all (Thomas, 1990). It accepts demographic attributes of people but extends its concerns to deep-level behavioural differences in attitudes, cultural styles, functional backgrounds, cognitive styles and beliefs within the workforce (Oswick and Noon, 2014, pp. 5, 6). Inclusion is concerned with the processes that incorporate differences into organisational practices and thereby help to realise the "value" of differences within the workforce (Oswick and Noon, 2014, p. 8). Equity has replaced equality in recent DEI literature on maternal mortality (Wilunda et al., 2015). It refers to fair coverage, as in maternal and neonatal care, based on managing diversity for inclusion (Luchenski et al., 2018; Oswick and Noon, 2014; Wilunda et al., 2015). DEI are already captured and reflected in PNG's 2011–2020 National Health Plan's vision and respective national health policies on gender, human resources, infrastructure and community health centres. However, pragmatic integration within the health system is hampered by public health funding, poor management and leadership, inadequate physical facilities, infrastructure and equipment and inadequate physicians, nurses and midwives, further constrained by inadequate transport, road, environment and geographical factors acting as barriers in translating rhetoric to practice (WHO, 2019).

The nature, spatial, scale, extent, context and directional intricacies and the institutionalised manifestations of maternal mortality determinants render this a complex and multidimensional phenomenon. We need an organisational framework to unpack the complex functional relationships contributing to maternal mortality, an official health agenda of government and its various stakeholders. Organisational psychologist Edgar Schein (2004) proposed the "organisational system", defined as the structure of how an organisation is set up, how each positional role functions and with employee compliance with role play and reporting forming its culture. He pinpoints four organisational systems' components of common purpose, coordinated effort, division of labour and hierarchy of authority and its four characteristics of control, departmentalisation, centralisation and decentralisation. He argues that each component and characteristic represents a critical aspect of an effective structure. Schein's (2004) organisational systems components emerge via Zaccaro and Klimoski's (2001) conceptualisation of their leadership management models: organisational systems (or common purpose), strategic decision making and management (or coordinated effort), leadership effectiveness and social imperatives (division of labour), and social and interpersonal exchange (or hierarchy of authority). Two critical behaviour patterns characterise the internal leadership transactional linkages or coordination of responsibilities: movement in one part of the organisation has predictable movements in other parts and there is "susceptibility to shifting environmental dynamics at resource procurement and output receptivity" (Zaccaro and Klimoski, 2001, p. 17). This system is open to inputs and outputs and interactional flows between them.

Organisational system represent the "health system" or health system culture but organisational systems or health systems capture the broader inter-sectoral or stakeholder management context represented in this editorial of *Reproductive Health Matters*:

> The papers are still about women dying in vain, and how horrific that is, and they still show that the poorest and the youngest women are the ones most at risk of dying as a consequence of gross negligence. But they aren't only calling on someone else to do something about it any longer. Instead, they are about women and their communities, women's health and human rights advocates and organisations, and more and more, about health professionals, governments and inter-governmental agencies taking action to hold countries, governments, health services, themselves and each other to account. (Berer, 2012, p. 5)

Depicted here is PNG's maternal mortality situation and its health systems' constitution of community, stakeholders, status of women and motherhood (Mola and Kirby, 2013; NDoH, 2009). Its descending structural linkage ranges from supra-national UN and its agencies, including WHO (2019), to the national health minister and Secretary of the Department of Health, to provincial health authorities and provincial hospitals or private health-care providers, to district-level health/sub-health centres and community clinics.

Strategic decision making and management advance the notion that senior organisational leaders enact coalignment between their organisation's goals and the environmental parameters, and how to manage this fit. Environmental parameters such as "resource availability, the fit of the organization with its environmental niche, and the strategic predisposition of the organization primarily account for organizational outcomes" (Zaccaro and Klimoski, 2001, p. 17). In PNG's case, the SDGs, including SDG 3.1, are an UN hand-down. The PNG government and senior health leadership articulated SDG 3.1 to reduce the global maternal mortality ratio to less than 70 per 100,000 live births by 2030 as KPA 5 to improve maternal health in PNG's National Health Plan 2011–2020. Leadership principles must be underpinned by DEI processes and the UN's sustainable development of economic, social and environmental processes aimed at translating resources into practical outcomes (Penchen and Squires, 2017).

Maternal health improvement will be the key sustainable social inclusion strategy for maternal mortality reduction. All rhetoric must translate to "whole or open systems thinking" (Penchen and Squires, 2017, p. 87) that requires practical top-down and cross-leadership management of stakeholder inter-connections, linkages, interaction and collaboration to achieve equality and social inclusion of diverse populations, reduce poverty, enhance livelihood prosperity and strengthen leadership and resource procurement yielding pos-itive outputs, outcomes and impact (Penchen and Squires, 2017; Zaccaro and Klimoski, 2001). Such interconnections signify "cross systems approaches" or effective collaborations and flexible local partnerships required for effective SDG 3.1 implementation (Penchen and Squires, 2017, p. 85). Intersectoral or interstakeholder collaborations of health with the likes of transport, education and communication are necessary because maternal mortality is embedded in other SDGs such as elimination of poverty (Goal 1), water and sanitation (Goal 6), economic productivity (Goal 8), equity (Goal 10) and access to education (Goal 4) (Penchen and Squires, 2017).

Collaboration between health stakeholders, authorities and health workers can guarantee the implementation of KPA 5: improve family planning cover-age (KPA 5.1), provision of safe and supervised deliveries (KPA 5.2), improve access to emergency obstetric care (EmOC) (KPA 5.3) and improve sexual and reproductive health for adolescents (KPA 5.4). Extra strategic decision making, alignment and management of goals with environmental parameters are required to strengthen PNG's "deficient health systems" or the health system's culture of high institutional risks and neglectful maternal deaths (DNPM, 2015, p. 30): at least 85 per cent of maternal deaths in PNG were pre-ventable and occurred even in health facilities (Mola and Kirby, 2013; NDoH,

2009). Zaccaro and Klimoski (2001) attribute the ineffective health system to ineffective senior health leadership and inadequate employee qualifications, training, professional development and performance, and/or the inappropriate placements of qualified personnel within the health system. Penchen and Squires (2017) attribute the defective health system to the inadequacy in skills of whole-system thinking, hence a failure to enact linkages between goals, and political issues of resource allocation, trade-offs and unintended consequences. Government and senior health officials who accept DEI inclusion and sustainable development as the background from which to improve the health system will undoubtedly address these issues.

Social and functional relationships are required between top leadership and subordinates responsible for goal or objective implementation. Leaders must provide critical direction setting, guidance and activity structuring to a collective, and members of the collective, in turn, grant their leader the legitimacy to lead (Zaccaro and Klimoski, 2001). An effective health leader can direct and motivate his/her followers by implementing KPA objectives for the benefit of the organisation. An effective leader will achieve his/her leadership performance imperatives. These imperatives are cognitive (problem solving), social (behavioural complex), personal (timely delivery on demand), political (acquisition, timely and judicious use of power), technology (ICT savvy), financial (source of pressure) and senior staff skills, disposition and capabilities (Zaccaro and Klimoski, 2001). Thus, a functional health system enables obstetricians and midwives to best perform maternal health-care imperatives (Patel et al., 2020). Public health beneficiaries can, in turn, trust and access health facilities and skilled attendants for obstetric care and EmOC.

KEY LITERATURE

We have introduced the research questions, offered organisational system and leadership management conceptualisations in relation to the complexity and multidimensionality of maternal mortality (Schein, 2004; Zaccaro and Klimoski, 2001) and linked these with DEI processes and SDGs. We now integrate evidence of maternal mortality in PNG's health system with DEI outcomes in the achievement of SDG 3.1 and KPA 5.

Without the practical inclusions of DEI strategies, SDGs and the effective management by health systems of maternal health service delivery programs, various maternal mortality determinants in PNG (Andrew et al., 2014; Bolnga et al., 2014; Mola and Kirby, 2013; NDoH, 2009; Vallely et al., 2015) signify systemic discrimination against women and children of their basic rights to life through inclusive and equitable health-care (Berer, 2012). "Discrimination is a pervasive and insidious phenomenon which affects organisations and communities in fundamental and enduring ways ... consequences of discrimination are potentially far more significant" (Oswick and Noon, 2014, p. 26). Some serious consequences of discrimination are that 85 per cent of maternal deaths are preventable (NDoH, 2009) and women encounter high risks for unsupervised births and maternal deaths even in hospitals and health facilities (Mola and Kirby, 2013). The inclusion of DEI strategies introduces anti-discriminant approaches (Oswick and Moon, 2014) against maternal mortality and removes obstacles for maternal health-care access embedded in PNG's health system's culture (NDoH, 2009).

The country violates its commitments to both the Universal Declaration of Human Rights (UDHR), Articles 25.1 and 25.2, and the Convention of Elimination of Any Form of Discrimination against Women (CEDAW). UDHR's Article 25.1 calls for equality or "sameness" in access of all to health, wellbeing and basic needs. UDHR's Article 25.2 specifies equal opportunity or affirmative action (Zaccaro and Klimoski, 2001) and equitable special care and assistance to mothers and children including those born out of wedlock. Equality is the goal and outcome of CEDAW to protect women in all stages of their life against any form of discrimination such as maternal mortality. With maternal mortality as a human rights issue, "anti-discriminant solutions" of DEI (Oswick and Noon, 2014, p. 1) must accompany efforts to achieve SDG 3.1 and KPA 5. DEI strategies must now translate as rights inclusion for mothers and neonates rather than mere discourse facets and fashions within management practice literature (Oswick and Noon, 2014). These DEI strategies (Oswick and Noon, 2014, p. 1), integrated with health goals and resource procurement, human resource management, health service delivery activities and outcomes, should enable a systemic or sustainable development shift away from discriminative culture to achieving KPA 5 in the long term (Zaccaro and Klimoski, 2001). Therefore, waning interest in equality (Oswick and Noon, 2014, pp. 6, 8) requires re-examination in the light of women and children's basic rights to health-care.

Diversity and an unequal and inequitable culture characterise maternal health-care availability and access to antenatal care, birth supervision and postnatal care, hence low attendance: 76 per cent of pregnant mothers of 2007 attended an antenatal clinic, 55 per cent delivered in a health facility but only 46 per cent with a skilled birth attendant, and only 46 per cent of mothers and 46 per cent of newborns received a postnatal check two days after delivery (NSO and ICF, 2019). As a qualifier, rural women with no income and who are distant from health facilities (NSO and ICF, 2019) especially will have no access to care. About 55 per cent of rural women who lived within the proximity of a health facility accessed basic EmOC while 30 per cent in remote rural areas accessed no functional EmOC (Mola and Kirby, 2013). With these disparities in maternal access and coverage for health-care, the reality of maternal deaths remains unknown. Therefore, PNG's maternal mortality ratio of 733 per 100,000 live births (NDoH, 2009) or 500 per 100,000 live births and other proposed international and national ratios are estimates, with relevant implications for planning. Inequitable culture is reflected in the treatment of mothers in the absence of vital registration systems yielding accurate and consistent maternal mortality data. Mola and Kirby (2013) use the HIS data of 2009 to calculate these national maternal mortality ratios: 295 in provincial hospitals, 386 in government health centres, 624 in church agency health centres and 457 in 2010 from supervised births. Somehow, health workers in all health facilities still provide less than quality care to pregnant women: 35 per cent had not attended an antenatal clinic during their pregnancy, including 30 per cent of those in remote rural regions. In their health facilities' sample, only 38 per cent of births were supervised by a skilled attendant in 2010 (Mola and Kirby, 2013).

Others have attributed the unequal treatment of mothers to the poor management of "3 delays": (1) delay in deciding to seek care for pregnancy complications; (2) delay in reaching a health facility to obtain EmOC; and (3) delay in receiving care in the health facility. What has been described reflects a health system's culture for discrimination and violation of UDHR and CEDAW rights of women and children. Any intentional organisational interventions must embed SDG 3.1 and KPA 5 in DEI strategies and processes for gap bridging and enacting a paradigm shift in health systems' practice (Oswick and Noon, 2014).

Health determinants or direct causes of maternal death refer to clinical causes of their deaths. The major direct cause is obstetric haemorrhage or postpartum haemorrhage (Mola and Kirby, 2013; NDoH, 2009). Puerperal sepsis and sepsis is another major cause: for example, a retrospective review of 21 maternal deaths in Goroka Base Hospital, in the period 2005–2008, yielded 48 per cent maternal mortality from this cause. Ectopic pregnancy and its associated postpartum haemorrhage has caused deaths too (Sanga et al., 2010). Haemorrhage, hypertensive disorders and infections determined 122 near misses and nine maternal deaths in a Port Moresby study (Tanimia et al., 2016). These direct causes of maternal deaths amplify a culture of diversity in the treatment of mothers and children, weak national and regional management and leadership in health service delivery policies, poor funding and human resourcing and weak human resource and activity coordination within the health system (WHO, 2019).

The non-health determinants of maternal mortality are inherent in issues of maternal access to social services and health-care for the individual woman, her household and community in the wider development and environmental context. Among those cited are lack of income and distance from a health centre (NSO and ICF, 2019), poverty (Mola and Kirby, 2013), geography, lack of transport (Sanga et al., 2010), geographical distance and costs, rural versus urban, literacy versus illiteracy, poor versus well-to-do, customary beliefs versus health knowledge, and low status of women (Andrew et al., 2014; Vallely et al., 2013). Bolnga et al. (2014) found in Madang life-threatening conditions of 153 near misses and 10 maternal deaths of those who are nulliparous, illiterate, from rural communities, lack formal employment, are referred from peripheral health facilities, unbooked, had history of still births and anaemic. We have illustrated the multiplicity and complexity of maternal mortality determinants and suggest the need for a flexible research methodology facilitating the interactive analyses of the determinants.

THE RESEARCH PROCESS, METHODS AND FRAMEWORK

Maternal mortality research in PNG has been the domain of medical practitioners competent in quantitative analyses of health determinants with occasional anecdotal reference made to non-health and organisational system aspects. Neither accurate longitudinal data exist nor analyses of an interplay of health and non-health determinants effects on maternal mortality (Mola and Kirby, 2013). DEI inclusion is reflected and represented in the SDGs, national health plans and policies of the country but hampered by weaknesses in health system management and leadership, limited physical infrastructure and financial and human resources. Still 85 per cent of maternal deaths are preventable (NDoH, 2009) and nearly 90 per cent of maternal deaths which occur in PNG hospitals are preventable (WHO, 2019) and we must explain what is going on to inform planning and practice. The aim of this research is to attempt to explain these knowledge gaps through Penchen and Squires' (2017) model of systems, holistic, interactive linkages or iterative processes of maternal mortality determinants leading to women's deaths. We suggest that understanding of maternal mortality determinants is rendered possible through the application of mixed-methods research (MMR). MMR permits the use of both quantitative and qualitative approaches in a study but is distinguished by the integration of these approaches at multiple levels or different stages: design level, methods level and interpretation level and reporting of research that can happen in a variety of ways – connecting, building, merging or embedding (Berman, 2017; Creswell and Plano Clark, 2011; Fetters et al., 2013; McCrudden and McTigue, 2019; Schoonenboon and Johnson, 2017). Integration is necessitated by pragmatics (Bazeley, 2012; Creswell, 2003), defined by Subedi (2016) as "actions, situations and consequences that arise in real time situations of the researched phenomenon" (pp. 570–571). Integration also is influenced by the purpose of research and implementation sequence of data collection (Bazeley, 2012). The latter is summarised by Creswell (2003) and Schoonenboon and Johnson (2017) in terms of dependent and independent implementations of data collection: dependent sequential exploratory (qualitative then quantitative) or sequential explanatory (quantitative then qualitative) or sequential transformative, and independent concurrent triangulation, concurrent nested or concurrent transformative. Our research applies the dependent explanatory sequential data collection strategy involving quantitative data collection and analysis in phase 1 followed by qualitative data collection and analysis in phase 2, with interpretation and integration of findings at the end of each phase. Figure 16.1 contains a visual illustration of the explanatory sequential MMR data collection strategy with procedures and product from each procedure.

Our limited knowledge about maternal mortality statistics about the Gulf province influenced our decision to apply a MMR explanatory sequential design where quantitative data collection and analysis precedes qualitative data collection which explains, elaborates, refines or extends the quantitative results (Schoonenboon and Johnson, 2017; Subedi, 2016). Deficiencies in health systems highlighted the ineffectiveness of hospital employees in maternal mortality data management, reporting and monitoring of maternal health for addressing DEI concerns. Hence, only three Maternal Mortality Registers were located between the provincial health office and Kerema General Hospital. From the Obstetric Registry Records of 2011–5 May 2014, 385 obstetric cases were received in Kerema General Hospital: about 128 each year for the three years, ten cases each month and two cases each week. Maternal access to antenatal care or health facility or skilled birth attendant was generally unavailable.

A total of 587 admission cases were reported in the Obstetric Admissions' Records between July 2006 and April 2011: an average of 117 each year for each of the five years, nine each month and two each week. Demonstrated here is a high maternal inaccessibility to Kerema Provincial Hospital facilities for antenatal care, health facilities and accessing skilled attendants at birth. Records of any incidences of maternal mortality during this period are absent highlighting a hospital culture of poor staff reporting attributed in the survey to fear over potential reprisals from maternal deaths. The latter was affirmed by the qualitative survey. Obstetric admissions and case registries were typed into Excel and SPSS analysis was conducted for descriptive statistics, mainly frequencies and percentages to detect risk patterns for maternal mortality and inferential statistics, reported in Table 16.1. Thirty-five per cent of invisible women identified under the category *Born before Arrival* (BBA) deliver neonates before their arrival at Kerema Provincial Hospital. Another 35 per cent presented with different risky morbidities and 13 per cent with abortions. Between four and six per cent of total admissions comprised our research village sample of six "high" incidence BBA-associated village communities of Meii, Sori 1, Mamuro, Siviri, Apeama and Karama. Our expectation was that the "source village" of the mother affects her "final diagnosis" or BBA

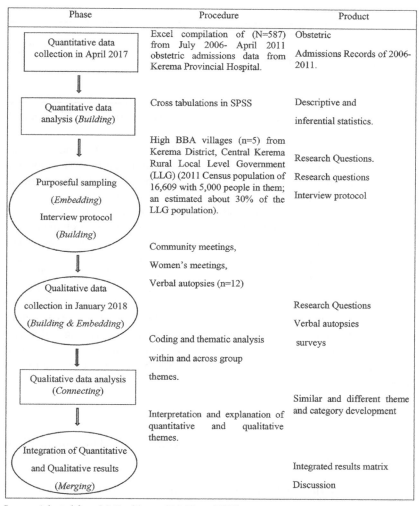

Phase	Procedure	Product
Quantitative data collection in April 2017	Excel compilation of (N=587) from July 2006- April 2011 obstetric admissions data from Kerema Provincial Hospital.	Obstetric Admissions Records of 2006-2011.
Quantitative data analysis (*Building*)	Cross tabulations in SPSS	Descriptive and inferential statistics.
Purposeful sampling (*Embedding*) Interview protocol (*Building*)	High BBA villages (n=5) from Kerema District, Central Kerema Rural Local Level Government (LLG) (2011 Census population of 16,609 with 5,000 people in them; an estimated about 30% of the LLG population).	Research Questions. Research questions Interview protocol
Qualitative data collection in January 2018 (*Building & Embedding*)	Community meetings, Women's meetings, Verbal autopsies (n=12)	Research Questions Verbal autopsies surveys
Qualitative data analysis (*Connecting*)	Coding and thematic analysis within and across group themes.	Similar and different theme and category development
Integration of Quantitative and Qualitative results (*Merging*)	Interpretation and explanation of quantitative and qualitative themes.	Integrated results matrix Discussion

Source: Adapted from McCrudden and McTigue (2019).

Figure 16.1   A visual display of the explanatory sequential design with integration strategies, procedures and product

status when she arrives at the hospital. We performed SPSS cross-tabulations on "source village" and "final diagnosis" to test the null hypothesis (H_o) of no relationship between the two variables and H_A that there is a relationship. At df=35649, significance level of 0.05, and p=<.001, we reject the null hypoth-

Table 16.1   Chi square test results

Chi-square tests	Value	df	Asymptotic significance (two-sided)
Pearson chi-square	39493.523[a]	35649	<.001
Likelihood ratio	3141.604	35649	1
Number of valid cases	587	–	–

Note: [a] 36,035 cells (100.0 per cent) have expected count less than 5. The minimum expected count is .00.

esis of no relationship between the "source village" of a mother and her "final diagnosis" and support the alternate hypothesis that a significant relationship exists between the two variables. The low likelihood ratio of 1 means being from a source village does not necessarily increase the final diagnosis.

Verbal Autopsy Reports asking about the cause of maternal deaths during the past year were held in community meetings and women's group interviews and from which representational narratives of maternal mortality experiences emerged. The outcomes validated our research approach, design and methods used to provide baseline data. Methods were altered in addressing high rural male and female illiteracy hence poor communication skills, cultural inhibitions or shame of speaking about experiences, and gender-related violence determinants of maternal mortality. Any weaknesses of the explanatory sequential design may apply to either priority, weight, sequencing and development given to type of data collection and analyses and managing stages of quantitative and qualitative research, connecting them and integrating results (Subedi, 2016, p. 571).

KEY FINDINGS AND DISCUSSION

We have structured our findings and discussion around addressing the three research questions.

RQ1: What Are the Health Determinants of Maternal Mortality?

Multiple obstetric complications compounded by a lack of proper management of diversity issues such as individual demographics, community, environment and defective health systems produce precursors to clinical conditions resulting in maternal mortality. The major cause of rural maternal death in our study villages was unmanaged postpartum haemorrhage (Mola and Kirby, 2013; NDoH, 2009). From verbal autopsies, Sori 1 village narratives offer an illustration on eight separate occasions in 2017, eight mothers in labour, each taking up to a six-hour canoe trip to deliver in Kerema General Hospital; each lost their neonates and their own lives to retained placenta-related postpartum haemorrhage. Even Siviri village, only 15 minutes' walk to the hospital, had a maternal death from postpartum haemorrhage in 2010. Mamuro also experienced a death in 2014 of a mother on a stretcher due to postpartum haemorrhage. Meii experienced a death in 2011 to the same cause from lack of money for transport to Kerema Hospital only a 30-minute boat ride away. These findings support NDOH (2009), WHO (2019) and high survival rates of BBA mothers at hospital that these reported deaths are preventable. Obstetric Registries record successful hospital management of women experiencing postpartum haemorrhage within the red-zone ranges of 500 ml to 2,700 ml. When managed, near-miss incidences can result in positive outcomes (Bolnga et al., 2017), underscoring maternal access to both health facility and skilled attendant at birth as crucial for maternal mortality prevention. Under health systems, morbidity, access issues to basic antenatal services, unbooked status of mothers, lack of health facilities for supervised delivery and no access to a skilled birth attendant all pose risks for maternal mortality.

RQ2: What Are the Non-Health Determinants of Maternal Mortality?

Qualitative interviews in the form of meetings with the community and women reports identified non-health determinants of maternal mortality under the categories individual woman's experiential attributes, household attributes, community attributes, economy DEI processes and environmental attributes. Maternal vulnerability to mortality can be gauged from the nature, degree and duration of any one or more of these individual women's experiences: being too young, fearful and shameful of male health workers, overwork during pregnancy, inadequate diet, poor health, victim of domestic violence, illiterate and ignorant of health information, fear of antenatal clinics and staff, past history of BBA and indecision to access antenatal care, site of delivery and treatment of neonate. Maternal vulnerability to mortality can result also from her household or community's experiential traits: adult illiteracy, ignorance of health information, malnutrition, of remote or rural subsistence origin, distant from town hospital, absence of income, lack of fast transport, traditional values and beliefs in sorcery, gender power and resource ownership and community demographics. Any one or a combination of more of these individual, household and community experiential traits can act as impediments in women's attempts to access antenatal care, health facilities, supervised births and postnatal care. Under environmental determinants, physical geographical and environmental isolation and constraints (e.g. rivers, mountains) trap communities, households and individual women and compound their access issues to health facilities and skilled attendants at birth.

RQ3: How Does the Interplay of Health and Non-Health Determinants Contribute to Maternal Mortality?

Having established a significant relationship between the source village of a mother and her final diagnosis in Kerema Hospital, we draw relevant inferences about maternal mortality from qualitative source village data. Qualitative reasoning about BBA experiences from Sori 1 maternal deaths indicate these important conclusions. First, rural women experiencing pregnancy-related complications or morbidities or are in labour will undertake emergency trips to access EmOC, a health facility and skilled attendants. Without such conditions, rural women, with nil or minimal access to health facilities and skilled attendants, will choose to deliver their babies at home. That is why over 77 per cent of 587 obstetric admissions to Kerema General Hospitals between 2006 and 2011 were recorded as "home" referrals: 16 per cent of obstetric admissions had safe deliveries at home and a mere 16 per cent were referred from a health facility or antenatal clinic. Second, mortality risks affect rural, illiterate, ignorant or unbooked women with no antenatal care at the onset of labour, or with a BBA status, and who require urgent access to a health facility or Kerema General Hospital and skilled birth attendants. Third, despite their personal, household or community attributes or distant source villages, pregnant rural women in labour or experiencing pregnancy-related complications and life-threatening morbidity will risk their lives to travel to access EoMC or a health facility and skilled attendants. To illustrate, of the 587 obstetric admissions of 2006–2011 in Kerema General Hospital, 83 per cent presented with BBA-related complications and life-threatening morbidities: 27 per cent included women in labour, experiencing a breech delivery, a still birth, twins, triplets, puerperal sepsis, lifestyle diseases and threatened or incomplete abortion, and only one case reported postpartum haemorrhage; 11 per cent were in the process of delivering their babies on arrival; 10 per cent presented with urinary tract infections in pregnancy; 10 per cent with completed abortion; 6 per cent with malaria; 5 per cent with placental retainment complications; 3 per cent with BBA-related severe tears including a vaginal and cervical tear; and 3 per cent with anaemia to severe anaemia.

Applying this information to the Sori 1 narratives of eight maternal deaths due to postpartum haemorrhage, it is possible that these women in labour had other morbidity conditions. In the absence of health system linkages with this village, the trip to Kerema General Hospital had to be made in order to access EmOC. Being in labour meant temporal access to hospital and specialist care was urgent. The trap was lack of access to fast transport along with no hire fee. UDHR and CEDAW prioritises the right to life or survival as important enough for both issues to be addressed by government and the health department or stakeholders. A six-hour canoe trip of about 200 kilometres through meandering waterways was critical for each woman and her baby's survival. This scenario suggests a lack of health service delivery activities linking rural woman and populations with the provincial health department and hospital staff or rural extension program staff to enact maternal access, coverage and distribution of antenatal care, EmOC and health facilities to rural women who needed these services the most. The inclusion of DEI strategies in the service delivery activities of national, provincial and local health authorities must drive the implementation of SDG 3.1 and KPA 5 thereby bridging diversity gaps and actively promoting inclusion of all. The SDGs already show the way forward to create equality and quality treatment of mothers and children and a more equitable society and quality of life for all (Penchen and Squires, 2017).

CONCLUSION/KEY RECOMMENDATIONS FOR FUTURE RESEARCH

Health determinants of maternal mortality denote clinical causes of death while non-health determinants denote the characteristics of women, their households, communities, government services and health department systems and environmental factors. Because maternal mortality is a human rights issue, inclusion of DEI strategies can bridge health system delivery gaps and enact processes that contribute to the realisation of SDG 3.1, the reduction of maternal mortality and the achievement of KPA 5 objectives in order to improve maternal health. We applied an adapted MMR explanatory sequential design to merge the data to create holistic maternal mortality narratives. Our findings demonstrate that the interactions between health and non-health maternal mortality determinants better explain maternal deaths. For a long-term effect of this approach on the health system or department, we advocate further for DEI strategies to also drive the achievement of economic, social and environment-related SDGs. This chapter fills a research gap on maternal mortality and argues for the integration of DEI processes and approaches in health systems and their service delivery thinking, inputs, activities, outcomes and impact to ensure better maternal health and lower maternal mortality.

Our first recommendation for immediate future research is to define and map out a conceptual model about the complex and multidimensional nature, context, scale and linkages between maternal mortality determinants. This model must include DEI strategies as drivers that define, clarify and enact linkages between these complex and multidimensional determinants. The model should inform onward stakeholder and health department research, planning, policy, decision making and practice that ultimately impact SDG 3.1 for KPA 5 objective achievements.

Another recommendation for immediate future research is the need for a long-term qualitative and quantitative research and monitoring approach to DEI inclusion in health departments' maternal health service delivery programs and activities, such as antenatal clinics, health facility access, skilled attendant access, EmOC and their overall impact on maternal mortality reduction and maternal health improvement. To begin with, rapid strengths, weaknesses, opportunities and threats analyses benchmarked against goals and objectives are needed for the whole agenda of obstetric handling by the health department authorities and staff. Health workers are key to the achievement of SDG 3.1 and KPA 5. Lessons learnt must be applied to improve the inculcation of DEI processes in health systems. A further key recommendation is to take a national sample of rural remote communities or villages with no access to health services, especially health facilities and skilled attendants, and through action research explore pathways for traditional birth systems to be integrated to improve maternal health and prevent maternal mortality. Such research should explore strategies of bringing mobile EmOC and maternal and child health services to the communities that bridge gaps in the health departments' maternal health coverage and promote the rights of mothers and newborns to life. More research is required into funding options and rural health service delivery models based on those options that would improve health-care quality in the Gulf province and PNG as a whole. In all of these, qualitative research is still needed to identify high-risk mothers and propose strategies for mitigating risks for maternal survival.

IMPLICATIONS FOR RESEARCHERS, PRACTITIONERS, ORGANISATIONS AND MANAGERS

1. This research is ground breaking in its inclusion of an MMR approach in unpacking the complex and multidimensional nature of maternal mortality. MMR analyses of the interactions of health and non-health determinants of maternal mortality, underpinned by DEI strategies, enact a paradigm shift in thinking and ultimately impact health system practices that improve maternal health. Recommendations for future research in the final part of this chapter can contribute greater insight towards a conceptual framework of an integration model of maternal mortality determinants.

2. International agencies, national leaders, health systems authorities and medical practitioners can learn from the flexibility permitted, in the organisational system's framework, through incorporating DEI strategies to effectively alter aspects of organisational culture for achieving SDG 3.1 to reduce maternal mortality and the PNG's National Health Plan's 2011–2020 KPA 5 to improve maternal health. Practical health incorporation of DEI strategies should influence medical pursuits for maternal

health improvement (KPA 5) while reaping the rewards in maternal mortality reduction (SDG 3.1).

3. Adopting DEI strategies within the organisational system's approach can alter the deficient health system's leadership culture as this approach facilitates and influences simultaneous and dynamic spatial arrangements for active partnerships and collaborations in the achievement of SDG 3.1 and KPA 5.

4. Even at provincial through to local level, health systems or department leaders and managers can enact through a system's linkages and interactions a coalignment of resources with SDG 3.1 and KPA 5 prioritising leadership accountability to DEI strategies in strategic decision making, resource procurement and coordination and management of activities for the achievement of SDG 3.1 and KPA 5.

REFERENCES

Andrew, E. V. W., Pell, C., Angwin, A., Auwun, A., Daniels, J., Mueller, I., and Pool, R. (2014). Factors affecting attendance at and timing of formal antenatal care: Results from a qualitative study in Madang, Papua New Guinea. *PLOS ONE, 9*(5), e93025.

Bazeley, P. (2012). Integrative analysis strategy for mixed data sources. *American Behavioral Scientist, 56*(6), 814–828.

Berer, M. (2012). Maternal mortality or women's health: Time for action. *Reproductive Health Matters, 20*(39), 5–10.

Berman, E. A. (2017). An exploratory sequential mixed methods approach to understanding researchers' data management practices at UVM: Integrated findings to develop research data services. *Journal of eScience Librarianship, 6*(1), 1–24.

Bolnga, J. W., Hamura, N. N., Umbers, A. J., Rogerson, S. J., and Unger, H. W. (2014). Insights into maternal mortality in Madang province, Papua New Guinea. *International Journal of Gynecology and Obstetrics, 124*(2), 123–127.

Creswell, J. W. (2003). *Research Design: Qualitative, Quantitative and Mixed Methods Approaches*. London: Sage.

Creswell, J. W. and Plano Clark, V. L. (2011). *Designing and Conducting Mixed Methods Research* (2nd ed.). Thousand Oaks, CA: Sage.

DNPM (2015). *Millennium Development Goals 2015: Summary Report for Papua New Guinea*. www.planning.gov.pg/images/dnpm/pdf/MDG-Summary-Report -2015_Opt.pdf

Fetters, M. D., Curry, L. A., and Creswell, J. W. (2013). Achieving integration in mixed methods designs: Principles and practices. *Health Services Research, 48*(6), 2134–2156.

Haupt, A., Kane, T. T., and Haub, C. (2011). *PRB's Population Handbook*. Washington, DC: Population Reference Bureau.

Kelly, E., and Dobbin, F. (1998). How affirmative action became diversity management. *American Behavioral Scientist, 41*, 960–984.

Kossek, E. E., and Pichler, S. (2006). EEO and mangement of diversity. In P. Boxell, J. Purcell and P. M. Wrigh (eds), *Handbook of Human Resource Management* (pp. 251–272). Oxford: Oxford University Press.

Luchenski, S., Maguire, N., Aldridge, R. W., Hayward, A., Story, A., Perri, P., Withers, J., Clint, S., Fitzpatrick, S., and Hewett, N. (2018). Review: What works in inclusion health: Overview of effective interventions for marginalised and excluded populations. *Lancet*, *391*, 266–280.

McCrudden, M. T, and McTigue, E. M. (2019). Implementing integration in an explanatory sequential mixed methods study of belief bias about climate change with high school students. *Journal of Mixed Methods Research*, *13*(3), 381–400.

Mola, G., and Kirby, B. (2013). Discrepancies between national maternal mortality data and international estimates: The experience of Papua New Guinea. *Reproductive Health Matters*, *21*(42), 191–202.

NDoH (National Department of Health) (2009). *Ministerial Taskforce on Maternal Health in Papua New Guinea*. Port Moresby: National Department of Health. http://health.gov.pg/pdf/Ministerial%20Taskforce%20Report.pdf

NSO (National Statistical Office) and ICF (2019). *Papua New Guinea Demographic and Health Survey 2016–18*. Port Moresby and Rockville, MD: NSO and ICF.

Oswick, C., and Noon, m. (2014). Discourses of diversity, equality and inclusion: Trenchant formulations or transient fashions? *British Journal of Management*, *25*(1), 23–39.

Patel, P., Meagher, K., El Achi, N., Ekzayer, A., Sullivan, R., and Bowsher, G. (2020). Having more women humanitarian leaders will help transform the humanitarian system: Challenges and opportunities for women leaders in conflict and humanitarian health. *Conflict and Health*, *14*(1), 1–5.

Penchen, D., and Squires, N. (2017). Invited review: Sustainable Development Goals (SDGs), and their implementation. A national global framework for health, development and equity needs a systems approach at every level. *British Medical Bulletin*, *124*, 81–90.

Sanga, K., de Costa, C., and Mola, G. (2010). A review of maternal deaths at Goroka General Hospital, Papua New Guinea 2005–2008. *Australian and New Zealand Journal of Obstetrics and Gynaecology*, *50*(1), 21–24.

Schein, E. H. (2004). *Organisational Culture and Leadership* (3rd ed.). San Francisco, CA: Jossey-Bass.

Schoonenboon, J., and Johnson, R. B. (2017). How to construct a mixed methods research design? *Kolner Z Soz Sozpsychol 69*(Supplement 2), 107–131.

Subedi, D. (2016). Explanatory sequential mixed method design as the third research community of knowledge claim. *American Journal of Educational Research*, *4*(7), 570–577.

Tanimia, H., Jayaratnam, S., Mola, G. L., Amoa, A. B., and Costa, C. (2016). Near-misses at the Port Moresby General Hospital: A descriptive study. *Australian and New Zealand Journal of Obstetrics and Gynaecology*, *56*(2), 148–153.

Thomas, D. A. (1990). Diversity as a strategy. *Harvard Business Review*, *82*(9), 98–108.

Vallely, L. M., Homiehombo, P., Kelly-Hanku, A., Vallely, A., Homer, C. S. E., and Whittaker, A. (2015). Childbirth in a rural highlands community in Papua New Guinea: A descriptive study. *Midwifery*, *31*(3), 380–387.

WHO (World Health Organization). (1996). *Revised 1990 Estimates of Maternal Mortality: A New Approach by WHO and UNICEF*. Geneva: WHO, April.

WHO (World Health Organization). (2019). Independent state of Papua New Guinea health system review. *Health System Review*, *9*(1).

Wilunda, C., Putoto, G., Riva, D. D., Manenti, F., Atzori, A., Calia, F., Assefa, T., Turri, B., Emmanuel, O., Straneo, M., Kisika, F., and Tarmbulini, G. (2015).

Assessing coverage, equity and quality gaps in maternal and neonatal care in SubSaharan Africa: An integrated approach. *PLOS ONE*, 1–15.

Zaccaro, S. J., and Klimoski, R. J. (2001). The nature of organizational leadership: An introduction. www.researchgate.net/publication/242546000

Zureick-Brown, S., Newby, H., Choiu, D., Mizoguchi, N., Say, L., Suzuki, E., and Wilmoth, J. (2013). Understanding global trends in maternal mortality. *International Perspectives on Sexual and Reproductive Health, 39*(1), 32–41.

17. Complexity and opportunity in diversity challenges in Singapore

Amy Lim and Peter Waring

INTRODUCTION

Equality and inclusion are principles forged within the first stanza of Singapore's National Pledge which commits citizens to build a democratic society based on justice and equality, 'regardless of race, language or religion'. The extension of these principles to Singapore's workplaces, however, remains an unfinished project. A global survey by consulting firm Kantar in 2019 placed Singapore as the second worst performing country (of 14 developed countries) for workplace diversity and inclusion practices. Moreover, the Council for Board Diversity (established by the Ministry of Social and Family Development) indicated that just 18 per cent of directors of Singapore's top 100 companies were women (Council of Board Diversity, 2021). These statistics contrast sharply with Singapore's otherwise stable multicultural and merit-based society and suggest that the city-state's rich demographic diversity is not necessarily fully reflected in its workplaces. Although the literature on the economic and social benefits of diversity is compelling (see Low et al., 2015), it does not appear to be a strong business imperative in Singapore and there remain significant structural and cultural impediments to realising these gains in many Singaporean workplaces. Tensions and restrictive practices continue to be observed over age, gender and religious, disability and sexual orientation diversity issues, in spite of well-intentioned efforts by policymakers. In this chapter we unravel this complexity which has its roots in history and culture and discuss the opportunity that greater diversity and inclusiveness presents for Singapore's economy. Following this introduction, we briefly outline the research approach used to inform this chapter's analysis before characterising in broad terms Singapore's diversity and inclusion profile.

The narrative then turns to consider the barriers to improved workplace diversity in Singapore. Drawing upon insights from social-psychology, economics and employment relations, we argue that in spite of a broad consensus on the merits of greater diversity, there remain substantial cultural, psychological and economic blockages to the achievement of diversity and inclusion. The penultimate section discusses possible solutions to clearing these barriers and blockages. Here we note both the important role to be played by the state and outline some private-sector responses to achieving more effective management of diversity and inclusion. The concluding section draws together the key findings from the chapter and offers guidance to those seeking a deeper understanding of this topic in the Singapore context.

THE RESEARCH APPROACH

The analysis of diversity and inclusion issues in Singapore has been informed through a variety of 'desktop' research methods. These include a thorough review of the extant literature including relevant 'grey literature'. Additionally, the contemporary and evolving nature of these issues makes it important to critically evaluate documents in the public domain. These include policy statements from government, political speeches and legislation, published opinion pieces by key stakeholders such as unions and advocacy groups as well as news articles. Finally, the research approach has included the analysis of relevant secondary data where these help to illustrate progress and continuing challenges.

DIVERSITY AND INCLUSION IN SINGAPORE

> Singapore can turn its racial and religious diversity into a source of strength and advantage on the world stage.
> (Deputy Prime Minister Heng Swee Keat, in Koh, 2019)

Being an ethnically diverse society, the Singapore government has instituted various policies based on the principles of multiculturalism and equality that have structured, and continue to structure, contemporary Singapore society. This policy context embraces the diversity of ethnic, cultural heritage and ensures that all ethnic groups are accorded equal treatment in economic participation, education, religious and cultural expression and practice so that Singapore achieves and remains a harmonious society (Hill and Lian, 1995; Mathews and Chiang, 2016).

Singapore's success at managing its diverse society is internationally renowned and has contributed to the workforce diversity found in local industry. With English used in everyday life, a stable political system and a reputation for a safe and clean living environment, Singapore has positioned itself as an attractive destination for businesses and expatriates. Thus, Singapore's multiculturalism is regarded as an asset for Singapore in attracting and connecting with businesses from all over the world.

Despite the success in managing demographic diversity and maintaining a stable multicultural society, Singapore has not seen much progress in workplace diversity. It is evident that workplace diversity is beneficial for companies, and Singapore possesses expertise in managing diversity, yet Singapore trails behind other countries in workplace diversity. As such, this calls for a deeper understanding of the barriers to achieving diversity in order to comprehend this perplexing phenomenon.

BARRIERS TO ACHIEVING DIVERSITY AND INCLUSION

Gender

A considerable number of factors exist that limit and constrain women's participation in the workforce. One of the more prominent factors is a workplace climate where women feel unwelcome and experience discrimination in their workplaces (Sandler and Hall, 1986). Inequities in the distribution of workplace resources (e.g., salary) and work opportunities that exclude women (e.g., manufacturing jobs considered too dangerous) have a significant impact in restricting the options of women (Betz, 2006; Fassinger, 2005). Women face additional workplace barriers when they are excluded from information and social networks that support advancement (e.g., 'old boy networks') and are subjected to added responsibilities as a result of tokenism (Betz, 2006; Fassinger, 2005, 2008). Additionally, the failure to consider and address the lack of encouragement for achievement, coupled with the lack of female role models in male-dominated fields (e.g., science, technology, engineering and medicine) and higher management, dissuades women from participating in the workforce and pursuing career advancement (Betz, 2006; Bettinger and Long, 2005; Dasgupta and Asgari, 2004; Fassinger, 2008; McIntyre et al., 2011). Moreover, women are frequently evaluated negatively when they demonstrate competence and achieve accomplishments at work (Rudman and Phelan, 2008). Such unfair evaluation practices contribute to an undesirable environment for women in the workplace.

Harassment of female employees remains one of the most egregious obstacles to gender diversity in the workplace. This manifests in two ways: gender harassment and sexual harassment. Gender harassment occurs when hostile sexist acts in the form of sexist jokes, displays of sexist or suggestive materials and the devaluation of women are directed at women in the workplace (Gelfand et al., 1995). In contrast, sexual harassment occurs when female employees are exposed to unwanted sex-related behaviours from others in the workplace; this includes sexual coercion (e.g., threats unless sexual favours are granted), unwelcome sexual attention and other forms of sexual harm

(Fitzgerald et al., 1995). Extensive literature has documented the adverse consequences of workplace harassment; harassment experiences are associated with the deterioration of mental and physical health, decreased satisfaction with life, withdrawal from work, worse interpersonal relationships at work, decreased job satisfaction and lower organisational commitment (see Sojo et al., 2016; Willness et al., 2007).

In the Singapore context, technology-facilitated sex offences (such as digital voyeurism and image-based sexual abuse) have increased in recent years according to advocacy groups (Rosli, 2019). Yi (2019) reported that incidents of digital sexual violence in Singapore had tripled from 2016 to 2018. To combat this, the penal code was amended in January 2020 to criminalise the making and distribution of (or threat to distribute) voyeuristic recordings and intimate images. Further, a new offence of sexual exposure was introduced, which criminalises the non-consensual sending of unsolicited images of genitals – sometimes referred to as 'cyber flashing' (Ministry of Law, 2019). This growing societal problem demonstrates that even the most well-intentioned diversity and inclusion practices can be weakened by errant behaviours found in broader society.

Commonly held assumptions regarding women's family responsibilities may also undermine diversity and inclusion. Singaporean women are often socially expected to shoulder the burden of managing the household, childcare and care of other family members; these responsibilities to home and children result in the perception that women are unreliable and distracted workers (see Betz, 2006; Fassinger, 2005). Furthermore, studies have found that women, especially mothers, were held to higher performance standards than men (i.e., fathers), even though they were perceived as being less competent and committed to the organisation than their male counterparts (Fuegen et al., 2004). Such perceptions led to a reduced interest to hire, promote and educate women with childcare responsibilities (Cuddy et al., 2004). Collectively, women find themselves in a predicament where not only are they perceived to be less competent (due to their responsibility to the family), but their capability of managing their duties at home and work is often underestimated.

Race

Racism, broadly referred to as the belief that members of different racial categories possess distinctive characteristics and the differential treatment of people based on their racial group, is often the main factor attributed to the lack of ethnic/racial diversity in workplaces. Racial minorities face barriers such as limited access to support networks and a lack of role models, which undermine their motivation and stunt career advancement (Fassinger, 2008). Moreover, at times, racial minorities assume the role of 'cultural ambassadors' to commercialise the organisation's diversity efforts; such tokenism increases their workload (i.e., needing to engage in race-related task forces and training) and adds to existing pressures they face at work (i.e., having to prove their competence) (Fassinger, 2008; Roberts et al., 2019). As a result, racial minorities often report feeling less supported, engaged and committed to their jobs (see Roberts et al., 2019).

In Singapore, a recent survey on racial harmony revealed that a large proportion of racial minorities felt that they had been discriminated against in hiring practices and promotional decisions, and this perceived level of workplace racial discrimination has risen since 2013 (Mathews et al., 2019). A significant portion of respondents also reported that beyond ability, factors such as language and race of the job applicant were also important in hiring decisions (Mathews et al., 2019). Anecdotal evidence corroborated these survey findings that race remains an issue in many workplaces. Personal accounts from European immigrants reported difficulty integrating with the Chinese majority due to the stereotypes they hold about Caucasians – European immigrants are typically avoided as they are stereotypically thought to be associated with wealth and power (Hof, 2018). That said, however, this may be a manifestation of the ignorance in interacting with members of other racial groups within the workplace. To elaborate further, it is likely that the Chinese majority were confused over how to treat these European immigrants who do not conform to the Caucasian stereotype (i.e., hold middle and higher management positions) (Hof, 2018). The incongruence between people's stereotypical beliefs regarding different racial groups and reality may lead to behaviours (e.g., avoidance) that could be construed as racism, even though the underlying reason is a lack of knowledge in dealing with the incongruity.

Age

Progress towards age diversity in the workplace is typically hindered by the assumptions and stereotypes held by employers about older workers. Older workers are perceived as being slower in work, less able to adapt to new technologies, less technologically oriented, less able to train, slower in learning, less risk taking and more prone to health problems compared to their younger counterparts (Darwin and Palanisamy, 2015). Due to such perceptions, older workers are often considered to generate lower returns on training investment by employers. Consequently, older workers face issues such as lower performance ratings and reduced opportunity for promotion and career progression (McGregor and Gray, 2002). Such perceptions persist even when studies have shown that there is no association between a worker's age and their work performance (Ilmarinen et al., 2005).

Singapore has an ageing demographic, which continues to be a source of concern. One in four Singaporeans will be 65 and older by 2030, while the resident working-age population will peak in 2020. To address this challenge, Prime Minister Lee announced in his National Day Rally speech of 2019 that the retirement age in Singapore would be raised from 62 to 63 in 2022 and to 65 by 2030. Singapore's ageing demographic profile, therefore, represents a conundrum on a number of levels for policymakers. The government needs to increase labour market opportunities for older workers while also encouraging the adoption of technology, which may erode such opportunities.

With the raising of Singapore's retirement age, it is critical to ensure that older workers are not discriminated against in the workplace. Unfortunately, the perception that older workers are less productive than younger workers continues to be observed in Singapore. Research within Singapore revealed that people hold negative attitudes towards employing older workers due to stereotypical expectations about older workers' likelihood of withdrawing from work, health and their decision-making abilities (Ko, 2019).

Stereotype Threat: The Psychology behind Sexism, Racism and Ageism

The threat of stereotyping manifests in the attitudes and behaviours of both employers and co-workers. Members of these stereotyped groups are also aware of these attitudes and are susceptible to them. The heightened consciousness of their stereotyped status and fear of conforming to the stereotypes lead members of stereotyped groups to perform worse and achieve less at work – a phenomenon known as stereotype threat (Steele, 1997). Stereotype threat has been demonstrated extensively among women and racial minorities (i.e., African Americans), where members of stereotyped groups perform more poorly on tasks associated with negative stereotypes of their group when they are made aware of the stereotypes (Nguyen and Ryan, 2008; Spencer et al., 1999; Steele, 1997). In recent years, stereotype threat effects have also been observed in older adults; exposure to negative age-related stereotypes undermined older adults' memory and physical performance (Armstrong et al., 2017; Lamont et al., 2015). The preponderance of evidence on stereotype threat establishes the pernicious impact stereotypes have on employees. Stereotypic expectations of different demographic groups discourage diversity in the workplace as high turnover rates would be expected from members of stereotyped groups; this lack of diversity is further perpetuated through stereotype threat experiences by remaining members of stereotyped groups.

Cultural

Diversity extends beyond physical attributes into less observable characteristics such as sexual identity. An increasing number of studies examining sexual minority issues in the workplace have found that heterosexism, discrimination against gay people, is pervasive (Croteau et al., 2008). Workers who were more open with their sexual orientation were often discriminated against (Croteau et al., 2008). Hence, sexual minorities engage in constant vigilance about sharing information of themselves and may attempt to pass off as heterosexual in order to conceal their sexual preferences; this results in them having to cope with feelings of dishonesty, inauthenticity and isolation and they eventually experience burnout (Croteau et al., 2008; Fassinger, 2008). Additionally, sexual minorities commonly experience depression, distress, lower self-esteem, lower job satisfaction, decreased organisational commitment and are likely to be absent and withdraw from work (Croteau et al., 2008). Discriminatory practices against sexual minorities discourage participation of these individuals in workplaces, which not only restricts career options for sexual minorities but also perpetuates occupational segregation and a lack of diversity in the workplace (Croteau et al., 2008; Fassinger and Gallor, 2006).

Singapore is generally considered a conservative society with conservative views of homosexuality (Straits Times, 2007). An example of this conservatism can be seen in the long-running debate over whether Section 337A of the criminal law, which criminalises sex between consenting men, should be repealed. In defending the legal status quo, Prime Minister Lee Hsien Loong stated that:

> The family is the basic building block of this society. And by family in Singapore, we mean one man, one woman marrying, having children and bringing up children within that framework of a stable family unit ... I acknowledge that not everybody fits into this mould. Some are single, some have more colourful lifestyles, some are gay. But a heterosexual, stable family is a social norm. (Prime Minister Lee Hsien Loong, in Straits Times, 2007)

Several efforts have been made to ensure that homosexuality is not encouraged; for instance, advertisements that target the LGBTQI community are not allowed for broadcasting, and gay role models have been barred from giving talks in Singapore (Beh, 2019). Additionally, Singapore does not recognise same-sex marriages, and the government aims to strengthen adoption laws to prevent adoption from same-sex couples as it considers that this contradicts the ideal that family units should consist of heterosexual parents (Ungku, 2019). As of the time of writing this chapter, laws concerning the protection of sexual minorities from discrimination in the workplace do not exist. While Singaporeans have become more accepting of gay sex and marriage in recent years, the majority remain conservative on issues concerning homosexuality (Cheng, 2019). The continuation of this approach somewhat contradicts the positioning of Singapore as being a modern, open economy that attracts talent on merit considerations alone.

Public and Private Approaches to Achieving Diversity and Inclusion in Singapore

In recent times there has been a robust public debate in Singapore concerning the merits of introducing anti-discrimination laws to promote greater workforce diversity and inclusion. The debate has largely been led by the Association of Women for Action and Research (AWARE), which has strongly advocated for the introduction of broad-based anti-discrimination law in Singapore, and more recently, for age-based discrimination law in particular.

AWARE's advocacy for discrimination law has been rebutted by both the Singapore National Employers Federation and the Ministry of Manpower. In a reply to AWARE's public advocacy, the Singapore National Employers Federation defended the existing arrangements and penalties for discrimination and predicted that anti-discrimination law would result in lengthy and costly disputes with employers potentially facing 'vexatious' claims (Sim, 2020). A spokesperson for the Ministry of Manpower was more circumspect, stating that 'While keeping an open mind on new laws to address workplace discrimination, we should also recognize the good outcomes achieved through a multi-pronged approach' (Lee, 2020). Rather than hard regulation, Singapore's Tripartite Alliance for Fair and Progressive Employment Practices provides a number of guidelines for all workplaces in Singapore to follow. These include:

- Employers should treat employees fairly and with respect and create progressive human resource management systems.
- Reward employees fairly based on performance, ability, contribution and experience.
- Provide employees with equal opportunities to be considered for training and development to help them reach their potential. This should be based on the strengths and needs of the individual.
- Recruit and select on merit regardless of gender, religion, marital status, age, race, family responsibilities or disability.
- Comply with all labour laws and abide by the Tripartite Guidelines on Fair Employment Practices.

In his annual National Day Rally Speech in 2021, Prime Minister Lee acknowledged that there had been calls from Singapore's labour movement and other advocacy groups to pass Anti-Discrimination laws as they considered the Tripartite Guidelines as 'lacking teeth'. Prime Minister Lee explained that the government had been reluctant to go down this legislative path as it did not wish to see disputes become 'legalistic or confrontational'. However, in his speech, he promised that 'after consulting tripartite partners' Singapore will 'enshrine the TAFEP [Tripartite] guidelines in law'. While the exact provisions and mechanics of the law are yet to be disclosed, this marks a very significant step in state regulation of discrimination in Singapore (Channel News Asia, 2021). Another significant influence on the private sector are the practices of multinational corporations in Singapore. The Economic Development Board claims that up to 7000 multinationals have their regional headquarters in Singapore (EDB, 2021). Many of these (especially from the United States) have introduced sophisticated diversity and inclusion practices such as unconscious bias training, which is designed to bring to the surface individual biases or learned stereotypes that are said to be deeply ingrained but nonetheless can influence managerial decisions and behaviour (see Lee, 2005). These practices tend to be limited to larger multinationals, and it is unclear as to whether they influence local views towards diversity and inclusion practices, or the Singaporean institutional context more broadly.

CONCLUSION

At the beginning of this chapter, we made specific reference to the principles of 'justice' and 'equality', which are words spoken by those reciting Singapore's National Pledge. Our exploration of the topic of diversity and inclusion in the context of Singapore demonstrates that these principles are evident in many aspects of Singaporean society and less evident in others. Our analysis has shown that the country has been both a beneficiary and exemplar of diversity and inclusion when it comes to race and religion. Its ethnic and religious diversity is undoubtedly a strength and supports the notion of Singapore as a welcoming entrepot. This image, however, is challenged by the reality that Singaporean women are far less likely to be found in senior management and on company boards. Further, the country's conservative views of homosexuality contrast sharply with the diversity and inclusion policies and practices of the multinational corporations it hopes to attract.

What might be considered best practice in diversity and inclusion, therefore, remains unfinished business for most Singapore workplaces. The recent move to adopt anti-discrimination law represents progress towards more diverse and inclusive workplaces, but it will take time for regulation to produce change. Further, strongly held cultural values that remain contrary to diversity and inclusion principles mean that progress is likely to be sluggish in an otherwise dynamic, modern, open economy.

RESEARCH FIELD TIPS

Given the pivotal role played by government in Singapore society, it is important for researchers to have a good grasp of policy issues. The Ministries of Manpower and Law and key agencies are important information sources. Similarly, researchers should consider the role of AWARE. AWARE is an important advocacy group in Singapore that participates in public debates over diversity and inclusion issues. Finally, researchers should be cognisant that Singapore workplaces are somewhat influenced by the role of multinational corporations in the local economy and the policies and practices they have introduced.

REFERENCES

Armstrong, B., Gallant, S. N., Li, L., Patel, K., and Wong, B. I. (2017). Stereotype threat effects on older adults' episodic and working memory: A meta-analysis. *The Gerontologist*, *57*(suppl. 2), S193–S205.

Beh, L. Y. (2019). Gay DJ pulls out of Singapore TEDx talk over censorship. *Reuters*, 5 July.

Bettinger, E. P., and Long, B. T. (2005). Do faculty serve as role models? The impact of instructor gender on female students. *American Economic Review*, *95*(2), 152–157.

Betz, N. (2006). Basic issues and concepts in the career development and counselling of women. In W. B. Walsh and M. H. Heppner (Eds), *Handbook of Career Counselling for Women* (pp. 55–84). Routledge.

Channel News Asia (2021). NDR 2021: Singapore to enshrine into law workplace anti-discrimination guidelines.

Cheng, K. (2019). 'Marriage between man and woman remains norm, despite more liberal attitudes on homosexuality: MSF'. *Today*, 5 May.

Council for Board Diversity (2021). Progress of women on boards. www.coun cilforboarddiversity.sg/

Croteau, J. M., Bieschke, K. J., Fassinger, R. E., and Manning, J. L. (2008). Counseling psychology and sexual orientation: History, selective trends, and future directions. *Handbook of Counseling Psychology*, *4*, 194–211.

Cuddy, A. J., Fiske, S. T., and Glick, P. (2004). When professionals become mothers, warmth doesn't cut the ice. *Journal of Social Issues*, *60*(4), 701–718.

Darwin, J., and Palanisamy, C. (2015). The effects of work force diversity on employee performance in Singapore organisations. *International Journal of Business Administration*, *6*(2), 17–29.

Dasgupta, N., and Asgari, S. (2004). Seeing is believing: Exposure to counterstereotypic women leaders and its effect on the malleability of automatic gender stereotyping. *Journal of Experimental Social Psychology*, *40*(5), 642–658.

Fassinger, R. E. (2005). Theoretical issues in the study of women's career development: Building bridges in a brave new world. In W. B. Walsh and M. L. Savickas (Eds), *Contemporary Topics in Vocational Psychology: Handbook of Vocational Psychology: Theory, Research, and Practice* (pp. 85–124). Lawrence Erlbaum Associates Publishers.

Fassinger, R. E. (2008). Workplace diversity and public policy: Challenges and opportunities for psychology. *American Psychologist, 63*(4), 252–268.

Fassinger, R. E., and Gallor, S. M. (2006). Tools for remodeling the masters' house: Advocacy and social justice in education and work. In R. L. Toporek, L. H. Gerstein, N. A. Fouad, G. Roysicar and T. Israel (Eds), *Handbook for Social Justice in Counseling Psychology: Leadership, Vision, and Action* (pp. 256–275). Sage.

Fitzgerald, L. F., Gelfand, M. J., and Drasgow, F. (1995). Measuring sexual harassment: Theoretical and psychometric advances. *Basic and Applied Social Psychology, 17*(4), 425–445.

Fuegen, K., Biernat, M., Haines, E., and Deaux, K. (2004). Mothers and fathers in the workplace: How gender and parental status influence judgments of job-related competence. *Journal of Social Issues*, 60(4), 737–754.

Gelfand, M. J., Fitzgerald, L. F., and Drasgow, F. (1995). The structure of sexual harassment: A confirmatory analysis across cultures and settings. *Journal of Vocational Behavior, 47*(2), 164–177.

Hill, M., and Lian, K. F. (1995). *The Politics of Nation Building and Citizenship in Singapore*. Routledge.

Hof, H. (2018). Worklife pathways to Singapore and Japan: Gender and racial dynamics in Europeans mobility to Asia. *Social Science Japan Journal, 21*(1), 45–65.

Ilmarinen, J., Tuomi, K., and Seitsamo, J. (2005, June). New dimensions of work ability. *International Congress Series*, 1280, 3–7.

Ko, C. (2019). Seniors do well at their jobs yet ageist myths and negative stereotypes persist: Commentary. *Channel News Asia*, 25 August.

Koh, F. (2019). Singapore can turn its racial and religious diversity into a strength globally: DPM Heng Swee Keat. *Straits Times*, 12 August.

Lamont, R. A., Swift, H. J., and Abrams, D. (2015). A review and meta-analysis of age-based stereotype threat: Negative stereotypes, not facts, do the damage. *Psychology and Aging, 30*(1), 180.

Lee, A. (2005). Unconscious bias theory in employment discrimination litigation. *Harvard Civil Rights–Civil Liberties Law Review, 40*(Rev 481).

Lee, C. (2020). Workplace discrimination: Laws part of approach to tackle employment issues. Forum letter. *Straits Times*, 4 November.

Mathews, M., and Chiang, W. F. (Eds). (2016). *Managing Diversity in Singapore: Policies and Prospects*. Imperial College Press.

Mathews, M., Lim, L., and Selvarajan, S. (2019). IPS-OnePeople. Sg indicators of racial and religious harmony: Comparing results from 2018 and 2013. *Institute of Policy Papers Working Paper*, 35.

McGregor, J., and Gray, L. (2002). Stereotypes and older workers: The New Zealand experience. *Social Policy Journal of New Zealand*, 163–177.

McIntyre, R. B., Paulson, R. M., Taylor, C. A., Morin, A. L., and Lord, C. G. (2011). Effects of role model deservingness on overcoming performance deficits induced by stereotype threat. *European Journal of Social Psychology, 41*(3), 301–311.

Ministry of Law (2019). Commencement of amendments to the Penal Code and other legislation on 1 January 2020. www.mlaw.gov.sg

Nguyen, H. H. D., and Ryan, A. M. (2008). Does stereotype threat affect test performance of minorities and women? A meta-analysis of experimental evidence. *Journal of Applied Psychology, 93*(6), 1314–1334.

Roberts, L. M., Mayo, A. J., and Thomas, D. A. (2019). *Race, Work, and Leadership: New Perspectives on the Black Experience*. Harvard Business Press.

Rosli, T. (2019). Number of tech-based sex crimes soars: Aware. *AsiaOne*.

Rudman, L. A., and Phelan, J. E. (2008). Backlash effects for disconfirming gender stereotypes in organizations. *Research in Organizational Behavior, 28,* 61–79.

Sandler, B. R., and Hall, R. M. (1986). The campus climate revisited: Chilly for women faculty, administrators, and graduate students. https://eric.ed.gov/?id=ED282462

Sim, G. (2020). Workplace discrimination: Disputes best resolved amicably. Forum letter, *Straits Times,* 4 November.

Sojo, V. E., Wood, R. E., and Genat, A. E. (2016). Harmful workplace experiences and women's occupational well-being: A meta-analysis. *Psychology of Women Quarterly, 40*(1), 10–40.

Spencer, S. J., Steele, C. M., and Quinn, D. M. (1999). Stereotype threat and women's math performance. *Journal of Experimental Social Psychology, 35*(1), 4–28.

Steele, C. M. (1997). A threat in the air: How stereotypes shape the intellectual identities and performance of women and African Americans. *American Psychologist, 52,* 613–629.

Straits Times (2007). Full parliamentary speech by PM Lee Hsien Loong in 2007 on Section 377A. www.straitstimes.com/politics/full-parliamentary-speech-by-pm-lee -hsien-loong-in-2007-on-section-377a

Ungku, F. (2019). Singapore may tighten adoption law after gay father adopted son. *Reuters,* 14 January.

Willness, C. R., Steel, P., and Lee, K. (2007). A meta-analysis of the antecedents and consequences of workplace sexual harassment. *Personnel Psychology, 60*(1), 127–162.

Yi, B. (2019). Pervasive digital sexual violence against women skyrockets in Singapore. Reuters, 25 November.

USEFUL WEB RESOURCES

AWARE: www.aware.org.sg
Ministry of Law: www.mlaw.gov.sg
Ministry of Manpower: www.mom.gov.sg
Tripartite Alliance for Fair and Progressive Employment Practices: www.tal.sg

18. Equality, diversity and inclusion in the South African workplace: the paradox of legislation

Shaun Ruggunan, Kathryn Pillay and Kantha Dayaram

INTRODUCTION

One measure of workplace diversity in South Africa is to assess the quantitative indicators of racial and gender transformation in the labour market. Such data show contrasting transformation projects. The public sector reflects the most diversity whereas the private sector lags significantly behind. The first part of the chapter describes and assesses legislative attempts in post-apartheid South Africa to create more equitable and inclusive workplaces. The chapter then provides an assessment of the current state of the country's labour market in terms of racial diversity. While we acknowledge that there are other forms of diversity in the workplace, given South Africa's protracted history of colonialism and apartheid and how legislation (based on race) from this time period still profoundly affects the world of work presently, this chapter focuses on racial diversity and inclusion.

The second part of this chapter discusses whether 'transformation by numbers' is sufficient to redress the legacy of apartheid. It argues that performative acts of diversity marginalise people of colour within the existing organisational culture. It suggests that initiatives to shift organisational culture beyond white comfort zones is necessary to achieve meaningful inclusion. In addition, organisations must become allies advocating for diverse employees rather than perpetuating a colour-blind organisational discourse which serves to further entrench white privilege and patterns of behaviour that exclude black South Africans and women from meaningful workplace participation while forcing them to assimilate into an organisational culture (specifically in the private sector) designed to support whiteness.

The chapter concludes by suggesting that despite a plethora of diversity legislation, and some notable quantitative achievements in diversity, a range of tacit and qualitative factors such as organisational culture, professional gate-keeping and overt and covert discrimination contribute to hampering equality, diversity and inclusion in South Africa's labour market. While legislation is vital, transformation of 'hearts and minds' is core in the support of such legislation as this will allow for authentic and sustainable diversity.

LITERATURE

Centuries of colonialism and decades of apartheid (separate development) have shaped the racialised and gendered nature of South Africa's labour markets (Dubow, 1989). Inevitably, the democratic post-apartheid government would enact legislation to address these inequalities. Employment equity legislation is now over two decades old in South Africa and has achieved mixed results (Oosthuizen et al., 2019). The legislation was conceived to achieve quantitative racial and gendered transformations of the workplace. This has most successfully been achieved in the public sector, with the state being able to more actively intervene in hiring policies. The private sector continues to exclude black people from its labour markets (despite black people being a majority of the population) and especially at senior levels of management (Republic of South Africa Department of Labour, 2020).

Organisations are key stakeholders in transforming society and have increasingly faced pressures by society to accurately reflect the demographics of their consumer base and the communities within which they operate. In as much as organisations have a profit motive, this is being tempered by state and activist pressures to also assume social justice agendas in their operations. In highly unequal countries, with traumatic colonial and racialised pasts such as South Africa, organisations are even more pressed to demonstrate their commitment to making themselves microcosms of democracy and social justice (Nkomo, 2021). One way of achieving this is by committing to principles of equality and equity in the workplace by showing their compliance with equity legislation. Many work organisations, including multinationals, were complicit with the apartheid and colonial regimes in supporting racist employment practices (Ruggunan and Sooryamoorthy, 2018). Post-apartheid these organisations now have to comply with equity legislation to 'ensure diversity and inclusion through employment equity plans' (Oosthuizen et al., 2019: 1). All literature cited throughout the various sections of this chapter is considered seminal and serves as a suggested reading list for researchers wanting to work in this area.

Four types of literature inform the debates on inclusivity and diversity in South African organisations (Ruggunan and Sooryamoorthy, 2018). Researchers need to be aware of these areas, since the area is multidisciplinary and fieldwork and writing in the area is seldom considered complete without consulting work from these four interrelated sets of literature.

- The human resources management, industrial psychology and management studies literature. This literature is produced by scholars from commerce and business schools in South Africa. The work is chiefly quantitative, positivist and treats race and other identities as fixed and objective categories. Examples of key work in this area include Wöcke and Sutherland (2008), Oosthuizen and Naidoo (2010), Olckers and van Zyl (2016) and Bergh and Hoobler (2018). The *South African Journal of Industrial Psychology* and the *South African Journal of Human Resources Management* are also notable sources for this literature.
- The social science and critical race theory literature. This includes scholarship from sociologists, critical management scholars, psychology and other social sciences that view identities including race as socially constructed. They therefore critique post-apartheid categorisations of race for example and argue that such categorisations are tantamount to the original apartheid racial classification systems. The literature here is qualitative, hermeneutic and interpretive. Notable work here includes Maré (2013, 2014), Pillay (2019), Erasmus (2012) and Pirtle (2021).
- The legal studies literature produced by law scholars that focuses on case law. This includes discrimination cases, challenges against the Employment Equity (EE) Act 55 pf 1998 and Broad Based-Black Economic Act 53 of 2003 (B-BBE). It is mainly produced by scholars in industrial relations and labour law departments. Seminal work here shifts given the dynamic nature of labour legislation in South Africa. However, work by MacEwen et al. (2004), Nkomo (2011), Roman and Mason (2019) and Matotoka and Odeku (2021) give a firm sense of chronological developments in this regard.
- Grey literature including state policy documents and company EE reports are the fourth domain of literature. Given the dynamic nature of inclusivity and diversity, researchers need to consult the latest reporting on EE by the South African Department of Labour as well as individual work organisations. The reports are too numerous to list but the websites of the South African Department of Labour and Statistics South Africa contain over two decades of reports. These can be accessed at www.labour.gov .za/documentcenter. Further work can be found at www.labourguide.co .za/employment-equit/776-employment-equity18 and Boonzaaier's (2021) article on the alignment between the Employment Equity and B-BBE Acts is a good primer.

LEGISLATIVE FRAMEWORK

The South African Constitution makes possible the EE legislation. Section 9 of the Constitution of South Africa provides a right to equality, which includes the full and equal enjoyment of all rights and freedoms. Section 9(2) of the Constitution states that to 'promote the achievement of equality, legislative and other measures designed to protect or advance persons, or categories of persons, disadvantaged by unfair discrimination may be taken' (Republic of South Africa Department of Labour, 2020: 4).

The two pillars of legislation that prop up the constitutional goals of achieving diversity in the workplace are (1) the EE Act No 55 of 1998, as amended, and (2) the B-BBE Act 53 of 2003, as amended. The former is targeted at creating transformation in the workplace, and the latter seeks racial transformation in the ownership of businesses. Combined, these two acts hope to achieve a more inclusive economy for the majority of South Africans. Both acts view transformation as the barring of all forms of discrimination in the workplace (not just racial discrimination) and the B-BBE Act promotes the 'economic participation of black people, women, persons with disabilities and youth in the mainstream South African economy' (Republic of South Africa Department of Labour, 2020: 5). The EE Act can be viewed as achieving labour market parity while the B-BBE Act has a broader goal of mitigating the still profound inequalities in the racialised economy of South Africa. It is viewed as an ambitious, if necessary, act to deal with macro-economic inequalities such as business ownership, management control, skills development and economic self-determination (Republic of South Africa Department of Labour, 2020: 4). Given the country's triple challenges of poverty, unemployment and inequality, such legislation is crucial in achieving goals of diversity and transformation, as organisational life cannot be divorced from the wider political economy. It should be noted, however, that while legislation exists to compel racial transformation of the workplace, and penalties are in place to enforce this, similar legislation to compel *inclusivity* does not exist. Thus, only transformation to the racial demographics of employees in the workplace is legislated.

OUTCOMES OF THE LEGISLATION

South Africa has a population of 58.56 million people (World Bank, 2019). Of this, 38.5 million people are considered to be of working age (18 years and older) and 16.4 million people are employed in the formal sector, with another 3 million estimated to be employed in the informal sector. The group most excluded from employment are young black South Africans aged between

18 and 35 years old. Youth unemployment is double that of adult unemployment. The population is classified as 80.7 per cent black African, 8.8 per cent coloured South African, 2.6 per cent Indian/Asian South African and 7.9 per cent white South African (www.statssa.gov.za).

However, when one looks at the demographic trends in the private sector, we find that top management positions remain dominated by white people (66.5 per cent). Black African people occupy 6 per cent of top management posts, coloured people occupy 3 per cent and Indian people occupy 4 per cent. In terms of gender, the country is almost evenly split between men and women. However, in the workplace we find that 87 per cent of men are in top management posts, most of whom are white male (Republic of South Africa Department of Labour, 2020). Further, most women in top management are white women. People with disabilities comprise less than 1.5 per cent of top management (Republic of South Africa Department of Labour, 2020). The equivalent trend in representations occurs at senior and middle levels of management in the private sector. The same holds true for professionally qualified employees. There is parity in terms of gender amongst professionally qualified people when controlling for race. In contrast, the South African public sector has 76 per cent of black African people in its top management positions, which aligns more with the overall demographics of the country (Republic of South Africa Department of Labour, 2020: 6).

The EE Act is premised on self-regulation of inclusiveness and equity, and no mandatory quotas are required. However, over 20 years after the promulgation of the EE Act, self-regulation is failing as private-sector organisations are not able to shift to practices of equity and inclusivity in a country where the majority are excluded from positions of authority in the workplace. While financial penalties, as well as possible imprisonment, have been mandated to enforce legislation aimed at redressing this, it has not been sufficient to compel compliance. As long as organisations are able to prove that they are making every attempt to transform the demographics in their business and have been reporting regularly to the Department of Labour, they are unlikely to be prosecuted or fined (Strata-G, 2017).

RESEARCHING 'RACE'

Despite the emphasis by the state and organisations on quantitative methods of achieving transformation, researchers need to be aware of the various critical discourses around race, racism and racial categories in South Africa. Social constructionists argue that researchers should study the taken-for-granted assumptions which inform everyday social practices, such as 'race' (Jacobs and Manzi, 2000). However, if these practices are taken for granted then the question remains, how do researchers go about doing this as active members of society who take these practices for granted themselves? Gunaratnam (2003) argues that an important concern for researchers engaged in knowledge production on race and ultimately issues of diversity, inclusion and transformation is to consider how such knowledge about race is produced without reifying these socially and politically constructed categories, as by its very nature researching race has the unintended effect of upholding particular notions about race in society, rather than challenging these constructs. In order for researchers to effectively do this, Schutz (1944) advocates for the importance of researchers becoming 'strangers' in the societies they are studying. This implies not taking for granted norms and values which, by definition, almost everyone does in their everyday lives and interactions.

Researchers then should not identify participants based on race, which would give credence to the process of identifying race based on physical markers such as skin colour and accent. In addition, questions should not be posed in order to classify the individual as 'Indian', 'black', 'white' or 'coloured' but instead allow for any categorisation, naming or classification to proceed organically from the response of the participants. Although race is not a biological reality, the effects of the social construction of race have nevertheless impacted the lives of research participants. In this regard, once respondents speak about their experiences or categorise themselves researchers would then be able to discuss further what this self-identification means to them historically and in contemporary South African society within their organisations. Race and ethnicity are constructed through social discourse and, as Alexander (2007) points out, even though racial identities are constructed they nevertheless hold significance for individuals, as they are not aware of the historical, social and political ways in which their identities have been formed. In our experience in the field, forms of classification and the 'natural' taken-for-granted ability to self-classify is revealed by participants in the stories that they tell, as people who have lived through apartheid and through discriminatory legislation based on race or as young people in post-apartheid South Africa trying to navigate difficult conversations on race. As researchers attempting to research as 'strangers' to classification and everyday assumptions, we are mindful to constantly reflect critically on the research process so as not to fall into the trap of legitimating essentialist understandings of race.

TRANSFORMATION BY NUMBERS

Workplace transformation cannot only be about numbers, and often the terms diversity and inclusion are used together and sometimes interchangeably when discussing issues of redress in the workplace. However, practitioners and researchers globally define the terms diversity and inclusion in many different ways. What then should researchers, researching in South Africa particularly, consider when entering this research terrain?

As mentioned earlier, given the history of colonialism and apartheid in South Africa, researchers need to be mindful of how critical understandings of race impact research on diversity and inclusion, and their working definitions of these concepts which ultimately will inform the analysis of the findings of their study. However, in addition, it is equally important at the outset to determine how individual organisations and leadership within these organisations conceptualise issues of transformation, diversity and inclusion that in turn inform their policies and practices within the organisation. This is critical as it has implications for the construction of interview guides and surveys.

Based on the employment/transformation statistics cited earlier, for research to have a meaningful impact on organisational change in South Africa, studies need to focus on developing tools to help organisations to unlearn their existing conceptions of transformation, diversity and inclusivity and drive a transformation programme that has systemic impact. What does it mean to have authentic representation and inclusion? How can organisations work towards this? Researchers studying issues of race, racism, diversity and inclusion need to be mindful that South Africa, as one of the most unequal societies in the world (World Bank, 2019), is still dealing with the legacy of separate development nearly three decades after the democratic transition and grappling with issues of systemic racism. How does leadership within organisations take responsibility and accountability to actively support and promote change and model the behaviours they expect to see from employees, and be transparent in the transformation process? For instance, inclusion involves creating a working environment where diverse workers feel welcomed, included and valued in the organisation. However, are employers hiring defensively because it's the law, and in so doing employees then are made to feel like they are 'employment equity' candidates? Do diverse employees feel that they are able to share their perspectives easily and safely in the same way as employees who are a 'cultural fit' with the organisation? Do they feel heard and that their voices matter? Who is diversity working for? When research focuses on inclusion and not just transformation and diversity, there is greater value in impacting organisational change and policies for employee well-being. There thus needs to be a commitment to changing organisational culture and character. It is important to identify organisational gaps that perpetuate racial inequity in organisations and obstacles to inclusion. This will help to eradicate performative or self-serving acts of transformation and diversity that continue to marginalise black people within the existing organisational culture. Performative acts of diversity and inclusion do not require critical assessment from organisations as the intentions are not meaningful change but only seen to be making change regardless of actual impact.

Researchers need to consider that racism is not only about personal views of individual employees or management, but also about systemic practices. In this regard, racism can be entrenched in both the structure and culture of organisations and thus, for example, performative acts of firing or suspending individuals who display racist behaviour in their actions or in the name of the organisation, or anti-racism training efforts to change behaviour, will never be enough on their own to deal with systemic issues within organisations. It is imperative therefore that researchers probe white supremacist organisational culture and environments and not be fearful of discussing what inclusion and integration of black people into those environments entails and the repercussions thereof. What does this mean for the well-being of black employees placed in hostile, untransformed spaces? The difference between an environment that welcomes diverse people as opposed to spaces created with diverse people in mind needs to be examined.

Researching diversity and inclusion therefore needs to have a focus on equity at the core of the study. Researchers need to be mindful that industry and corporate spaces were not designed with black people in mind. Separate development legislation, the cornerstone of apartheid, included the 1911 Mines and Works Act that reserved skilled mining jobs for whites, while the 1913 Land Act prevented black people from owning land in white-designated areas (Bhorat et al., 2014). The Job Reservation legislation under apartheid meant that black people were not meant to be included in corporate society but to remain on the periphery, while white society was built around them.

Democracy and the repeal of the Group Areas Development Act 1955 and Population Registration Act 1950 in theory meant that society would now be integrated. However, black people 27 years later are being expected to integrate into organisations designed around and for whiteness. Researchers therefore need to consider critical discussions around integration and inclusion within South African organisations, being mindful that suggested policies do not integrate black people 'into a burning house' (Martin Luther King, Jr., cited in Jones, 2020).

SHIFTING ORGANISATIONAL CULTURE BEYOND WHITE COMFORT ZONES

> [W]hite South Africans cannot move forward unless they confront the extent to which their identities and personal expectations have been shaped through asymmetrical power relations, both internally within South Africa, and globally through enmeshment within Western historical processes and ideologies.
>
> (Steyn, 2001: xxxii)

In researching diversity and inclusion, it is imperative to analyse the foundations of the culture of the organisation and leadership. A historical analysis is necessary to examine as organisations, rooted in white supremacy, were created to support and accommodate whiteness and for white comfort. Organisations in contemporary South African society are still seen as bastions of white privilege. Research initiatives are needed to shift organisational culture beyond white comfort zones to achieve meaningful inclusion, where existing organisational culture maintains whiteness. In these instances, organisational culture, including language contained in policies, patterns of behaviour, 'professionalism' linked to whiteness, white and western dress codes and accents and centring white concerns and issues further strengthen white privilege (Wildman, 2005). White supremacy is expressed not only structurally but also interpersonally. Researchers need to be mindful of the complexity of such organisations, as these 'norms' and 'standards', while not named as such, are reflected in the behaviours and actions of not only white people in the organisation but also people of colour who perpetuate these practices. According to Clare et al. (2019: 7), 'these attitudes and behaviours can show up in any group or organization, whether it is white-led, predominantly white, people of colour-led, or predominantly people of colour'. Even though people of colour may be marginalised, they can nevertheless still be complicit in perpetuating a workplace culture rooted in white supremacy. While white supremacy is associated with violent right-wing groups such as the Afrikaner Weerstandsbeweging in South Africa or the Ku Klux Klan in the United States, and we are taught to identify white supremacy as such, researchers need to focus on the characteristics of white supremacy that institutionalise whiteness as the norm and as superior. The systemic nature of white privilege within organisations that extends beyond the individual must thus be examined to unpack the conflation of white supremacy and privilege with the norm or as 'the way things are'. According to Mahoney (1995), 'the way things are ... tends to make prevailing patterns of race, ethnicity, power, and the distribution of privilege appear as features of the natural world'.

Such organisations may perform diversity and have a 'colour-blind' organisational culture which does not 'see colour'. However, in contemporary South African society, and around the globe, by not 'seeing' someone's race, it implies that you are unable to see the person's socio-economic circumstances, history and race-based challenges that they have faced. Trauma caused by apartheid and the legacy thereof lives on and being colour blind negates a person's trauma and lived experiences, acting as though apartheid did not happen and the legacy of the Group Areas Act is still not prominent. South African organisations do not have the luxury of being colour blind because of pre-existing inequities and inequalities. South African employees do not all start from the same place. While some people start their journey jumping over hurdles of oppression from a distance, others only need a few steps to cross the finish line. In addition, by not acknowledging racial trauma, whiteness too gets ignored. And if whiteness is not acknowledged then the systems that uphold it within the organisation and the people that benefit from it remain invisible.

Researchers, therefore, should be mindful and address the ways systemic racism and normalised whiteness continue to shape the world of work, particularly in South Africa. Researchers should also be conscious of power dynamics, in that while black African people make up the majority of the population they are underrepresented in management and leadership positions, and researchers need to be mindful not to centre white voices in research over those who are marginalised.

IMPLICATIONS OF THE RESEARCH FOR ANALYSIS, PRACTICE OR POLICY

South Africa presents an interesting case for doing work on equality, diversity and inclusion in the workplace that sets it apart from contexts in the global north. South Africa is ranked either as the first or second most economically unequal country in the world on an annual basis (World Bank, 2021). The 2021 official unemployment rate is 32.5 per cent and unofficially is said to be closer to 50 per cent (Stats SA, 2021; World Bank, 2021). This in itself presents challenges in researching inclusion in formal workplaces. Whilst discussions in the northern hemisphere are dominated by the inclusion of minority groups, in South Africa the focus remains on the inclusion of the majority in workplaces. This specifically applies to racial inclusion. The implications of the South African context are twofold. First, the transferability of the global north's research findings and research design are contextually limited and therefore require specific South African-based diversity and inclusion research. Second, the vocabulary of racial classification is part of the South African discourse in ways that may make some non-South African researchers uncomfortable. For example, the use of the word 'coloured' to indicate a particular group of South Africans of 'mixed' descent is an official racial categorisation. Whereas for instance in the United States the term 'coloured' is considered pejorative or racist. Simultaneously, researchers also need to be mindful that race in South Africa is very much a contested idea, and that there is often a mismatch between the official use of racial classification terms and the ways in which people choose to classify themselves (or not) racially. Scholars must not make assumptions of participants' racial identities based on their phenotype.

RESEARCH FIELD TIPS

- The Employment Equity Act 55 of 1998, Section 2(b), has as its basis affirmative action to 'redress the disadvantages in employment experienced by designated groups' (Republic of South Africa Department of

Labour, 1998). Designated groups, according to the Act, refers to 'black people, women and people with disabilities'. However, 'black' is further broken down into 'Africans', 'Coloureds' and 'Indians'. Appointments to workplace positions then are based on physical external appearance and hinge, in the first instance, on self-classification. In order to obtain employment, people are compelled to classify themselves whether or not they identify with any one of the racial categories outlined in the EE Act. It should be noted that there are no longer any legal definitions of each race as the Population Registration Act has been rescinded. Classification then is left open to interpretation by the persons classifying, but ultimately classification can only occur within the confines of the phenotype of the person being classified, and no other variables are considered. The above is an indication of the fluidity and social construction of the concept of race in South Africa.

- When designing questionnaires for quantitative studies, the race categories as laid out in the EE Act, i.e., African, Indian, Coloured and White, must be included, as well as categories of 'other' or 'prefer not to say'.
- Many researchers have reported poor compliance with items on racial classification in quantitative studies due to the poor wording or understanding of the discourses of race in the country.
- There are challenges with quantitative studies, particularly with smaller sample sizes that do not elicit meaningful data on correlations of variables with race. For example, forcing a participant to classify themselves racially in a cross-sectional survey design study might provide contradictory results when that same participant is interviewed about their racial heritage and classification.
- Race is the predominant indicator of inclusion and exclusion in South Africa, but researchers need to be aware of how race intersects with other markers of identity such as gender. For example, in South Africa, much debate occurs on whether white women should benefit from equity and affirmative action policies. Awareness of these debates is critical for the researcher. Statistics indicate that white women have been some of the main beneficiaries of EE in South Africa.
- Given the overwhelming focus on race in South Africa, other areas of diversity remain underexplored, and researchers are encouraged to add to the scholarship in areas of inclusion of LGBTQIA+ people, neurodiverse people and differently abled people.

CONCLUSION

Organisations in South Africa have not shown that they are truly engaged with the legislation to make a real impact. The focus has primarily been on transformation by numbers, with old, apartheid, white colonial culture remaining, and diverse employees forced to assimilate into a system designed mainly for white men and women. Organisations must become allies advocating for people of colour rather than perpetuating a colour-blind organisational discourse. This serves to further entrench white privilege and patterns of behaviour that exclude people of colour from meaningful workplace participation while forcing them to assimilate into an organisational culture designed to support whiteness. In order for this to take place, research on diversity and inclusion should focus on critical examinations of transformation as more than just a numerical outcome. Organisational culture in South Africa must be actively anti-racist.

For researchers in other contexts, the case of South Africa is instructive in the following ways. First, our chapter shows racial identities everywhere are contested and socially constructed and mobilised to serve political and economic ambitions. Second, legislation does not always serve as a panacea for inclusion, diversity or transformation, even when penalties apply. Researchers should be mindful of this when researching other contexts. The South African example signals how important organisational culture is, and how extant organisational cultures can impede the transformation intentions of equity legislation. This is often not captured in the main, especially quantitative methodological approaches to studying diversity. We particularly encourage organisational ethnographic work as one way of capturing the roles of organisational cultures in different countries. Third, whilst whiteness is central to the South African context as a marker of privilege and power, other countries will have other markers, and these may include a range of other identities including but not limited to ethnicity and race. Whatever these identities are, researchers need to note their enmeshment with power and privilege. Finally, inequality and its exacerbation, whilst acute in South Africa, is growing globally. Where inequality is unchecked, be it in the global north or global south, diversity, inclusion and organisational transformation will always be lagging. There are material consequences of this beyond work organisations as the recent insurrection in South Africa demonstrates.

REFERENCES

Alexander, N. (2007). Affirmative action and the perpetuation of racial identities in post-apartheid South Africa. *Transformation*, 63, 92–108.

Bergh, C. and Hoobler, J. M. (2018). Implicit racial bias in South Africa: How far have manager–employee relations come in 'The Rainbow Nation'?, *Africa Journal of Management*, 4(4), 447–468.

Bhorat, H., Naidoo, K. and Yu, D. (2014). Trade unions in an emerging economy: The case of South Africa. *World Institute for Development Economic Research Working Paper*, 2014/055.

Boonzaaier, F. (2021). The alignment between the Employment Equity and B-BBEE Acts. *TFM Magazine*, 21, 32–34.

Clare, E.Y., Briones, E., Page, K. and Angers-Trottier, P. (2019). *White Supremacy Culture in Organizations*. Quebec: Centre for Community Organisations.

Dubow, S. (1989). *Racial Segregation and the Origins of Apartheid in South Africa, 1919–1936*. New York: Palgrave Macmillan.

Erasmus, Z. (2012). Apartheid race categories: Daring to question their continued use. *Transformation: Critical Perspectives on Southern Africa*, 79, 1–11.

Gunaratnam, Y. (2003). *Researching 'Race' and Ethnicity: Methods, Knowledge and Power*. London: Sage.

Jacobs, K. and Manzi, T. (2000). Evaluating the social constructionist paradigm in housing research. *Housing, Theory and Society*, 17, 35–42.

Jones, M. (2020). Integrating into a burning house: Remembering the other MLKs. www .stlamerican.com/mlk/integrating-into-a-burning-house/article_34da83c8-3821-11ea-979a-9bbe0dba31b8.html

MacEwen, M., Dupper, O., Louw, A. (2004). Employment equity: A South African case study. *International Journal of Discrimination and the Law*, 6(2), 165–193.

Mahoney, M. R. (1995). Segregation, whiteness, and transformation. *University of Pennsylvania Law Review*, 143(5), 1659–1684.

Maré, G. (2013). The cradle to the grave: Reflections on race thinking. *Thesis Eleven*, 115(1), 43–57.

Maré, G. (2014). *Declassified: Moving beyond the Dead End of Race in South Africa*. Johannesburg: Jacana.

Matotoka, M. D. and Odeku, K. O. (2021). Untangling discrimination in the private sector workplace in South Africa: Paving the way for Black African women progression to managerial positions. *International Journal of Discrimination and the Law*, 21(1), 47–71.

Nkomo, S. M. (2011). Moving from the letter of the law to the spirit of the law: The challenges of realising the intent of employment equity and affirmative action. *Transformation: Critical Perspectives on Southern Africa*, 77(1), 122–135.

Nkomo, S. M. (2021). Reflections on the continuing denial of the centrality of 'race' in management and organization studies. *Equality, Diversity and Inclusion*, 40(2), 212–224.

Olckers, C., van Zyl, L. (2016). The relationship between employment equity perceptions and psychological ownership in a South African mining house: The role of ethnicity. *Social Indicators Research*, 127, 887–901.

Oosthuizen, R. M. and Naidoo, V. (2010). Attitudes towards and experience of employment equity. *SA Journal of Industrial Psychology/SA Tydskrif vir Bedryfsielkunde*, 36(1), Art. 836.

Oosthuizen, R. M., Tonelli, L. and Mayer, C.-H. (2019). Subjective experiences of employment equity in South African organisations. *SA Journal of Human Resource Management/SA Tydskrif vir Menslikehulpbronbestuur*, 17, a1074.

Pillay, K. (2019). The 'Indian' question: Examining autochthony, citizenship, and belonging in South Africa. In Essed P., Farquharson K., Pillay K. and White E. (eds), *Relating Worlds of Racism*. Cham: Palgrave Macmillan.

Pirtle, W. N. L. (2021). Racial states and re-making race: Exploring coloured racial re-and de-formation in state laws and forms in post-apartheid South Africa. *Sociology of Race and Ethnicity*, 7(2), 145–159.

Republic of South Africa Department of Labour (1998). Employment Equity Act, No. 55 of 1998. www://labour.gov.za/DOL/legislation/acts/employment-equity/employment-equity-act

Republic of South Africa Department of Labour (2020). 20th Commission for Employment Equity Annual Report 2019/2020. www.labour.gov.za/DocumentCenter/Reports/Annual%20Reports/Employment%20Equity/2019%20-2020/20thCEE_Report_.pdf

Roman, L. J. and Mason, R. B. (2019). Employment equity in the South African retail sector: Legal versus competence and business imperatives. *African Journal of Employee Relations*, 39(2), 84–104.

Ruggunan, S. and Sooryamoorthy, R. (2018). *Management Studies in South Africa: Exploring the Trajectory in the Apartheid Era and Beyond*. New York: Springer.

Schutz, A. (1944). The stranger: An essay in social psychology. *American Journal of Sociology*, 49(6), 499–507.

Steyn, M. E. (2001). *Whiteness Just Isn't What It Used to Be: White Identity in a Changing South Africa*. Albany, NY: State University of New York Press.

Stats SA Statistics (2021). South Africa Quarterly Labour Force Survey, 1st Quarter 2021. www.statssa.gov.za/?page_id=1854&PPN=P0211&SCH=72943

Strata-G (2017). Employment equity: Compliance and penalties. www.strata-g.co.za/wp-content/uploads/EMPLOYMENT-EQUITY-%E2%80%93-COMPLIANCE-AND-PENALTIES-14-dec.pdf

Wildman, S. M. (2005). The persistence of white privilege. *Washington University Journal of Law and Policy*, 18, 245.

Wöcke, A. and Sutherland, M. (2008). The impact of employment equity regulations on psychological contracts in South Africa. *International Journal of Human Resource Management*, 19(4), 528–542.

World Bank (2019). Population, South Africa. https://data.worldbank.org/indicator/SP.POP.TOTL?locations=ZA

World Bank (2021). Overview of South Africa. www.worldbank.org/en/country/southafrica/overview

USEFUL WEB RESOURCES

Centre for Social Science Research, South Africa, University of Cape Town: www.cssr.uct.ac.za/cssr/ssu/projects/race

Creative Methodology for Researching Race: www.dreamingworkshops.org.za/index.html

Department of Employment and Labour South Africa: www.labour.gov.za/

Human Sciences Research Centre, South Africa: www.hsrc.ac.za

Power and Privilege: https://theedgefund.files.wordpress.com/2013/04/neon-power-and-privilege-intro-guide.pdf

Statistics South Africa: www.statssa.gov.za/

19. Social enterprise performance measurement using a diversity and inclusion approach: implications for equitable and inclusive smallholder farmers' improved wellbeing

Peter Musinguzi, Renato A. Villano and Derek Baker

INTRODUCTION

Social enterprises (SEs) are seen as enablers of growth that employ diversity and inclusion to achieve social and economic development (Kiss et al., 2020; OECD, 2018a). SEs then contribute to solving the world's intractable challenges, such as poverty and inequality, targeted by the United Nations Sustainable Development Goals (SDGs) (Littlewood and Holt, 2018). Indeed, SEs have been noted as possessing a high propensity for operationalising SDGs locally through their interventions to deliver positive social change in the form of social value and/or wellbeing improvement.

There are few quantitative studies that address SEs' performance (Short et al., 2009). This constrains prediction of SE outcomes and formulation of generalised approaches to improving SEs' performance in the delivery of social value for beneficiaries. In particular, such studies from the perspective of diversity, equality and inclusion (DEI) research are lacking. This perspective addresses heterogeneity within social groups, rather than treating beneficiaries as a homogenous aggregate. There remain questions such as the extent to which diversity and inclusion are reflected in SEs' interventions regarding performance/social value creation efforts. In other words, how are these diverse groups' wellbeing influenced by SEs' interventions?

Studies on diversity and inclusion in social entrepreneurship are still emerging (Kiss et al., 2020; Meltzer et al., 2018). Meltzer et al. (2018) focus on diversity and inclusion of people with disabilities, and describe their social participation, personal autonomy and wellbeing at emotional, physical and material levels. Kiss et al. (2020) examine organisational and societal inclusion levels through an analysis of SE objectives, activities, operations and barriers that affect the SE's contributions to inclusion with a focus on disadvantaged groups. Despite some focus on disadvantaged groups in developed countries (Kiss et al., 2020), few studies address smallholder farmers (e.g., Doherty and Kittipanya-Ngam, 2021). Extant SE studies generally are mostly conducted in developed countries and there are calls for SE research in developing/ emerging country contexts (Holt and Meldrum, 2019). Most of the SE studies in developed country contexts do not focus on the rural context and there are calls for a focus on this context (Steiner et al., 2019).

Smallholder farmers are an important focus for development efforts in developing countries as they comprise the largest proportion of vulnerable and poor people in rural areas and their main activity is smallholder agriculture or related enterprise (Doherty and Kittipanya-Ngam, 2021). Rural areas suffer disproportionately from limited services provided by government and the private sector (Steiner and Teasdale, 2019). A few qualitative studies on these topics have emerged from researchers (e.g., Doherty and Kittipanya-Ngam, 2021) and SE support agencies, e.g., the World Bank (Tinsely and Agapitova, 2018). In addressing smallholders and rural development in developing countries through SEs' interventions, we define diversity and inclusion by adapting Klingler-Vidra's (2019, p.14) understanding of both concepts. Diversity is defined as differences in attributes among marginalised smallholder rural farmers which can be observable or unobservable – we offer insights primarily on observable attributes including gender and age. Inclusion is synonymous with social inclusion and is defined as the promotion of the full participation of diverse smallholder rural farmers in SEs' interventions.

This study contributes to filling the gaps outlined above. First, we target a rural developing country context, Uganda, where the majority (76 per cent) of the adult population live in rural areas. Further, this population is mostly smallholder farmers and contributes 89 per cent of national poverty numbers (UBOS, 2018, p. 42). Second, we use the capabilities approach lens (Kato et al., 2018; Weaver, 2018) in selecting variables for multidimensional consideration of social value accruing to smallholder farmer households. We refer to this as the wellbeing derived from the SEs' interventions. We operationalise this wellbeing as capacity, adaptability and resilience scores estimated using network data envelopment analysis (network DEA) based on Villano et al. (2020). Third, we employ quantitative methods, i.e., network DEA, together with a diversity/class analysis approach that involves the identification of patterns of similarities and differences in wellbeing across a diverse group of beneficiaries (men, women and youth) of a rural agriculturally focused SE and we compare these with non-SE beneficiaries in a similar context. Implications of these contributions for theory and practice beyond the study area in similar developing/emerging country contexts and beyond are presented. Box 19.1 presents a conceptualisation of key concepts as they apply to this chapter.

BOX 19.1   OPERATIONALISATION OF KEY CONCEPTS USED IN THIS CHAPTER

1. Social value is conceptualised in line with Weaver's (2018) understanding that it encompasses efforts and activities engaged in by SEs to address intractable challenges, e.g., poverty and inequality, which affect human development. Thus, social value is improved wellbeing derived by the SEs' beneficiaries from the SEs' interventions.
2. Wellbeing is conceptualised as a composite consisting of interrelated variables (cf. White, 2018) and we view it as being synonymous with social value. Thus, social value equals wellbeing which is derived by beneficiaries from the SEs' interventions, and we operationalise it in terms of capacity, capability and resilience scores (see Methods section).
3. The term beneficiaries is synonymous with clients.
4. Within diversity, equality, and inclusion research, we focus on two elements, i.e., diversity and inclusion. We contend that this could in the long term contribute to achieving equality (i.e., fairness in accessing tools/opportunities needed to improve wellbeing) within marginalised rural communities.

RELEVANT LITERATURE

Social entrepreneurship, encompassing SEs, is an emerging field that, as noted above, targets intractable challenges and offers opportunities for achieving the SDGs (Littlewood and Holt, 2018). SEs' performance takes the form of social value creation (Kato et al., 2018; Weaver, 2018) in pursuit of positive social change. Despite the acknowledgement of SEs' social value creation by many scholars, methods for its empirical measurement are not established. Such measurement relates to the results of SEs' efforts and activities addressing intractable challenges, so some researchers advocate the capability approach because of its multidimensional reach (Kato et al., 2018; Weaver, 2018). SEs' actions, in boosting capability, enhance the supply of goods and services that transform beneficiaries' opportunities into functionings which are 'the desired or achieved outcomes' (Robeyns, 2005, cited in Kato et al., 2018, p. 560). An example is training and employment provision (Kiss et al., 2020; Steiner and

Teasdale, 2019), which are vital particularly in rural areas. The design of SE interventions must address participation and be synonymous with inclusion (Kiss et al., 2020; OECD, 2018), to ensure that the supply of services and goods reach marginalised and poor beneficiaries.

Emerging studies of inclusion and diversity from DEI literature in social entrepreneurship are mostly descriptive in nature (e.g., Kiss et al., 2020; McKague et al., 2021; Meltzer et al., 2018). Inclusion and diversity are important because different members of groups are affected differently by intractable challenges (Bishop-Sambrook et al., 2017; Kiss et al., 2020; McKague et al., 2021; Meltzer et al., 2018), and benefit differently, from participation in SE initiatives. McKague et al. (2021), for example, note that female community health workers benefit less in social and economic terms than do their male counterparts. Further, youths have been shown to encounter poverty and marginalisation differently than do adults (Bishop-Sambrook et al., 2017).

Inclusion is linked to various political, social, cultural and economic indicators such as opportunity and service access, employment, earning an income and being able to participate in the community and society (Kiss et al., 2020). SEs use mechanisms of inclusion such as provision of products/services for their beneficiaries, so as to increase access to opportunities. This requires an emphasis on building capabilities and skills. However, there are barriers to inclusion that are closely associated with SE challenges, such as financial unsustainability, failure to scale up SEs' interventions and a poor legal and policy environment, especially in developing countries (Kiss et al., 2020). Thus, in addressing diversity and inclusion, SEs can be aided by proper targeting of their interventions to beneficiaries (Bishop-Sambrook et al., 2017).

The foregoing portrays SEs as tools for steering inclusive social and economic development achieved through social value creation services that improve their beneficiaries' capabilities and functionings. Social value is a multidimensional concept and a capability approach lens is instrumental in its measurement. Smallholders whose mainstay is agriculture are the majority in developing countries' rural areas and, thus, focusing on agricultural-oriented SEs that offer services to rural smallholder farmers offers potential for solving intractable challenges such as poverty and inequality and contributing to the achievement of the SDGs. Diversity and inclusion, and the class analysis perspective in social entrepreneurship research, are vital as both challenges and solutions affect differently the diverse members of marginalised groups. Targeting can reinforce this perspective in the efforts of reaching and enabling marginalised groups to participate and benefit from SE interventions. The participation of marginalised groups ensures that factors that deter or facilitate their wellbeing improvement are understood and considered by SE practitioners and supporting agencies.

METHODS

This study is based on a 2020 household survey in rural Uganda involving members and, for comparison, non-members of an agricultural-focused SE (subsequently 'the SE') with its interventions in Nyabuharwa sub-county, Kyenjojo district. A sample of 1,021 (523 members and 498 non-members) household respondents was assembled after considering missing and incomplete data. This is an appropriate sample size for analysis based on the Cochran formula (Cochran, 1953), applied in a pilot survey conducted in Nyabuharwa sub-county before rolling out the main survey where it was found that five out ten households randomly selected for interviews were members of the SE. A 5 per cent level of precision was assumed.

Nyabuharwa sub-county has been the SE's core intervention area since 2009. Interventions in the area include agricultural production and productivity programs focusing on coffee, vegetables and orphaned crops. In these agricultural programs, agricultural development-focused training is conducted, for example, on good agronomic practices, practising farming as a family business in the efforts of gender integration into the agricultural value chains. The financial inclusion and financial literacy improvement program includes the promotion of village savings and loans associations and associated training in selection, planning and management of different income-generating activities.

In sampling, SE members were randomly selected from the SE's membership register, while non-members were randomly selected from the local council's registration lists for the same villages where the SE members live. Thus, both members and non-members were from the same locality in similar geographic and social-economic conditions.

Quantitative data were collected using a pre-tested survey instrument (approved by relevant human research ethics in both Australia and Uganda) and deployed on an android-enabled platform. Data were captured in a secure server and processed using appropriate software including Microsoft Excel, Stata (Stata's two-sample mean-comparison test calculator was used for estimating statistical differences within the estimated scores) and network DEA for developing the relevant indicators. In analysing the data, a diversity/class analysis approach lens (Shucksmith, 2012) was applied to capture differences amongst the respondents defining 'youth' as those aged between 18 and 30 years (UBOS, 2018, p. xxv). This approach has been noted as vital for advancing diversity/inclusion studies, especially in rural contexts (Shucksmith, 2012).

We employ a capability approach lens in selecting indicators of SEs' performance. There are key terms for contextualising the capability approach viz capability and functioning (Shucksmith, 2012) and we use performance indicators, operationalised as capacity, adaptability and resilience. Capacity (similar to capability) is defined as an available opportunity/resource that a household may or may not have to help achieve its goals. The capacities we measure are in terms of a means to an end (i.e., to achieve functionings) rather than the end itself (Kato et al., 2018; Weaver 2018). SEs' interventions facilitate maximising or converting this capacity into further opportunities, termed adaptability, in improving the households' wellbeing. The households' wellbeing is measured as a resilience score which is computed from the capacity and adaptability scores. Thus, through improved capacity and adaptability, the households' resilience score increases.

We employed a linear programming approach to obtain capacity, adaptability and resilience scores for individual households, distributed on a [0, 1] interval where 1 indicates full potential using existing and available resources. The process of maximising these scores is akin to a multistage production process in which each household is a decision-making unit. Using existing resources and available social support and capital, we calculate a resilience score composed of capacity and adaptability scores. We first record capacity scores, where the linear programming objective is to maximise outputs (measured as total crop and livestock income) in the presence of households' assets such as farm size, household size, crop diversity and tropical livestock units. In a second stage, adaptability score was delivered by maximising a multidimensional poverty index (Alkire and Foster, 2011). The output in the first stage becomes an intermediate input to the second stage, along with the value of assets. A composite resilience score was derived for each household by equally weighting capacity and adaptability scores. A network DEA, following Villano et al. (2020, pp. 70–73) was used to examine the linkages between these measures. The network DEA is an extension of the standard DEA model, which offers the advantages of allowing for (in our case equal) weighting of multiple performance measures of households.

RESULTS

As Table 19.1 shows, with respect to capacity, no significant difference exists in the mean scores of non-SE and SE beneficiaries at the aggregate level nor at the youth level. However, results are significantly different when the sample is disaggregated for female and male SE beneficiaries (female non-SE and SE beneficiaries, $p=0.0013$; male non-SE and SE beneficiaries, $p=0.0000$). The SE beneficiaries in both of these categories exhibit higher mean capacity scores than do non-SE beneficiaries. Within SE beneficiaries, results indicate significant differences between male and female beneficiaries' capacity mean scores even within the youth category, with the female youths having higher scores (male SE and female SE beneficiaries, $p=0.0178$; male youth SE beneficiaries and female youth SE beneficiaries, $p=0.0777$). We infer that at an aggregate level, the SE's services did not lead to changes in smallholder capacities. However, diversity/class analyses of the smallholders reveal that the SE improved both the female and male beneficiaries' capacities as compared to the non-SE beneficiaries. The within-SE beneficiary differences between male and female smallholders including male and female youth category indicate that the SE contributes more to female, and to youth, smallholder capacity development as compared to the males, and to non-youth, respectively.

For adaptability, there are no significant differences between female and male non-SE and SE beneficiaries' mean scores, but differences appear between non-SE and SE beneficiaries at the aggregate level (p=0.000) and from the diversity/class analysis level of youth (non-SE and SE youth beneficiaries, p=0.0031). Comparisons of female and male SE beneficiaries including the youth category show no significant differences in the adaptability mean scores. We infer that the SE has enabled its beneficiaries in general, and in particular the youth category, to improve their adaptability.

For mean resilience scores, comparisons of non-SE and SE beneficiaries at the aggregate level (non-SE and SE beneficiaries, p=0.0002) and diversity/ class analysis levels (female non-SE and SE beneficiaries, p=0.0006 and non-SE and SE youth beneficiaries, p=0.0265) show significant differences, with higher scores for the SE beneficiaries. We identify no difference between male non-SE and SE beneficiaries. Comparisons within SE beneficiaries show a significant difference between female and male smallholders (p=0.1033), with females having a higher resilience score whereas no difference exists between the male and female youth scores. These results indicate that the SE improved the resilience of its beneficiaries, specifically the females and youths as compared to the males.

DISCUSSION

This study begins a conversation about the contribution of diversity/class analysis (Shucksmith, 2012) in improving the performance and/or effectiveness of SEs. We particularly address SEs operating in developing countries with marginalised and poor rural smallholder farmers. Our merging of diversity and inclusion together with class analyses has global implications for SE practitioners and for supporting actors in development. SEs face resource constraints (Kiss, 2020; Steiner and Teasdale, 2019; Steiner et al., 2019), so they need to develop organisational policies, interventions and implementation strategies that facilitate wellbeing improvement and related opportunities among diverse groups of people (cf. Bishop-Sambrook et al., 2017).

We identify and measure the performance of the SE in terms of its social value creation (i.e., its contribution to the wellbeing of smallholder rural farmers when compared to non-SE smallholder farmers). As found in other

Table 19.1   Household capability, adaptability and resilience scores across the aggregate and diversity/class analysis lens: comparing non-SE and SE households and within SE households in Nyabuharwa sub-county, Kyenjojo district, Uganda

| | Aggregate analysis | | Diversity/class analysis | | | | | | Comparison within SE members | | | |
| | | | Comparison with non-SE members | | | | | | | | | |
	Non-SE HHs (N=498)	SE-HHs (N=523)	F-non SE HHs (N=116)	F-SE HHs (N=188)	M-non SE HHs (N=382)	M-SE HHs (N=335)	Y-non-SE (N=157)	Y-SE (N=130)	F-SE HHs (N=188)	M-SE HHs (N=335)	MY-SE HHs (N=81)	FY-SE HHs (N=49)
Capacity												
Mean	0.294	0.271	0.243	0.369	0.373	0.312	0.354	0.345	0.369	0.312	0.304	0.412
p-value	*0.1332*		*0.0000*		*0.0013*		*0.7970*		*0.0178*		*0.0777*	
Std.Dev	0.237	0.252	0.202	0.272	0.260	0.245	0.264	0.318	0.272	0.245	0.284	0.361
Min	0.016	0.009	0.091	0.060	0.033	0.065	0.052	0.009	0.060	0.065	0.018	0.009
Max	1.000	1.000	1.000	1.000	1.000	1.000	1.000	1.000	1.000	1.000	1.000	1.000
Adaptability												
Mean	0.253	0.345	0.337	0.382	0.324	0.349	0.288	0.398	0.382	0.349	0.381	0.427
p-value	*0.0000*		*0.1602*		*0.2002*		*0.0031*		*0.1961*		*0.4137*	
Std.Dev	0.204	0.252	0.258	0.290	0.261	0.260	0.236	0.298	0.290	0.260	0.282	0.325
Min	0.059	0.060	0.016	0.010	0.062	0.081	0.059	0.060	0.010	0.081	0.120	0.060
Max	1.000	1.000	1.000	1.000	1.000	1.000	1.000	1.000	1.000	1.000	1.000	1.000
Resilience												
Mean	0.225	0.274	0.235	0.329	0.297	0.291	0.268	0.338	0.329	0.291	0.310	0.384
p-value	*0.0002*		*0.0006*		*0.7394*		*0.0265*		*0.1033*		*0.1895*	

| | Aggregate analysis | | Diversity/class analysis | | | | | | | | | |
| | | | Comparison with non-SE members | | | | | | Comparison within SE members | | | |
	Non-SE HHs (N=498)	SE-HHs (N=523)	F-non SE HHs (N=116)	F-SE HHs (N=188)	M-non SE HHs (N=382)	M-SE HHs (N=335)	Y-non-SE (N=157)	Y-SE (N=130)	F-SE HHs (N=188)	M-SE HHs (N=335)	MY-SE HHs (N=81)	FY-SE HHs (N=49)
Std.Dev	0.189	0.228	0.204	0.264	0.243	0.239	0.225	0.293	0.264	0.239	0.265	0.333
Min	0.058	0.048	0.058	0.050	0.063	0.060	0.060	0.048	0.050	0.060	0.084	0.048
Max	1.000	1.000	1.000	1.000	1.000	1.000	1.000	1.000	1.000	1.000	1.000	1.000

Note: Non-SE HHs = non-social enterprise households; SE-HHs = social enterprise households; F-non SE HHs = female-headed non-social enterprise households; F-SE HHs = female-headed social enterprise households; M-non SE HHs = male-headed non-social enterprise households; M-SE HHs = male-headed social enterprise households; Y-non SE = youth-headed non-social enterprise households; Y-SE = youth-headed social enterprise households; MY-non-SE HHs = male youth-headed non-social enterprise households; MY-SE HHs = male youth-headed social enterprise households; FY-non-SE HHs = female youth-headed non-social enterprise households; and FY-SE-HHs = female youth-headed social enterprise households.

Source: Authors' calculations, based on data from Household Survey (2020).

studies on SEs and their wellbeing outcomes (Kiss et al., 2020; Steiner and Teasdale, 2019; Weaver, 2018), the studied SE contributed to the smallholder farmers' improvement in terms of wellbeing through expanding their capabilities and functionings. Also concurring with other studies (e.g., Kiss et al., 2020), the SE contributed to increasing its beneficiaries' inclusion in the local economy by supplying services and products that improved their wellbeing. Relevant SE support agencies and governments could count on and embrace SEs as development players, contributing to inclusive social and economic growth.

We identify variation in the SE beneficiary smallholder farmers' wellbeing, delivered by the SE. This offers important insight, particularly as SEs may select beneficiaries, and design and implement interventions so as to target certain groups. Our results contribute to understanding of such heterogeneity amongst beneficiaries: men, women and youth in this study. This heterogeneity might also influence the ability of the men, women and youth smallholder farmers to seize social and economic opportunities provided by the SE to improve their wellbeing (cf. Bishop-Sambrook et al., 2017), as portrayed in this study by female and youth smallholder farmers outperforming their male counterparts. We suggest that there may be beneficiaries' characteristics (demographic, socio-economic, competence in accessing health services, exercise of access to and control over resources, education, age, etc.) that shape their ability to participate and benefit from the SEs' interventions. These are important for SE practitioners, support agencies and researchers to consider, although they lie beyond this chapter's scope and are suggested as subjects for future research.

CONCLUSION AND CONTRIBUTION OF THE STUDY

Our results point to differential performance by SEs within their disaggregated beneficiary groups. They support the application of the capability approach in the identification of variables for performance measurement in SEs, which together with network DEA enable the creation of social value in the form of wellbeing scores that are multidimensional in nature. Indeed, the differential social value created by the SE for its beneficiaries in the form of wellbeing (measured in terms of capacity, adaptability and resilience) was not apparent in most cases without the diversity/class analysis. The differential wellbeing achieved for instance was high for women and the youth in most cases, as compared to men. This shows the importance of considering a diversity/class analysis perspective in SE interventions and other related development interventions targeting marginalised poor beneficiaries. It further suggests that there are barriers for men in this particular context that need to be removed to improve their wellbeing given that male-headed households persist as the majority. We advocate consideration of context, including diversity and inclusion issues, before SEs and other related development interventions are designed and implemented.

This study makes a research contribution by addressing gaps in the emerging social entrepreneurship field. It targets a developing country's rural and agricultural setting, a less studied context in the social entrepreneurship field. We introduce diversity and inclusion elements of DEI literature into social entrepreneurship research and highlight their importance for improving SE performance. We reinforce social value creation for wellbeing as a performance measure, and its improvement for diverse marginalised poor people.

We contribute to methods of measuring SE performance/value creation by: (1) using network DEA to advance SE performance measurement; and (2) identifying variables and processing them into multidimensional wellbeing scores for measurement of the SE's social value using the capability approach. The use of network DEA allows us to disentangle the internally determined and inherent characteristics of SEs alongside externally driven factors.

By applying a diversity/class analysis approach, the study brings to SEs' practitioners and supporters' attention that aggregate-level SE performance is problematic. In our rural development setting, this means that smallholder rural farmers should be approached as a diverse group. In improving their performance, SEs should use a diversity/inclusion approach in explicit targeting of the constituents of diverse smallholder groups.

KEY RECOMMENDATIONS FOR SE PRACTITIONERS, SUPPORTERS AND GOVERNMENT

Our results indicate that diversity and inclusion should play a significant role in the design and implementation of SE interventions, and in the measurement of their performance. This advance toward achieving equitable and inclusive growth can contribute to the achievement of the SDGs. It would also enable SEs to understand and address smallholder poverty and marginalisation, and has implications for reducing gaps in development opportunities amongst diverse groups. Consideration of diversity and inclusion also enables better engagement (cf. Bishop-Sambrook et al., 2017) and characterisation of challenges such as access to resources, skills, services and markets.

FUTURE RESEARCH DIRECTIONS

The identified differential performance of an SE's interventions across diverse smallholder farmer groups suggests that there are other factors which facilitate or deter participation and performance. Future studies should aim to identify these factors. This will progress the identification of the separate needs and priorities of rural men, women, youth and other vulnerable categories which can be considered and integrated into SEs' interventions.

Future studies could apply and refine the capability lens and network DEA as tools for measuring SE performance. This might include the examination of alternate scores for multidimensional performance measurement. DEA is a powerful non-parametric-based approach that is reliant on the assumptions imposed on the behaviours of the decision-making units, in this case, households. Consideration of discretionary and non-discretionary factors that are beyond the control of decision makers and how they influence the SE performance is imperative. Moreover, rigorous analytical techniques (e.g., propensity score matching) can be refined and fed back to elements of SE intervention design, implementation and performance measurement. This study also points to the importance of DEI elements' consideration in SE research for inclusive growth and wellbeing improvement of marginalised poor communities, and contributions to the achievement of the SDGs. Our study considered two DEI elements (diversity and inclusion). A suitable extension for future studies is to include the equality element. These steps would move forward the quantitative SE performance research agenda and enable comparability of SEs' performance in terms of their ability to improve the wellbeing of marginalised smallholder rural populations.

REFERENCES

Alkire, S., and Foster, J. (2011). Counting and multidimensional poverty measurement. *Journal of Public Economics*, *95*(7–8), 476–487.

Bishop-Sambrook, C., Cooke, J., D'Souza, J., Hartl, M., and Camaleonte, V. (2017). *Poverty targeting, gender equality and empowerment*. www.ifad.org/en/web/knowledge/publication/asset/40241536

Cochran, W. G. (1953). *Sampling Techniques*. University of California Press.

Doherty, B., and Kittipanya-Ngam, P. (2021). The role of social enterprise hybrid business models in inclusive value chain development. *Sustainability*, *13*(2), 499.

Holt, D., and Meldrum, B. (2019). Hybrid social entrepreneurship in emerging economies: A research agenda. In A. de Bruin and S. Teasdale (Eds), *A Research Agenda for Social Entrepreneurship* (pp. 145–154). Edward Elgar Publishing.

Kato, S., Ashley, S. R., and Weaver, R. L. (2018). Insights for measuring social value: Classification of measures related to the capabilities approach. *Voluntas*, *29*(3), 558–573.

Kiss, J., Primecz, H., and Toarniczky, A. (2020). Patterns of inclusion: Social enterprises targeting different vulnerable social groups in Hungary. *Journal of Social Entrepreneurship*, 1–23.

Klingler-Vidra, R. (2019). *Global review of diversity and inclusion in business innovation*. https://assets.publishing.service.gov.uk/government/uploads/system/uploads/attachment_data/file/777640/Global_Review_LSE_Consulting_2019.pdf

Littlewood, D., and Holt, D. (2018). How social enterprises can contribute to the Sustainable Development Goals (SDGs): A conceptual framework. In R. N. Nikolaos

Apostolopoulos, H. Al-Dajani, D. Holt and P. Jones (Ed.), *Entrepreneurship and the Sustainable Development Goals* (pp. 33–46). Emerald Publishing.

McKague, K., Harrison, S., and Musoke, J. (2021). Gender intentional approaches to enhance health social enterprises in Africa: A qualitative study of constraints and strategies. *International Journal for Equity in Health*, *20*(1), 98.

Meltzer, A., Kayess, R., and Bates, S. (2018). Perspectives of people with intellectual disability about open, sheltered and social enterprise employment: Implications for expanding employment choice through social enterprises. *Social Enterprise Journal*, *14*(2), 225–244.

OECD (2018). Social enterprises and inclusive SMEs. In *SME Policy Index: ASEAN 2018: Boosting Competitiveness and Inclusive Growth*. OECD Publishing.

Short, J. C., Moss, T. W., and Lumpkin, G. T. (2009). Research in social entrepreneurship: Past contributions and future opportunities. *Strategic Entrepreneurship Journal*, *3*(2), 161–194.

Shucksmith, M. (2012). Class, power and inequality in rural areas: Beyond social exclusion? *Sociologia Ruralis*, *52*(4), 377–397.

Steiner, A., and Teasdale, S. (2019). Unlocking the potential of rural social enterprise. *Journal of Rural Studies*, *70*(May), 144–154.

Steiner, A., Farmer, J., and Bosworth, G. (2019). Rural social enterprise: Evidence to date, and a research agenda. *Journal of Rural Studies*, *70*, 139–143.

Tinsely, E., and Agapitova, N. (Eds). (2018). *Reaching the last mile: Social enterprise business models for inclusive development*. World Bank. http://documents .worldbank.org/curated/en/370641521094121368/pdf/124302-WP-14-3-2018-16-1 -20-bmibookMar.pdf

UBOS (2018). *Uganda Bureau of Statistics: 2018 statistical abstract*. www.ubos.org/ wp-content/uploads/publications/05_2019STATISTICAL_ABSTRACT_2018.pdf

Villano, R. A., Magcale-Macandog, D. B., Acosta, L. A., Tran, C. D. T. T., Eugenio, E. A., and Macandog, P. B. M. (2020). Measuring disaster resilience in the Philippines: Evidence using network data envelopment analysis. *Climate and Development*, *12*(1), 67–79.

Weaver, R. L. (2018). Re-conceptualizing social value: Applying the capability approach in social enterprise research. *Journal of Social Entrepreneurship*, *9*(2), 79–93.

White, L. (2018). A cook's tour: Towards a framework for measuring the social impact of social purpose organisations. *European Journal of Operational Research*, *268*(3), 784–797.

20. Beyond expanding an acronym: strategies for supporting LGBTQ+ people in schools

Peggy Shannon-Baker and Nikki DiGregorio

INTRODUCTION

As globalization advances, populations continue to change in novel ways and, in turn, diversification within employment settings follows. Research has indicated that a diverse workplace can foster growth in a number of ways. For example, companies with gender diverse employees are 27 percent more likely to financially outperform their homogenous counterparts (Hunt et al., 2018). Additionally, being around diverse people makes one smarter (Harvard Business Review, 2016). It is clear that organizations, management, and employees all stand to benefit from supporting diversity, equity, and inclusion (DEI) efforts in workplace settings. These findings are particularly salient with respect to educational institutions, as they have the capacity to shape students' learning experiences and understandings of DEI.

Despite increasing efforts to address DEI issues in educational settings in the United States (USA), surface-level approaches and a limited scope have hampered their effectiveness. This poses a significant barrier to the cultivation of a diverse workforce. DEI work that specifically addresses the needs of people who identify as LGBTQ+ (lesbian, gay, bisexual, trans/transgender, queer/questioning, and more) is paramount to the success of broader initiatives. LGBTQ+ people face discrimination and violence internationally (OHCHR, 2019), which educational institutions must work to understand if they aim to recruit and retain LGBTQ+ leaders, teachers, and staff. This chapter highlights historical and contemporary policies and practices that have discriminated against LGBTQ+ individuals. Through analysis of various contexts, the chapter illustrates the need for intentional DEI work in these areas. Additionally, this chapter highlights several key strategies educational institutions can use to support LGBTQ+ people. For the purposes of this chapter, we intentionally take a broad approach to the framing of educational institutions to include formal institutions and informal environments that engage in schooling, while focusing on the unique circumstances of these settings that set them apart from other arenas. This approach is grounded in our contexts, which we briefly describe at the international, national, personal, and theoretical levels. Lastly, the chapter provides a series of research-informed best practices and recommendations to support LGBTQ+ students and school employees in management and research capacities.

Language and LGBTQ+ Experiences

Prejudice and discrimination against LGBTQ+ people pervade all spheres of life, including where one is employed (OHCHR, 2019). In addition to overt discrimination, LGBTQ+ individuals are significantly more likely to experience microaggressions, or the subtle, frequent, often unintended verbal or behavioral slights against individuals in oppressed groups (Haines et al., 2018). Perhaps unsurprisingly, approximately 35 percent of LGBT employees report feeling compelled to lie about their personal lives at work (Human Rights Campaign Foundation, 2014). Since the late 1960s, the phrase "in the closet" has described someone who hides the fact that they are gay; this phrase has now expanded to include other identities (Kushnick, 2010). Schools that do not support the expression of gender and sexual diversity further perpetuate the minoritization, or ascribe lower visibility and status, of LGBTQ+ identities (Linley and Kilgo, 2018). The perceived pressure to remain closeted goes against the most central tenets of DEI work. Creating and maintaining workplaces that are genuinely inclusive, in rhetoric and in practice, is vital for educational institutions to overcome histories often rife with exclusionary norms.

One area where LGBTQ+ activists and advocates have intervened directly to change exclusionary practices has been that of language. Language serves as an incredibly powerful communication tool. The effectiveness and meaningfulness of new terms, or the changing definitions of existing words and phrases, are relative to their adoption within society. Generally, language referring to LGBTQ+ individuals has had very negative associations, such as social deviance, immorality, condemnation, and mental illness (LeVay et al., 2019). The ongoing change of this language illustrates the power of self-labeling, and that of being labeled, with respect to experiences related to DEI. For example, the LGBTQ+ acronym has undergone numerous changes in recent decades and continues to evolve. Historically, it was simply GLB (gay, lesbian, and bisexual). However, social movements advocated for representation of other communities. Insomuch as the general US population continues to grapple with DEI issues related to LGBTQ+ people within its various establishments, LGBTQ+ communities also struggle with inclusivity. The continued efforts around inclusive language have helped to bring LGBTQ+

DEI issues within education and other social institutions to the forefront of US politics. The prejudice and discrimination LGBTQ+ people face has only been acknowledged in policy arenas during the last several decades, largely in part because of the aforementioned shifts in language.

THEORETICAL AND CONTEXTUAL FRAMEWORKS

Theoretical Frameworks

Ontologically we approach this chapter with the view that experiences are shaped by social structures, such as racism (the ideology that affords privilege to white people and people perceived as white; Solórzano and Yosso, 2002) and heteronormativity (defined in the next section). This is informed by theoretical frameworks related to intersectionality (that individuals at the intersections of identity are further marginalized by social structures; Crenshaw, 1991), feminist standpoint theory (a theory positing that individuals engage in critical analysis of dominant ideologies and examine their interactions and experiences with them based on their social locations in society; Harding, 1986), and queer theory (a theory that disrupts heteronormative policies, practices, and representations to construct more affirming spaces for queer people broadly; de Lauretis, 1991).

Global Contexts

LGBTQ+ communities represent an expansive array of identities, including, but not limited to, those related to gender and sexuality. As a result, LGBTQ+ people may be violating social norms with respect to gender as well as those associated with sexuality in any particular setting. Globally, social norms are largely heteronormative. Heteronormativity refers to the ideology that affords privilege to those whose gender and sex match what they were assigned at birth while also identifying as heterosexual (LeVay et al., 2021; Robinson, 2005). This perpetual support and belief in the gender binary (one is either a woman or a man), heterosexuality, and conventionally structured relationships positions these identities as natural and implicitly superior (LeVay et al., 2021).

Historically and contemporarily, these social norms have played an essential role in the institution of policies and laws governing the expression of LGBTQ+ identities. Efforts to dismantle exclusionary laws and policies that persecute LGBTQ+ people have been met with opposition for many years. German researcher, Magnus Hirschfeld, is credited with having organized the Scientific Humanitarian Committee in 1897 with the goal of removing negative laws criminalizing homosexuality (LeVay et al., 2021). Since then, a social movement has continued across the globe with stark degrees of success and resistance. Currently, macro-level laws, policies, and social norms governing the rights and protections of LGBTQ+ people vary significantly depending upon location. Presently, the United Nations Sustainable Development Goal 5 works toward achieving gender equality; however, it is largely focused on women and girls. Significant variation exists globally when considering the criminalization and discrimination against LGBTQ+ identities (OHCHR, 2019). In some parts of the world, laws are designed to support violence against LGBTQ+ populations. For example, same-sex relationships are still illegal in more than 70 countries around the world and punishable by death in seven countries. More specifically, over 2.5 billion people currently live in parts of the world where LGBTQ+ legal protections are lacking (DiGregorio and Trask, 2020). It is evident that acts of violence and discrimination continue to be committed against LGBTQ+ people around the world (OHCHR, 2019). A considerable amount of work remains to be done with respect to affording LGBTQ+ individuals the same rights and protections as their heterosexual and cisgender counterparts around the world.

The Context of the United States

National-level LGBTQ+ policies in the USA have undergone changes in a number of areas. The 2015 US Supreme Court ruling in favor of marriage equality provides a notable example. However, state-level policies, that vary significantly in terms of protection, tend to more directly influence the daily experiences of LGBTQ+ individuals. Moreover, experiences of hate crimes, harassment, and abuse persist even when protective laws are in place. Despite the fact that approximately 54 percent of the LGBTQ+ population lives in states in the USA with hate crime laws covering sexual orientation and gender identity, hate crimes continue to increase across the country (Ronan, 2020).

Unwritten policies and social norms serve to govern daily behaviors more so than formal laws. Governmental policies written with inclusive language can only be influential within societies when they are coupled with accountability and embodied by management. The same applies to policies and practices within organizations. LGBTQ+ individuals are only beginning to be recognized by local, state, and federal institutions in the USA as protected citizens (Payne and Smith, 2018) and any significant influences on LGBTQ+ workplace experiences have yet to be fully realized. Within the workplace, approximately 68 percent of LGBTQ+ employees have experienced employment discrimination (Badgett et al., 2007, cited in Gates, 2012); it is evident that strategies for protecting LGBTQ+ employees have largely failed.

Additionally, at the time of writing this chapter, there are over 80 anti-transgender laws being proposed in the USA that, for example, make it illegal to provide transgender youth with gender-affirming medical care or disallow transgender girls to play on girls' afterschool sports teams. Transgender and gender non-conforming people are at a greater risk for developing mental illness and are more likely to attempt suicide than their gender-conforming peers (Payne and Smith, 2018). Black and Brown transgender women are particularly targeted for harassment and violence in the USA (LeVay et al., 2021). The ripple effects of these policies throughout the education system within the USA are felt by all, whether directly or indirectly, as they create additional barriers to cultivating DEI.

Personal Contexts

This work is further influenced by our own personal experiences and contexts. We aim to capture some of those contexts here. I (Peggy) come to this work as a queer white person living on the ancestral homelands of the Mvskoke (Muscogee/Creek) and Yamasee people (known now as Savannah, Georgia, USA). My experiences in primary and secondary school were marred by homophobia, transphobia, sexism, and other forms of discrimination. Most microaggressions and more overt discriminatory acts were not addressed by teachers or administrators. I was in the closet through college until I studied abroad in Ireland where, at the time, the LGBTQ+ community was much more visible. During my graduate schooling, I was able to find a community on and off campus of LGBTQ+ people where it took years of advocacy to get a full-time staff person and dedicated space on campus to work on programming, education, and advocacy to support the LGBTQ+ community. During this time, I was able to witness the powerful impact that administrators who openly advocate for LGBTQ+ people can have on schools and workplace climate. These experiences fuel my own advocacy, teaching, and research as a university faculty member.

I (Nikki) am a queer white person who was born outside of Boston, Massachusetts, grew up outside of Philadelphia, Pennsylvania, and I have been cascading down the east coast of the USA ever since, landing in Statesboro, Georgia. I was, colloquially, a "late bloomer," not reaching puberty until I turned 17, at which point my years of gender non-conformity began to make more sense to me. My adolescence was shaped by queerphobia and once outed by peers, homophobia. As a result of these experiences I was truant throughout high school and did not pursue college upon graduation. When I finally circled back to education, I always attended as a commuter student and did not contribute to, or benefit from, extant LGBTQ+ campus culture. It was not until my mid-20s when I found my stride as an individual and am grateful to have remained persistent. I hope to help foster more inclusive educational experiences for LGBTQ+ youth, faculty, and staff by employing my own experiences to inform my work.

KEY LITERATURE ON LGBTQ+ WORK IN EDUCATIONAL INSTITUTIONS

LGBTQ+ people in schools, including students, staff, teachers, and administrators, face discrimination globally that includes bullying, being pushed out or expelled, harassment, and violence (OHCHR, 2019). Attempts to integrate DEI work into schools in the USA specific to LGBTQ+ identities are often fragmented and short lived as a result of obstacles specific to these populations as well as those unique to the USA's education system. For example, the intersection of workplace DEI initiatives and religious beliefs can pose unique challenges for LGBTQ+ individuals, with some organizations facing backlash from employees who believe that their identities are morally wrong (Robinson, 2005). Additionally, school administrators are sometimes resistant to LGBTQ+ professional development for their staff, claiming it is not relevant to schooling or that it would attract enmity from parents and community members (Payne and Smith, 2018).

In early childhood education settings in particular, LGBTQ+ topics are seen as risky or inappropriate due to the perception that children are unaware of sexuality, gender, gender roles, and other related topics (Shannon-Baker, 2020). Teachers view talking about LGBTQ+-related topics as too risky, stressful, and inappropriate or that it will in some way convince the children to become LGBTQ+ (Robinson, 2005; Shannon-Baker, 2020). However, it is well established that children conceptualize gender differences and sex categories by the age of three (LeVay et al., 2021). Additionally, research demonstrates that children are not only knowledgeable about their own and others' sexuality and gender, but they also actively construct their own gender in relation to others (Robinson, 2005). As such, waiting until secondary or even postsecondary education may be "too late" to address the "harassment, ostracism from colleagues, the questioning of their own sexual identities or the loss of employment" and the risks public educational institutions in the USA face like those associated with backlash from parents and the loss of funding from community members or local and state governments (Robinson, 2005, p. 177). LGBTQ+ topics are rarely covered in teacher education or educational administrator preparation programs around the globe (e.g., Bartholomaeus et al., 2017; Young and Middleton, 2002). As a result, teachers are often "misinformed and ill-prepared" to work with LGBTQ+ students (Clark, 2010, p. 704).

Moreover, educators often frame LGBTQ issues as "risk" and LGBTQ individuals as "victims" or "problems" and, thus, approach DEI work in these areas as obligatory (Payne and Smith, 2018). Consequently, DEI initiatives risk being superficially inclusive of LGBTQ+ communities (Robinson, 2005). Similarly, failed DEI initiatives are those that treat LGBTQ+ identities as commodities and often tokenize members of LGBTQ+ communities. Strategies that offer cosmetic approaches to supporting LGBTQ+ identities such as posting rainbow flags only during Pride celebrations are not sustainable and do not encourage tangible change in the lives of LGBTQ+ students, staff, teachers, and administrators. Clearly, there are barriers at multiple levels to LGBTQ+ DEI efforts that educational leaders and researchers must address.

CHALLENGES TO FIELDWORK AND RESEARCH IN EDUCATIONAL CONTEXTS

There are several challenges to DEI fieldwork that are specific to educational contexts. For example, the disclosure of diverse gender and/or sexual identities may present a complex problem for LGBTQ+ people working in school settings. The decision to come out at work is regarded as one of the most important career decisions LGBTQ+ employees face (Ward and Winstanley, 2005) and is a complex and ongoing process. Despite possible negative consequences, LGBTQ+ employees may choose to come out for a variety of reasons, such as a sense of responsibility to self and others, authenticity, or educating colleagues by raising awareness (Prock et al., 2019). However, disclosure of LGBTQ+ identities is strongly related to organizational climate, indicating that the workplace plays a substantial role in determining whether or not employees feel safe and comfortable doing so. Discriminatory organizational policies, negative perceptions, anti-LGBT curricula, as well as interpersonal and community factors influence how LGBTQ+ employees engage in sexual identity management (Wax et al., 2018).

The reality of having to manage one's sexual identity illustrates another challenge for LGBTQ+ people living and working in heteronormative environments. This adversity also influences how LGBTQ+ students, as well as the larger general student body, experience educational settings. Insomuch as LGBTQ+ employees may be reluctant to come out, LGBTQ+ students may be, too. Additional barriers exist when considering LGBTQ+ youth and how to best support this population within school settings, which are further compounded by the variability and relative inconsistency of DEI initiatives in education. Furthermore, unique challenges exist with respect to accessing LGBTQ+ youth in schools, as there are ethical concerns regarding age, individual awareness and desire to come out, and social pressures associated with conformity that may be particularly strong during early and mid-adolescence (Russell et al., 2010).

Harassment of LGBTQ+ individuals in schools is a significant problem. For example, LGBTQ students are at higher risk of academic failure, dropping out of school, depression, self-mutilation, and suicidal ideation and actions (Sadowski, 2016). Facing continued discrimination and harassment during schooling can impact an LGBTQ+ person's ability to find fulfilling employment in the future (OHCHR, 2019). Moreover, LGBTQ stigma affects educators, particularly in schools where sexual orientation is not part of non-discrimination policies. Research has illustrated that a lack of legal protection can increase the fear experienced by some LGBTQ+ faculty and staff and make it difficult for them to do their jobs (Mayo, 2008, cited in Graff and Stufft, 2011). Thus, self-identifying as LGBTQ may be dangerous for employees and students alike, as school culture often reflects the heteronormative biases and stigmas present within the larger societal context (Graff and Stufft, 2011). Collectively, these factors contribute to the reluctance of LGBTQ+ individuals to participate in DEI efforts within school settings.

RESEARCH-INFORMED BEST PRACTICES AND KEY STRATEGIES TO SUPPORT LGBTQ+ PEOPLE IN SCHOOLS

There are many ways that school leaders, teachers, staff, and researchers can demonstrate their support of LGBTQ+ people from individual practices to system-wide policies. This section provides an overview of research-informed best practices and key strategies (see Figure 20.1).

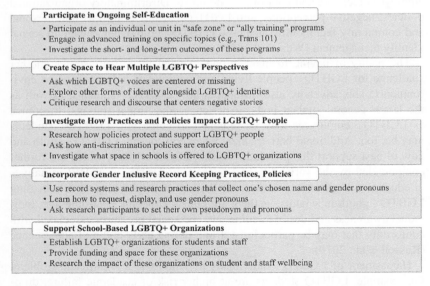

Figure 20.1   Research-informed best practices and key strategies to support LGBTQ+ people in schools

Participate in Ongoing Self-Education about LGBTQ+ Experiences

Engaging in ongoing education is a mainstay for working with LGBTQ+ people and others from minoritized communities. New terms are being created to reflect a wider diversity of experiences and identities in the LGBTQ+ community (LeVay et al., 2021). Researchers have investigated the nature of school-based "safe zone" training or LGBTQ+ "ally training" (Fox and Ore, 2010; Poynter and Tubbs, 2008; Woodford et al., 2014). These trainings cover basic information about the differences between sex, gender, and sexual orientation, how these impact one's daily life, and how to support LGBTQ+ people. Participants can typically choose to include a sign on their office door, laptop, or email signature indicating completion of this training. Researchers have argued that, rather than just focusing on an individual's personal actions and disposition, units collectively can engage in training to see how their unit culture and the institution as a whole supports LGBTQ+ people (Woodford et al., 2014). Ongoing training typically entails going to more advanced training on particular topics or identities (e.g., Trans 101, how to request/use/display gender pronouns) and renewing one's "safe zone" designation (Poynter and Tubbs, 2008). Researchers can investigate the short- and long-term effects of these educational programs on student and staff dispositions toward LGBTQ+ topics and people, professional gender-inclusive practices, instances of bullying, etc.

Create Space to Hear Multiple Perspectives from LGBTQ+ People

The LGBTQ+ community is diverse (LeVay et al., 2021). The experiences of one's identities related to sex, gender, and sexuality influence and are influenced by other identities such as race, nationality, age, languages spoken, and more. This influencing process is known as intersectionality (Crenshaw, 1991). As a result, the LGBTQ+ community is not monolithic; there are many experiences and identities within this community locally and globally. Recognizing the diversity and intersectionality of experiences of people in the LGBTQ+ community entails asking whose voices are centered, elevated, missing, or negated. This also entails engaging in open dialogue and education about other forms of identity (such as those presented in other chapters in this volume), including but not limited to race, disability, language use, nationality, ethnicity, and religion. Be critical of research that seems to maintain a primary focus on negative stories, emphasize deficits in people, or portray LGBTQ+ people as always having a story of struggle; we do struggle, but this is not our only experience. Qualitative methods that are more open-ended can be particularly beneficial for encouraging diverse experiences and perspectives to come through in your research.

Investigate How Practices and Policies Impact LGBTQ+ People

School policies and curricula play a role in defining who and what is (or is not) important for the school, including gender diverse students and staff (Robinson, 2005). These policies set the tone for the community about how inclusive it is for LGBTQ+ people. Researching these practices and policies entails asking how LGBTQ+ people are protected, supported, and/or empowered (or not) in the policies governing school staff and students. For example, what are the school's policies for discrimination and bias response, bullying, dress code, hiring, asking for students' and staff gender pronouns, and continuing education? How are these policies enforced? How are these policies related to or disconnected from the school culture? This research should then be contextualized within the micro-level practices on the interpersonal level, meso-level policies within schools and school systems, and macro-level laws and policies within the region, nation, and world. These contexts vary greatly but have important influences on the rights, protections, and support for LGBTQ+ people. Research into these practices and policies also entails asking about the space provided on site for student organizations such as a gay–straight alliance, gender-inclusive bathrooms for students and staff, and an employee resource group for LGBTQ+ people. Larger schools or school systems may also have a resource center to support both students and staff, housing specifically for LGBTQ+ students, or housing policies that recognize transgender and non-binary students. It is through intentional, consistent application of best practices that educational systems and research within these contexts can develop and foster places for working and learning that truly value DEI.

Incorporate Gender-Inclusive Practices and Policies for Record Keeping

Schools that support gender diverse students and staff have policies and practices related to displaying and using someone's chosen name and correct pronouns. In response to continued advocacy, some school systems use student record systems that include information about students' names (beyond those assigned to them at birth) and gender pronouns. This information is then listed on student records and class rosters (Linley and Kilgo, 2018). English gender pronouns include she/her and he/him. Non-binary and gender neutral pronouns include ze (pronounced like the letter Z) and hir (pronounced like "here"). Pronouns can be listed in email signatures, at the end of names on web-conferencing platforms like Zoom, on name tags at workshops or events, and in professional biography pages. In training on gender identity and pronouns, school staff and researchers can learn the importance of using someone's correct gender pronouns. It is considered best practice to no longer ask for "preferred" pronouns as this gives an impression that using pronouns is a choice rather than a reflection of who a person is or how they identify (GLSEN, 2020). Rather than asking for "preferred" pronouns, ask for pronouns (e.g., what pronouns do you use?). During data collection for research or employee on-boarding, demographic questions about gender, pronouns, and/or sexual orientation should be framed recognizing the diversity of identities in the LGBTQ+ community. A best practice for collecting demographic information is to offer a textbox for participants to enter in their own identities that can later be grouped by the researcher. Such forms can ask separate questions for sex, gender identity, sexual orientation, etc. (Ford et al., 2021). Additionally, rather than assigning pseudonyms, asking participants to create their own name and gender pronouns provides additional agency in how they are referred to in research or reports.

Establish and Support LGBTQ+ Student and Staff Organizations

Another way that schools have demonstrated support for LGBTQ+ people is in establishing and supporting LGBTQ+-focused student and staff organizations. Examples of these organizations include gay–straight alliances open to students in the LGBTQ+ community and their straight peers and LGBTQ+ employee resource groups. Researchers can investigate the impact of these organizations for student and staff wellbeing, academic success, and retention. Particularly for new students or employees, such organizations can provide a more welcoming environment to help them adjust to the school culture. Support for these organizations is demonstrated by providing funding for events, collective professional development, and community building. Support can also be demonstrated by openly acknowledging the group in school-wide meetings, webpages, and social media as well as by providing physical space on school grounds for the organization and the LGBTQ+ community in general. These spaces can include gender-inclusive housing, a resource center with staff, books, movies, and other materials on site, and gender-inclusive bathrooms.

CONCLUSIONS

In this chapter, we discussed how those working and researching in educational settings can support LGBTQ+ people. We situated this discussion in the international context for rights for LGBTQ+ people and within our personal and USA-based contexts. Next, we provided a summary of key literature and best practices and strategies used to support LGBTQ+ people informed by research (e.g., Ford et al., 2021; Fox and Ore, 2010; LeVay et al., 2021; Robinson, 2005; Woodford et al., 2014). These practices include actions individual researchers and employees can take (e.g., engaging in ongoing training, hearing stories from the diverse voices in the LGBTQ+ community), systems units put into place (e.g., using record-keeping practices that allow for gender-inclusive input), and supporting school-based LGBTQ+ organizations. We recommend that researchers investigate the short- and long-term effects of educational programming on dispositions toward LGBTQ+ topics and people; critique research that only shares negative and deficit-oriented portrayals of LGBTQ+ people's experiences; engage in more qualitative research methods that recognize the micro, meso, and macro contexts of LGBTQ+ people's experiences; examine the existence and enforcement of policies related to protecting and supporting LGBTQ+ people; and collect open-ended demographic data including gender identity, pronouns, and/or sexual orientation (cf. Ford et al., 2021; GLSEN, 2020; Woodford et al., 2014). We offer additional sources in Figure 20.2 for further learning. With ongoing education and continued advocacy, employees and researchers in educational contexts can better support LGBTQ+ people.

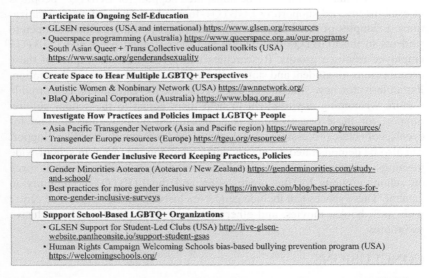

Participate in Ongoing Self-Education
- GLSEN resources (USA and international) https://www.glsen.org/resources
- Queerspace programming (Australia) https://www.queerspace.org.au/our-programs/
- South Asian Queer + Trans Collective educational toolkits (USA) https://www.saqtc.org/genderandsexuality

Create Space to Hear Multiple LGBTQ+ Perspectives
- Autistic Women & Nonbinary Network (USA) https://awnnetwork.org/
- BlaQ Aboriginal Corporation (Australia) https://www.blaq.org.au/

Investigate How Practices and Policies Impact LGBTQ+ People
- Asia Pacific Transgender Network (Asia and Pacific region) https://weareaptn.org/resources/
- Transgender Europe resources (Europe) https://tgeu.org/resources/

Incorporate Gender Inclusive Record Keeping Practices, Policies
- Gender Minorities Aotearoa (Aotearoa / New Zealand) https://genderminorities.com/study-and-school/
- Best practices for more gender inclusive surveys https://invoke.com/blog/best-practices-for-more-gender-inclusive-surveys

Support School-Based LGBTQ+ Organizations
- GLSEN Support for Student-Led Clubs (USA) http://live-glsen-website.pantheonsite.io/support-student-gsas
- Human Rights Campaign Welcoming Schools bias-based bullying prevention program (USA) https://welcomingschools.org/

Figure 20.2   Website resources for the best practices to support LGBTQ+ people in schools

REFERENCES

Bartholomaeus, C., Riggs, D. W., and Andrew, Y. (2017). The capacity of South Australian primary school teachers and preservice teachers to work with trans and gender diverse students. *Teaching and Teacher Education, 65*, 127–135.

Clark, C. T. (2010). Preparing LGBTQ-allies and combating homophobia in a US teacher education program. *Teaching and Teacher Education, 26*(3), 704–713.

Crenshaw, K. (1991). Mapping the margins: Intersectionality, identity politics, and violence against women of color. *Stanford Law Review, 43*(6), 1241–1299.

de Lauretis, T. (1991). *Queer Theory: Lesbian and Gay Sexualities*. Indiana University Press.

DiGregorio, N., and Trask, B. S. (2020). Working toward reducing violence against LGBTQQIA+ populations. In W. Leal Filho, A. M. Azul, L. Brandli, A. Lange Salvia, and T. Wall (Eds), *Gender Equality* (pp. 1–10). Springer International Publishing.

Ford, K. S., Rosinger, K. O., Choi, J., and Pulido, G. (2021). Toward gender-inclusive postsecondary data collection. *Journal of Literacy Research, 50*(2), 46–67.

Fox, C. O., and Ore, T. E. (2010). (Un)covering normalized gender and race subjectivities in LGBT "safe spaces." *Feminist Studies, 36*(3), 629–649.

Gates, T. G. (2012). Why employment discrimination matters: Well-being and the queer employee. *Journal of Workplace Rights, 16*, 107–128.

GLSEN (2020). *Pronouns: A resource: Supporting transgender and gender nonconforming (GNC) educators and students*. www.glsen.org/sites/default/files/GLSEN %20Pronouns%20Resource.pdf

Graff, C., and Stufft, D. (2011). Increasing visibility for LGBTQ students: What schools can do to create inclusive classroom communities, *Current Issues in Education, 14*(1), 1–27.

Haines, K. M., Boyers, C. R., Giovanazzi, C., and Galupo, M. P. (2018). "Not a real family": Microaggressions directed towards LGBTQ families. *Journal of Homosexuality, 65*, 1138–1151.

Harding, S. (1986). *The Science Question in Feminism*. Cornell University Press.

Human Rights Campaign Foundation (2014). *The cost of the closet and the rewards of inclusion: Why the workplace environment for LGBT people matters to employers*. Fidas.

Hunt, V., Prince, S., Dixon-Fyle, S., and Yee, L. (2018). *Delivering Through Diversity*. McKinsey & Company.

Kushnick, H. L. (2010). In the closet: A close read of the metaphor. *AMA Journal of Ethics, 12*(8), 678–680.

LeVay, S., Baldwin, J., and Baldwin, J. (2021). *Discovering Human Sexuality* (5th ed.). Sinauer.

Linley, J. L., and Kilgo, C. A. (2018). Expanding agency: Centering gender identity in college and university student records systems. *Journal of College Student Development, 59*(3), 359–365.

OHCHR (Office of the United Nations High Commissioner for Human Rights) (2019). *Born free and equal: Sexual orientation and gender identity in international human rights law* (2nd ed.). www.ohchr.org/en/issues/discrimination/pages/ bornfreeequalbooklet.aspx

Payne, E. C., and Smith, M. J. (2018). Safety, celebration, and risk: Educator responses to LGBTQ professional development. *Teaching Education, 23*, 265–285.

Poynter, K. J., and Tubbs, N. J. (2008). Safe zones: Creating LGBT safe space ally programs. *Journal of LGBT Youth*, *5*(1), 121–132.

Prock, K. A., Berlin, S., Harold, R. D., and Groden, S. R. (2019). Stories from LGBTQ social work faculty: What is the impact of being "out" in academia? *Journal of Gay and Lesbian Social Services*, *31*, 182–201.

Robinson, K. H. (2005). "Queerying" gender: Heteronormativity in early childhood education. *Australian Journal of Early Childhood*, *30*(2), 19–28.

Ronan, W. (2020). New FBI hate crimes report shows increases in anti-LGBTQ attacks. *Human Rights Campaign*. www.hrc.org/press-releases/new-fbi-hate-crimes -report-shows-increases-in-anti-lgbtq-attacks

Russell, S. T., Horn, S., Kosciw, J., and Saewyc, E. (2010). Safe schools policy for LGBTQ students and commentaries. *Social Policy Report*, *24*(4), 1–25.

Sadowski, M. (2016). More than a safe space: How schools can enable LGBTQ students to thrive. *American Educator*, *40*, 4–9.

Shannon-Baker, P. (2020). Unlearning heteronormative discourse: Let's talk about LGBTQI children in early childhood teacher education. In C. A. R. Brant and L. Willox (Eds), *Teaching the Teachers: LGBTQ Issues in Teacher Education* (pp. 39–52). Information Age Publishing.

Solórzano, D. G., and Yosso, T. J. (2002). Critical Race methodology: Counter-storytelling as an analytical framework for education research. *Qualitative Inquiry*, *8*(1), 23–44.

Ward, J., and Winstanley, D. (2005). Coming out at work: Performativity and the recognition and renegotiation of identity. *The Sociological Review*, *53*, 447–475.

Wax, A., Coletti, K. K., and Ogaz, J. W. (2018). The benefit of full disclosure: a meta-analysis of the implications of coming out at work. *Organizational Psychology*, *8*, 3–30.

Woodford, M. R., Kolb, C. L., Durocher-Radeka, G., and Javier, G. (2014). Lesbian, gay, bisexual, and transgender ally training programs on campus: Current variations and future directions. *Journal of College Student Development*, *55*(3), 317–322.

Young, A. J., and Middleton, M. J. (2002). The gay ghetto in the geography of education textbooks. In R. M. Kissen (Ed.), *Getting Ready for Benjamin: Preparing Teachers for Sexual Diversity in the Classroom* (pp. 91–102). Rowman and Littlefield.

21. Women's careers in SME accounting firms in Australia, Malaysia and India

Alison Sheridan and Sujana Adapa

INTRODUCTION

Historically, the accounting profession attracted more men than women, but over the past two decades this pattern has been disrupted by increasing numbers of women studying accounting. Despite the rising numbers entering the profession, women remain underrepresented in senior roles within accounting firms internationally (Joyce and Walker, 2015). While there is a growing body of research outlining the gendered nature of the accounting profession, this research is mostly drawn from large firms in Western contexts (Del Bado et al., 2019).

We consider three quite different cultural and economic contexts, Australia, India and Malaysia (Singh, 2014), to gain a deeper understanding of the factors constraining women's movement into senior roles in the profession internationally. As most accountants are found in small and medium-sized enterprises (SMEs), this is where we focus our attention. Through this cross-cultural comparative analysis, we add to theory by making visible how 'doing gender' (West and Zimmerman, 1987) impacts women's careers in accounting SMEs, identifying common practices across the countries as well as teasing out specific manifestations in the different cultural contexts to make visible how gender, class and race mutually reinforce inequality regimes (Acker, 2006). We track how culturally defined meanings enacted in the daily practices and processes of accounting SMEs impact women's accounting careers, showing how accounting as practised in these SMEs is a gendered and gendering institution (Carmona and Ezzamel, 2016). Across the three countries, the similarities in the (deficit) framing of women's roles and their capabilities are remarkable given the different cultural contexts and stages of development the countries are at. It seems the alignment of masculinity and accountancy remains potent, with SME accounting practices remaining inflexible and the senior ranks largely impenetrable to women.

CAREERS IN ACCOUNTING FIRMS

Internationally, the accounting profession has traditionally been dominated by men. Since 1999 women have comprised more than 50 per cent of those studying accounting in Australia (Jackling and Calero, 2006). In India and Malaysia, women's enrolments in accounting programs have been increasing, and in both countries they now represent almost half of the accounting graduates (Financial Reporting Council, 2018). With their increasing participation in higher education, it is often assumed that, in time, women's representation in the senior ranks of accounting firms will increase to parity with men. This is known as the 'pipeline' argument, which attributes women's absence from senior positions as a function of timing. This argument assumes that as more women enter a profession, it is simply a matter of time before they take on the senior roles. However, women have been entering the profession in significant numbers for more than two decades, and the retention of women in accounting firms and their lack of progress into more senior roles continues to be a challenge for the profession.

The gendered nature of the accounting profession has attracted significant attention (Haynes, 2016). There is a growing body of literature charting the factors impacting the career progression of female accountants but much of the research is related to large accounting firms in Western contexts. Common findings from these studies suggest women's careers are limited by informal and formal processes that display gendered hierarchies (Joyce and Walker, 2015) and gender stereotyping (Anderson-Gough et al., 2005) in careers. Temporal norms of work and homosocial reproduction reinforcing the privileging of the white male are common. While the large accounting firms capture most attention, the reality is the majority of accountants are employed in small and medium-sized accounting practices, and it is timely to make visible their experiences. The overarching aim of this study is to understand: What are the factors that impact women's career progression in accounting SMEs in Australia, Malaysia and India?

INEQUALITY REGIMES

In seeking to understand careers in accounting SMEs, we draw on West and Zimmerman's (1987) 'doing gender' where they recognize gender as sustained, reproduced and rendered legitimate through interaction. Gender is done, because to not do so risks being held accountable and judged against prevailing normative expectations of gender. There are consequences of conforming or not. In recognizing the performativity of gender, we can examine gender beyond the labels 'man' or 'woman'. While West and Zimmerman's

(1987) original work was based in a Western context, the framing of it as dynamic allows for the different manifestations of it in cultural contexts, as the normative conceptions are shaped by local conditions.

Acker (1990) extended this work through the theory of gendered organizations, disrupting the notion of organizations as neutral entities. 'Doing gender' also impacts the structural processes and dynamics within organizations. Acker's theorizing enabled the identification and labelling of the commonly accepted organizing practices that reinforce gender inequality in organizations, challenging the individual-centred approach that underpinned earlier explanations for women's absence from senior roles. Acker's work paved the way for Western scholars to contest the individual-level explanations for gender inequality, with an extensive body of work calling out the social construction of gender in workplaces, the differential power in gender relations and the daily processes privileging men and marginalizing women.

Syed and Özbilgin (2009) developed a relational framework focusing on three interconnected levels – macro-societal, meso-organizational and micro-individual – to capture the concerns of (in)equality. Syed and Özbilgin (2009) describe the macro-national context as the all-encompassing domain, arguing the historical context in which the macro environment operates cannot be ignored in understanding the generation and maintenance of inequalities at all levels, not just around gender, but around class and race, too. The intersectionality of these axes of difference interact to render qualitatively different experiences. The meso-level environment captures the firms' existing structures and prevailing hierarchies that privilege men and restrict women from taking up senior roles within the profession. The micro-level environment focuses on exploring the influence exerted by class, family and other demographic variables at the individual level that may enable or hinder career progression in a specific context (Holvino, 2010).

METHODOLOGY

The accounting practices in Australia, Malaysia and India have been influenced by the professional standards developed in the United Kingdom. We reviewed the cultural context at the country level and applied an interpretive methodology to build an understanding of the contextualized experiences of accountants in SMEs. By conducting semi-structured interviews with male and female principals and partners in each of the countries, we explored women's progression to senior roles, the nature of everyday work, gender equality/inequality in the profession, women's career opportunities and work and family (im)balance.

In each country, face-to-face semi-structured interviews were undertaken, with most running between 45 minutes to one hour, and participants were assured their anonymity would be respected.[1] In Australia, we conducted interviews with 31 accountants in regional and metropolitan locations (north-west New South Wales and Sydney), while in both Malaysia and India we interviewed 20 principals and partners in each of the metropolitan locations (Kuala Lumpur and Chennai) (Miles et al., 2014). The shift between the profiles of the Australian versus the Malaysian and Indian samples occurred as we were most interested in the views of those with decision-making powers. A comparative case study methodology was followed to synthesize the differences, similarities, practices and patterns across the respondents' narratives from the three different country contexts (Ruffa, 2019).

All of the interviews were audio recorded, transcribed and coded with NVivo 11 to identify themes with conceptual coherence. The limited literature concerning women's experiences as principals or partners in SME accounting businesses prompted us to make sense of the conversations by cross-referencing existing work, including West and Zimmerman's (1987) 'doing gender', Acker's (1990) gendered organizations and inequality regimes, Syed and Özbilgin's (2009) relational framework, and identifying new insights emerging from the field.

COUNTRY CONTEXTS

In explaining the country contexts, we have provided information from the latest available datasets (2017 and 2018).

Australia

With its population of 25 million (49.6 per cent male, 50.4 per cent female), Australia is one of the most multicultural populations in the world, and its diversity of religious identities reflects this. There are more than 300 different ancestries and 28 per cent of the population is born overseas (ABS, 2018). Australia is recognized as a developed country and with its per capita gross domestic product (GDP) at US$55,000 is ranked 10th internationally (International Monetary Fund, 2018). While gender equality in paid work has been a focus of public policy in Australia for nearly 50 years, structural inequality remains a feature of workplaces, with Australia remaining one of the most gender segregated of the Organisation for Economic Co-operation and Development (OECD) countries and its enduring gender pay gap (WGEA, 2018). Each of the professional associations associated with the accounting profession in Australia have expressed their commitment to gender equality.

Malaysia

Malaysia consists of the Sabah and Sarawak and has a population of 32 million people (50.7 per cent male, 49.3 per cent female) (Department of Statistics, 2018). While over 55 per cent of the population are Malays, non-Malay Bumiputeras make up 12 per cent, the Chinese nearly 25 per cent and Indians just over 7 per cent. Over 60 per cent of the population are Muslim, 20 per cent are Buddhist, 9 per cent are Christian and 6 per cent are Hindu. Malaysia's per capita GDP is US $9755 (ranked 68th internationally) (International Monetary Fund, 2018). The way religion infuses the workplace is often overlooked in organization studies (Essers and Benschop, 2009). Abdullah (2014) acknowledges the impact of religion in creating a thick 'glass ceiling' for women's progression in Malaysia. Women in Malaysia entered the skilled workforce in the 1960s (Saadin et al., 2016) and the Malaysian government amended Article 8(2) of the constitution to bar gender-based discrimination and ensure fairness in 1995. Although there has been an upsurge in skilled women professionals in Malaysia, only 10 per cent of women have progressed to senior roles in the public sector (Saadin et al., 2016).

India

With a population of 1.3 billion, India is the second most populous country in the world. It is described as a developing country and with a per capita GDP of US$1983, it is ranked 140th internationally (International Monetary Fund, 2018). Studies focusing on working women in India link the empowerment of women to the significant changes India has undergone from Western colonial rule to the freedom movement and the gaining of independence (Radhakrishnan, 2009). Women's education levels have been rising, but a positive flow onto employment rates has been less evident. Women make up 22 per cent of employment (Ministry of Statistics and Programme Implementation, 2017). India, like many Asian economies, is characterized by strong family networks, informality and forms of social capital that are different to Western economies (Eddleston et al., 2020). Accumulation of social capital in India depends on caste, family networks and political connections (Witt and Redding, 2013). The number of women working in professional services in India has increased over the past two decades, although women remain underrepresented in senior roles.

ANALYSIS OF INTERVIEWS

The participant profiles across the three cohorts demonstrated similar levels of education and years of experience (see Table 21.1). The range of incomes was

Table 21.1   Summary profile of participants

	Australia	Malaysia	India	Total
Female	14	9	7	30
Male	17	11	13	41
Total interviews	31	20	20	71
Age	37–64 years	35–62 years	38–62 years	
Annual income	A$100,000–A$270,000* (US$71,000–$191,000)	RM150,000– RM280,000** (US$36,000–$67,000)	R1500,000– R5000,000*** (US$21,000–$71,000)	
Education level	Diploma to master	Bachelor to master	Bachelor to master	
Number of years working	10–36 years	20–35 years	7–30 years	

Note: * A = Australian dollars; ** RM = Malaysian ringgits; *** R = Indian rupees.

consistent with the relative stage of the country's development and industry norms.

The themes to emerge from the responses suggest that while the interplay of macro, meso and micro factors influencing women's accounting careers vary according to cultural context, there are similarities in outcomes. We illustrate the themes with reference to quotes from each country.[2]

Macro/Societal Expectations

In considering participants' responses, the cultural context emerged as shaping the expectations about women's roles and associated gender stereotypes in two ways. First, social beliefs about gender entail a discounting of women's competences (Murray and Southey, 2020). Second, gendered roles in marriage and the family imprint social practices onto business practices (Yang and Aldrich, 2014).

Gender stereotypes

Across the three countries, the normative expectations held about family presumed men as the breadwinner and women as supporting their husbands' careers, as well as being responsible for childcare and the household. In the cultural contexts of Malaysia and India, women's participation in higher education has increased dramatically. However, with the relatively lower participation rates of women in the workforce and the prescriptive expectations about appropriate roles for women, there were frequent references to women

Table 21.2   Gender stereotypes

Australia	Malaysia	India
'Certain types of clients in the business need to be tackled with more power, control and tactics ... those (skills) are not possessed or simply cannot be demonstrated by women.'(P8, male, medium-sized firm)	'Many accounting firms in Malaysia do not have women in senior roles. Ethnicity intensifies the problem as well. Chinese women are seen as workaholics. You cannot find women from Malay origin or Indian origin taking on senior roles in the profession.'(P11, female, micro firm)	'Our clients as business owner-managers are men themselves and they would feel odd to meet up with a female senior accountant to discuss their taxes and accounts.' (P1, male, small firm)

'not being partner material' and that women limited their own opportunities (Table 21.2).

At the meso/organizational level and individual level, cultural differences informed organizational practices and individuals' opportunities. From the participants' responses across the three countries, we were able to see how at the micro level, family responsibilities may hinder women's career progression, while ethnicity, class and caste were also important in Malaysia and India.

Meso/Organizational-Level Factors

Practices within workplaces are shaped by wider social norms. From participants' responses, we identified how organizational culture and work practices, including the allocation of work and accessibility of flexible work, are inflected by gender norms and reinforce gender hierarchies within the SME accounting firms.

Allocation of work

The male and female principals and partners identified differences between the work allocated to male and female accountants within the practices, assigning women to particular functions and spheres (Joyce and Walker, 2015) and illustrating the everyday, small-scale actions and experiences of doing gender (see Table 21.3).

Similar to the distinction between the backstage (women's work) and frontstage (men's work) of accounting work identified by Lupu (2012), participants in Malaysia and India recognized how 'office work' is allocated to female employees and 'outside office work' is assigned to their male employees, with women's family responsibilities accounting for this division. In Australia, despite the higher rates of women's labour force participation and supposedly enlightened views on women's equal participation, similar sentiments

Table 21.3   Allocation of work

Australia	Malaysia	India
'[O]ften out of business hours networking is a compulsory activity. Our female employees have children and family commitments after the normal working hours. Only our male employees are available to engage in these networking activities and they have to be paid more in … incentives for their efforts.' (P6, male, small firm)	'I have to argue with my senior management … to give me out of office work to prove myself.'(P3, female, small firm)	'Female accountants are not often motivated to take up senior roles. They are aware they can operate very well within the office and are limited in external engagement activities with clients and professional bodies due to family and cultural restrictions.' (P18, male, medium-sized firm)

emerged. These out-of-office work practices and distinctions between front- and back-office work allow male accountants to earn more than their female counterparts, reinforcing a gender hierarchy (Carmona and Ezzamel, 2016).

Flexible work practices
In Western countries, the availability of flexible work options has been on the policy agenda for the past two decades, and while not uniformly embraced, is recognized as an important factor enabling women's continued participation in paid work (Young, 2018). The pattern of working hours in Australia is more polarized than many other OECD countries, with a relatively high incidence of very short weekly hours (15 or less) among female part-time workers and very long weekly hours (50 or more) among male full-time workers (OECD, 2017). While there were mixed responses from participants about the availability of part-time work in their accounting SMEs in Australia, with some smaller firms claiming they couldn't afford them, it seems those in Australia were more open to these adaptations than their Malaysian and Indian counterparts. For Malaysian and Indian participants, the lack of flexibility was clearly recognized and largely defended on the basis of competitive pressures. Table 21.4 shows the male breadwinner and female carer stereotypes are reinforced by this lack of flexibility, providing an example of how gender is done in the workplace.

For Malaysia, wider social norms around ethnicity impacted work practices, while for Indian businesses, caste and class impacted how they organized work and revealed that group membership is important to practice, shaping opportunities. For Australia's multicultural and inclusive society, these additional influences did not emerge from the narratives of participants.

Table 21.4   Lack of flexibility

Australia	Malaysia	India
'Gender equality to some extent in our firm is mainly due to the flexible work options and the support we give to our female employees.'(P4, female, small firm)	'Flexible work options is not a common practice and our firm is not prepared to forgo the number of working hours. The associated impact will be huge on our firm's profits.'(P1, male, family firm)	'Over the past two decades our firm never had a female principal or partner. Principals and partners (all senior men) have the power to change existing rules in the firm. We never thought about introducing flexible work options for our employees.'(P18, male, medium-sized firm)

Ethnicity and work practices

Reflecting Acker's (2006) description of the compounding of inequality through 'inequality regimes' are the constraints women face because of their ethnicity in Malaysia. These existing beliefs about men's primacy in the public space that emerged from the interviews were commonly linked to ethnic origins (Adapa and Sheridan, 2019). The male principals and partners described working Malaysian-Chinese women as 'too proactive', Malay women as 'religious' and Malaysian-Indian women as possessing many 'cultural inhibitions', which impacted negatively on firm performance. Malaysian cultural norms were also used to attribute confusion and a 'lack of confidence' by male clients if they had work with female accountants.

Caste and work practices

A majority of the Indian participants explained they belonged to the upper class and were in higher castes. These participants recognized they benefited from pursuing their education at high-quality institutions in India and the presence of at least one member in the immediate and/or extended family in the same profession provided guidance and support in devising their career strategies, reinforcing the importance of group membership. Approximately 20 per cent of the sample defined themselves as upper-middle class, which was supported by the level of income earned per annum.

It seems the macro layers of social class and caste stratifications impact a firm's performance as they impose several layers of cultural and social complexities to client interaction, communication and negotiation processes. With the combination of gender, class and caste, the career paths for women from less wealthy backgrounds and from lower castes are even more complex to navigate than those Western women face (Cassan, 2019).

Table 21.5   Attributions of women's reluctance to assume senior roles and/or their incapacity

Australia	Malaysia	India
'Women themselves are not interested in progressing to senior roles.' (P4, female, medium-sized firm)	'Female employees do not volunteer to take on additional responsibilities (... at work).'(P17, male, medium-sized firm)	'There was only one occasion where we had promoted a woman from junior to senior accountant. She had a baby and left the job as she was not prepared to cope with the timelines during the tax filing period.' (P18, male, medium-sized firm)

Micro/Individual Level

The interweaving of cultural norms and individuals' experiences manifested at the micro level with attributions about individual factors limiting women's opportunities, and how women themselves saw how they proscribed their activities in light of social norms.

Women's reluctance

The translation to the individual woman's reluctance and/or incapacity to assume a senior role by partners and principals conveniently shifts responsibility from the organization to the individual, reinforcing gender practices. As is common in other cultural contexts, motherhood, not fatherhood, was portrayed as limiting career trajectories. This attribution of women's lack of desire for progression (see Table 21.5) resonates with other studies on women's employment in Muslim countries (Alfouni and Karam, 2017).

Family roles: India

The lower participation rates of Indian women in the paid workforce suggest the norms around women working may be different to those in Malaysia and Australia. Beyond the expectations about women's childcare responsibilities which were common across all countries, reflecting the enduring gender division of labour in the household, insights emerged into the prescriptive roles Indian women face in terms of what is appropriate for women, even highly educated ones. Reference was made by some women to being answerable to their parents, and that working later (an indicator of commitment to the firm) would be frowned upon in their culture. These cultural norms are not evident in many of the Western studies and provide a more nuanced insight into how the cultural norms intersect with gender, shaping women's careers in India.

DISCUSSION

Discursive practices employed to justify women's absence from senior roles echo those evident in Western contexts (Anderson-Gough et al., 2005), reflecting the traditional, Anglo accounting model, where tasks are divided into front-office and back-office activities and a privileging of long hours worked. The barriers to progression for women in SME accounting firms include gendered work practices and stereotypes, with the added intersectionality of ethnicity and religion for Malaysia and class, caste and family expectations for India. While Australian firms were more open to flexible work practices, the social norms around women's roles in each country, particularly the primacy of family for women, emerged in many of the participants' attributions of women's absence from senior roles. Flexibility was not seen as a priority for the firms, and in fact was often framed as reducing a firm's competitiveness. The emergence of the macro and micro thematic factors suggests women's progress to the senior levels of the accounting profession remains slow. Perceived gains in terms of increases in women's representation at the firm level in accounting mask the continuation of historical patterns of gendered practices.

Even in a developed country such as Australia, where gender equity has featured on the policy agenda for decades, work practices within SME accounting firms remain remarkably intransigent to adaptation. The discourse of the primacy of the client and requirements for staff to be constantly available continue to inflect work practices. In India, women's opportunities are further curtailed by the social norms discouraging women's activities in public roles outside work hours. It seems there is little reflection by participants on how gendered work practices, including informal networking outside of normal hours, reinforce the 'doing of gender' in these firms. In Malaysia, the intersection of the doing of gender and ethnicity further limits the opportunities available to women. With membership of a particular ethnic group proscribing who works with whom, career opportunities for women in SME accounting firms are additionally constrained. In India, the influence of caste on interactions between businesses and their clients impacts on career opportunities and is seen as acceptable behaviour by their families.

Our study contributes to theory by making visible how doing gender and the relational framework impact women's careers in accounting SMEs internationally, identifying common practices across the countries as well as teasing out specific manifestations of intersectionality in the different cultural contexts. From a practical perspective, universities and professional associations are key institutional actors in addressing inequality at the macro level. We see a role for universities and professional associations in educating members on the need to support women's access to the breadth of work and challenge the discursive practices reinforcing the gender hierarchies embedded in the accounting profession. At the firm (meso) level, change will only happen through professionals – both men and women – questioning and challenging the daily practices and processes of accounting SMEs. Our research findings can inform policy makers and small business associations in their decision-making capabilities in devising gender-inclusive policies for all.

CONCLUSION

Through our exploration of accounting SMEs across the different cultural contexts, we sought to contribute to investigations addressing accounting and gendered workspaces. Across the three countries, the similarities in the (deficit) framing of women's roles and their capabilities are remarkable given the different cultural contexts and stages of development the countries are at. From our analysis, we conclude the norms associated with accounting firms across the three countries remain very much tied to the traditional, masculine Anglo accounting model from which the profession developed, where the 'doing of gender' is evident in the allocation of tasks within firms and the pervasiveness of the privileging of long hours worked which continue to proscribe women's career opportunities. For change to occur, it will not be enough for universities and professional associations to simply call for gender equity, they have a role to play in disrupting, subverting and emancipating from constraining gender norms and preparing current members and the professionals of the future to 'do accounting' in a more inclusive manner. Future studies could explore the doing of gender and relational frameworks in cross-country contexts using mixed methodological approaches.

NOTES

1. Ethics approval for the studies across the three countries was granted by the Human Research Ethics Committee of the University of New England prior to the data collection.
2. For anonymity, participants are referred to as P# for each country.

REFERENCES

Abdullah, S. (2014). The causes of gender diversity in Malaysian large firms. *Journal of Management and Governance, 18*(4), 1137–1159.
ABS (2018). *Interesting Facts about Australia's 25,000,000 population.* Canberra. www.abs.gov.au/
Acker, J. (1990). Hierarchies, jobs, bodies: A theory of gendered organizations. *Gender and Society, 4*(2), 139–158.

Acker, J. (2006). Inequality regimes gender, class, and race in organizations. *Gender and Society*, *20*(4), 441–464.

Adapa, S., and Sheridan, A. (2019). A case of multiple oppressions: Women's career opportunities in Malaysian SME accounting firms. *International Journal of Human Resource Management*, 1–27.

Alfouni, F., and Karam, C. (2017). Debusting myths surrounding women's careers in the Arab region: A critical reflective approach. In R. Sultane (Ed.), *Career Guidance and Livelihood Planning Across the Mediterranean: Challenging Transitions in South Europe and the MENA Region* (pp. 55–70). Sense Publishers.

Anderson-Gough, F., Grey, C., and Robson, K. (2005). 'Helping them to forget': The organizational embedding of gender relations in public audit firms. *Accounting, Organizations and Society*, *30*(5), 469–490.

Carmona, S., and Ezzamel, M. (2016). Accounting and lived experience in the gendered workplace. *Accounting, Organizations and Society*, *49*(February), 1–8.

Cassan, G. (2019). Affirmative action, gender and education: Evidence from India. *Journal of Development Economics*, *136*(1), 51–70.

Del Bado, M., Tiron-Tudor, A., and Faragalla, W. (2019). Women's role in the accounting profession: A comparative study between Italy and Romania. *Administrative Science*, *9*(2), 1–23.

Department of Statistics (2018). Demographic statistics, Malaysia 2017–18. www.dosm.gov.my/

Eddleston, K. A., Jaskiewicz, P., and Wright, M. (2020). Family firms and internationalization in the Asia-Pacific: The need for multi-level perspectives. *Asia Pacific Journal of Management*, *37*(2), 345–361.

Essers, C. and Benschop, Y. (2009). Muslim businesswomen doing boundary work: The negotiation of Islam, gender and ethnicity within entrepreneurial contexts. *Human Relations*, *62*(3), 403–423.

Financial Reporting Council. (2018). *Key Facts and Trends in the Accountancy Profession*. https://frc.gov.au/

Haynes, K. (2016). Accounting as gendering and gendered: A review of 25 years of critical accounting on gender. *Critical Perspectives on Accounting*, *43*, 110–124.

Holvino, E. (2010). Intersections: The simultaneity of race, gender and class in organisation studies. *Gender, Work and Organisation*, *17*(3), 248–277.

International Monetary Fund (2018). World Economic Outlook Database. www.imf.org/

Jackling, B., and Calero, C. (2006). Influences on undergraduate students' intentions to become qualified accountants: Evidence from Australia. *Accounting Education: An International Journal*, *15*(4), 419–438.

Joyce, Y., and Walker, P. (2015). Gender essentialism and occupational segregation in insolvency practice. *Accounting, Organisations and Society*, *40*(1), 41–60.

Lupu, I. (2012). Approved routes and alternative paths: The construction of women's careers in large accounting firms. Evidence from the French Big Four. *Critical Perspectives on Accounting*, *23*(4–5), 351–365.

Miles, M. B., Huberman, A. M., and Saldana, J. (2014). *Qualitative Data Analysis: A Methods Sourcebook* (3rd Ed.), Sage.

Ministry of Statistics and Programme Implementation (2017). *Women and men in India*. www.mospi.gov.in/

Murray, P. A., and Southey, K. (2020). Can institutionalized workplace structures benefit senior women leaders? *Asia Pacific Journal of Management*, *37*, 1193–1216.

OECD (2017). *Connecting people with jobs: Key issues for raising labour market participation in Australia*. OECD Publishing.

Radhakrishnan, S. (2009). Professional women, good families: Respectable femininity and the cultural politics of a 'new' India. *Qualitative Sociology, 32*, 195–212.

Ruffa. C. (2019). Designing and conducting the comparative case study method. In *Sage Research Methods Cases*. Sage.

Saadin, I., Ramli, K., Johari, H., and Harin, N. A. (2016). Women and barriers for upward career advancement: A survey at Perak state secretariat, Ipoh, Perak. *Procedia Economics and Finance, 35*, 574–581.

Singh, A. (2014). Indian diaspora as a factor in India–Malaysia relations. *Diaspora Studies, 7*(2), 130–140.

Syed, J., and Özbilgin, M. (2009). A relational framework for international transfer of diversity management practices. *International Journal of Human Resource Management, 20*(12), 2435–2453.

West, C., and Zimmerman, D. (1987). Doing gender. *Gender and Society, 1*(2), 125–151.

WGEA (2018). *Australia's gender pay gap statistics August 2018*. www.wgea.gov.au/

Witt, M., and Redding, G. (2013). Asian business systems: Institutional comparison, clusters and implications for varieties of capitalism and business systems theory. *Socio-Economic Review, 11*, 265–300.

Yang, T., and Aldrich, H. (2014). Who's the boss? Explaining gender inequality in entrepreneurial teams. *American Sociological Review, 79*(2), 303–327.

Young, Z. (2018). *Women's Work: How Mothers Manage Flexible Working in Careers and Family Life*. Bristol University Press.

PART III

22. Effectiveness of gender equality and diversity initiatives: a way forward

Erica French, Muhammad Ali, Marzena Baker and Lina Alsaree

INEQUALITY AT WORK

Globally, gender inequality results in extreme poverty rates that are 22 per cent higher for women than men during their peak productive and reproductive years (Oxfam, 2020). This inequality is spurred by the lack of recognition of care work which is largely the unpaid responsibility of women and girls 15 years and over and calculated as a $10.8 trillion industry, three times larger than the world's technology industry. Forty two per cent of working-age women are outside the paid labour force due to unpaid care responsibilities compared with only 6 per cent of men. Since the start of the coronavirus pandemic, 112 million women worldwide are at higher risk of losing their income or job than men because women are overrepresented in the sectors of the economy hardest hit by the pandemic (Oxfam, 2021). In Australia the Workplace Gender Equality Agency is charged with promoting and improving gender equality in Australian workplaces. Workplace gender equality refers to equal access to rewards, resources and opportunities regardless of gender. In Australia, despite significant progress towards gender equality, large gaps remain in pay equity, women in leadership, parental leave and flexible work opportunities (WGEA, 2021).

Despite worldwide identification, the legislation and social activity undertaken to address gender inequality has remained ignominious. United Nations (UN) Deputy Secretary-General Amina Mohammed described inequality as one of the leading challenges of our time and "gender inequality" as part of its leading edge; specifically, "The most pervasive and universal form of inequality". Gender inequality is deeply seated in structural, cultural and educational bias. When women do get access to work they are often poorly remunerated and overrepresented in the informal sector with a disproportionate burden of unpaid care work (United Nations Press Release, 2019). Meanwhile, the gender pay gap remains at a stagnated 20 per cent globally (ILO, 2018).

Although substantial action has called attention to the issues, this situation is not predicted to change anytime soon. "Young women are at risk of taking a back seat in the Fourth Industrial Revolution as their level of participation in Science, Technology, Engineering and Mathematics studies and employment is much lower than for young men" (World Economic Forum, 2018). Further, such disadvantages are enduring, following them for decades, adding up to a lifetime of disadvantage making it harder for women to lift themselves and their families out of poverty or to have income security in old age.

Yet, gender inequality need not be inevitable (G7 Gender Equality Advisory Council, 2019).

The UN 2030 Agenda for Sustainable Development adopted by all UN member states in 2015 (n=193) provides a plan for the shared peace and prosperity of the entire planet and its people. There are 17 detailed Sustainable Development Goals (SDGs), offering a call to action for all members. "They recognize that ending poverty and other deprivations must go hand-in-hand with strategies that improve health and education, reduce inequality, and spur economic growth – all while tackling climate change and working to preserve our oceans and forests" (United Nations Department of Economic and Social Affairs, 2018). However, implementing substantive change requires more than a focus on the end goal. Many systems and processes, customs and traditions will need to be modified. Two principal SDGs are linked to the focus of this chapter, and we identify the difficulties in addressing them. Goal 5 involves achieving gender equality and the empowerment of all women and girls. Goal 8 involves the promotion of sustained, inclusive and sustainable economic growth with full and productive employment and decent work for all.

The 2020 Goals Report on Sustainable Development acknowledges progress in meeting the goals but also recognizes the lack of achievement in some areas (United Nations Department of Economic and Social Affairs, 2020). For example, there are more girls in school worldwide compared to a generation ago, with gender parity reached in many areas in primary education. However, despite a growing percentage of women getting paid for their work there are still stark inequalities in work and wages with substantial unpaid "women's work" and gender discrimination in workplaces. Further, despite the number of developing countries growing their middle class over the past generation, job growth is not keeping pace with the growing labour force, reducing the outcomes for the goal of decent work for all women and men. The level of variation between different economic jurisdictions suggests how well different members are able to ensure fair access to opportunities such as education and jobs, and outcomes including fair wages for everyone, and how well they can design and implement effective practices and processes to address the complexity. In Australia, the gender pay gap is recognized at 14.2 per cent (WGEA, 2021). The gender pay gap measures the difference between the average pay rates of men and women. In Organisation for Economic Co-operation and Development terms Australia's gender pay gap is higher than the world average at 12.2 per cent (OECD, 2021), with Korea the highest at 31 per cent and Bulgaria the lowest at 3 per cent.

ADDRESSING INEQUALITY AT WORK

Designing and implementing effective practices and processes to achieve gender parity requires a broad focus yet complexity is a problem. "The UN sustainable development goals aim at tackling complex, multidimensional challenges faced by humankind and set the international agenda for 2030. So far, little is known about the interactions, relationships and potential conflicts between the set of SDGs" (Bottlenecks for Sustainable Development, 2018).

Ergül and Mehmet (2019) suggest the sustainable welfare targets should include three main pillars: economic growth, social inclusion and environmental protection. Ferrata (2019) advocates that ensuring access to financial services is a key enabler of Agenda 2030 and these services contribute to the achievement of most of the SDGs including gender equality and getting decent work. Overcoming financial exclusion, when combined with other forms of deprivation such as work, education and health, is vital to ensure the full contribution of those excluded. Ultimately, decision makers will have to implement measures to speed up digital financial inclusion like creating effective consumer protection systems, reducing physical and technological barriers, increasing the financial knowledge of the less educated and developing reliable and secure technical infrastructures.

When it comes to gender equality, the UN Guidance Note of the Secretary General (United Nations News, 2021) suggests inclusivity strengthens buy-in, accountability, transparency and sustainability. Stakeholders need to be broad and all-encompassing, and the emphasis should be on those who have been historically excluded, such as women and women's rights organizations. However, little is proposed about the means of achievement of inclusion or the challenges and conflicts. The Global Partnership for Education is pushing strongly for the recognition that laws alone won't be sufficient to achieve transformative change, highlighting that those laws are an imperfect litmus test of progress towards equality, that what is needed is programs and policies to implement change (G7 Gender Equality Advisory Council, 2019). The UN Development Programme suggests the longer an inequality exists the harder it is to address because it becomes entrenched in the political context (UNDP, 2019). The Workplace Gender Equality Agency advises "businesses who pay close attention to their own data, and who consistently scrutinize and apply their workplace policies, are the ones that have seen the most effective gender equality outcomes" (Cassells and Duncan, 2021, p. 6).

Oxfam (2020) advises going beyond income measures to counting unpaid care. In their latest report on inequality, Oxfam calls for "the transformative '4Rs' framework" (Oxfam, 2020, p. 2). First, recognize unpaid and poorly paid care work, primarily done by women. Second, reduce the amount of time spent on unpaid care via the better use of technology and support services. Third, redistribute unpaid care work within the household and within society to the government and the private sector. Finally, represent the most marginalized caregivers in the design and delivery of policies and services that will affect them (Oxfam, 2020). All this speculation points to the need for new and better policies of inclusiveness in social and self-determination. Gender equality and diversity initiatives (GEDIs) are increasingly called for to assist in the proactive inclusion of women in exclusive systems. This chapter uses GEDI as the comprehensive label for numerous equal opportunity policy types including diversity policies, equity policies, equal employment opportunity policies, etc. We explore the arguments and merits of various approaches to the design and implementation of GEDIs with a view to examining current research for substantive justice-based design and implementation to encourage more effective individual and organizational outcomes.

GENDER EQUALITY AND DIVERSITY INITIATIVES

Workplace GEDIs have been identified as potential solutions capable of assisting in the proactive inclusion of women and minorities within exclusive systems by increasing their recruitment, retention and promotion (Morello et al., 2018; Shrestha et al., 2020). However, past empirical research into the effectiveness of such initiatives has shown mixed results (French and Strachan, 2015; Härtel, 2004; Kalev et al., 2006; Konrad and Linnehan, 1995). Some authors suggest that the implementation of GEDIs has improved the employment status of women and people of colour (e.g., Ali, 2016; Cockburn, 1991; Konrad and Linnehan, 1995; Sheridan, 1995; Still, 1993). Ali (2016) found a positive impact of GEDIs on both management gender diversity and non-management gender diversity. Verbeek and Groeneveld (2012) and French and Strachan (2007, 2009, 2015) argue that the impact of GEDIs on women's representation in traditionally male-dominated industries and in management is limited. French and Strachan (2007, 2009, 2015) found no correlation between the use of some types of GEDI and the representation of women across organizational levels, whereas Galea et al. (2015) found that the design of GEDI policies impacts their capacity to genuinely challenge gendered norms, practices and narratives of the male-dominated industries. Baker et al. (2019b) note that formal GEDIs are not always effective in achieving intended outcomes and are generally unrelated to the increased employment of women. The mere increased presence of GEDIs does not necessarily result in increased representation of women (Baker et al., 2021b).

INEFFECTIVENESS OF GEDIs TO ACHIEVE EQUITY AT WORK

The question of why GEDIs are failing (Benschop et al., 2015; Dobbin et al., 2015; Holck, 2016) has been raised, with suggestions that effectiveness may be dependent on organizational leaders' design of GEDIs (Pitts et al., 2010; Strachan and French, 2015; Verbeek and Groeneveld, 2012), their translation into substantive policy and strategy (Hoque and Noon, 2004) and their implementation (Pitts, 2005; Pitts et al., 2010). O'Leary and Sandberg (2017) posit that understanding how GEDIs are designed and implemented may assist in developing more effective policy and strategy and creating substantive equality and inclusion outcomes. We argue that typology and approach are influential in the design and implementation of GEDIs and organizational outcomes. We further suggest the justice perspective of the individual and their organization are powerful determinants in the debate about what is identified as fair and just when it comes to design and implementation of GEDIs.

CHALLENGES IN GEDI DESIGN AND IMPLEMENTATION

Approach

Arguments debating the paradox of two approaches to GEDIs implemented for the purpose of improving gender equity indicate different results. First, identity-blind initiatives refer to activities which ignore group identity (such as gender, age, ethnicity, etc.) of individuals, encouraging identical decisions for all employees (Konrad and Linnehan, 1995, p. 788). The identity-blind approach into GEDI design and implementation proposes the equal treatment of everyone based usually on merit, with no acknowledgement of any past or current inequality of individuals or their groups. Employing the identity-blind approach to equality and diversity initiatives alone results in a system that maintains the current disparity between groups within those organizations (Krook and Mackay, 2011). Equal treatment initiatives have been identified as offering limited organizational or individual equality outcomes (French, 2001; Galea et al., 2015; Konrad and Linnehan, 1995; Windscheid et al., 2017). On the other hand, identity-conscious GEDIs explicitly consider structural, cultural and historical influences on group identity in the design of special measures. In addition to individual merit, demographic group identity should be considered in the implementation of initiatives to remedy discrimination, redress past injustices and achieve increased representation (Konrad and Linnehan, 1995). Identity-conscious initiatives have been positively associated with increased numbers of women and people of colour in management and across all organizational levels (Ali, 2016; Ali and Konrad, 2017; French, 2001; Konrad and Linnehan, 1995).

Eliminating discrimination and expanding the recruitment pool are often seen as policies that should be unbiased, rather than those that focus on using special measures or identity-conscious strategies (Cropanzano and Mitchell, 2005). Therein lies the paradox. Many organizations and their leaders have been reluctant to implement identity-conscious, special-measure initiatives because employees and others may perceive them as reverse discrimination (Windscheid et al., 2017). Indeed, Verbeek and Groeneveld (2012) challenged such measures as "hard" HR that should be avoided. However, by acknowledging legislative requirements and linking them to the broader business case for the organization, this paradox can be overcome to substantively address equality and diversity (Baker et al., 2021a; Shore et al., 2009; Windscheid et al., 2017).

Typology

Arguments debating the effectiveness of two types of GEDI are identified in the literature as human resource (HR) initiatives and work–life initiatives. French and Strachan (2007, 2009, 2015) note a difference between the "hard" HR strategies and the "soft" work–life initiatives. The HR strategies of GEDI include activities of recruitment, promotion and training and retention strategies to address systemic inequality and bias, while work–life initiatives involve the support for flexibility of employees with family and/or caring responsibilities. One encourages movement up through the structure of the organization and the other affords the flexibility to move in and out of the organization to meet care responsibilities. Findings indicate relatively few organizations develop proactive strategies in the "hard" HR areas, preferring to advocate for "equal treatment" as the primary driver for their lack of proactivity in this area (French and Strachan, 2009). Yet, such equal treatment is not linked to increased numbers of women employed or the numbers of women in management (see Konrad and Linnehan, 1995). Strategies that influence work and life opportunities do increase women's participation in the workforce by encouraging greater work flexibility, but they do not extend or increase the numbers of women in management or in leadership roles. Instead, they allow for greater numbers in the potential labour pool to move in and out of the workforce at the behest of management (French and Strachan, 2009).

Baker et al. (2019), in a study of more than 350 organizations, did find support for a positive relationship between GEDIs featuring work–life initiatives and the increased representation of women at both management and non-management levels. However, it is important to note that this relationship is only influenced by an increased number of women in the top management team. Specifically, the more women there are in the top management team the higher the representation of women in management and non-management areas when work–life initiatives are the GEDIs implemented.

In a second study, Baker et al. (2019a) found evidence for the relationship between women's increased representation in management and effective organizational financial performance. Using a sample of 932 organizations the findings identified the relationship between the increased numbers of women in management and increased financial organizational performance in male-dominated project-based organizations such as construction and engineering. However, it is also true that women in male-dominated industries may be unlikely to use work–life initiatives for fear of limiting their career progress (Baker et al., 2021b). Work–life initiatives may allow for greater flexibility, but they do not address existing structural and systemic inequality, which may be better addressed through well-implemented HR initiatives (Baker et al., 2021b). There is also support for a diversity environment as a moderator of the relationship between work–life initiatives and organizational financial outcomes, where a highly supportive diversity environment positively affects that relationship. This is consistent with earlier research, which identified the positive effects of a diversity environment on the diversity management–organizational performance relationship (Harrison and Klein, 2007; Jackson and Joshi, 2004; Williams and O'Reilly, 1998). For practitioners, these findings suggest that organizations may well need to consider changing their gender imbalances in management to capitalize on gender diversity benefits for substantive organizational outcomes.

Baker et al. (2021a) further note that the design of GEDIs by leaders specifically in male-dominated organizations is heavily influenced by coercive legislation and the pressure of industry norms. Equality and diversity are identified as a compliance-based requirement following the dictates of coercive legislation and mimicry of industry norms rather than any strategic objectives of the organization. Leaders design GEDIs based on their own personal views of what is fair and just, resulting in the neglect of substantive equality and diversity issues in their organization. While the range of GEDIs offered may be identified as extensive, the improvement of any outcomes for women has been minimal (Baker et al., 2019a). Leaders guided by their own need for "equal" treatment often reject proactive design and implementation of GEDIs that acknowledge historic or systemic disadvantage such as skewed recruitment practices, sexist attitudes, masculine organizational culture or a challenging working environment (Baker et al., 2021b; Fielden et al., 2015; Simons and Chabris, 1999). Although GEDIs designed to encourage equal treatment may be well intentioned, they often only alleviate symptoms of inequality, rather than address any systemic root causes to create lasting change. The execution of equal treatment GEDIs appears to support business outcomes but does little more than provide lip service to validate compliance with legal requirements, and any real change is slow (Baker et al., 2021a; Roberts, 2019; Scharmer, 2002). This study further highlights the importance of increasing leadership gender diversity, particularly board diversity, in order to improve the design and implementation of diversity initiatives and, in turn, improve organizational financial outcomes. Similarly, Ali and Konrad (2017) found a gender diverse top management team is positively associated with GEDIs which interact with lower through middle management gender diversity to improve financial performance.

Perspective

Organizational justice theory has been a primary paradigm within gender equality and diversity literature. Organizational justice is defined as employee perceptions of fairness regarding the policies and procedures established and carried out in the workplace by management (Greenberg, 2013). Colquitt and Rodell (2015) suggest justice perceptions may cause positive or negative behaviours in employees' performance, outcomes and attitudes. Studies have shown that perceptions of justice are not only important to employees' outcomes but are also crucial to organizational outcomes and organizational performance (Colquitt, 2013). However, the perspectives are complex and difficult to interpret and implement. Perspectives include distributive justice, procedural justice, interactional justice and informational justice (see Cohen-Charash and Spector, 2001; Colquitt et al., 2001; Cropanzano and Greenberg, 1997; Greenberg and Colquitt, 2005).

Distributive justice is generally defined as the fair distribution of resources (Greenberg and Colquitt, 2005). Within the organizational and HR literature, it has been shown to be positively related to organizational commitment (Poon, 2012) and negatively related to employees' turnover intention (e.g., Griffeth et al., 2000; Poon, 2012). This form of justice is most frequently linked to equity theory (Adams, 1965). According to Adams' equity theory, people determine fairness by a reasoned calculation and evaluation of their perceived contributions or inputs (i.e., participation, effort, performance or skills) compared to the outcomes (tangible and intangible rewards) they receive. They then compare this ratio to some standards to determine whether the outcomes they have received for their contributions are fair (Ambrose and Arnaud, 2005; Nowakowski and Conlon, 2005).

Procedural justice is referred to as the fairness of the process used to make decisions at the workplace (Konovsky, 2000). Within the HR management domain, research has shown positive relationships between HR management practice and procedural justice. For example, Meyer and Smith (2000) found a positive link between promotion, career development and training opportunities, and satisfaction with the employee benefits packages, performance appraisal and perceptions of procedural justice.

Interactional justice involves the human or social aspect of organizational practices (Chou, 2009). It focuses on the quality of interpersonal treatment (Cropanzano et al., 2002; Landy and Conte, 2004) and examines how managers allocate resources and rewards in the workplace toward their employees (Kernan and Hanges, 2002). Research has shown that interactional justice is positively related to organizational citizenship behaviour, organizational commitment and many other forms of employee behaviour and attitudes. Bies and Moag (1986) introduced this concept in the justice literature by focusing attention on the importance of the quality of the interpersonal treatment people receive when procedures are implemented.

Informational justice focuses on the amount and quality of information provided concerning procedures and outcomes (Colquitt, 2001; Greenberg, 1990). It refers to the explanations that supervisors offer during the decision-making process, the degree of communication between supervisors and subordinates and whether a thorough explanation is given to employees. It involves the truthfulness and adequacy of explanations of decisions and activities by management to their employees (Greenberg, 1993).

Rupp et al. (2014) suggest the four perspectives of justice characterize employees' perceptions of justice at work, namely whether the rewards they receive, the procedures used to determine outcomes and both the information conveyed about procedures and the interpersonal treatment given are perceived as fair and just. Although justice theory literature lacks studies about how organizational justice models are used in designing and implementing GEDIs, they are considered one of the main complex blocks in designing and implementing GEDI initiatives in the workplace today (Otaye-Ebede et al., 2016). Studies have shown that where employees are not treated fairly and justly, their output will be reduced, thus affecting organizational outcome as well as organizational performance (Cappelli and Keller, 2013). Moreover, Folger et al. (2007) highlight the importance of organizational justice and the necessity to develop a framework for understanding the concept of justice at the workplace. However, little work has yet been done to identify the different justice perspectives of employees and managers (Alsaree and French, 2020).

In a ground-breaking study of supervisors and subordinates' perspectives on justice, Alsaree and French (2020) found each group uses completely different justice lenses due to their dissimilar concerns of diverse organizational issues. Subordinates were more concerned with informational justice relative to organizational processes for change and their own inclusion in the amount and quality of information; while supervisors were more concerned about distributive and procedural justice as they focused on aspects of equality in rewards according to individual contributions. In fact, the findings indicate that supervisors are not concerned about change processes at all as they believe in following organizational rules and management decisions. This demonstrates a gap of communication and a disconnection between the major foci of supervisors and subordinates. It also identifies a difference in their perceptions of what is fair and just. This difference in their perspective has ramifications for the design and implementation of GEDIs and ultimately their effectiveness. Employees desire greater inclusion through more information and communication about the decisions and processes of justice (informational justice) while their supervisors are concerned with the fairness of the distribution procedures for resources (distribution and processual justice).

Baker et al. (2021a) applied the lenses of organizational justice theory (Cohen-Charash and Spector, 2001; Cropanzano and Greenberg, 1997; Greenberg and Colquitt, 2005) in their study to gain insights into leaders' decisions in GEDI design and implementation. They posit that the decisions of leaders were influenced by the complexity of justice (Otaye-Ebede et al., 2016) and the various arguments regarding its achievement, resulting in confusion and leading to inattention and neglect (Simons and Chabris, 1999). Inattention theory suggests that people fail to notice obvious things within organizations when focusing hard on something else (Simons and Chabris, 1999). They do what they know, which comes from an inner place that is a source of their attention when related to the world (Scharmer, 2002). This creates a unique climate within which policies and strategies are developed (Roberts, 2019; Schneider et al., 2013). Leaders have blind spots based on their past experience, and they may be unaware of the systems and practices within their organizations and remain oblivious to any inequality that can lead to inadequate and potentially discriminatory decisions (Roberts, 2019; Scharmer, 2002).

Rather than the design and implementation of GEDIs being based on the understanding of various arguments for different treatment and the use of special measures to meet cultural and systemic disadvantage, leaders focus on meeting legislative and industry requirements. They present fairness as solely being about the processes for delivery rather than for acknowledging or changing any unfair systems, outcomes or representations. They ignore the need to address a full justice spectrum as well as ensuring benefits and burdens are distributed equitably across all groups and individuals in the workplace (Greenberg and Colquitt, 2005). Further, the interactional justice elements that consider the greater dignity and respect for all are overlooked (Cropanzano et al., 2002), through what can be interpreted as leadership indifference and inattention to substantive equality and diversity based upon a lack of awareness and understanding of systemic discrimination issues (Baker et al., 2021a) and the use of special measures. Different treatment for different people in different situations may well be what is needed, as well as the balanced use of equal treatment with consideration for when and where each is required (French and Strachan, 2015).

DESIGNING AND IMPLEMENTING GEDIs FOR EFFECTIVENESS

Addressing the complexity and confusion of the multiple issues of gender and diversity and inequality is an issue for future research. Greater attention may need to be paid to looking beyond the numbers of women employed and their income (UNDP, 2019). Oxfam (2020) suggests going beyond income measures, to considering unpaid care which is so valuable in multiple societies but undertaken primarily by women and rarely counted. Their global report on inequality (Oxfam, 2020, p. 2), "Time to Care", calls for "the transformative '4Rs' frame-work". This framework advocates for better government policies to support and pay for care work, better jobs that result in wages for work valued by a society, new approaches to taxation of the world's wealthy to address care deficits and new and better policies of inclusiveness in social and self-determination.

In this chapter we explored how new and better policies of inclusiveness may be designed and implemented as GEDIs influenced by approach, type and perspectives in justice. Our findings indicate achieving gender equality and diversity at work through the design and implementation of specific initiatives is a complex business. While workplace GEDIs have been identified as a potential answer to addressing inequality, they appear to be failing in their objectives. Identity-conscious GEDIs that explicitly consider structural, cultural and historical discrimination issues and address them through the use of special measures have been positively associated with the increased numbers of women across all areas of management, yet apathy and inattention appear to dominate when it comes to their design and implementation. Further, the identity-blind and equal treatment approach to GEDI design and implementation has been ineffective in moving women into management or leadership areas without substantial numbers of women recruited into the top management team and the support of a strong diversity culture.

Approach

The challenge still remains in overcoming injustice present in the design of GEDIs and their translation into substantive organizational policy and strategy. Current designs seem to merely alleviate symptoms of inequality, rather than address any systemic root causes of injustice, and do not create any lasting change. The Australian Federation of Business and Professional Women's Association (2021) identified that it will take at least 26 years to address gender inequality specifically related to equal pay status in Australia given the slow progress made to date. This is the result in Australia, a country which is seen to be making progress in addressing gender equality. Many other countries are yet to show this level of progress (OECD, 2021). Future research should investigate the effects of identity-blind and identity-conscious gender diversity efforts that are relevant to a broader scope of organizations (i.e., including small and medium-sized enterprises) (Windscheid et al., 2017) and studies including awareness and value of specific quota programs designed to address specific inequities in different jurisdictions and their outcomes would be beneficial (Baker et al., 2019a, 2021a).

Type

Women experience work differently in terms of access, opportunities and rewards. Gender inequality at work is the result of how work is valued. In many cases, women earn less than men for doing jobs of equal value. The main cause is the way in which women's skills are valued compared to men. In addition, segregation in the labour market reinforces the gender pay gap. Women and men still tend to work in different jobs. Segregation is also frequently linked to stereotypes. In Europe, around 60 per cent of new university graduates are women, with a minority in fields like mathematics, computing and engineering. Consequently, fewer women work in scientific and technical jobs and many women work in lower-valued and lower-paid sectors of the economy. Further, more women than men choose to take parental leave. This, together with a lack of childcare facilities, means that women are often forced to leave the labour market (European Union, 2019). This variety in causes is best addressed through a variety of policy types. Belter et al. (2020) identify the importance of organizations to get two critical aspects right to support both increased diversity and increased inclusion, particularly when addressing the gender wage gap. The first is behavioural inclusion. It is necessary to create a culture of belonging where employees in the organization have a more inclusive mindset, making more inclusive decisions and taking more inclusive actions. This is the place for work and life balance policies to encourage inclusion as such policies allow the flexibility for greater inclusion. The second is structural inclusion, where organizations revisit practices and processes that may be holding underrepresented employees back, such as recruitment processes, job descriptions, performance evaluation checklists and reward practices. These can be replete with norms, behaviours and adjectives that inadvertently favour a bias toward the majority group. Baker et al. (2019a, 2021b) and Baker et al. (2021a) found that work–life strategies are popular in

Australia, however, these policies are only effective in addressing inequality where there are increased numbers of women in the top management team and where there is a supportive culture. More research is needed into the value of the "hard" HR policies and practices designed to encourage structural inclusion through addressing the underrepresentation of women in leadership and management positions and in non-traditional areas of work (French and Strachan, 2015) and the links to culture change.

Perspective

Applying the justice lens to GEDI policies is a further important future research area (Alsaree and French, 2020). This is particularly true in relation to understanding the differences between the justice perspectives of individuals across the various levels within the organization's decision-making and implementation areas. Ng and Sears (2020) also note the importance of the individual decision makers and the need for future research into the individual behaviours of the designers themselves, including chief executive officers and their influence on managers particularly to identify any potential for similarity bias. Further research is also needed to explore how line managers' beliefs and values contribute to the implementation and effectiveness of workplace diversity practices (Alsaree and French, 2020; Baker et al., 2021a).

Ultimately there can be no one best way to design and implement GEDIs to achieve substantive equality. Just as there are many causes of inequality there must be many solutions. The intersectionality of approach, type and perspective raises a further area for new research. A pluralist slant is called for, but the imperative remains that those making the decisions in the design and implementation of GEDIs need to be fully informed on the various causes, challenges and choices if global and systemic discrimination against women and the design of decent work for all is the objective.

REFERENCES

Ali, M. (2016). "Impact of gender-focused human resource management on performance: The mediating effects of gender diversity". *Australian Journal of Management*, 41(2), 376–397.

Ali, M., and Konrad, A.M. (2017). "Antecedents and consequences of diversity and equality management systems: The importance of gender diversity in the TMT and lower to middle management". *European Management Journal*, 35(4), 440–453.

Alsaree, L., and French, E. (2020). "What is just? How do today's workforce perceive justice at the workplace?" Presented at AIRAANZ Queenstown New Zealand, January.

Australian Federation of Business and Professional Women's Association (2021). "Equal pay day – 26 years is too long to wait to close the gap". www

.equalpayday.com.au/resources/Documents/BPWA%20EPD%202021%20Media %20Release.pdf

Baker, M., Ali, M., and French, E. (2019a). "Effectiveness of gender equality initiatives in project-based organizations in Australia". *Australian Journal of Management*, 44(3), 425–442.

Baker, M., Ali, M., and French, E. (2019b). "The impact of women's representation on performance in project-based and non-project-based organizations". *International Journal of Project Management*, 37(7), 872–883.

Baker, M., French, E., and Ali, A. (2021a). "Insights into ineffectiveness of gender equality and diversity initiatives in project-based organizations". *Journal of Management in Engineering*, 37(3), 04021013.

Baker, M., Ali, M., and French, E. (2021b). "Leadership diversity and its influence on equality initiatives and performance: Insights for Construction Management". *Journal of Construction Engineering and Management*, 147(10), 04021123.

Belter, C., McMullen, T., Riley, M., and Tapia, A.T. (2020). "Getting it right: Three types of pay equity gaps and how to fix them". *Journal of Total Rewards*, 29(1), 41–48.

Business Mirror (2018, January 24). "Bottlenecks for sustainable development". https:// gateway.library.qut.edu.au/login?url=https://www.proquest.com/newspapers/ bottlenecks-sustainable-development/docview/1990822325/se-2?accountid=13380

Cassells, R. and Duncan, A. (2021). "Gender equity insights 2021: Making it a priority", BCEC/WGEA Gender Equity Series, 6(March).

Cockburn, C. (1991). *In the Way of Women: Men's Resistance to Sex Equality in Organizations*. Ithaca, NY: Cornell University Press.

Cohen-Charash, Y., and Spector, P.E. (2001). "The role of justice in organizations: A meta-analysis". *Organizational Behavior and Human Decision Processes*, 86(2), 278–321.

Cropanzano, R., and Greenberg, J. (1997). "Progress in organizational justice: Tunnelling through the maze". In C. Cooper and I. Robertson (eds), *International Review of Industrial and Organizational Psychology*, 317–372. Chichester: Wiley.

Cropanzano, R., and Mitchell, M.S. (2005). "Social exchange theory: An interdisciplinary review". *Journal of Management*, 31(6), 874–900.

Cropanzano, R., Prehar, C.A., and Chen, P.Y. (2002). "Using social exchange theory to distinguish procedural from interactional justice". *Group Organization Management*, 27(3), 324–351.

Dobbin, F., Schrage, D., and Kalev, A. (2015). "Rage against the iron cage: The varied effects of bureaucratic personnel reforms on diversity". *American Sociological Review*, 80(5), 1014–1044.

Ergül H, and Mehmet, A.S. (2019). "Sustainable development from Millennium 2015 to Sustainable Development Goals 2030". *Sustainable Development*, 27(4), 545–572.

European Union. (2019). "Equal pay? Time to close the gap!" https://ec.europa.eu/info/ sites/default/files/factsheet-gender_pay_gap-2019.pdf

Ferrata, L. (2019). "Digital financial inclusion – an engine for 'leaving no one behind'". *Public Sector Economics*, 43(4), 445–458.

French, E. (2001). "Approaches to equity management and their relationship to women in management". *British Journal of Management*, 12(4), 267–285.

French, E., and Strachan, G. (2007). "Equal opportunity outcomes for women in the finance industry in Australia: Evaluating the merit of EEO plans". *Asia Pacific Journal of Human Resources*, 45(3), 314–332.

French, E., and Strachan, G. (2009). "Evaluating equal employment opportunity and its impact on the increased participation of men and women in the transport industry". *Transport Research Part A Policy and Practice*, 43(1), 78–89.

French, E., and Strachan, G. (2015). "Women at work! Evaluating equal employment policies and outcomes in construction". *Equality Diversity and Inclusion International Journal*, 34(3), 227–243.

Galea, N., Powell, A., Loosemore, M., and Chappell, L. (2015). "Designing robust and revisable policies for gender equality: Lessons from the Australian construction industry". *Construction Management and Economics*, 33(5–6), 375–389.

Greenberg, J., and Colquitt, J.A. (2005). *Handbook of Organizational Justice*. Mahwah, NJ: Lawrence Erlbaum.

Griffeth, R., Hom, P., and Gaertner, S. (2000). "A meta-analysis of antecedents and correlates of employee turnover: Update, moderator tests, and research implications for the next millennium". *Journal of Management*, 26, 463–488.

Harrison, D.A., and Klein, K.J. (2007). "What's the difference? Diversity constructs as separation, variety, or disparity in organizations". *Academy of Management Review*, 32, 1199–1228.

Härtel, C.E. (2004). "Towards a multicultural world: Identifying work systems, practices and employee attitudes that embrace diversity". *Australian Journal of Management*, 29, 189–200.

Holck, L. (2016). "Putting diversity to work: An empirical analysis of how change efforts targeting organizational inequality failed". *Equality Diversity and Inclusion International Journal*, 35(4), 296–307.

Hoque, K., and Noon, M. (2004). "Equal opportunities policy and practice in Britain: Evaluating the 'empty shell' hypothesis". *Work Employment and Society*, 18(3), 481–506.

International Labour Organization (2018). "Global wage report 2018/19: What lies behind gender pay gaps?" Geneva: ILO.

Jackson, S.E., and Joshi, A. (2004). "Diversity in social context: A multi-attribute, multilevel analysis of team diversity and sales performance". *Journal of Organizational Behavior*, 25, 675–702.

Kalev, A., Dobbin, F., and Kelly, E. (2006). "Best practices or best guesses? Assessing the efficacy of corporate affirmative action and diversity policies". *American Sociological Review*, 71(4), 589–617.

Konrad, A.M., and Linnehan, F. (1995). "Formalized HRM structures: Coordinating equal employment opportunity or concealing organizational practices?" *Academy of Management Journal*, 38(3), 787–820.

Krook, M.L., and Mackay, F. (2011). *Gender, Politics, and Institutions: Towards a Feminist Institutionalism*. Basingstoke: Palgrave Macmillan.

Morello, A., Issa, R.R.A., and Franz, B. (2018). "Exploratory study of recruitment and retention of women in the construction industry". *Journal of Professional Issues in Engineering Education and Practice*, 144(2), 04018001.

Ng, E.S., and Sears, G.J. (2020). "Walking the talk on diversity: CEO beliefs, moral values, and the implementation of workplace diversity practices". *Journal of Business Ethics*, 164(3), 437–450.

O'Leary, J., and Sandberg, J. (2017). "Managers' practice of managing diversity revealed: A practice-theoretical account". *Journal of Organizational Behavior*, 38(4), 512–536.

OECD (2021). "Gender wage gap (indicator)". doi: 10.1787/7cee77aa-en

Otaye-Ebede, L., Sparrow, P., and Wong, W. (2016). "The changing contours of fairness: Using multiple lenses to focus the HRM research agenda". *Journal of Organizational Effectiveness: People and Performance*, 3(1), 70–90.

Oxfam (2020). "Time to care: Unpaid and underpaid care work and the global inequality crisis". Oxford: Oxfam.

Pitts, D.W. (2005). "Diversity, representation, and performance: Evidence about race and ethnicity in public organizations". *Journal of Public Administration Research and Theory*, 15(4), 615–631.

Pitts, D.W., Hicklin, A.K., Hawes, D.P., and Melton, E. (2010). "What drives the implementation of diversity management programs? Evidence from public organizations". *Journal of Public Administration Research and Theory*, 20(4), 867–886.

Roberts, S. (2019). "Gender inequality: A review of the wilful blindness of leaderships in organizations". Proceedings, EURAM 2019: Exploring the Future of Management, Lisbon.

Scharmer, C.O. (2002). "Presencing: Illuminating the blind spot of leadership. Foundations for a social technology of freedom". www.researchgate.net/publication/237631506_Presencing_Illuminating_the_Blind_Spot_of_Leadership

Sheridan A.J. (1995). "Affirmative action in Australia: Employment statistics can't tell the whole story". *Women in Management Review*, 10, 26–34.

Shrestha, B.K., Choi, J.O., Shrestha, P.P., Lim, J., and Nikkhah Manesh, S. (2020). "Employment and wage distribution investigation in the construction industry by gender". *Journal of Management in Engineering*, 36(4), 06020001.

Simons, D.J., and Chabris, C.F. (1999). "Gorillas in our midst: Sustained inattentional blindness for dynamic events". *Perception*, 28(9), 1059–1074.

Still L.V. (1993). *Where to from Here? The Managerial Woman in Transition*. Sydney: Business and Professional Publishing.

United Nations (2019). Press release DSG/SM/1293-WOM/2184, 4 June. www.un.org/press/en/2019/dsgsm1293.doc.htm

United Nations (2021). News. https://news.un.org/en/story/2021/03/1086662

United Nations Department of Economic and Social Affairs (2018). "Do you know all 17 SDGs?" https://sdgs.un.org/goals

United Nations Department of Economic and Social Affairs (2020). The Sustainable Development Goals report 2020. https://unstats.un.org/sdgs/report/2020/

Verbeek, S., and Groeneveld, S. (2012). "Do hard diversity policies increase ethnic minority representation?" *Emerald Insight*, 41(5), 647–664.

Williams, K.Y. and O'Reilly, C.A. (1998). "Demography and diversity in organizations: A review of 40 years of research". In B.M. Staw and L.L. Cummings (eds), *Research in Organizational Behavior*, 77–140. Greenwich, CT: JAI Press.

Windscheid, L., Bowes-Sperry, L., Mazei, J., and Morner, M. (2017). "The paradox of diversity initiatives: When organizational needs differ from employee preferences". *Journal of Business Ethics*, 145(1), 33–48.

USEFUL WEB RESOURCES

G7 Gender Equality Advisory Council: www.globalpartnership.org/blog/inequality-not-inevitable-challenging-gender-discrimination-through-g7

Workplace Gender Equality Agency: www.wgea.gov.au/publications/australias-gender-pay-gap-statistics

World Economic Form: www.weforum.org/agenda/2018/01/gender-inequality-and-the
-fourth-industrial-revolution/

23. Implications for fieldworkers in diversity, equality, and inclusion research

Subas P. Dhakal, John Burgess and Roslyn Cameron

INTRODUCTION

As set out in Chapter 1, the book's purpose was to bring together various contributions that examine the multiple aspects of the diversity, equality, and inclusion (DE&I) agenda. This purpose is relevant within the context of meeting the 17 Sustainable Development Goals (SDGs), in particular, the 10th goal that aims to "empower and promote the social, economic and political inclusion of all irrespective of age, sex, disability, race, ethnicity, origin, religion or economic or other status" (UNDESA, 2015). In relation to the broad findings, the DE&I-related issues addressed in this edited volume ranges between gender inequality and caring for the intellectually disabled to the challenges faced by LGBTQI fly-in/fly-out workers to the social inclusion of indigenous people. Although the way the three elements within DE&I are defined and operationalised differ in differing contexts, it was posited (Chapter 2) that all three aspects are complementary to each other because they collectively contribute to highlight the significance of the need to overcome social inequalities due to various facets of social hierarchy and exclusion. This chapter summarises the key research topics concerning the DE&I agenda covered by this volume and discusses the practical implications of methods used for future research.

FINDINGS

DE&I-Related Topics Covered in This Volume

To investigate the key topics of the chapters in this volume, we carried out a word frequency analysis of abstracts as a starting point for identifying the prevalent research themes using the NVivo software. Figure 23.1 provides a synopsis of the top 20 topics (n≥5) and their weighted percentage as a relative strength of occurrence.

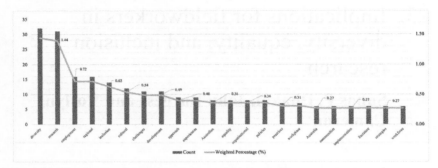

Figure 23.1   Frequent word occurrences within abstracts

These frequently occurring words, not surprising, were diversity, inclusion, and equality. A word cloud map (Figure 23.2) was created using the NVivo software from the frequency occurrences within abstracts. The word cloud provides a visual estimation of the relative emphasis of the topics. Nonetheless, as Roux et al. (2019) point out, word frequency analysis provides only a rough estimate of possible trends in the data analysed.

DE&I-Related Topics, the Country Represented, Methods Used, and Field Implications

Chapters included in this edited volume indicate that there is a diversity in the DE&I-related issues across developed as well as developing countries. Table 23.1 summarises the key findings regarding topics, methods used, and implications for future research. The table summarises a range of DE&I-related challenges such as gender, disability, age, and exclusion in all studied countries related to both their organisational as well as social functioning.

On the one hand, several researchers have identified the challenges relating to conducting field research in developing economies such as Bangladesh and Uganda. On the other hand, researchers in developed countries such as Australia have focused on issues surrounding people with disability and their families that have been marginalised by the Australian government's decision to nationalise disability-related funding. In addition, despite being an advanced economy with a broad consensus on the advantages of embracing the DE&I agenda, researchers in Singapore have identified substantial cul-

Figure 23.2   Word cloud of key topics within abstracts

tural, psychological, and economic impasses towards making progress in the DE&I agenda at the country level.

Field Implications

Each country and organisation experiences the challenges of overcoming exclusion and inequality differently due to the differing nature of the sectoral operating environment (see Georgiadu et al., 2019). However, there are a few common themes that penetrate a variety of contexts. Several chapters have proposed a range of remedial DE&I strategies, policies and programs for public, not-for-profit and private-sector organisations to implement to complement their existing DE&I initiatives. For example, the American case study highlights that the case of achieving equality and diversity is a complex policy challenge across educational institutions that necessitates a pluralist approach. More importantly, just because an organisation is operational in a developed economy does not mean the DE&I agenda is less challenging when compared to a developing economy.

Table 23.1   *DE&I related topics, the country represented, methods used, and field implications*

Topic	Country	Method used	Field implications
Closing the gap on Aboriginal and Torres Strait Islander employment disadvantage	Australia	Alternate methodologies based on philosophical positioning/epistemology consistent with an indigenous worldview	Future studies can extend this analysis to comprehensively evaluate and analyse labour market programs in Australia and other colonised countries to bridge the gap between indigenous and non-indigenous peoples
Regional business addressing the triple penalty of regional location, gender, and motherhood on women's careers	Australia	Case study approach to examine women's re-entry into the labour market following periods of unpaid care	Future case studies can investigate strategic positioning of the business and their openness to innovative workplace practices, leveraging of technology for enabling access to professional development, and the breaking down of geographical barriers
Researching skilled migrants in Australia	Australia	Interpretive multiple qualitative paradigms using a phenomenological study approach based on purposeful sampling	Future studies can use the method to examine skilled migrants' issues beyond South Asia to get a better understanding of habitus, sense-making, and acculturation to analyse the challenges
Valuing older workers in Australian universities' response to their ageing academic workforce	Australia	A case study approach to capture perceptions of older academics and the retirement intentions of more senior academics	Future studies can examine to what extent organisations adopt a proactive approach to fully leverage the knowledge and experience of their older workforce to fully gain competitive advantage
Creating an individualised foundation for genuine community inclusion	Australia	Phenomenological study approach to capture and examine individual experiences and perspectives on microboards based on semi-structured interviews	Future studies could explore how creating a microboard model can provide an opportunity for measuring changes in social inclusion, quality of life, and decision-making capacity of people with intellectual disabilities
Comparing women in small and medium-sized accounting firms	Australia, Malaysia, and India	Comparative analysis of the cultural context by applying an interpretive methodology	Future studies could examine gender and relational frameworks in cross-country contexts using mixed-method approaches

Topic	Country	Method used	Field implications
Examining LGB employees and their experiences of fly-in/ fly-out employment	Australia	An exploratory research process using semi-structured interviews via convenience and snowball sampling techniques	Future studies can build on this study by including research participants who actively avoid disclosing sexual orientation information amongst mining businesses
Improving garment sector workers' well being through international action	Bangladesh	Qualitative inquiry based on one-to-one, in-depth telephone interviews with managers	Future studies can extend the analysis by examining the researcher's social media presence and activities to interact with research participants
Conducting equity-related research in a developing country	Bhutan	Institutional ethnography to observe research participants as members of a society to uncover the culture shared within the broader social context	Future studies can build on this research to highlight the need for researchers to critically contemplate and demonstrate their subjectivity in other South Asian countries and beyond
Exploring workplace lessons on diversity, equity, and inclusion	Canada	Reflective practice that is aligned with both Inuit societal values and social work practice in cross-cultural settings	Future studies can complement lessons learned by conducting participative research through action learning to bring indigenous and multicultural voices forward
Examining gender mainstreaming	Indonesia	A feminist policy analysis	Future analysis can utilise this framework to examine the progress of gender mainstreaming in improving women's quality of life in emerging economies
Assessing affirmative action and equality, diversity, and inclusion	Malaysia	An integrated policy analysis approach to examine various structural, political, and socio-economic factors	Future studies could assess affirmative action policies in other country contexts such as South Asia or Southeast Asia, where ethnic disparities are prominent
Examining intersectional gender justice in professional design practice	New Zealand	Analysis of wicked problems using systems mapping as an action-oriented methodology	Future studies can explore the utility of systems mapping to comprehend how gender binaries manifest in their field or organisation

Topic	Country	Method used	Field implications
Determining organisational implications for diversity, equality, and inclusion strategies against maternal mortality	Papua New Guinea	A case study of health and non-health determinants of maternal mortality	Future case studies can extend the analysis by exploring strategies of bringing mobile health services to communities across the developing world
Learning from Kaupapa Māori research	New Zealand	Māori research methodologies, i.e., research involving Māori, Māori-centred research, and Kaupapa Māori methods	Future studies can utilise and extend these methodologies to examine the DE&I and indigenous nexus beyond New Zealand
Investigating complexity and opportunity in diversity challenges	Singapore	Policy analysis	Future studies can extend this analysis by examining how diversity and inclusion have manifested in multinational organisations across the developed parts of the Asia Pacific
Exploring the paradox of legislative reforms towards equality, diversity, and inclusion in workplaces	South Africa	Qualitative analysis of legislative frameworks	Future studies can build on this approach to complement quantitative methods to examine societal transformation in terms of adopting the diversity, equality, and inclusion agenda
Evaluating performance of social enterprise performance	Uganda	Quantitative analysis of social enterprises' performance based on a survey and network data envelopment analysis	Future studies could apply and refine the capability lens and network data envelopment analysis as tools for the recognition of key variables for capturing the social value of organisations
Supporting LGBTQ+ strategies in schools	United States	Policy and contextual analysis of the LGBTQ+ acronym and the importance of representation	Future studies could extend this analysis and examine ways to improve inclusive practices and policies around LGBTQ+ matters in secondary and tertiary educational settings

On the one hand, despite a broad consensus on the merits of greater diversity, there remain substantial cultural, psychological, and economic blockages to achieving diversity and inclusion in advanced economies like Singapore. On the other, participation in the labour market does not automatically empower women if the socio-economic and cultural aspects continue to be ignored in developing economies like Indonesia. Several authors have recognised the limitations of legislative advancements and recommended revising organisational practices in collaboration between all relevant stakeholders. For instance, organisations in South Africa must be willing to advocate for people of colour rather than perpetuate a colour-blind organisational discourse. In line with the nature of this book, chapters included in this volume have adopted a variety of methodological approaches that have a wide array of field implications. For instance, some have highlighted the limitations of traditional "western" methodological approaches in order to examine the DE&I agenda in the context of indigenous peoples, whereas others have utilised innovative approaches such as the network data envelopment analysis adopted to examine the performance of social enterprises in Uganda to capture the social value of organisations in other countries.

Limitations of the Book

The book provides a snapshot of various DE&I-related challenges across 13 countries around the world. However, there are limitations in terms of issues and regions covered. Since the call for chapters and the actual data collection and analysis occurred during the middle of the COVID-19 pandemic, the potential for original research was limited. Several initial expressions of interest received could not be completed. Additional limitations include the limited coverage of countries in Europe, organisations by industry classification, occupations and professions, and the different dimensions of diversity within diversity. Many of the case study chapters are confined to a single diversity dimension, with a few exceptions on the intersectionality across diversity dimensions – for example, gender, age and ethnicity are not evaluated. Again, with few exceptions, there is also an absence of comparative analysis, either across diversity dimensions, across organisations, or across countries. Then there are emerging issues that establish new forms of exclusion – for example, the COVID pandemic has led to working-from-home arrangements being implemented, but such arrangements bring with them challenges and access barriers (Dhakal et al., 2021; Wheatley et al, 2021). Emerging topics within the DE&I agenda such as technological advancements and artificial intelligence have not been addressed. For instance, the impact of the Fourth Industrial Revolution and the emergence of a digital divide that covers access, technology, and literacy compounds exclusion and inequality across the developed and developing economies (Dhakal and Tjokro, 2021; Nankervis et al., 2020). There are ongoing national and international crises associated with natural disasters, ecological degradation, and conflicts that cause population displacement, destroy public and private infrastructure, and disrupt and destroy industries and jobs. For example, global warming and the crisis associated with environmental degradation has put millions at risk and compounds existing inequalities and exclusion (United Nations Development Programme, 2020). From the limitations of the book emerge further areas for ongoing research and there is an opportunity for future DE&I-related research to address these limitations. The chapters in this volume certainly provide a strong foundation for further research.

REFERENCES

Dhakal, S. P. and Tjokro, S. (2021). Tourism enterprises in Indonesia and the Fourth Industrial Revolution – are they ready? *Tourism Recreation Research.* https://doi.org/10.1080/02508281.2021.1996687

Dhakal, S. P., Burgess, J. and Connell, J. (2022). COVID-19 crisis, work and employment: Policy and research trends. *Labour and Industry*, 31(4), 353–365.

Georgiadu, A., Gonzalez-Perez, M. A., and Olivas-Luján, M. R. (2019). Diversity within diversity management: Where we are, where we should go, and how we are getting there. In Georgiadou, A., Gonzalez-Perez, M. A., and Olivas-Luján, M. R. (eds), *Diversity within Diversity Management: Country-Based Perspectives*, 1–20. Emerald Publishing.

Nankervis, A., Connell, J., Montague, A. and Burgess, J. (2020). Meeting the workforce challenges of the Fourth Industrial Revolution. In Nankervis, A., Connell, J. and Burgess, J. (eds), *The Future of Work in Asia and Beyond*, 3–19. Routledge.

UNDESA (United Nations Department of Economic and Social Affairs) (2015). Reduce inequality within and among countries. https://sdgs.un.org/goals/goal10

United Nations Development Programme (2020). *Human Development Report 2020*. UNDP. https://hdr.undp.org/sites/default/files/hdr2020.pdf

Wheatley, D., Hardill, I. and Buglass, S. (2021). *Handbook of Research on Remote Work and Worker Well-Being in the Post-COVID-19 Era*. IGI Global.

Index

Printed and bound by CPI Group (UK) Ltd, Croydon, CR0 4YY

16/04/2025

14658487-0003